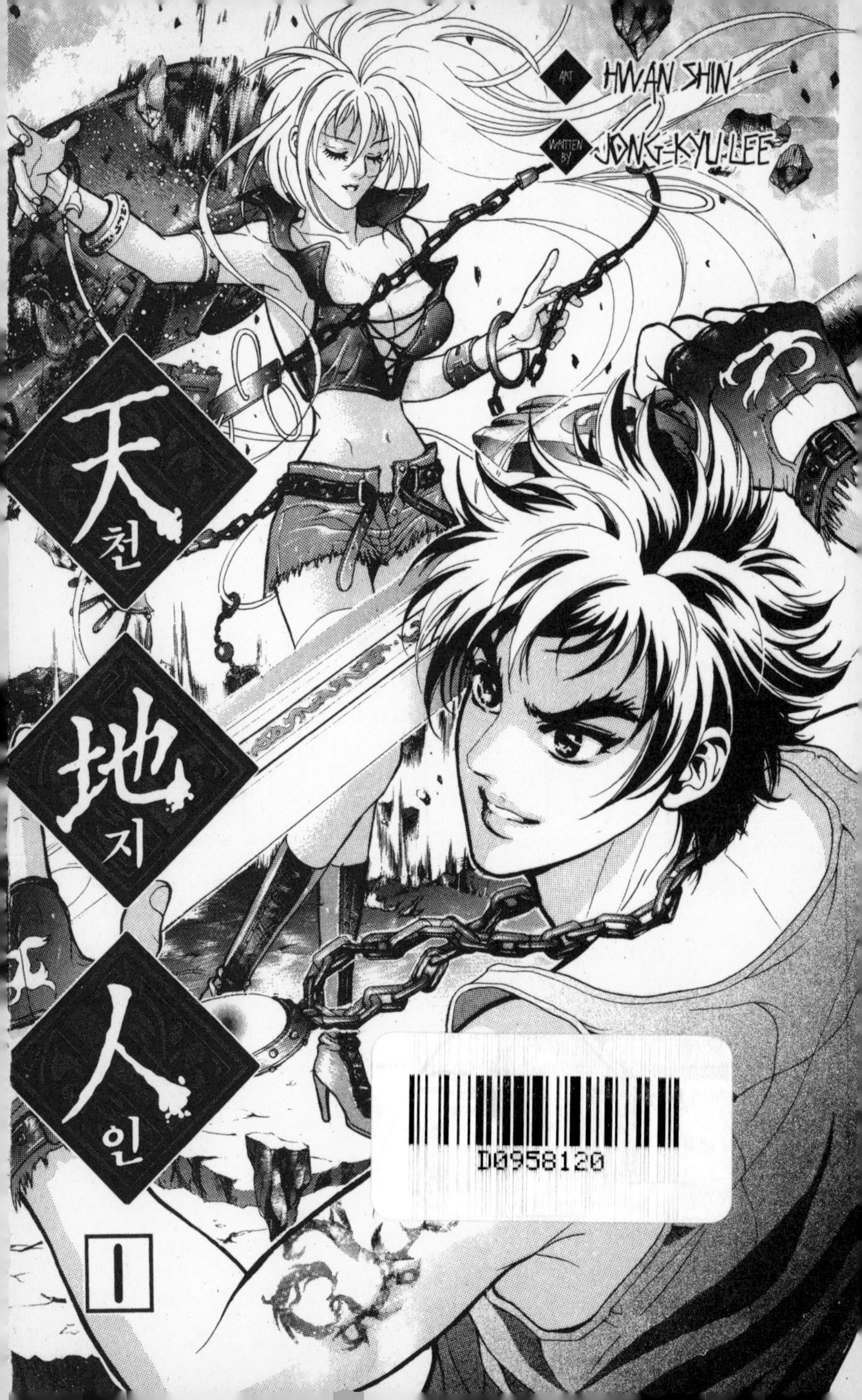
ART HWAN SHIN
WRITTEN BY JONG-KYU LEE
天 천
地 지
人 인
1

Translator - Seung-Ah Lee
English Adaptation - Anna Wenger
Retouch and Lettering - Haruko Furukawa
Cover Layout - Patrick Hook

Editor - Luis Reyes
Digital Imaging Manager - Chris Buford
Pre-Press Manager - Antonio DePietro
Production Managers - Jennifer Miller and Mutsumi Miyazaki
Art Director - Matt Alford
Managing Editor - Jill Freshney
VP of Production - Ron Klamert
President & C.O.O. - John Parker
Publisher & C.E.O. - Stuart Levy

E-mail: info@TOKYOPOP.com
Come visit us online at www.TOKYOPOP.com

A  Manga

TOKYOPOP Inc.
5900 Wilshire Blvd. Suite 2000
Los Angeles, CA 90036

Evil's Return Vol. 1

ISBN: 1-59182-784-1

First TOKYOPOP printing: July 2004

10 9 8 7 6 5 4 3 2 1

Printed in the USA

EVIL'S RETURN

VOLUME 1

ART: HWAN SHIN
WRITTEN BY: JONG KYU-LEE

LOS ANGELES · TOKYO · LONDON · HAMBURG

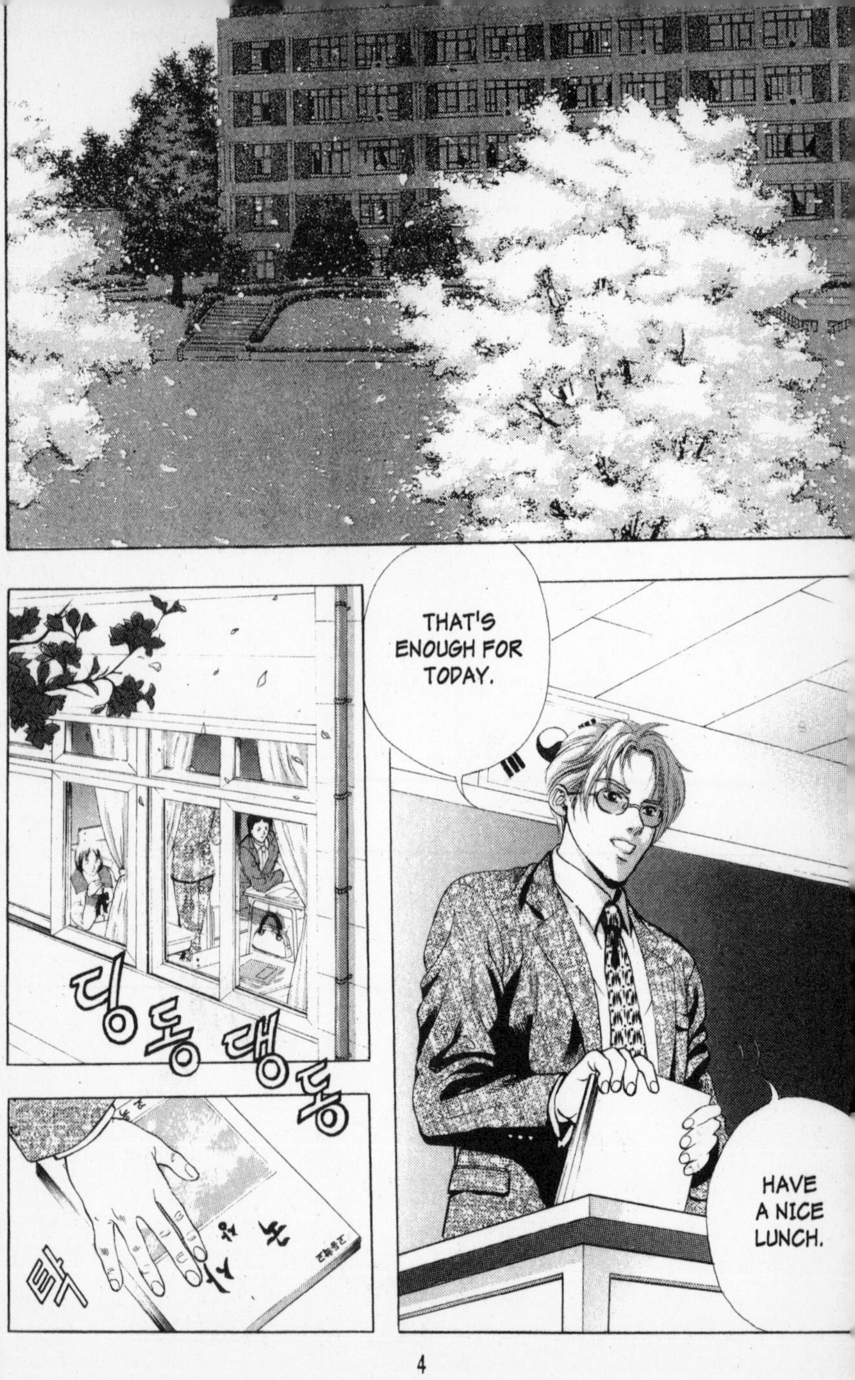
딩동댕동
THAT'S ENOUGH FOR TODAY.
HAVE A NICE LUNCH.

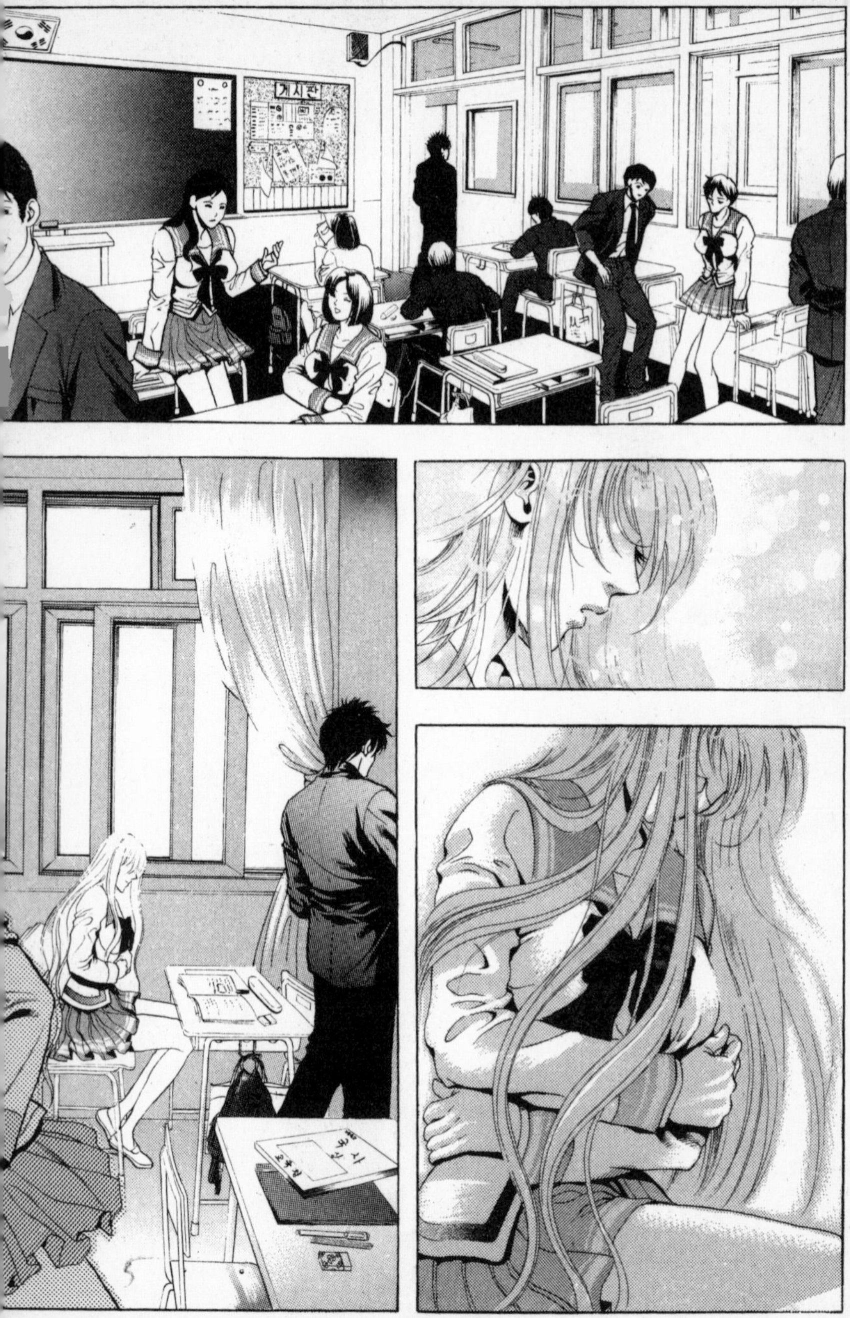
게시판

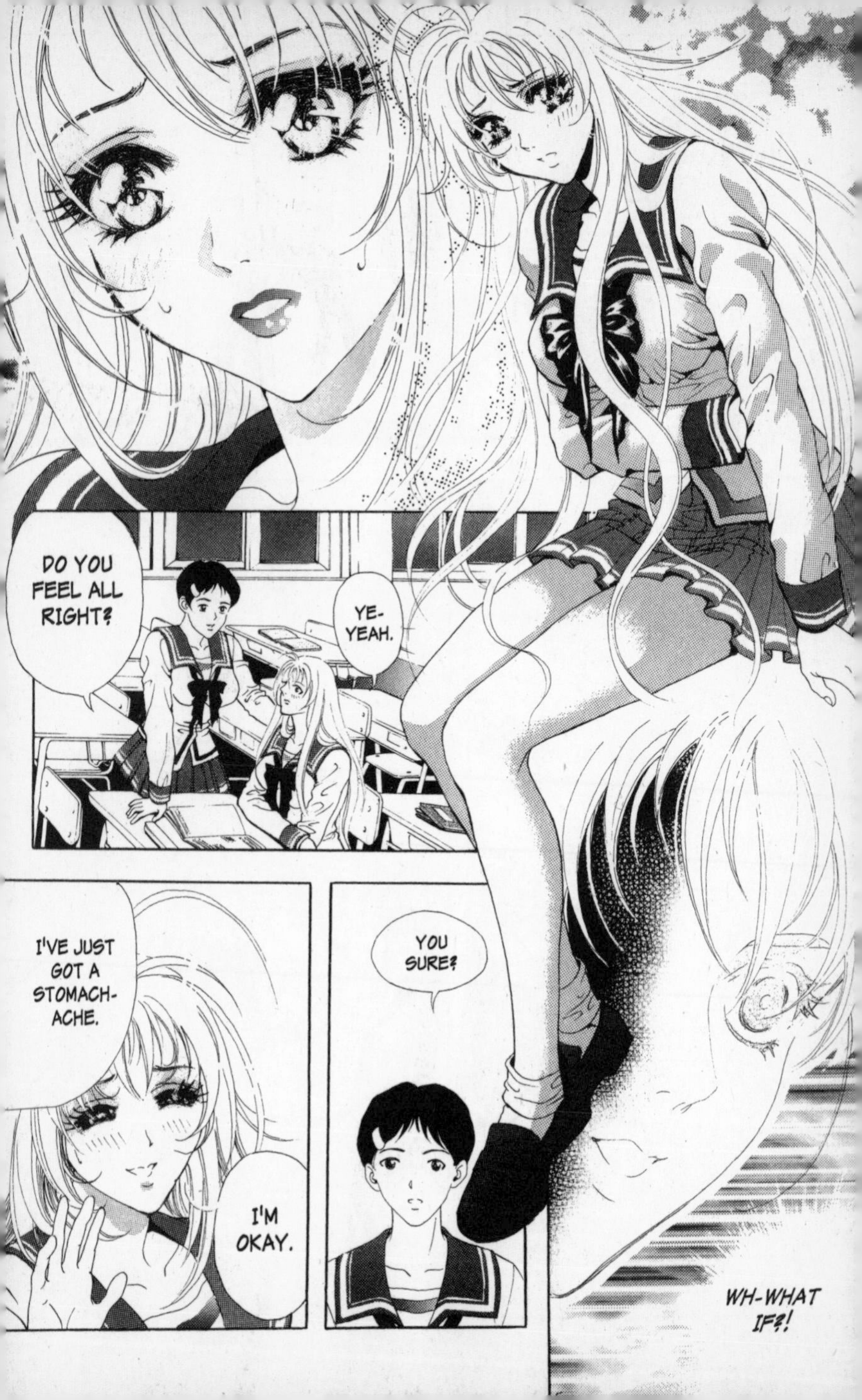
DO YOU FEEL ALL RIGHT?
YE-YEAH.
WH-WHAT IF?!
YOU SURE?
I'M OKAY.
I'VE JUST GOT A STOMACH-ACHE.

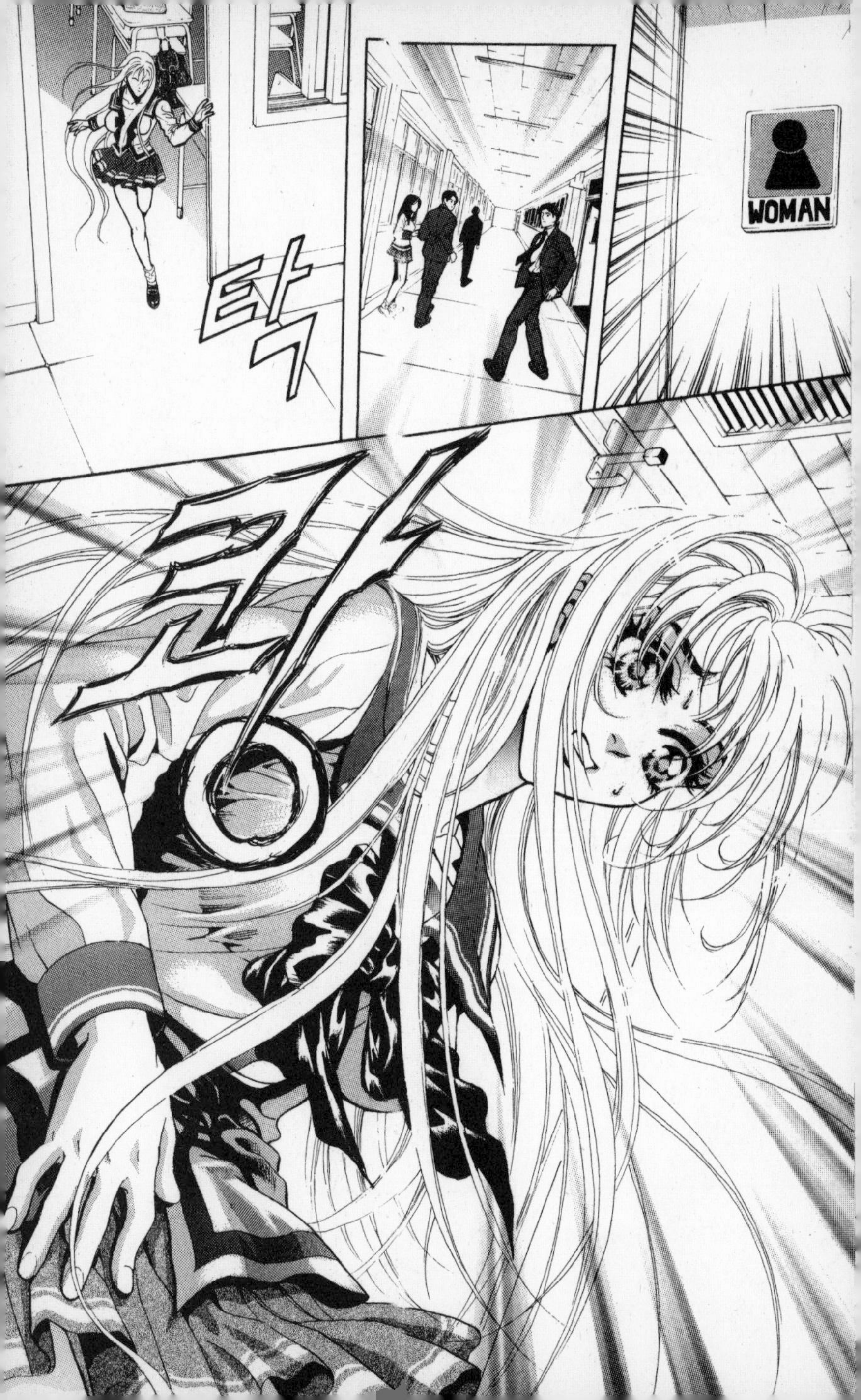
WOMAN
탁

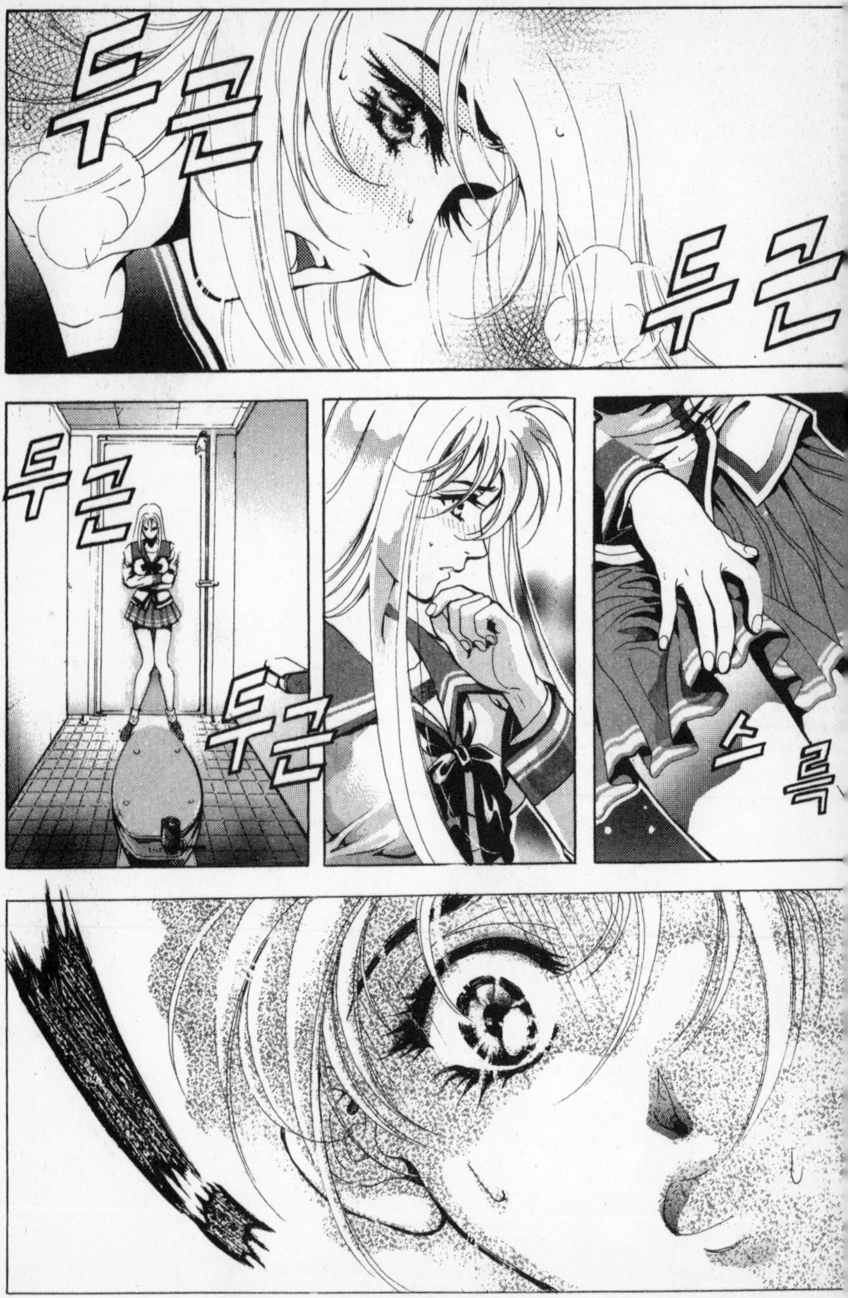
두근
두근
두근
두근
스륵

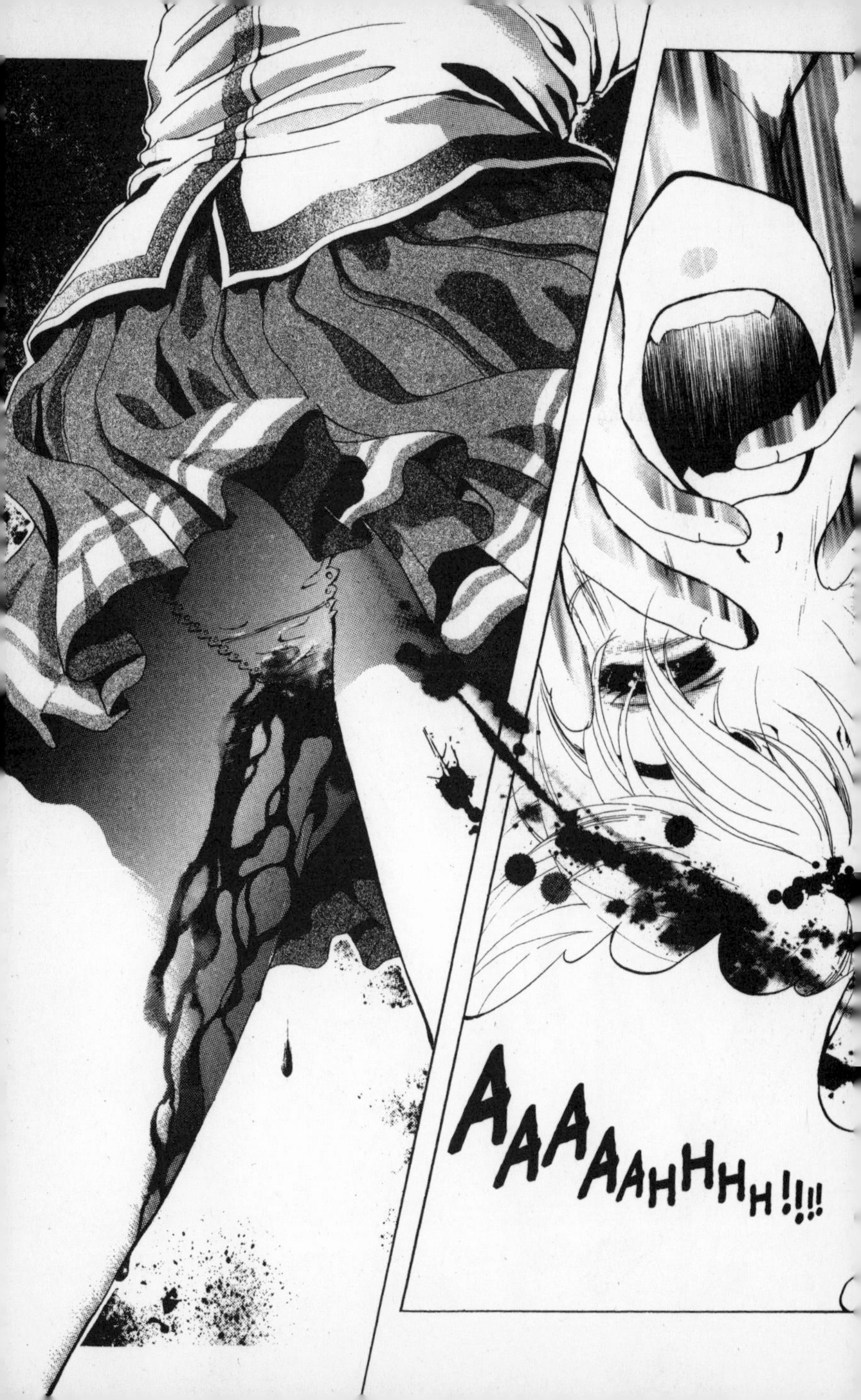
AAAAAHHHH!!!!

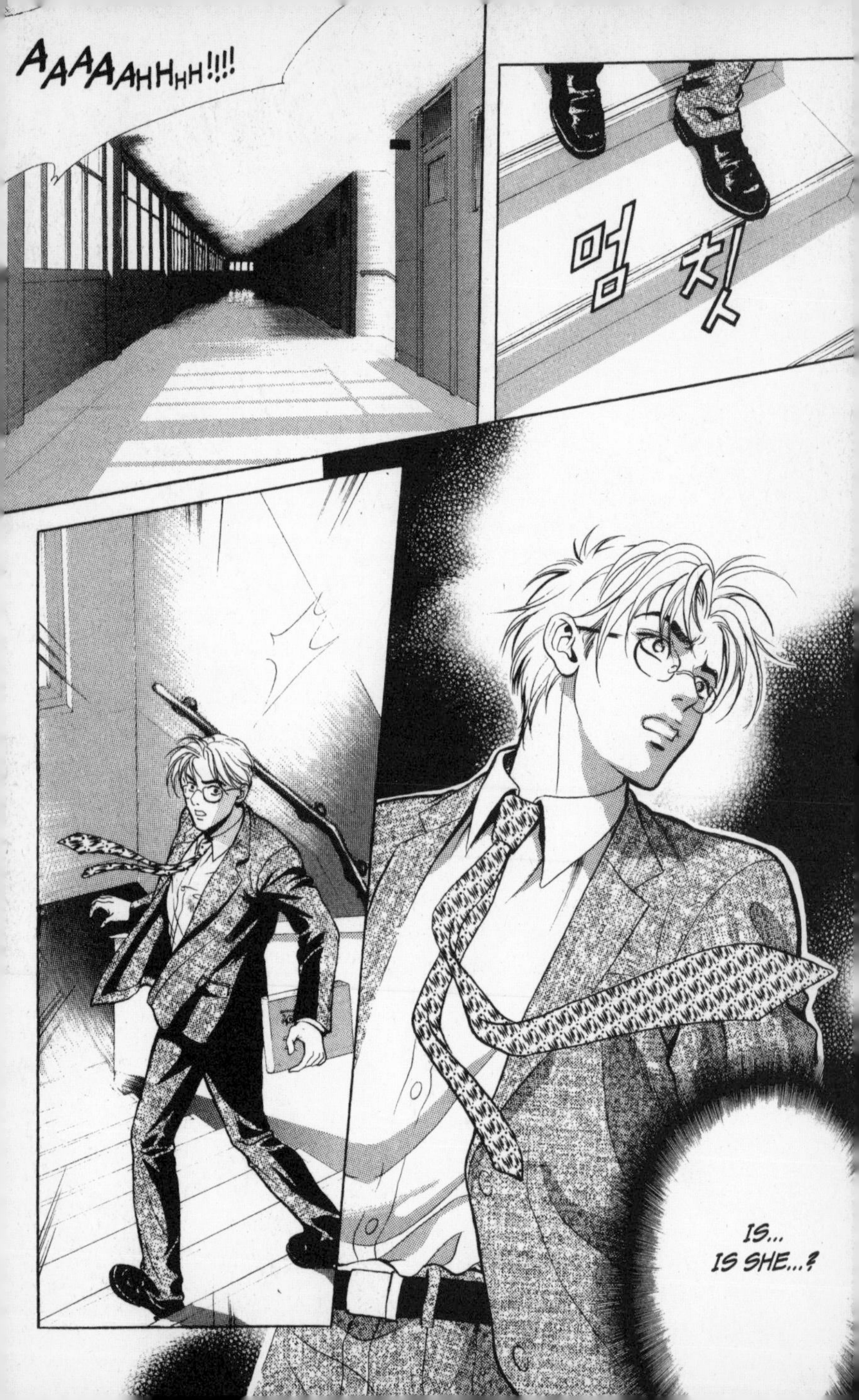
AAAAAHHHH!!!!
멈칫
IS...
IS SHE...?

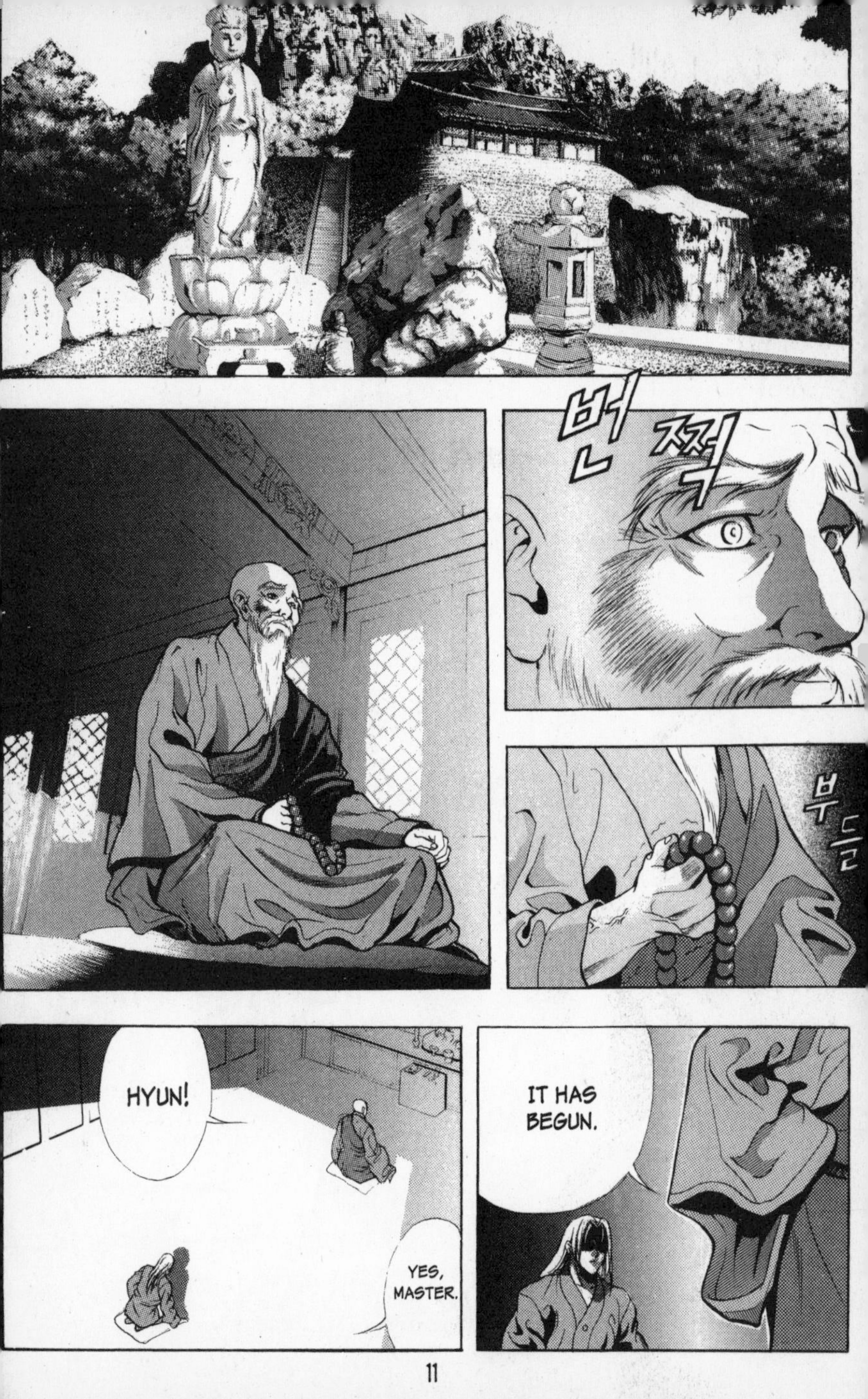
번쩍
부들
HYUN!
YES, MASTER.
IT HAS BEGUN.

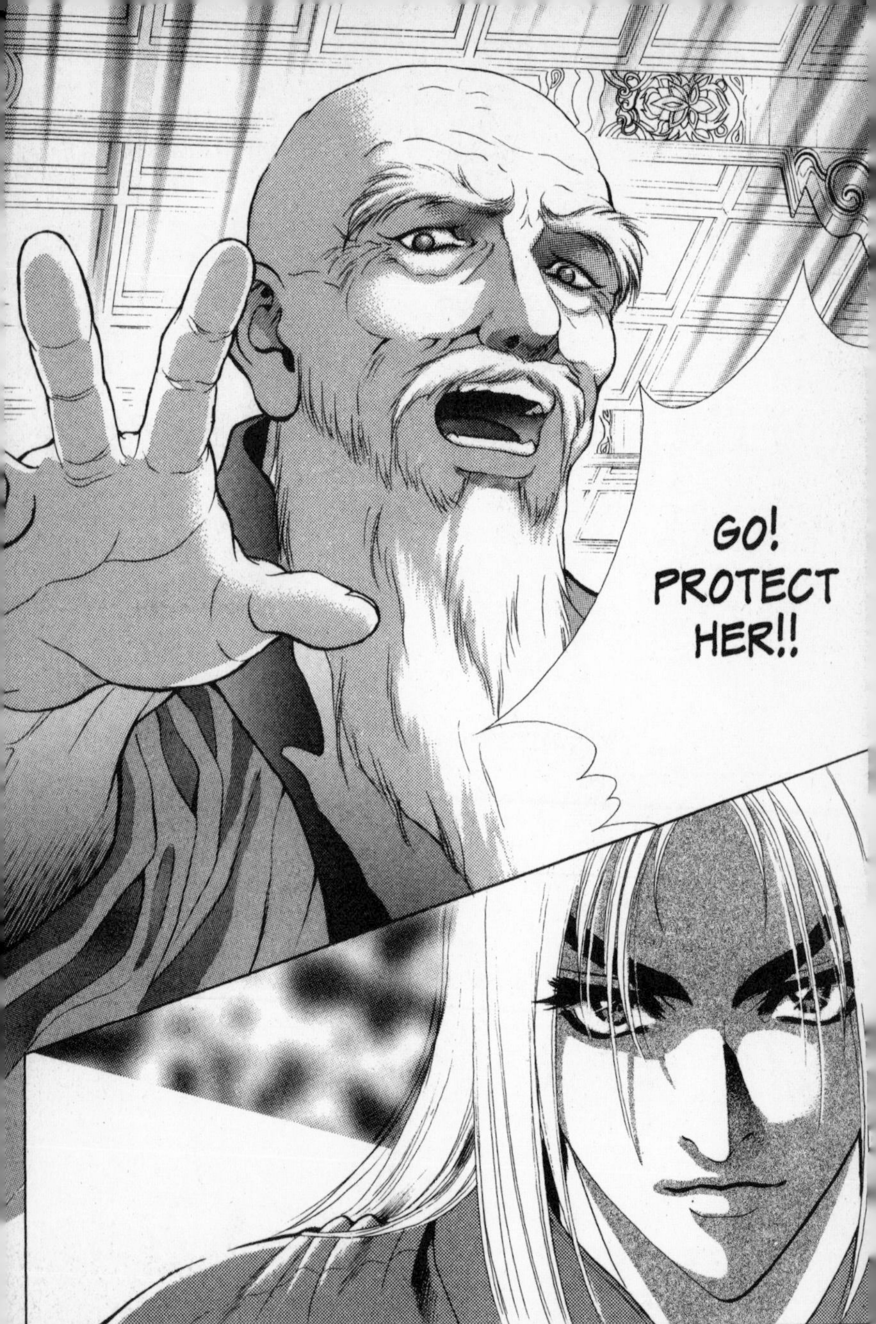
GO! PROTECT HER!!

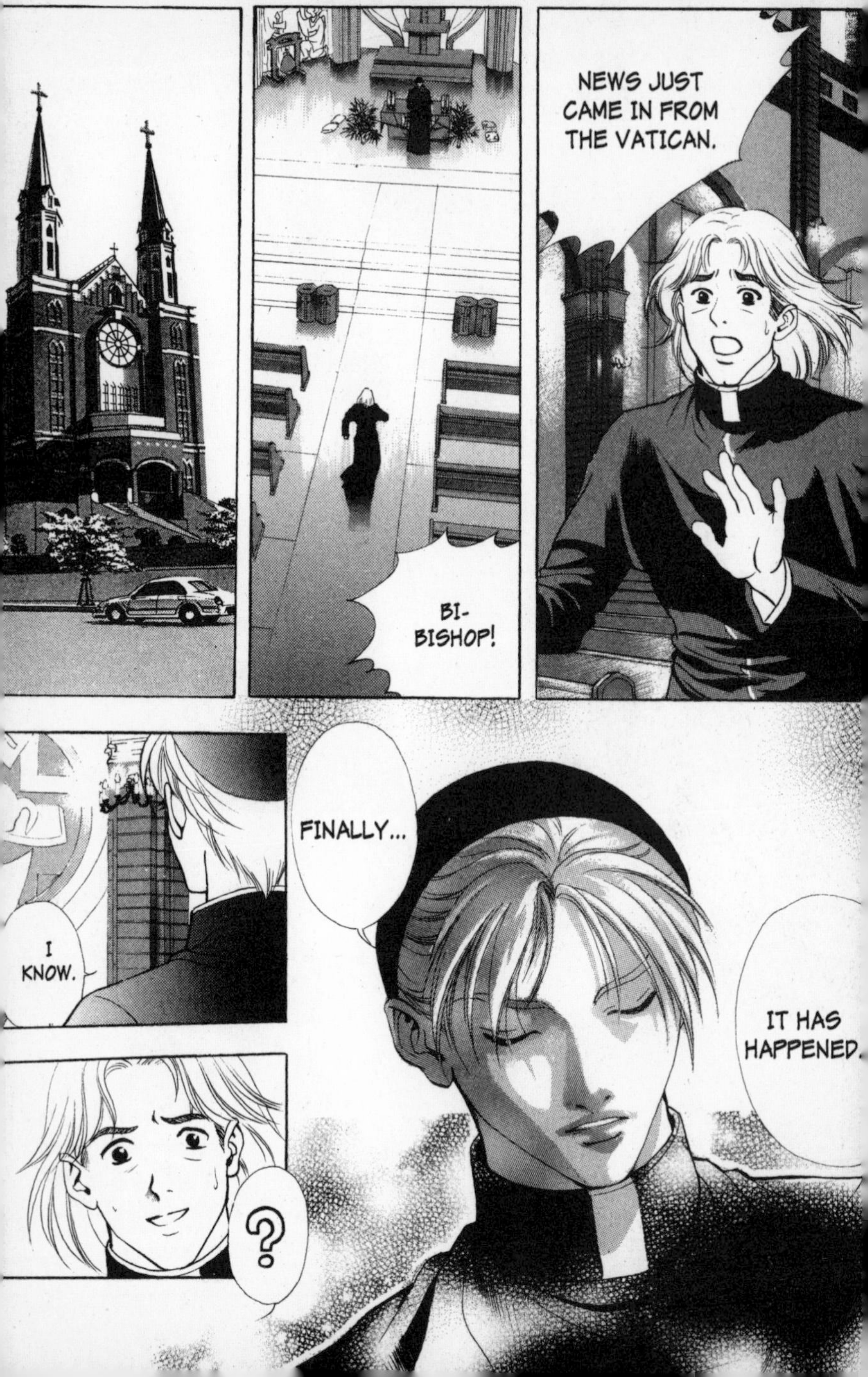
BI-
BISHOP!
NEWS JUST CAME IN FROM THE VATICAN.
I KNOW.
FINALLY...
IT HAS HAPPENED.
?

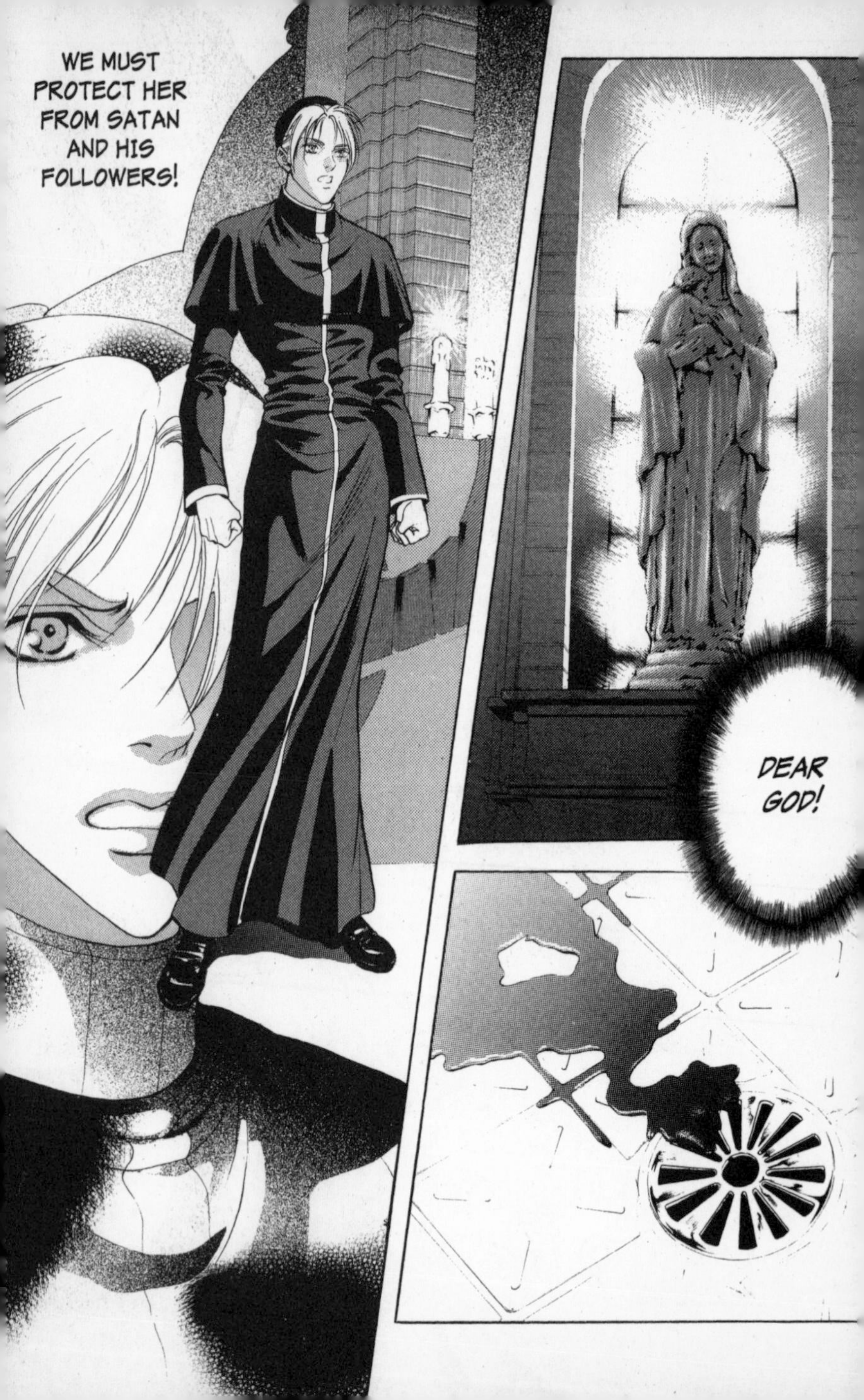
WE MUST PROTECT HER FROM SATAN AND HIS FOLLOWERS!
DEAR GOD!

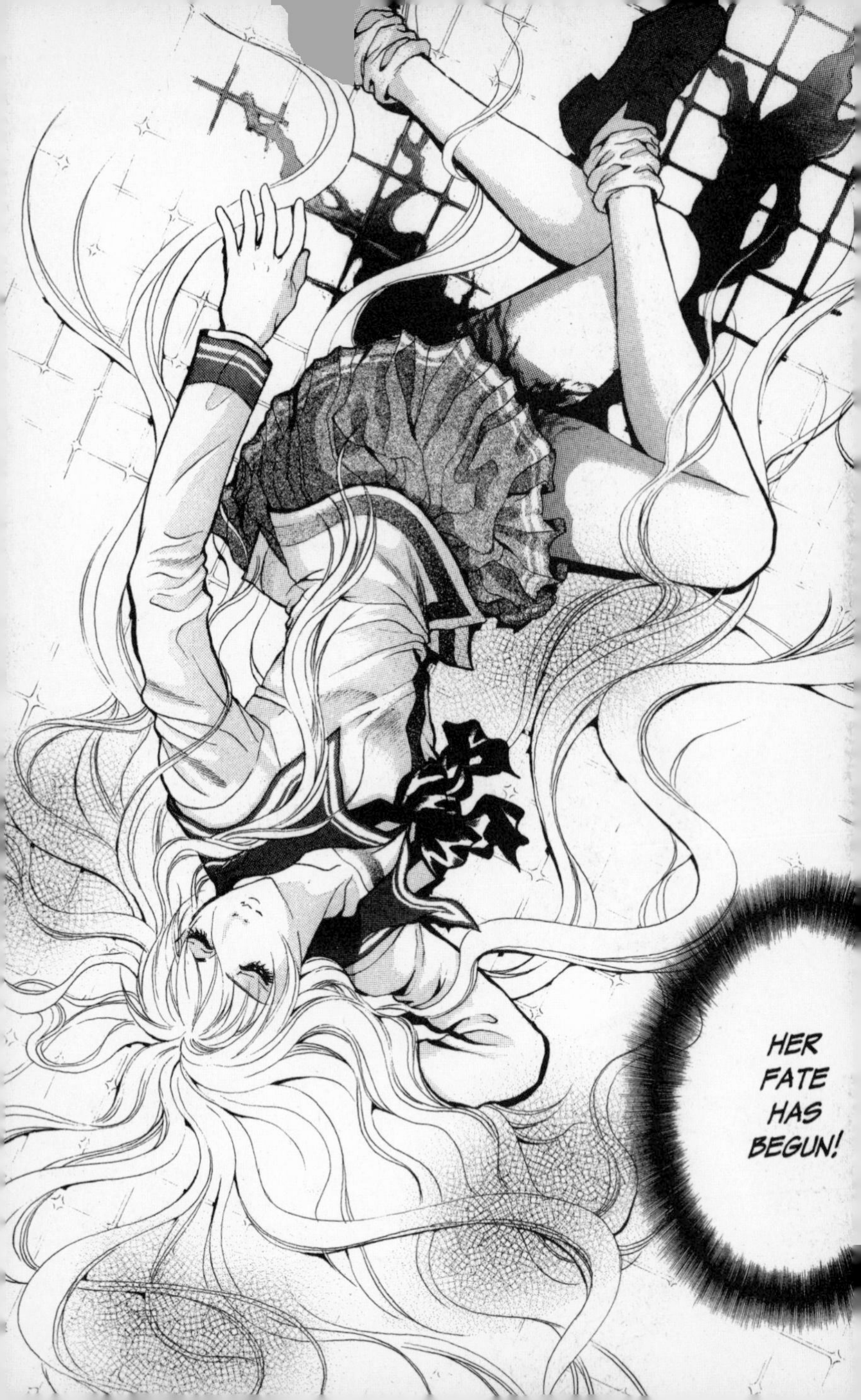
HER FATE HAS BEGUN!

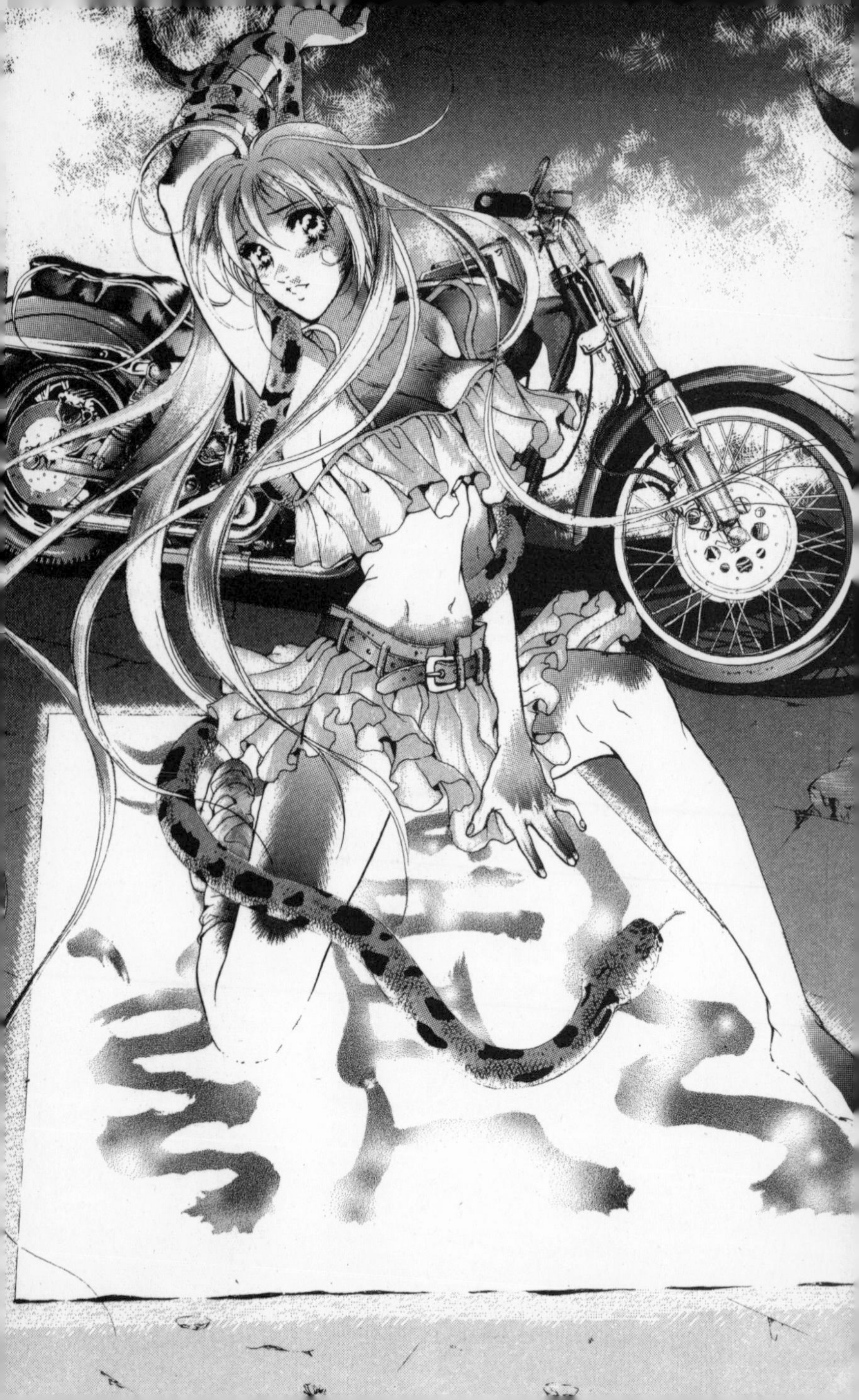

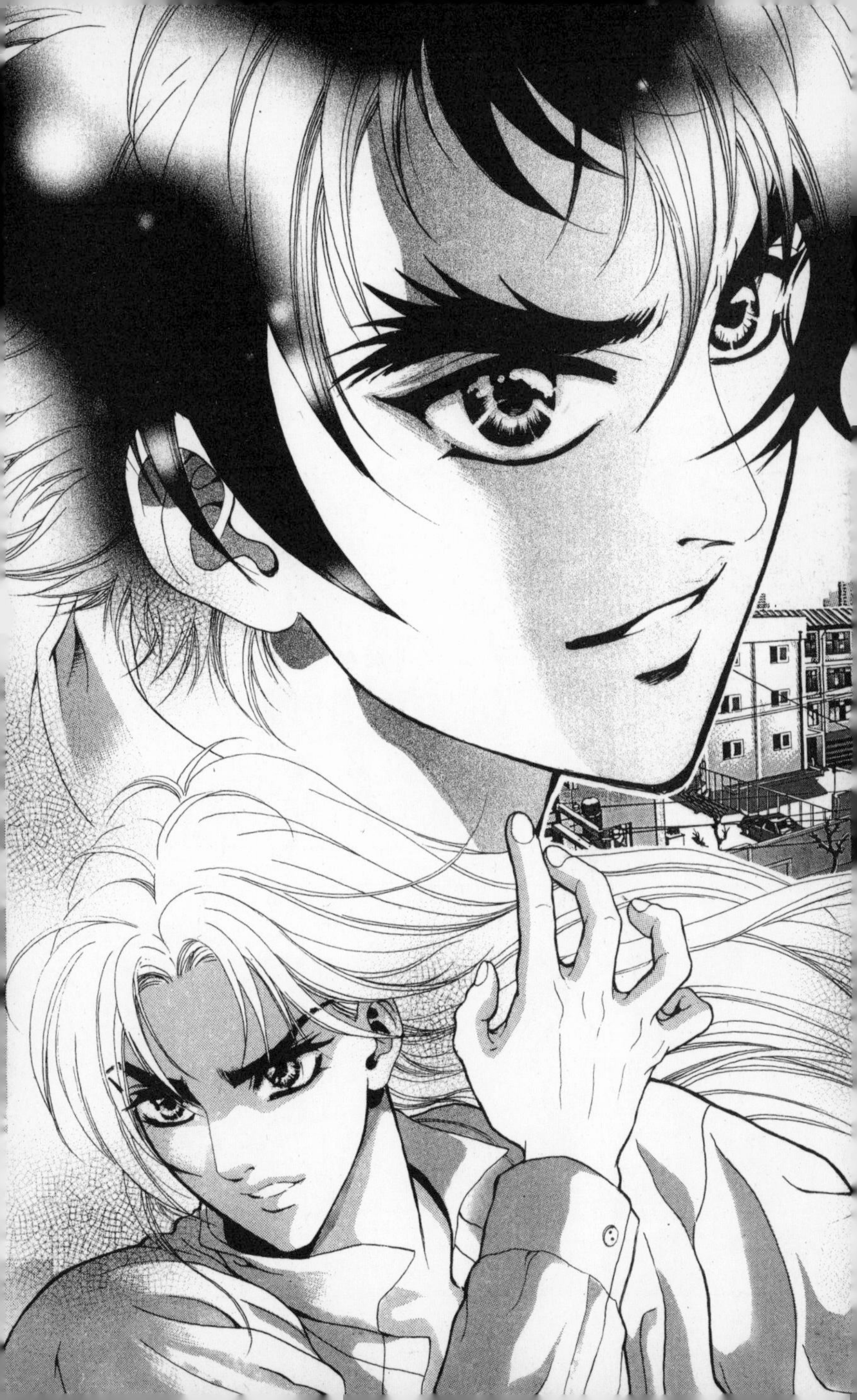

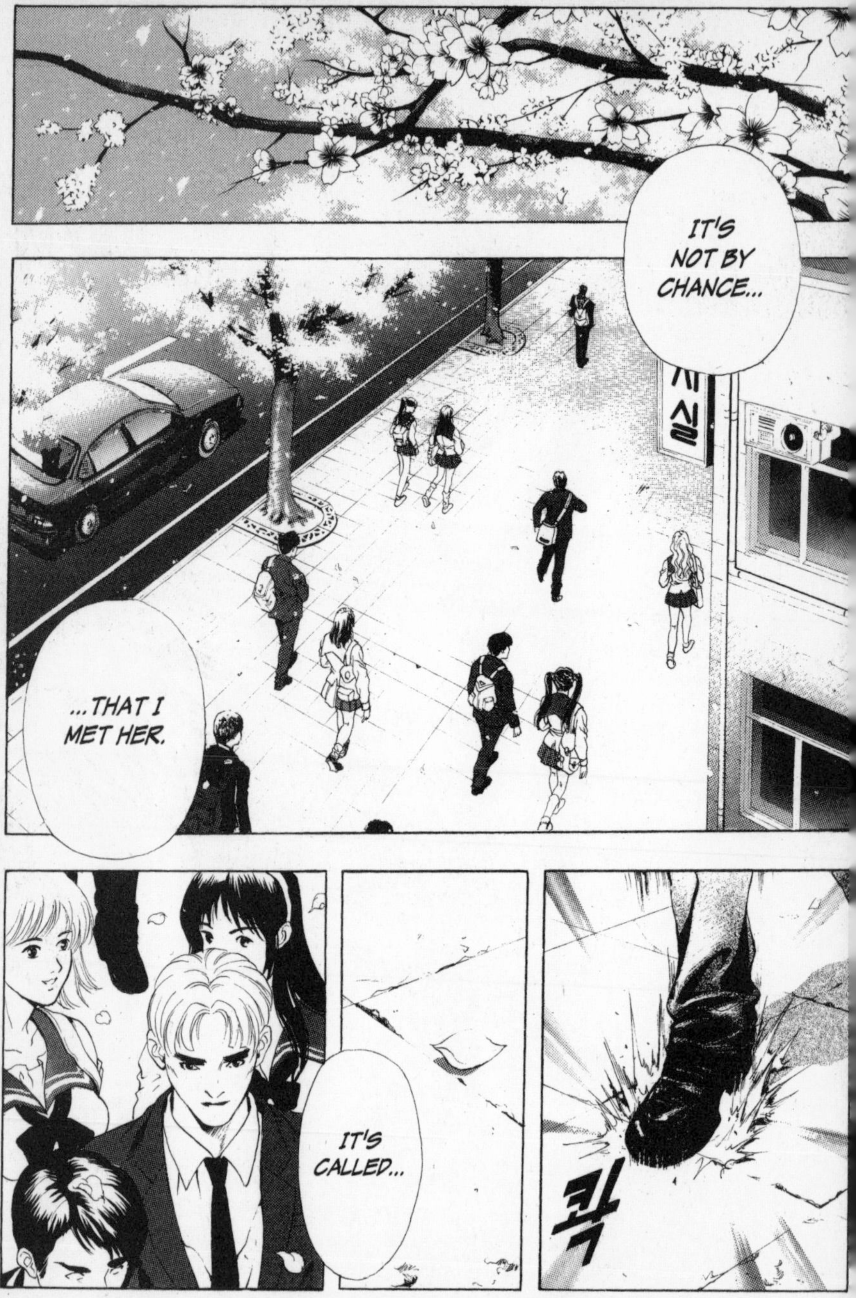
IT'S NOT BY CHANCE...
...THAT I MET HER.
IT'S CALLED...
콱

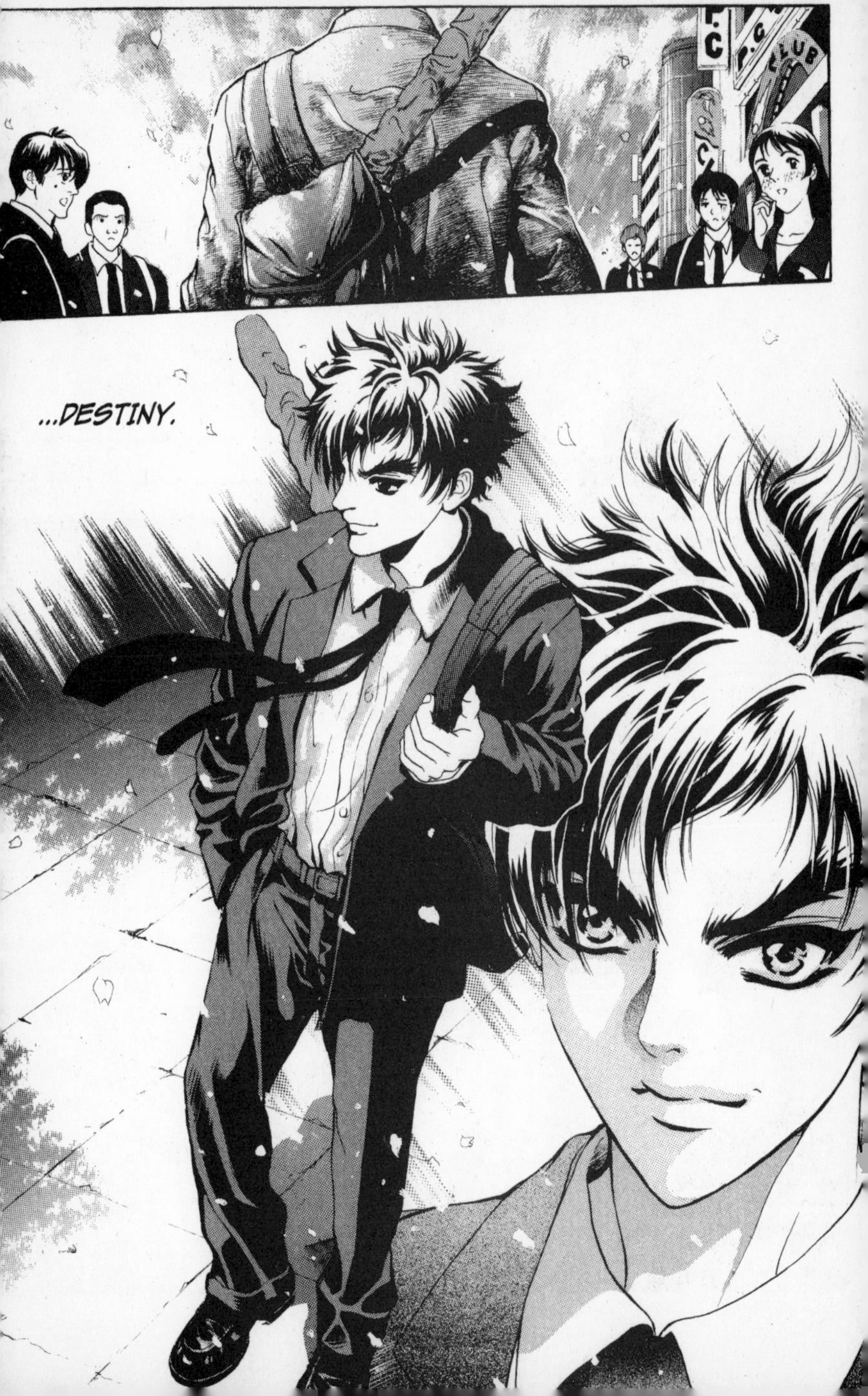
P.C
P.C CLUB
...DESTINY.

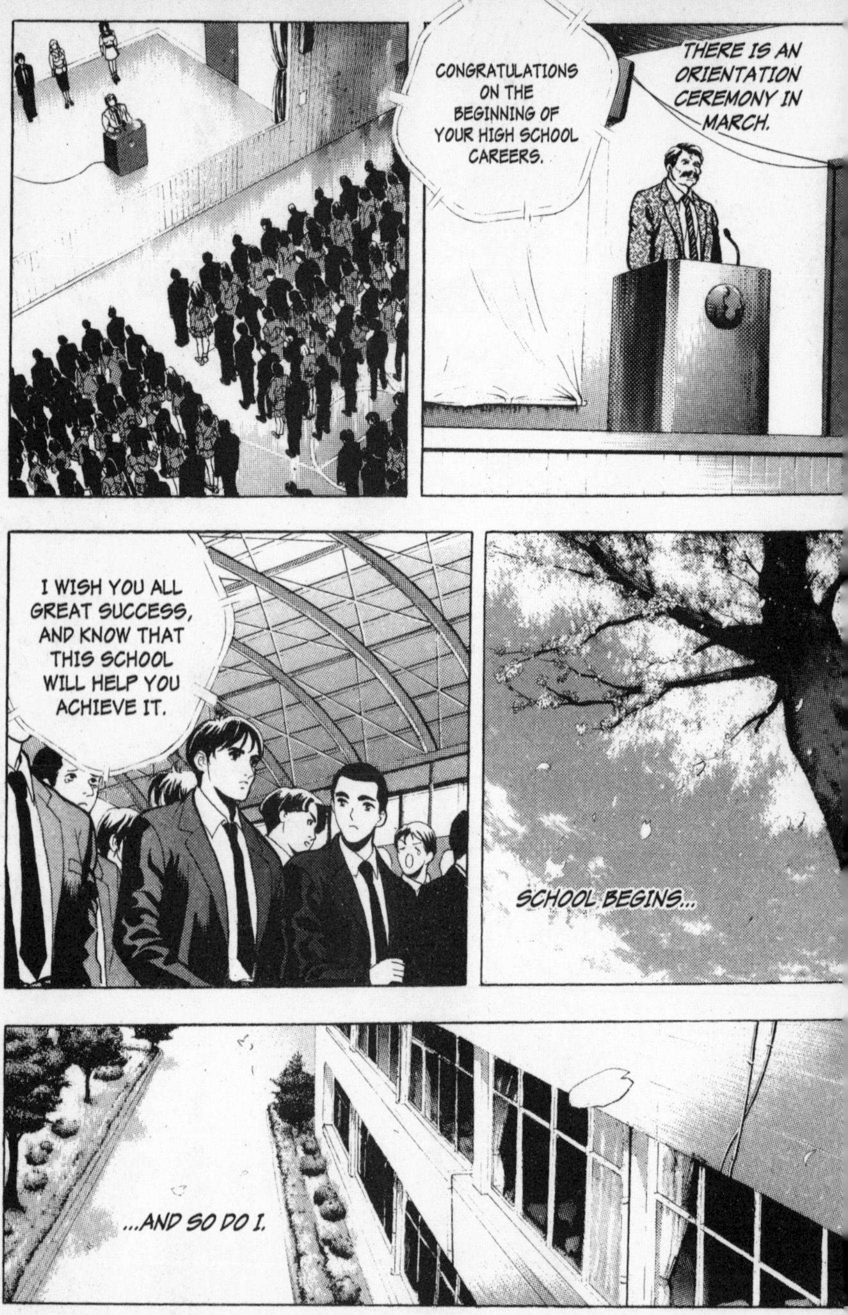
THERE IS AN ORIENTATION CEREMONY IN MARCH.
CONGRATULATIONS ON THE BEGINNING OF YOUR HIGH SCHOOL CAREERS.
I WISH YOU ALL GREAT SUCCESS, AND KNOW THAT THIS SCHOOL WILL HELP YOU ACHIEVE IT.
SCHOOL BEGINS...
...AND SO DO I.

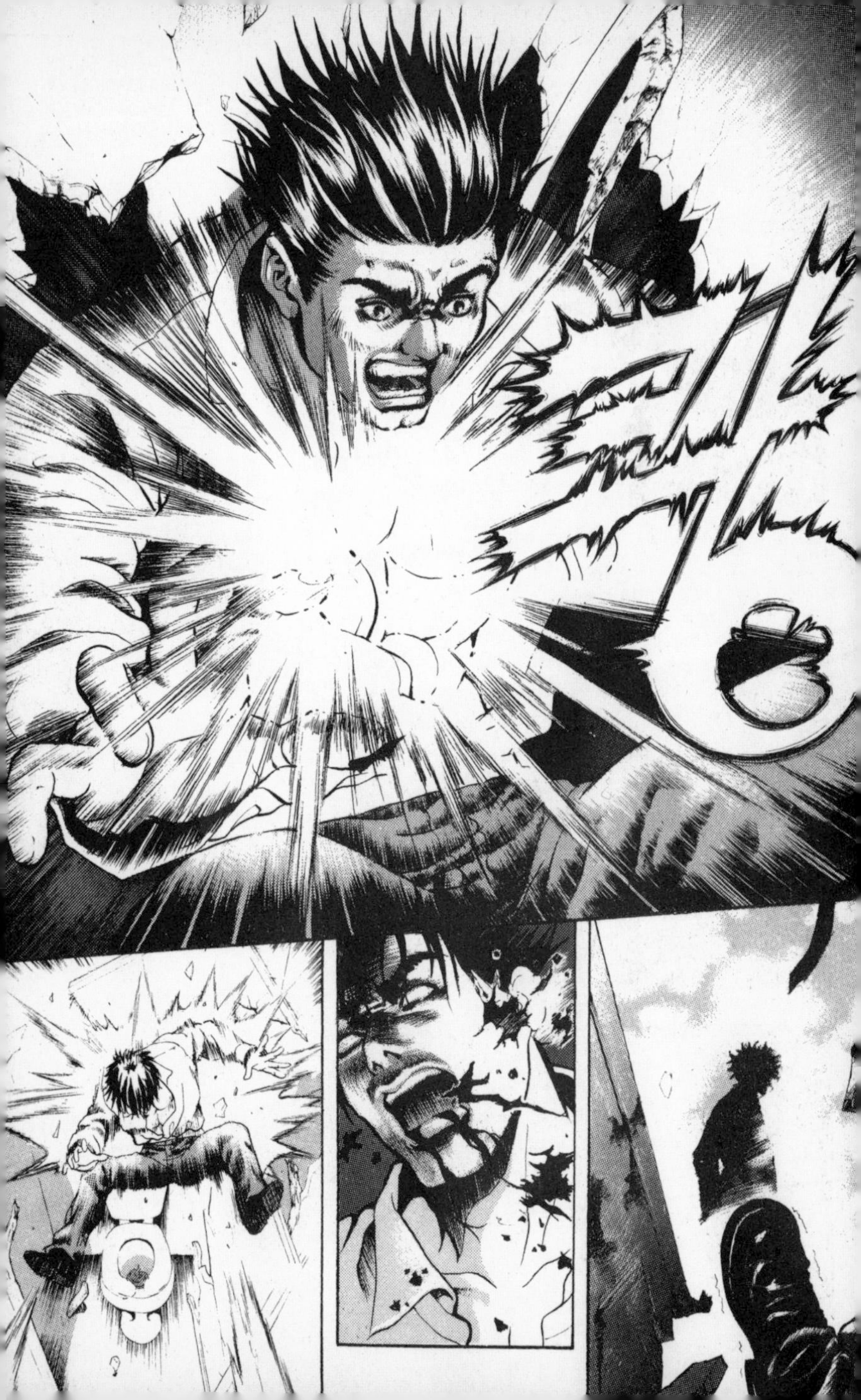

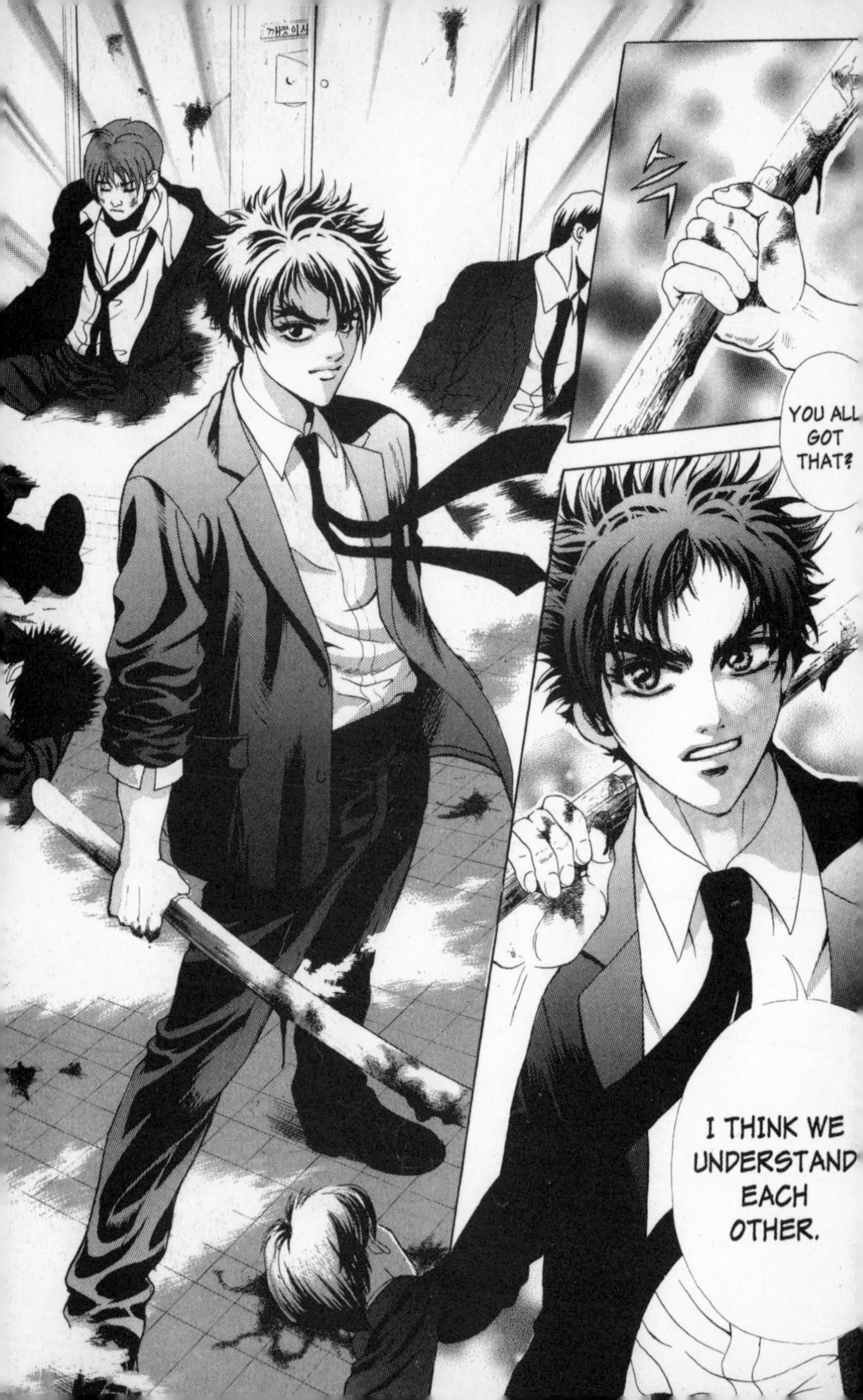
YOU ALL GOT THAT?
I THINK WE UNDERSTAND EACH OTHER.

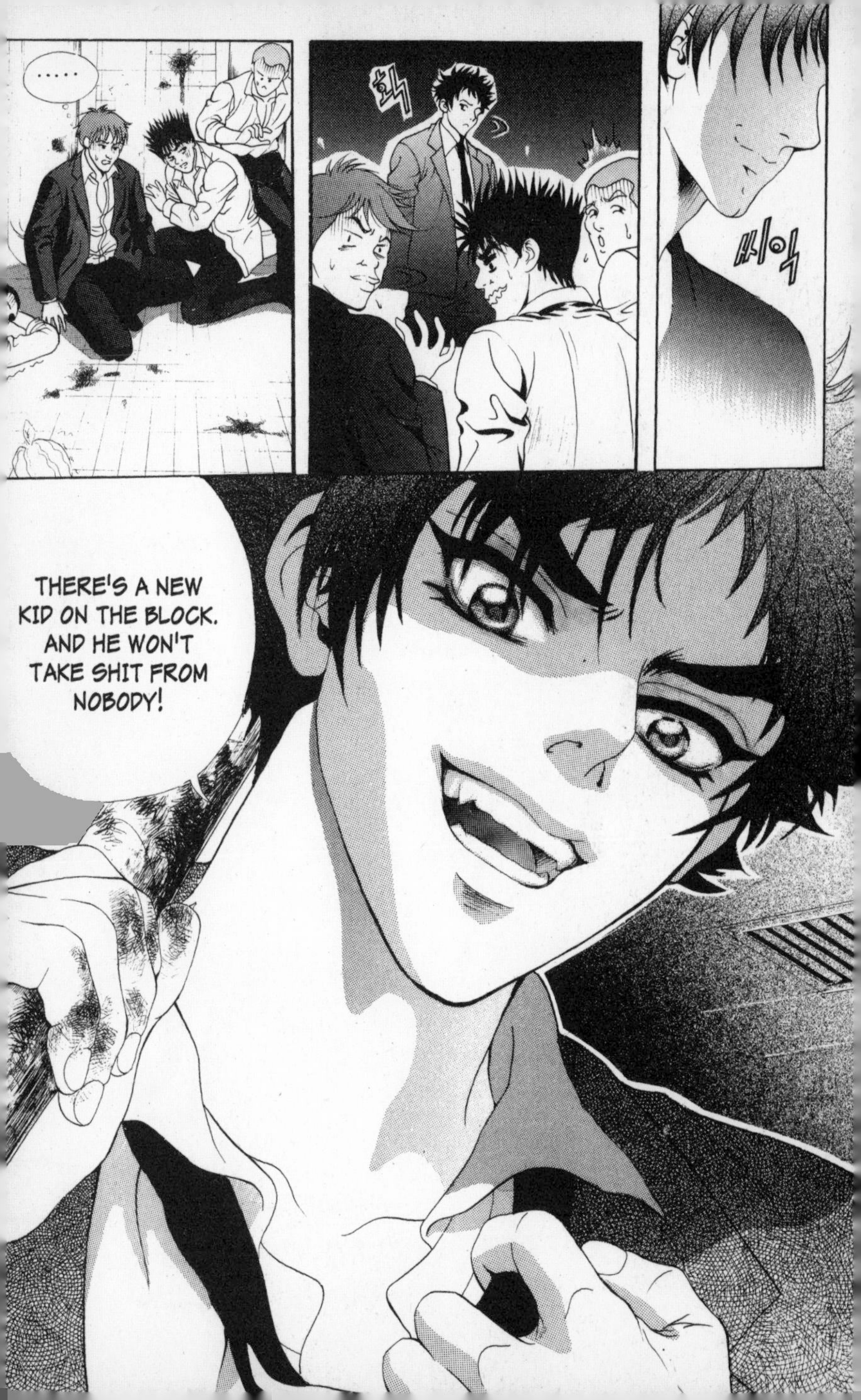
......
THERE'S A NEW KID ON THE BLOCK. AND HE WON'T TAKE SHIT FROM NOBODY!

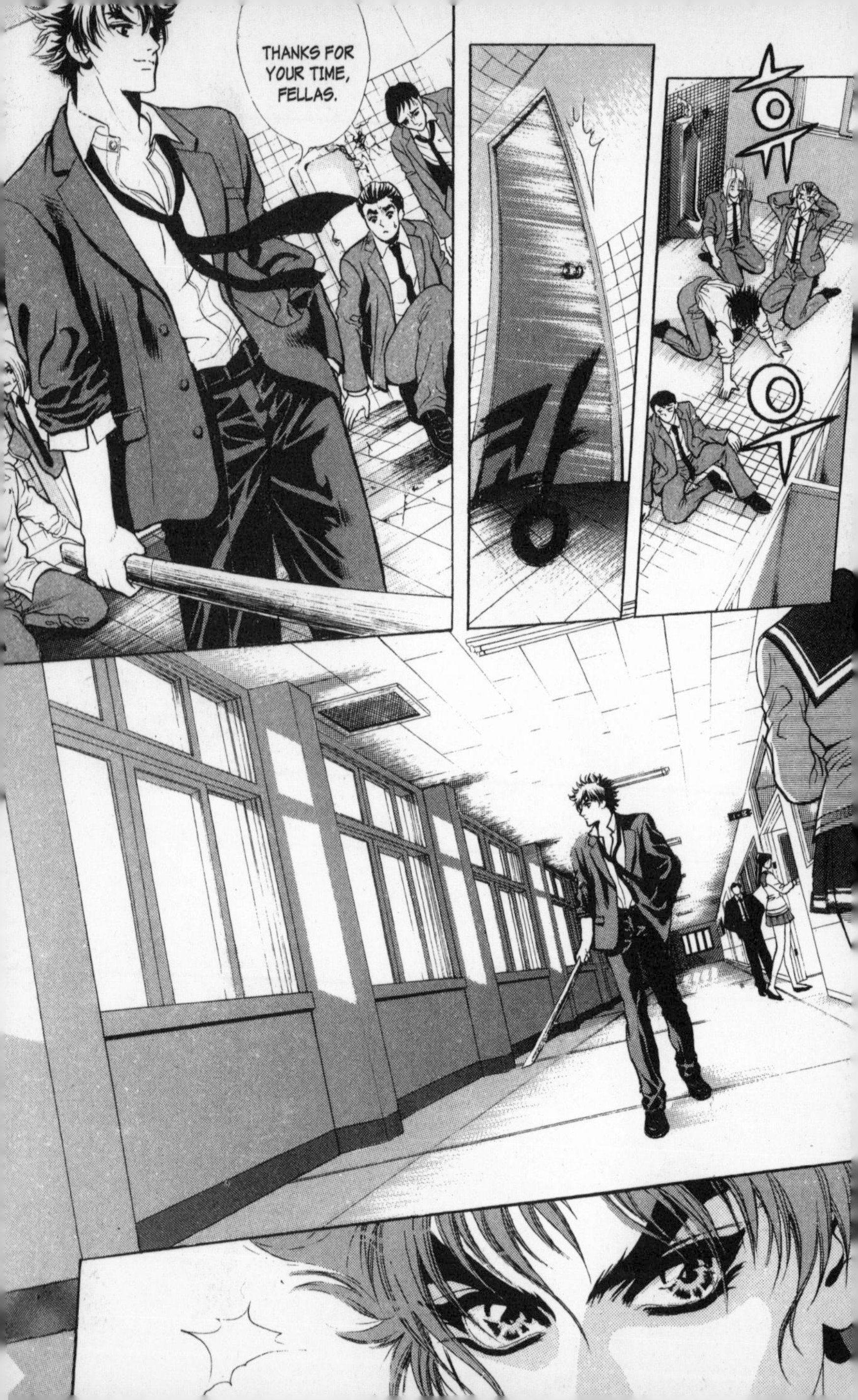
THANKS FOR YOUR TIME, FELLAS.

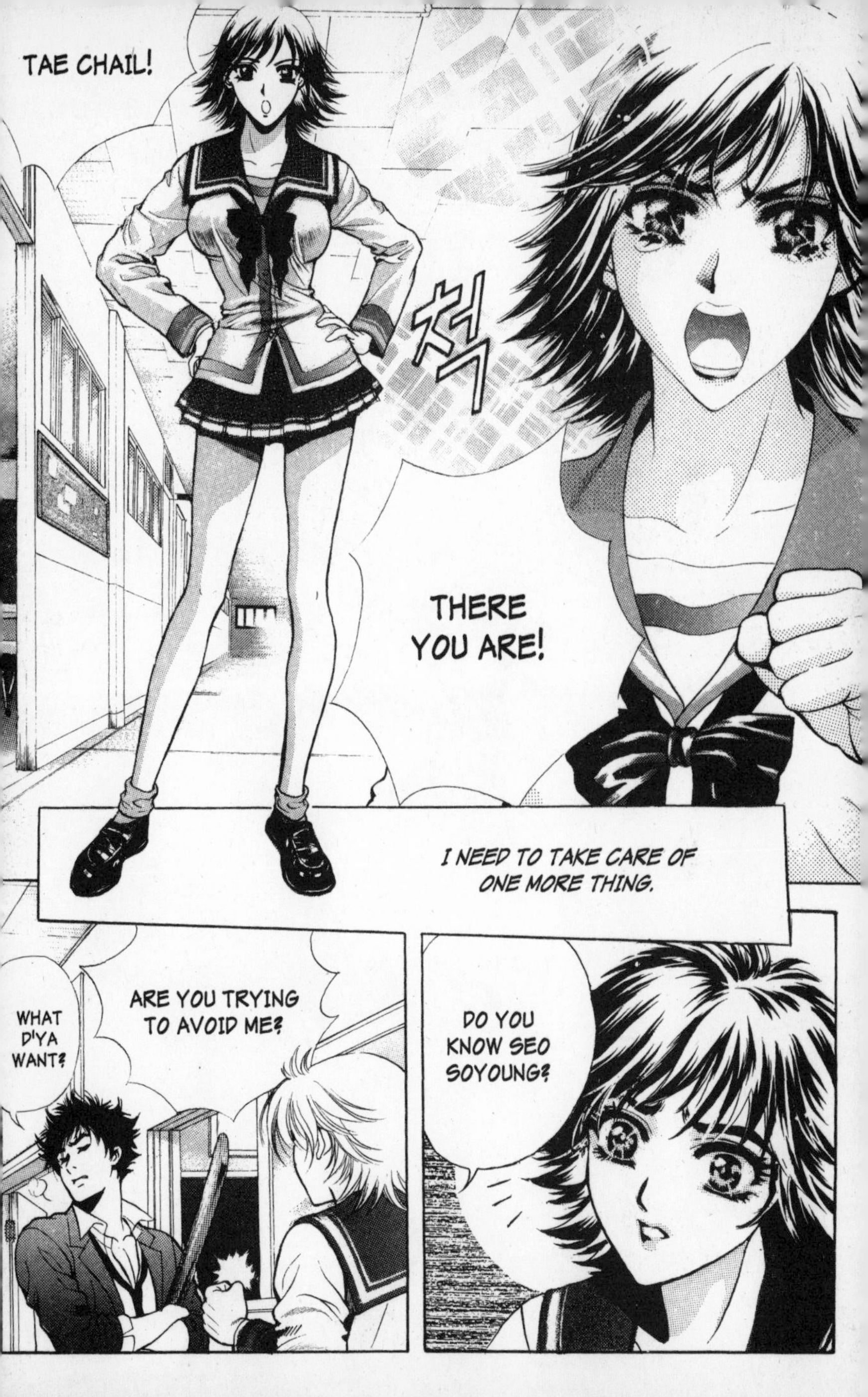
TAE CHAIL!
척
THERE YOU ARE!
I NEED TO TAKE CARE OF ONE MORE THING.
ARE YOU TRYING TO AVOID ME?
WHAT D'YA WANT?
DO YOU KNOW SEO SOYOUNG?

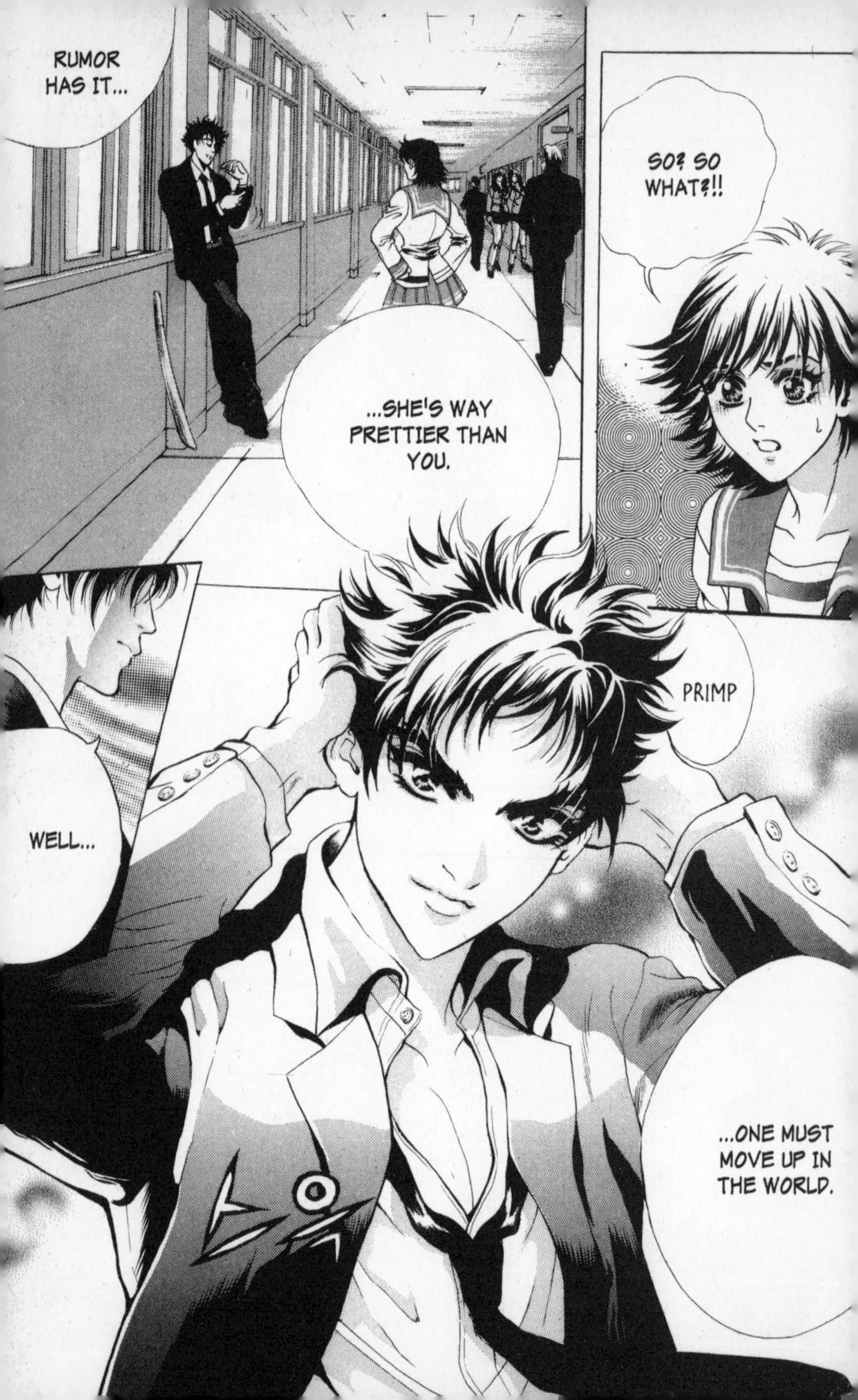
SO? SO WHAT?!!
RUMOR HAS IT...
...SHE'S WAY PRETTIER THAN YOU.
PRIMP
WELL...
...ONE MUST MOVE UP IN THE WORLD.

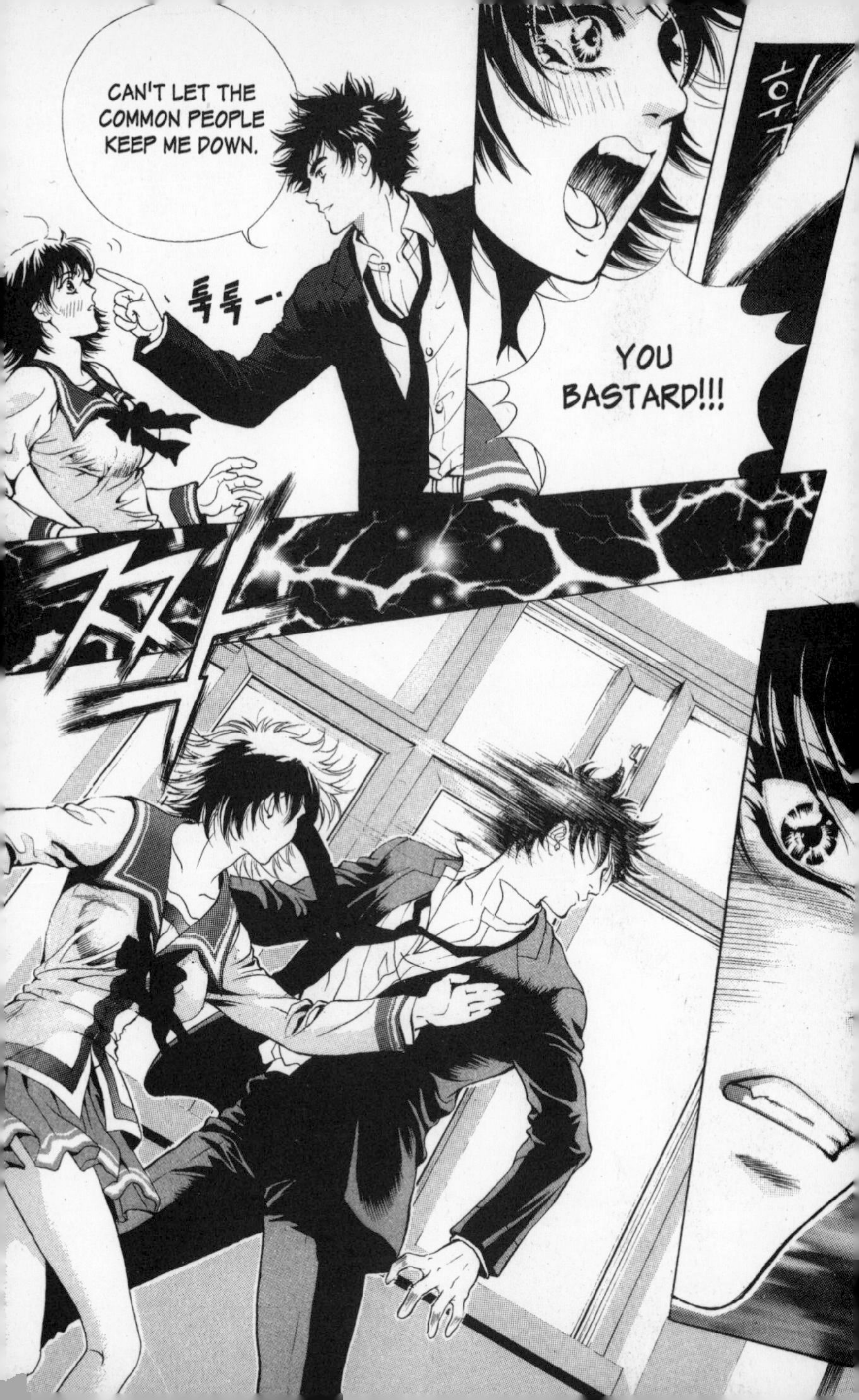

흐억
YOU BASTARD!!!
CAN'T LET THE COMMON PEOPLE KEEP ME DOWN.
톡톡 ─.

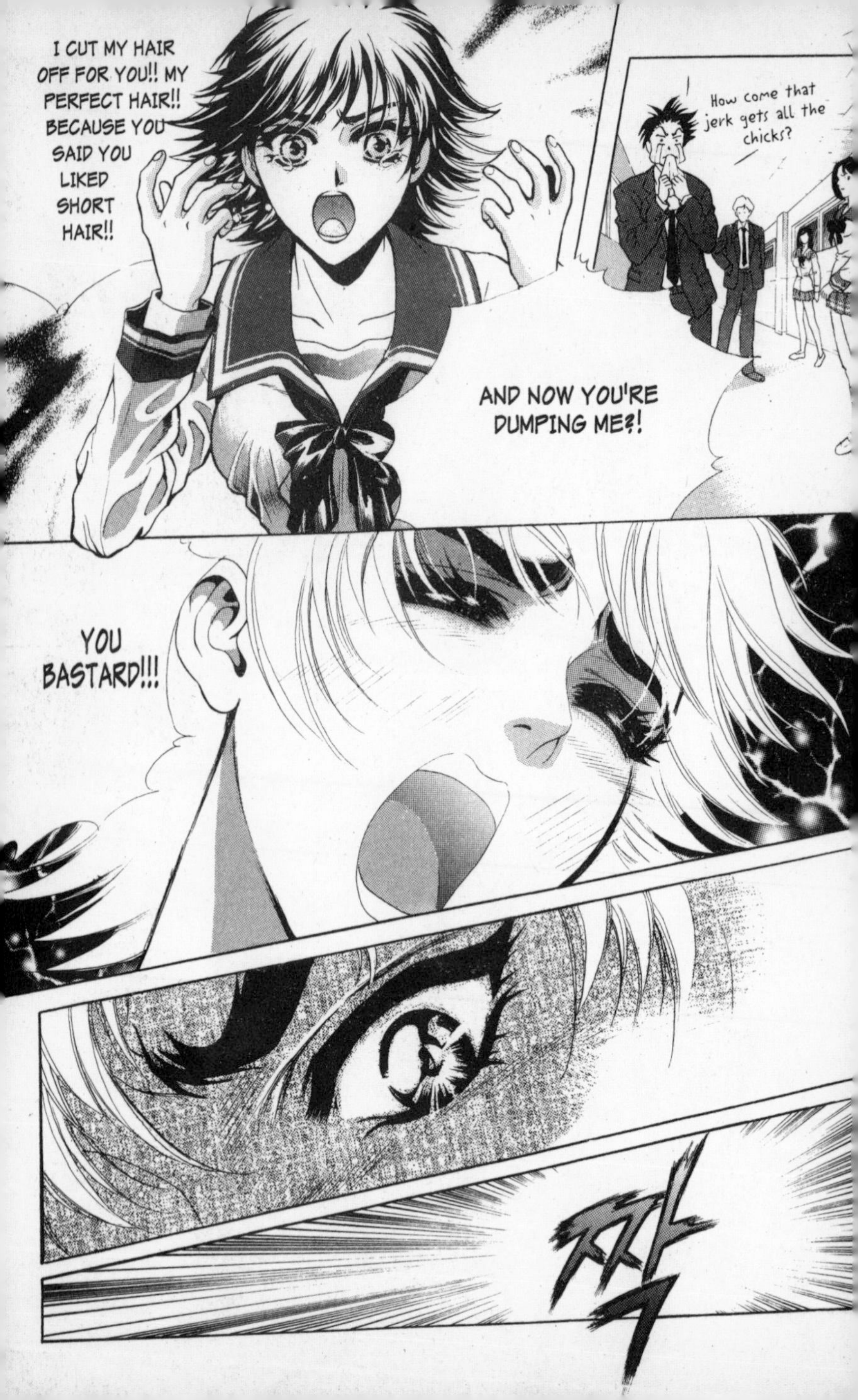

I CUT MY HAIR OFF FOR YOU!! MY PERFECT HAIR!! BECAUSE YOU SAID YOU LIKED SHORT HAIR!!
How come that jerk gets all the chicks?
AND NOW YOU'RE DUMPING ME?!
YOU BASTARD!!!

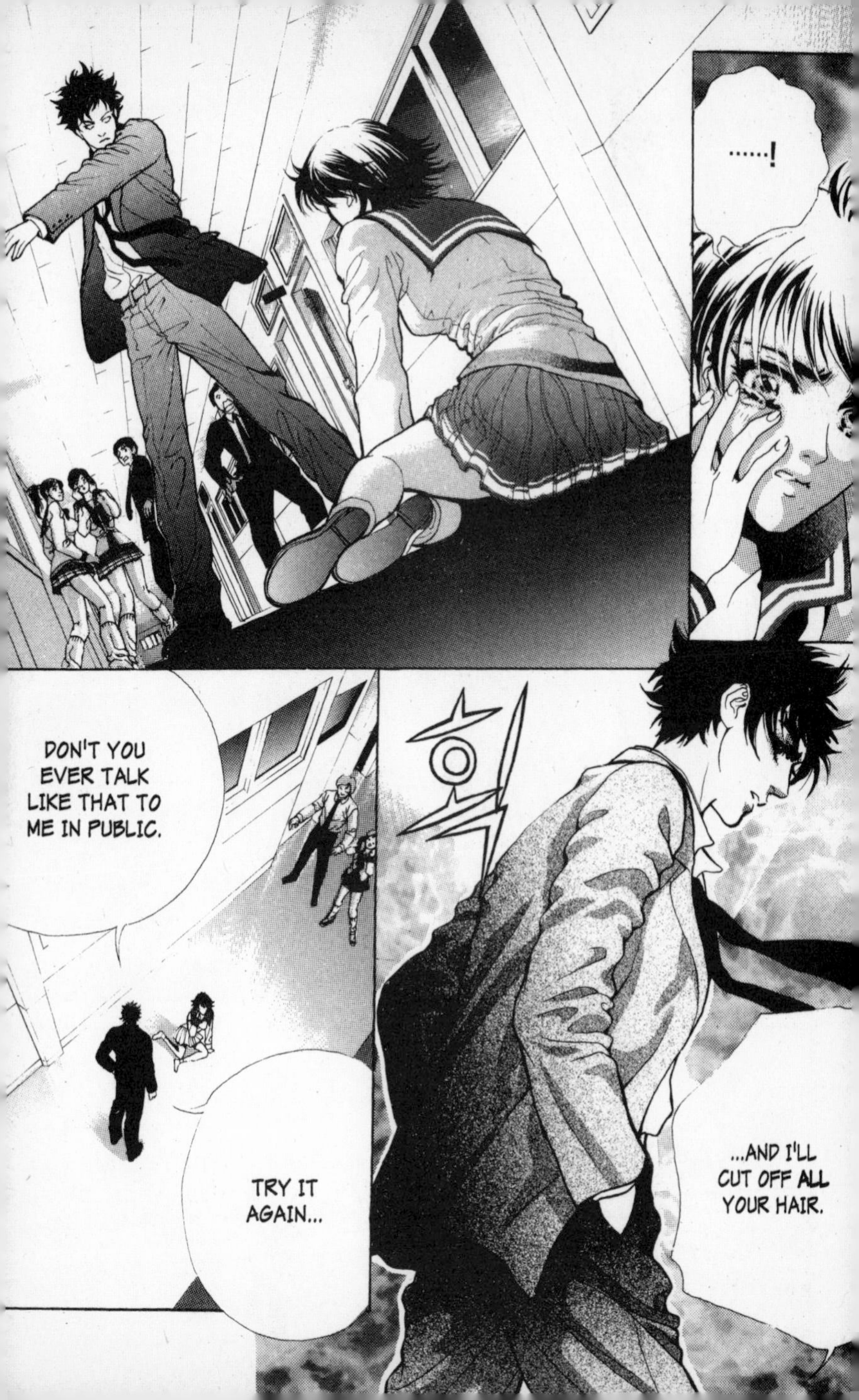
......!
DON'T YOU EVER TALK LIKE THAT TO ME IN PUBLIC.
TRY IT AGAIN...
...AND I'LL CUT OFF ALL YOUR HAIR.

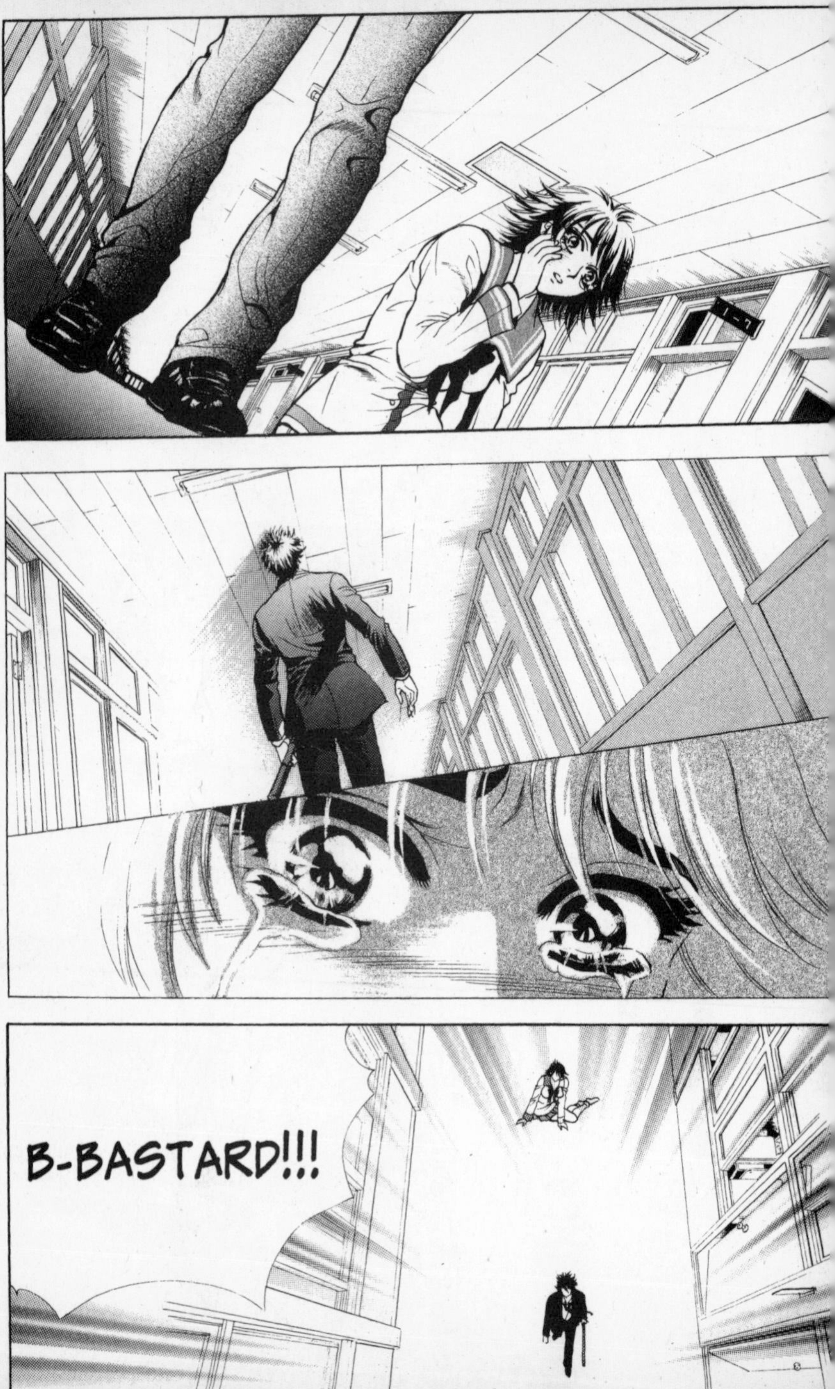
B-BASTARD!!!

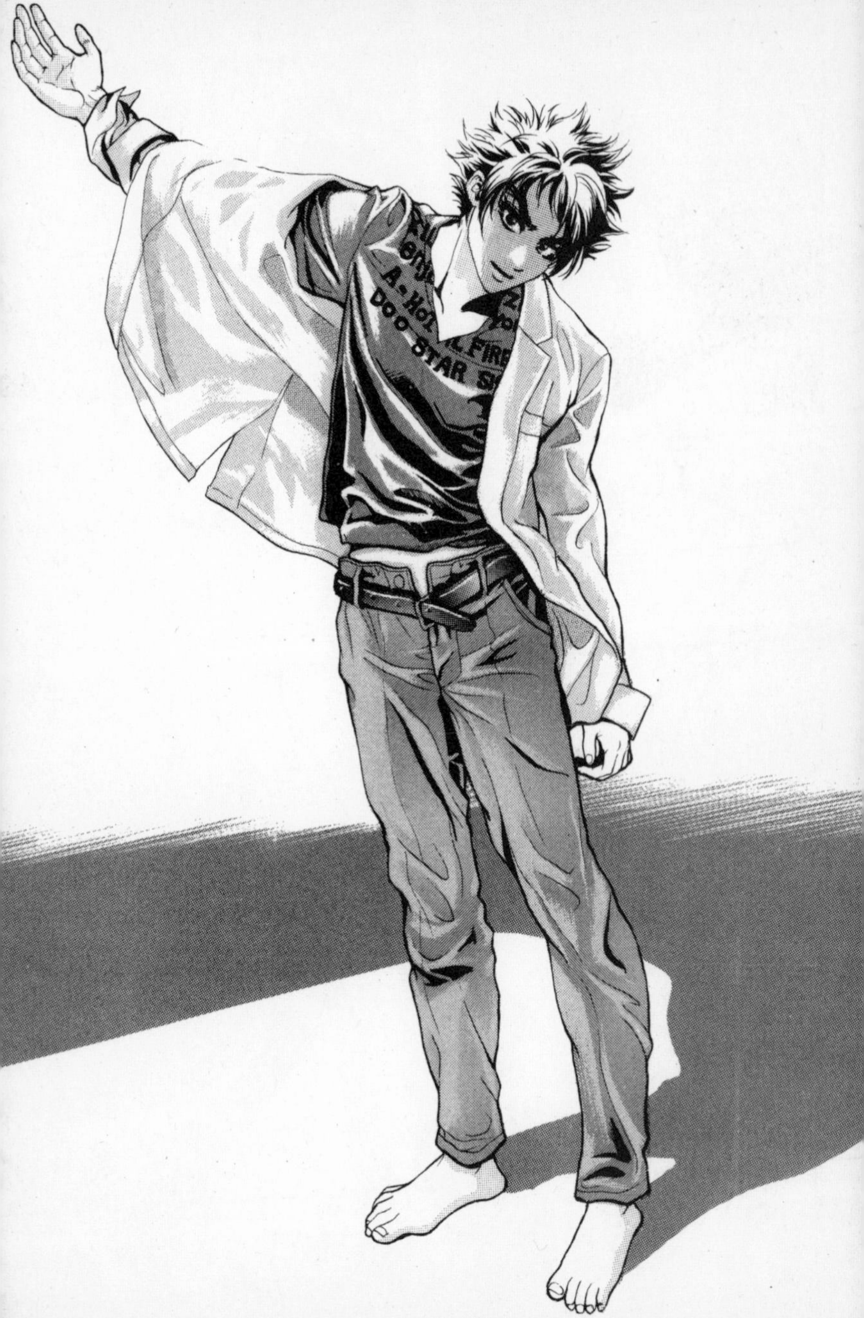

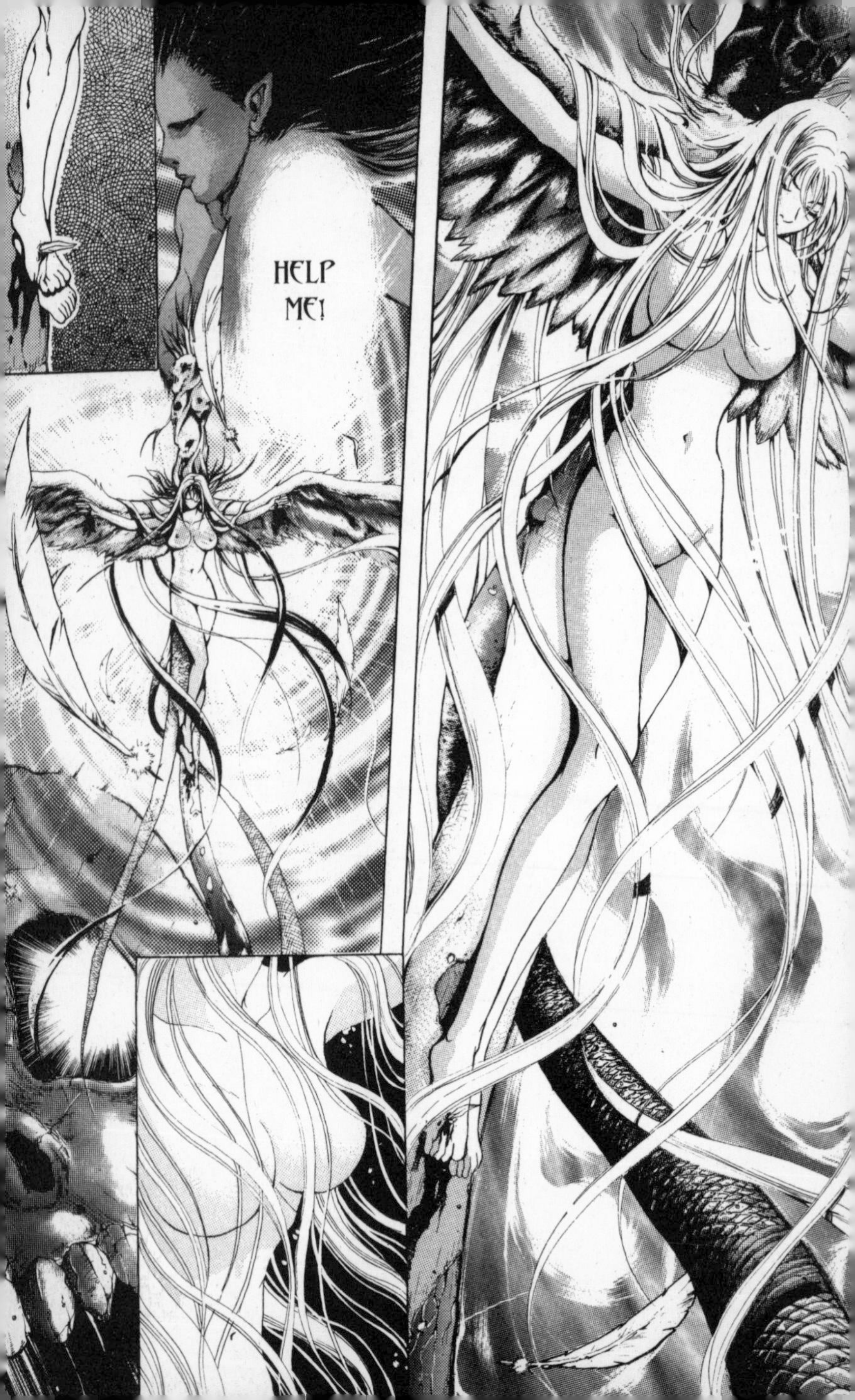
HELP ME!

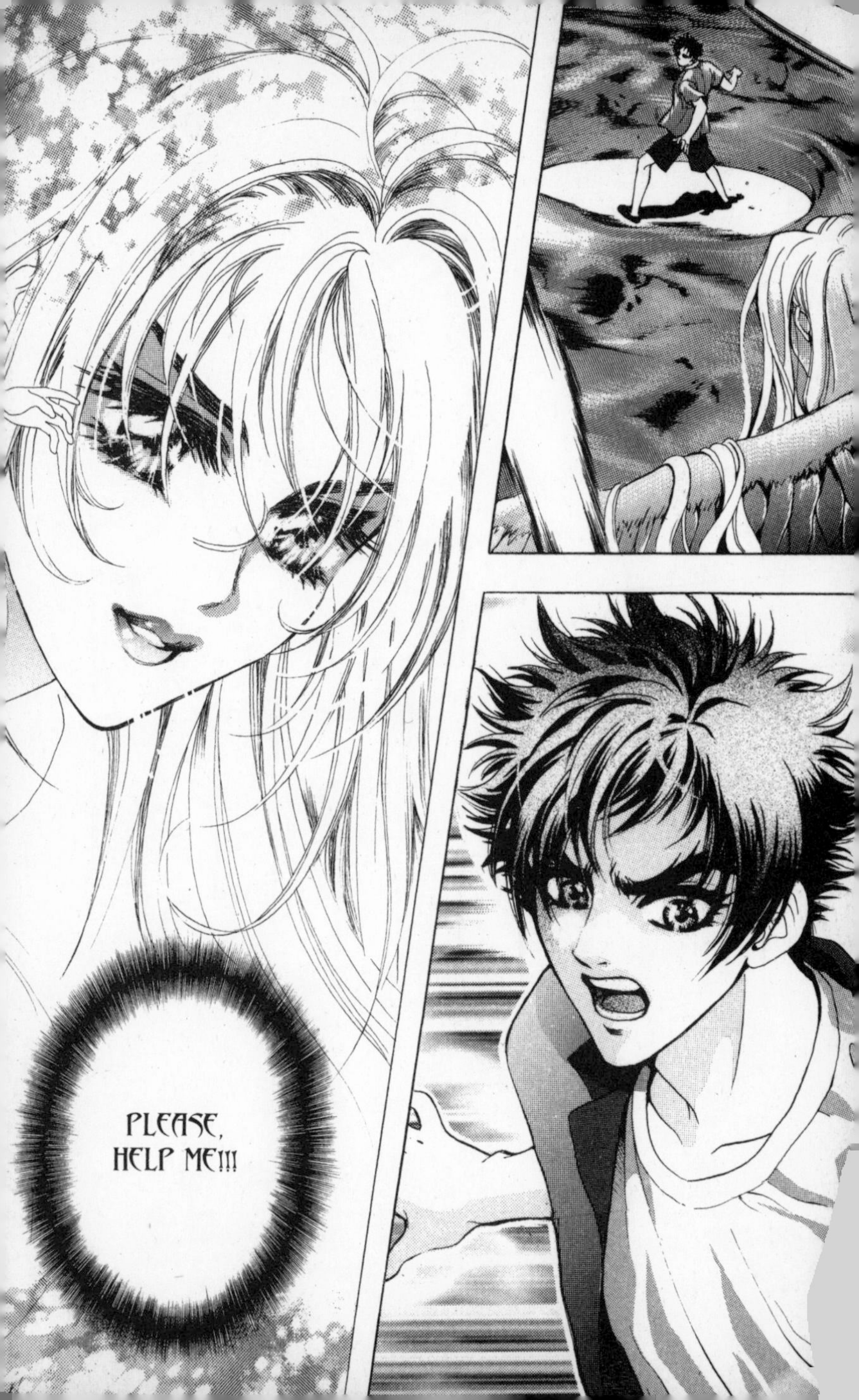
PLEASE, HELP ME!!!

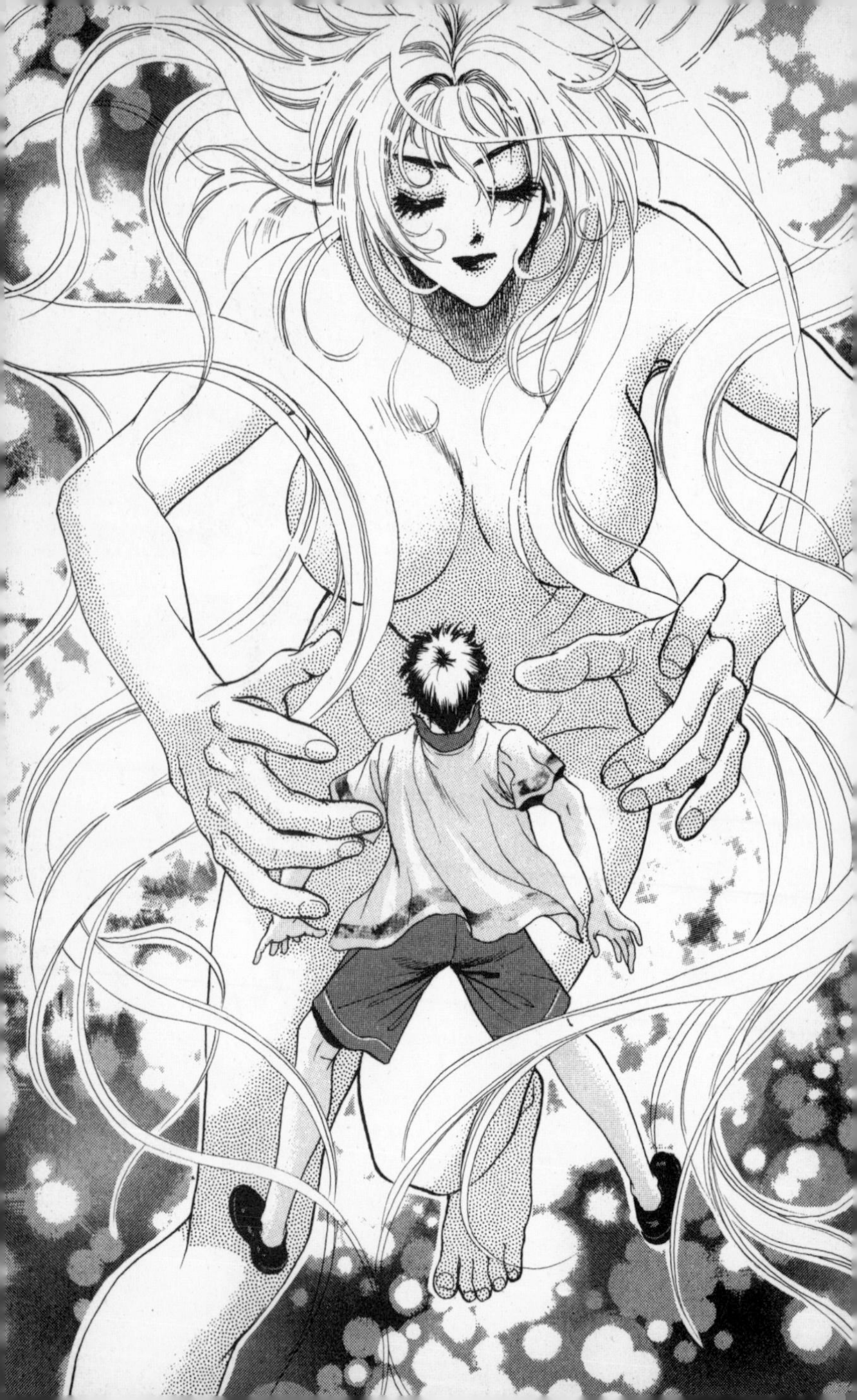

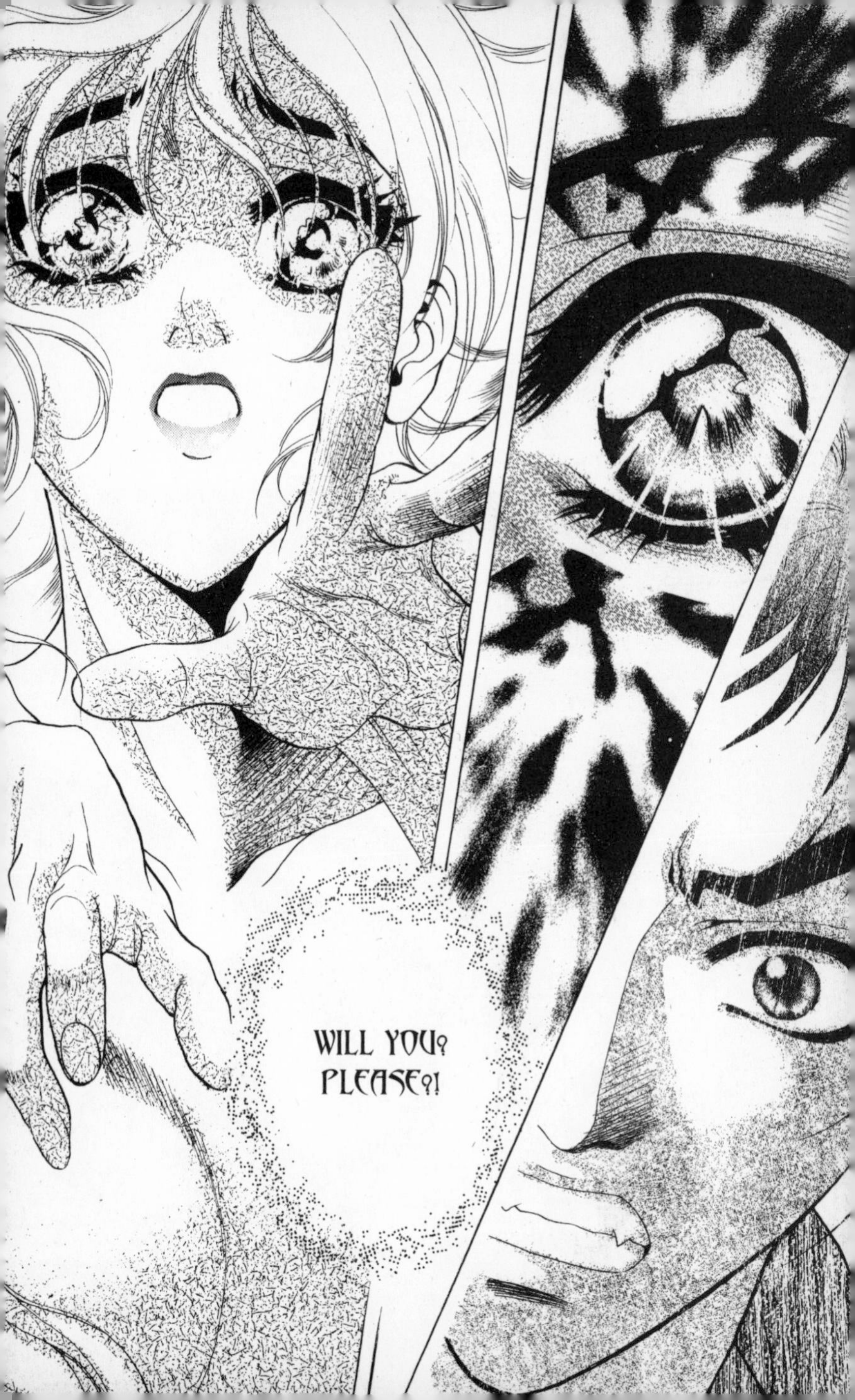
WILL YOU?
PLEASE?!

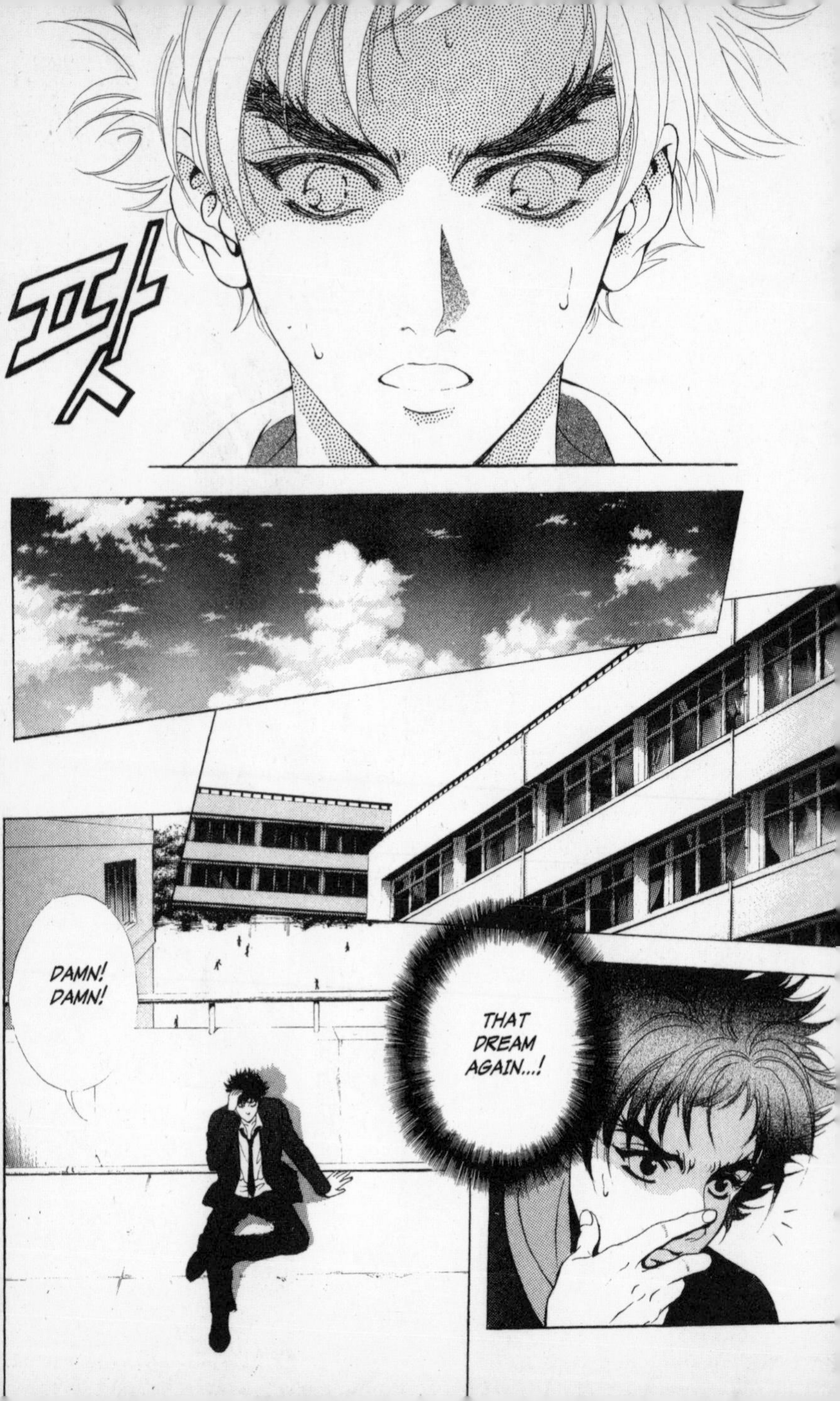
THAT DREAM AGAIN...!
DAMN! DAMN!

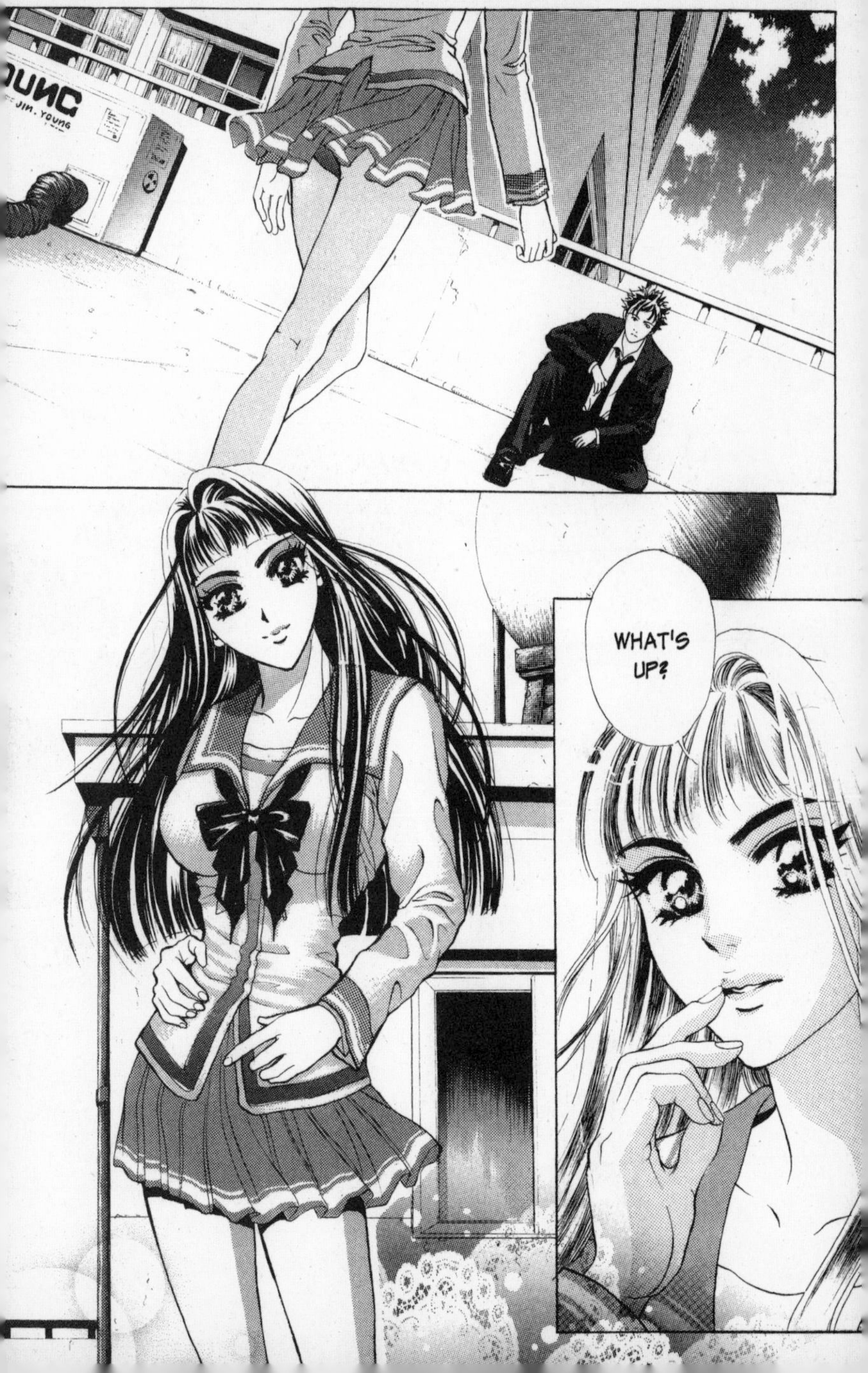
JIN. YOUNG
WHAT'S UP?

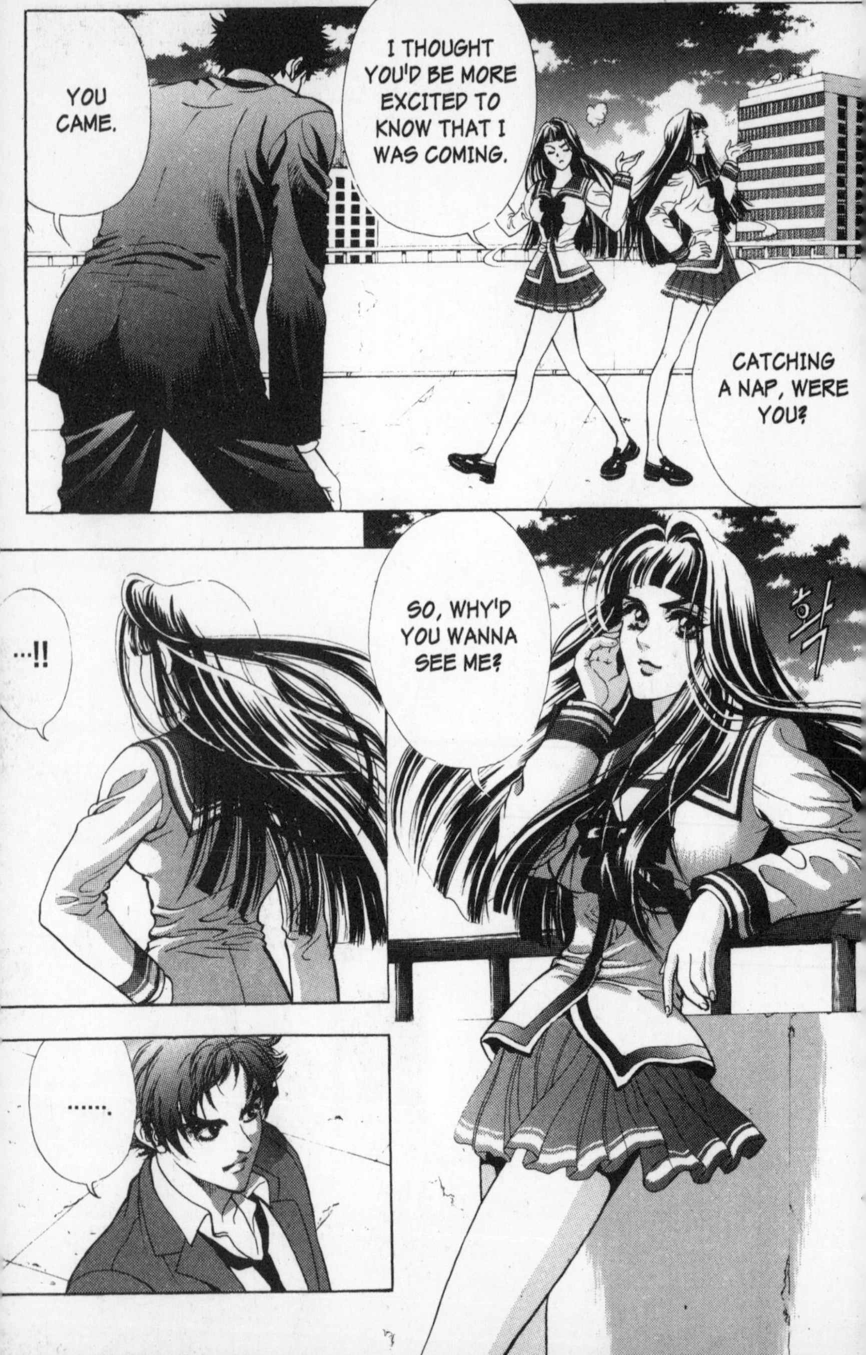
YOU CAME.
I THOUGHT YOU'D BE MORE EXCITED TO KNOW THAT I WAS COMING.
CATCHING A NAP, WERE YOU?
SO, WHY'D YOU WANNA SEE ME?
훅
...!!
......

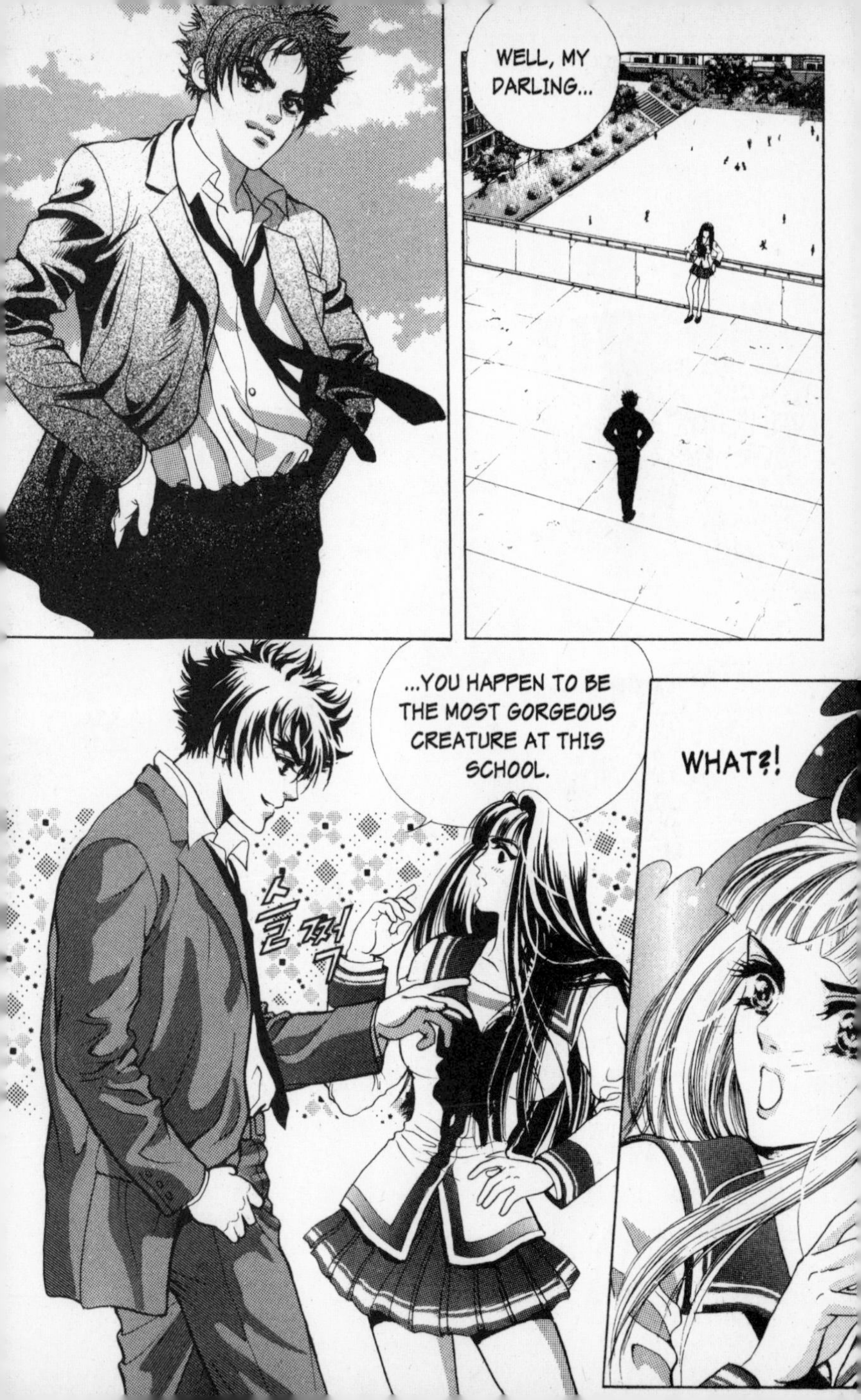
WELL, MY DARLING...
...YOU HAPPEN TO BE THE MOST GORGEOUS CREATURE AT THIS SCHOOL.
WHAT?!

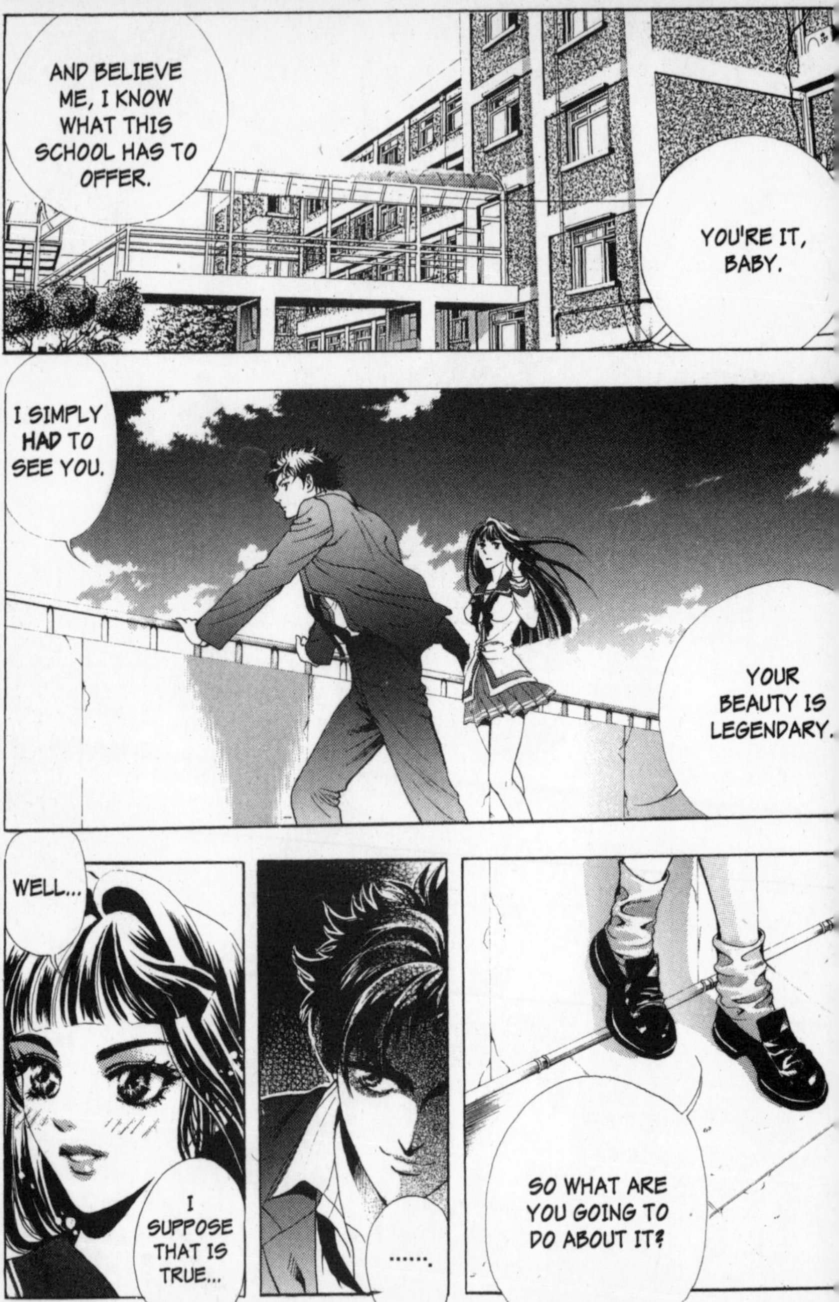
AND BELIEVE ME, I KNOW WHAT THIS SCHOOL HAS TO OFFER.
YOU'RE IT, BABY.
I SIMPLY HAD TO SEE YOU.
YOUR BEAUTY IS LEGENDARY.
WELL...
I SUPPOSE THAT IS TRUE...
....
SO WHAT ARE YOU GOING TO DO ABOUT IT?

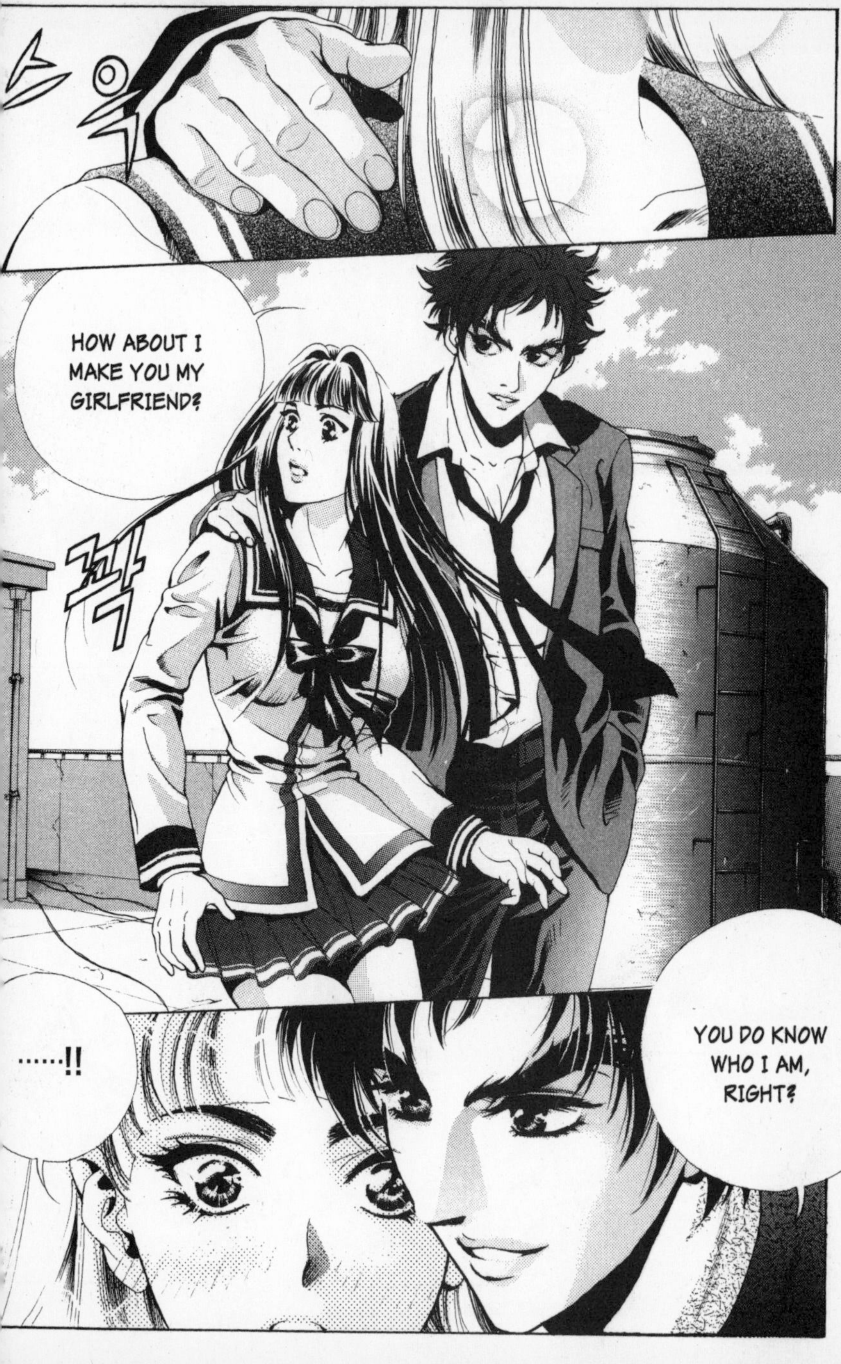
HOW ABOUT I MAKE YOU MY GIRLFRIEND?
......!!
YOU DO KNOW WHO I AM, RIGHT?

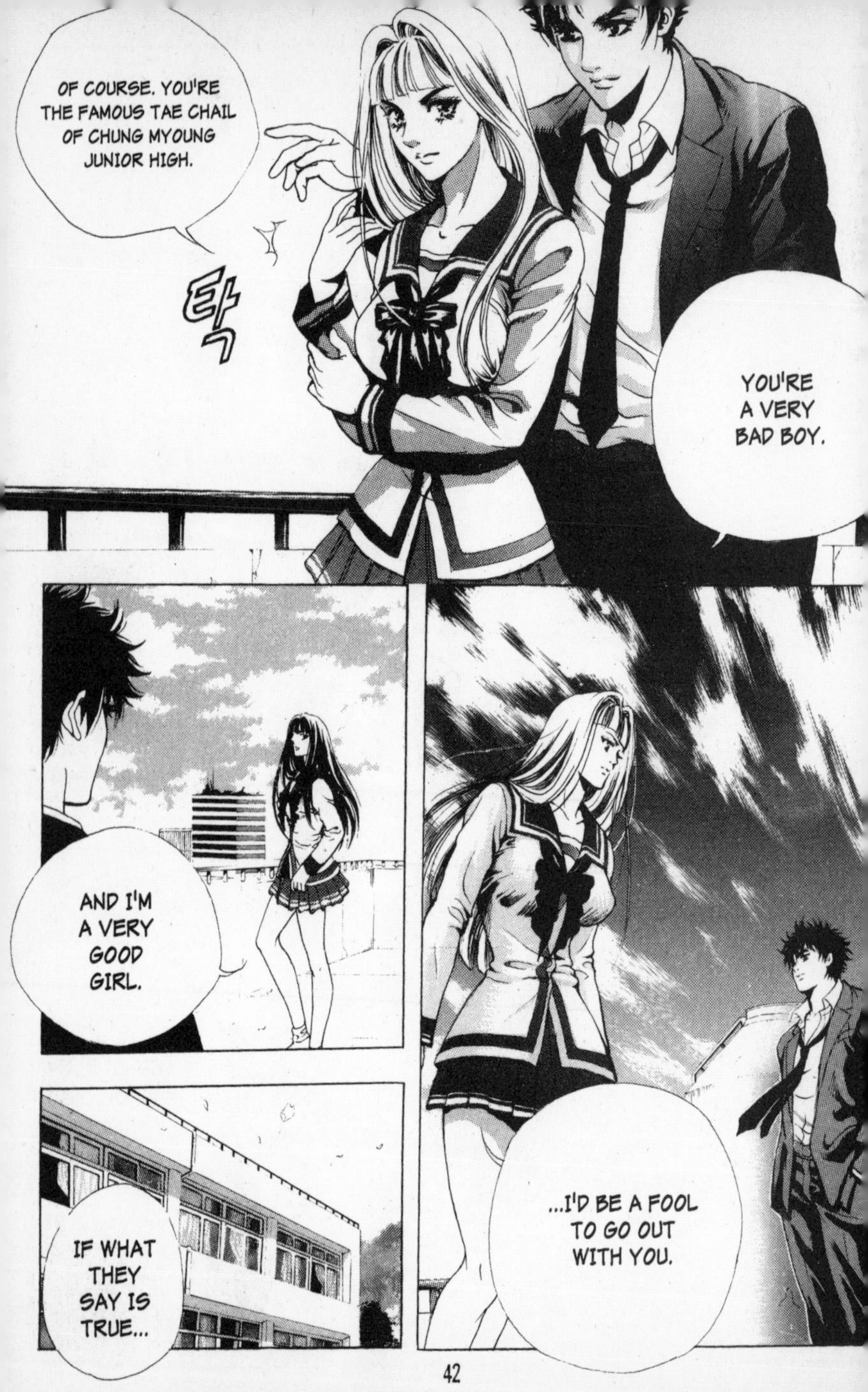
OF COURSE. YOU'RE THE FAMOUS TAE CHAIL OF CHUNG MYOUNG JUNIOR HIGH.
탁
YOU'RE A VERY BAD BOY.
AND I'M A VERY GOOD GIRL.
IF WHAT THEY SAY IS TRUE...
...I'D BE A FOOL TO GO OUT WITH YOU.

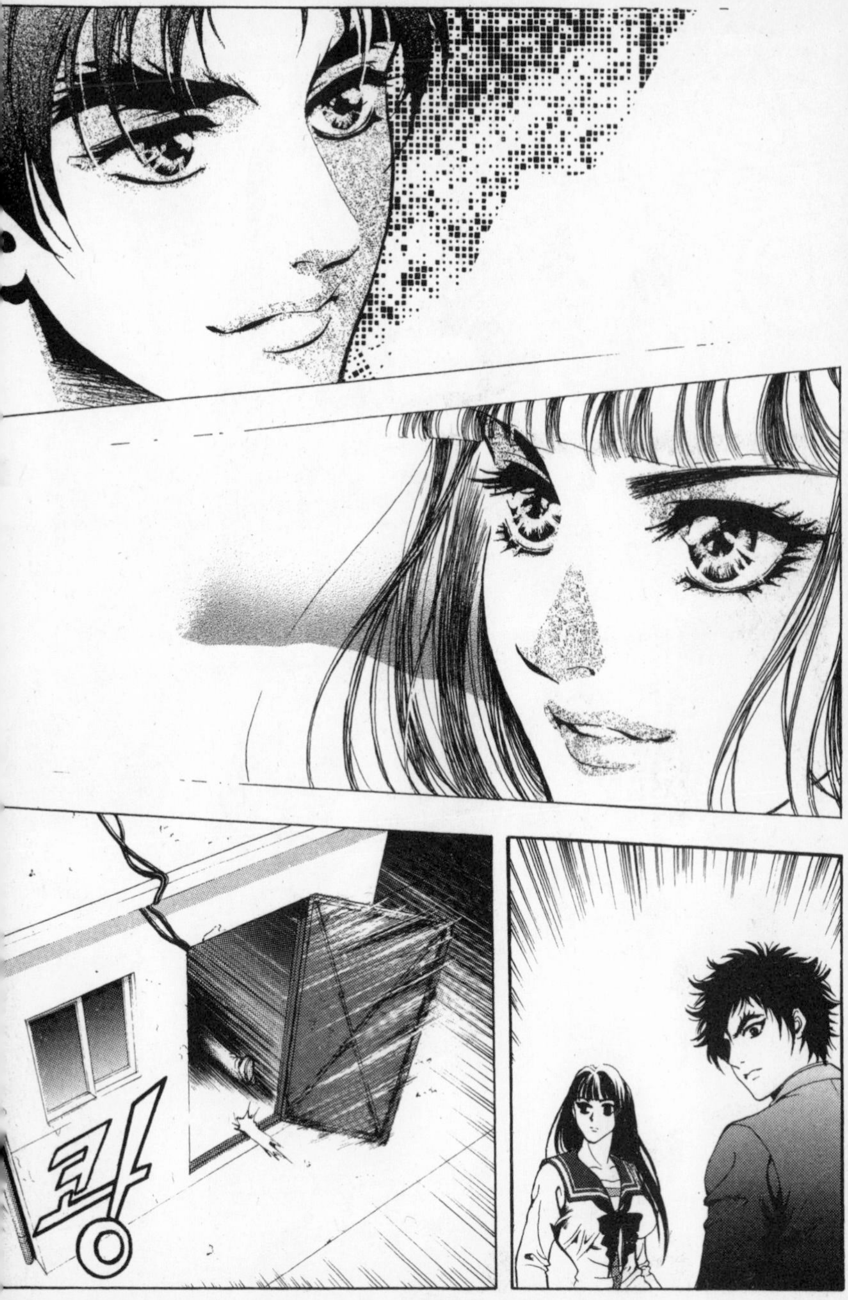
쾅

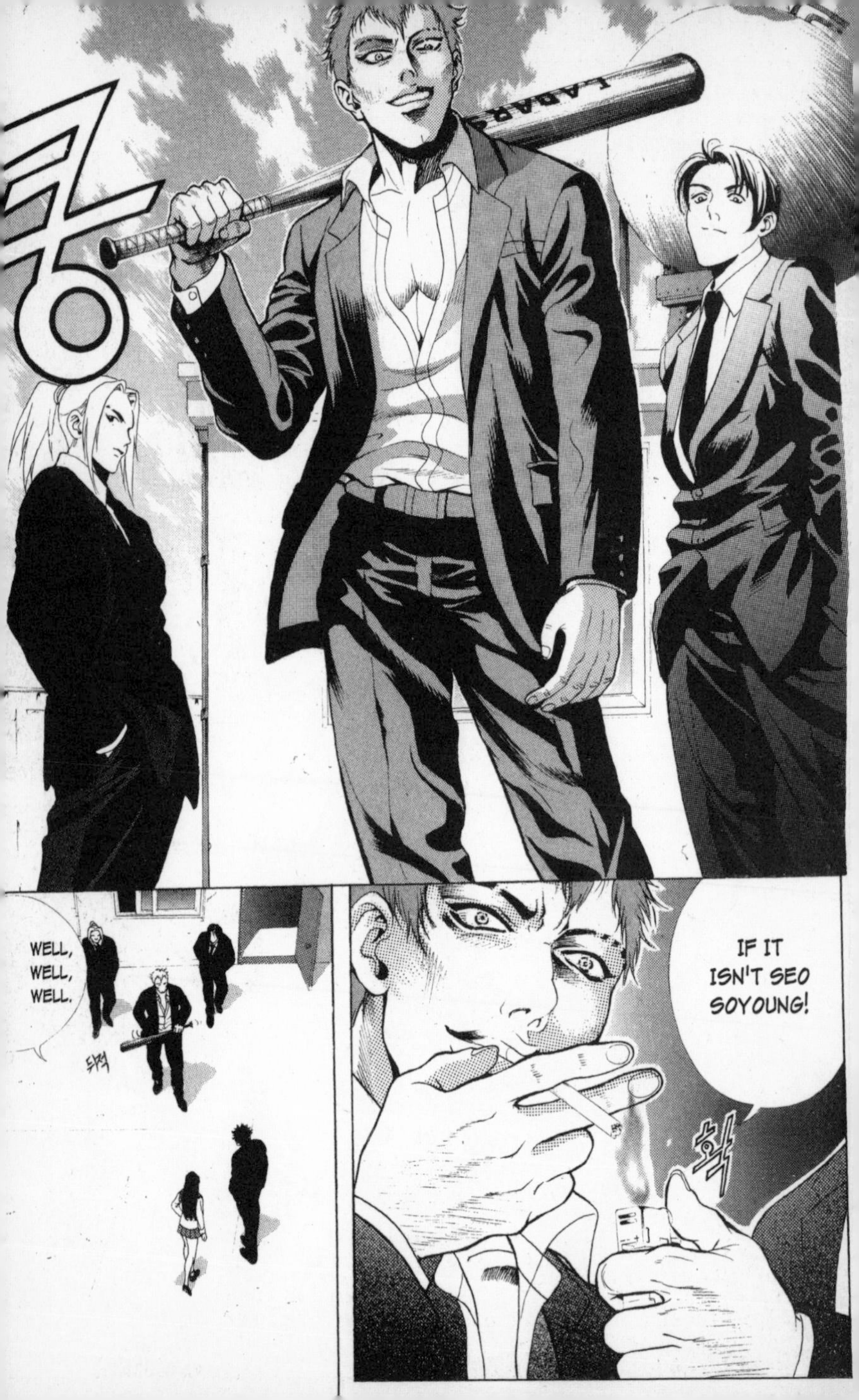
WELL,
WELL,
WELL.
IF IT ISN'T SEO SOYOUNG!

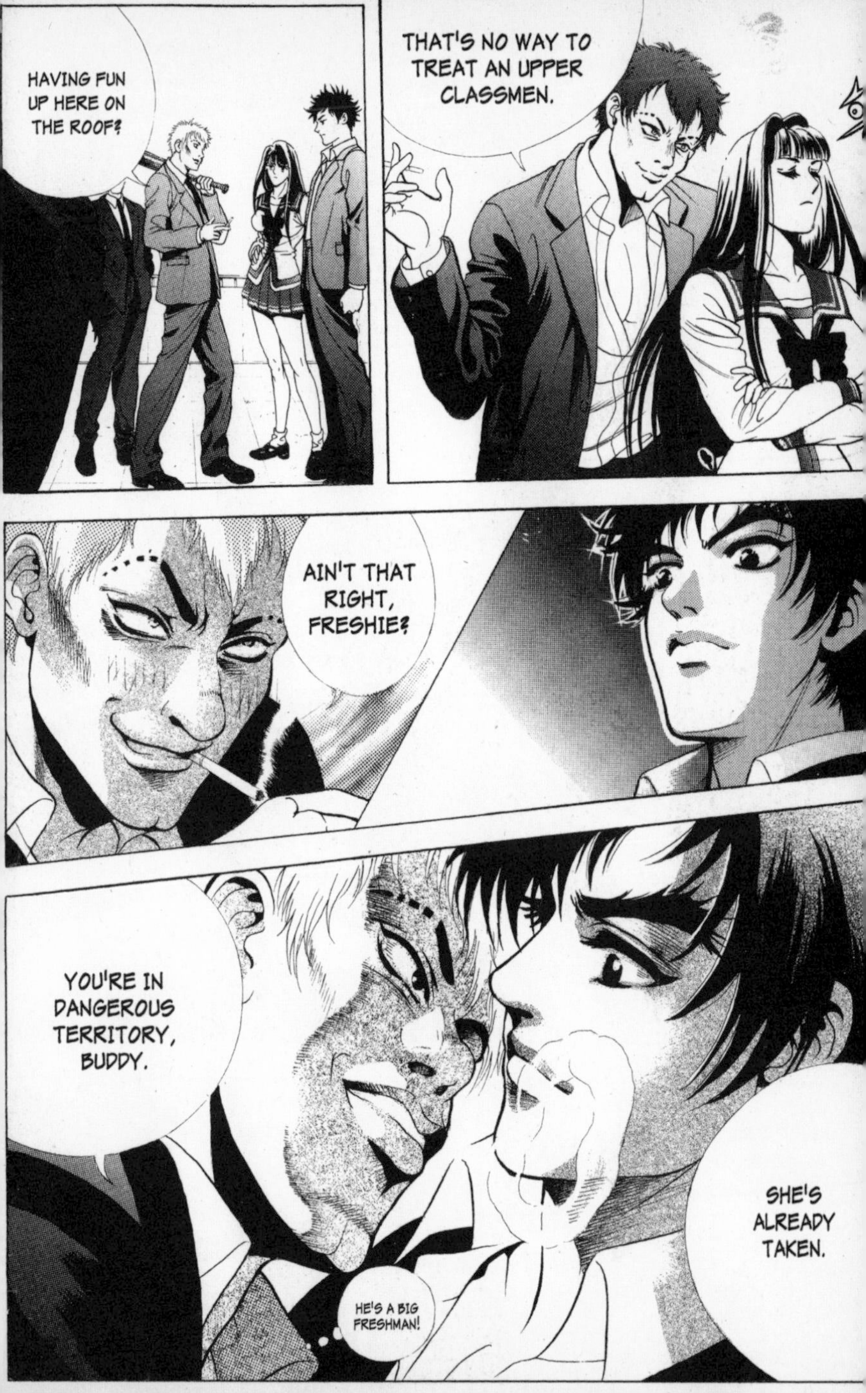
HAVING FUN UP HERE ON THE ROOF?
THAT'S NO WAY TO TREAT AN UPPER CLASSMEN.
AIN'T THAT RIGHT, FRESHIE?
YOU'RE IN DANGEROUS TERRITORY, BUDDY.
HE'S A BIG FRESHMAN!
SHE'S ALREADY TAKEN.

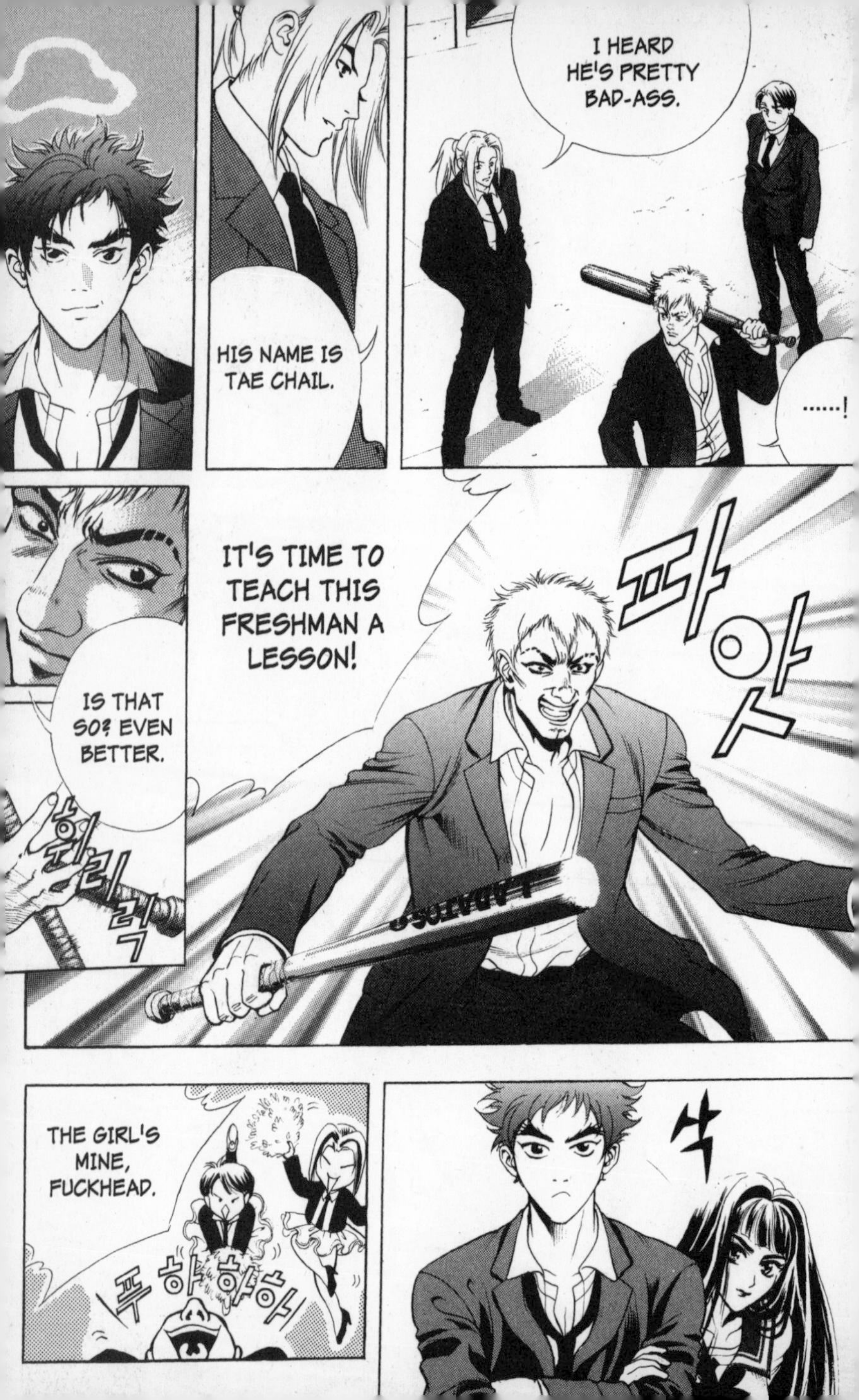
HIS NAME IS TAE CHAIL.
I HEARD HE'S PRETTY BAD-ASS.
......!
IT'S TIME TO TEACH THIS FRESHMAN A LESSON!
파앗
IS THAT SO? EVEN BETTER.
휘리릭
THE GIRL'S MINE, FUCKHEAD.
푸하하하
싹

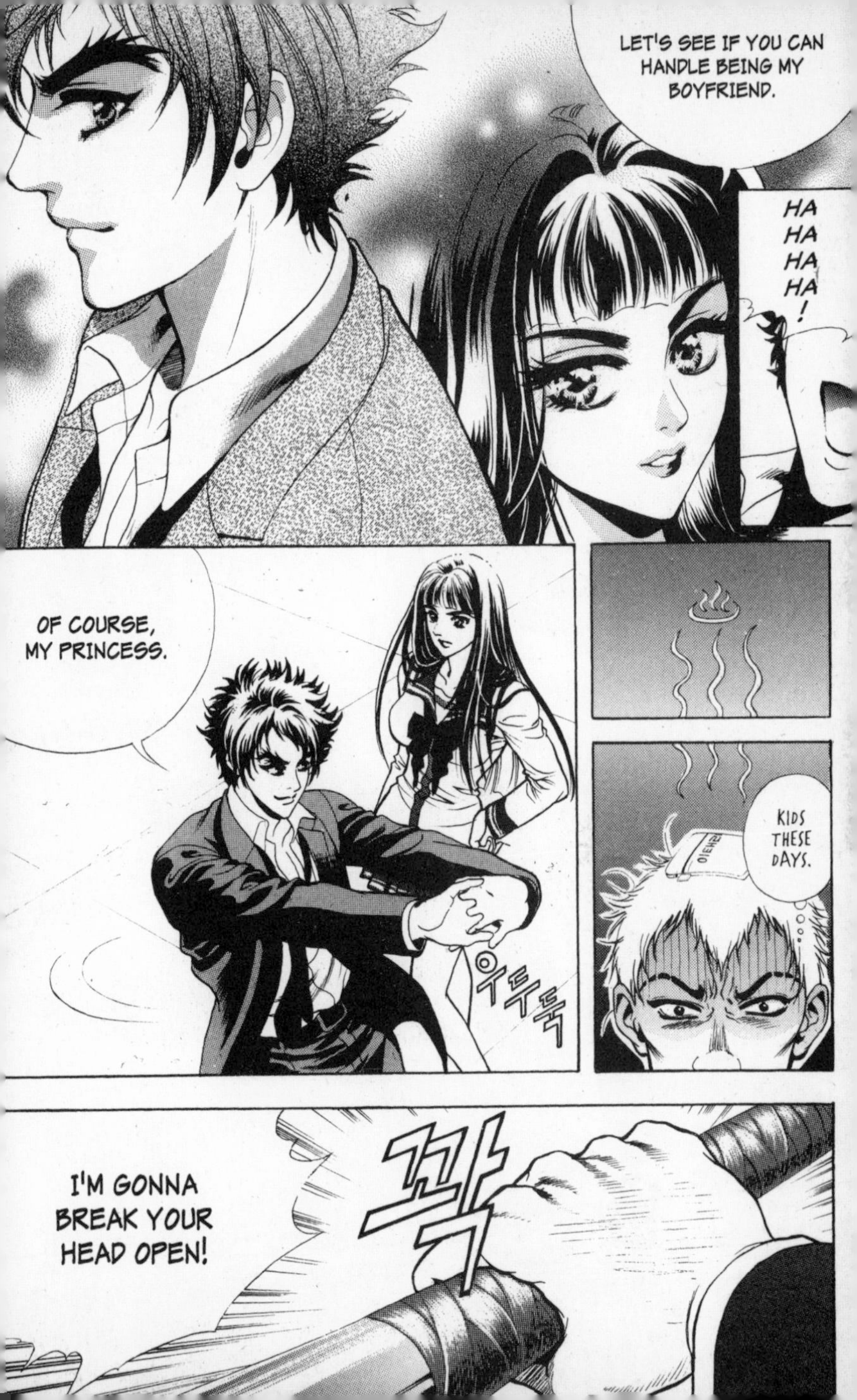
LET'S SEE IF YOU CAN HANDLE BEING MY BOYFRIEND.
HA HA HA HA!
OF COURSE, MY PRINCESS.
우드득
KIDS THESE DAYS.
I'M GONNA BREAK YOUR HEAD OPEN!
꽉

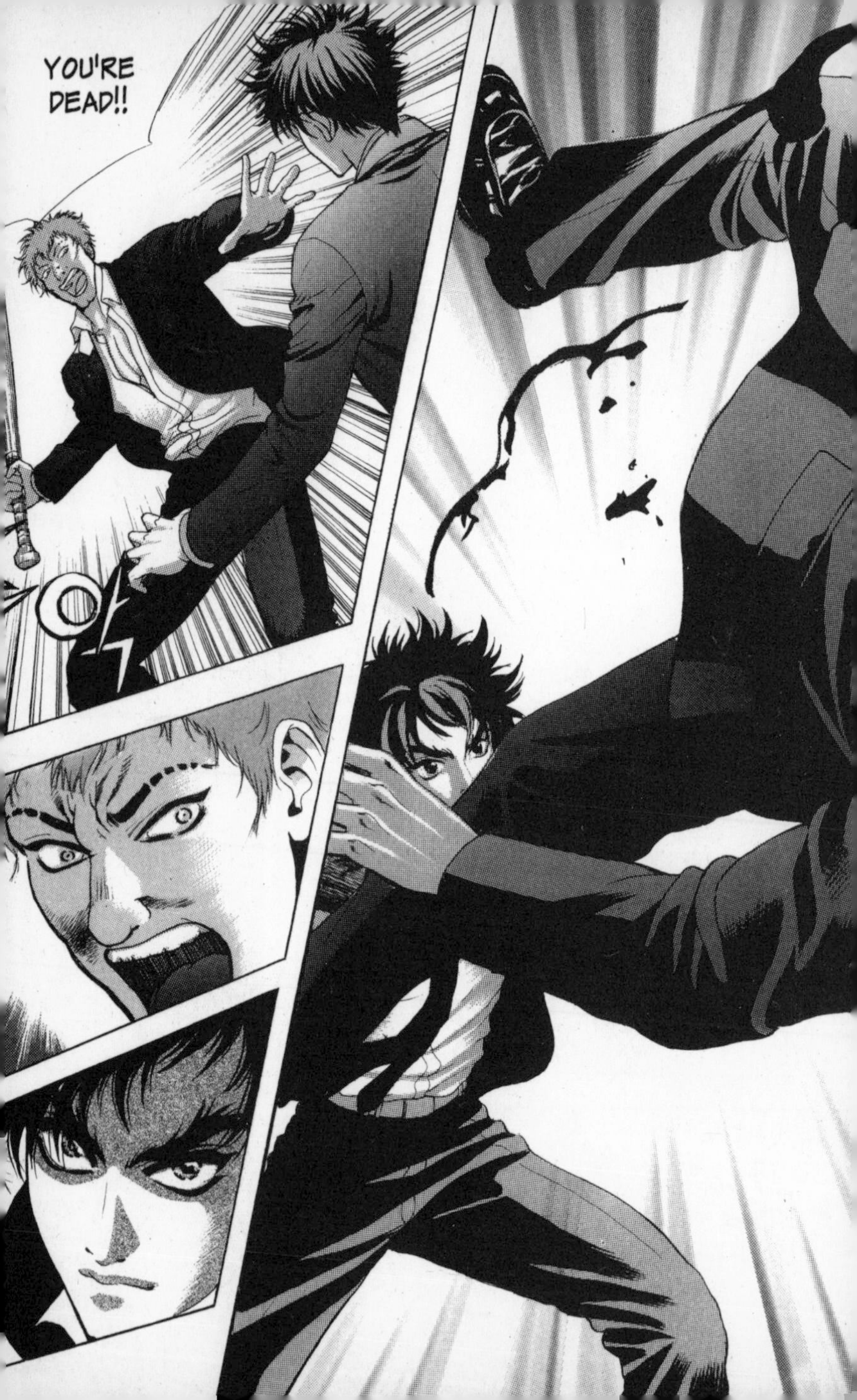
YOU'RE
DEAD!!

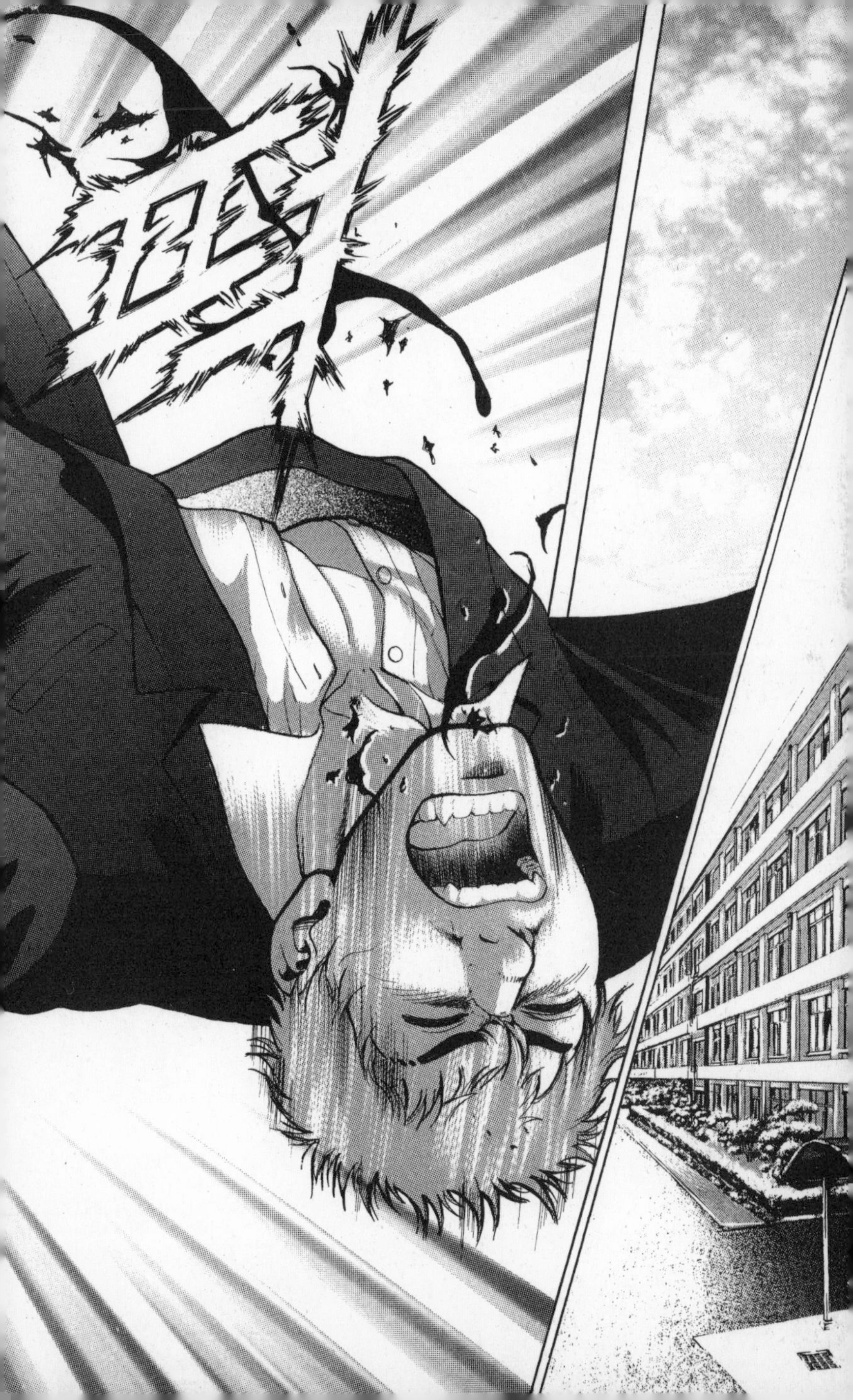

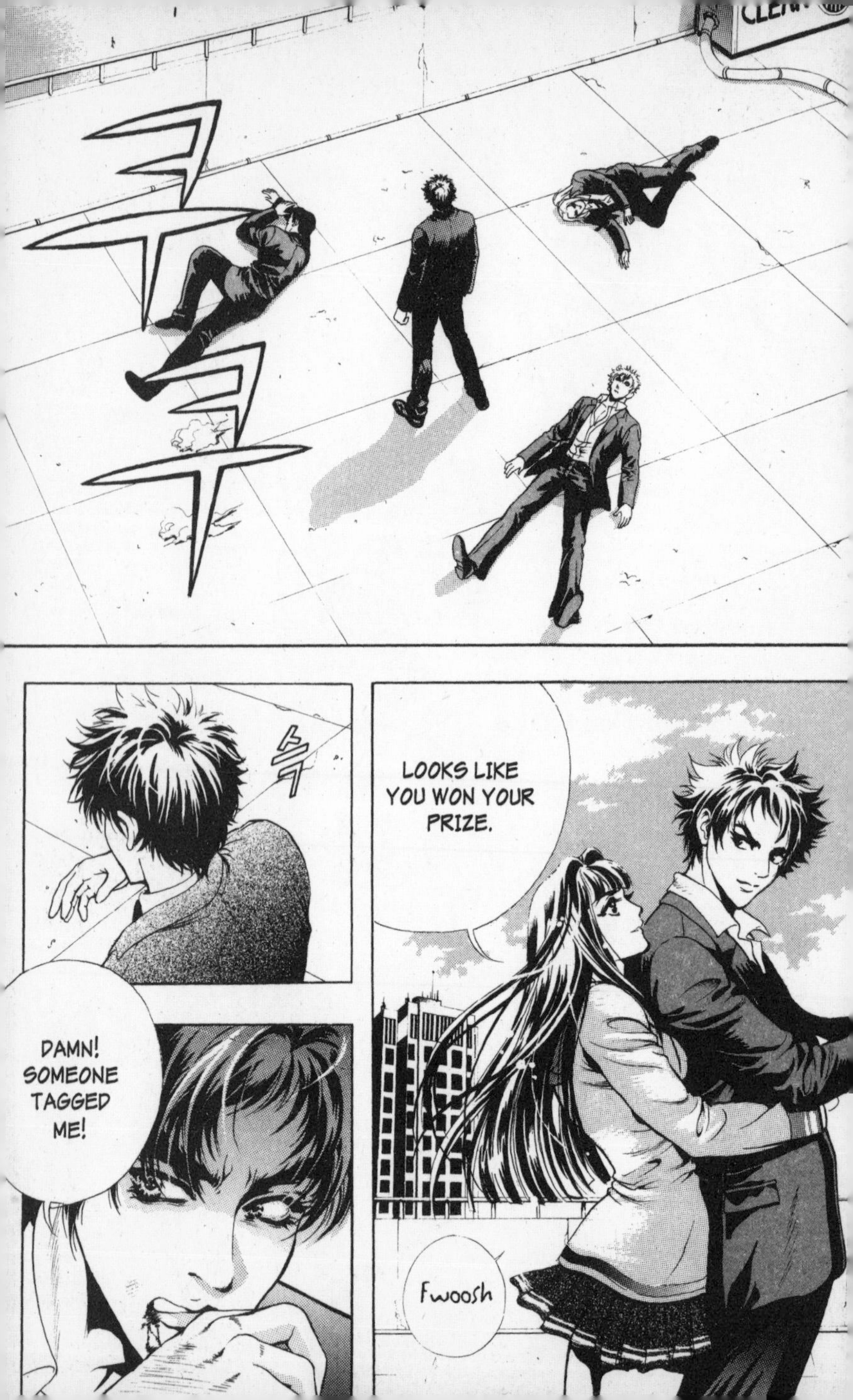
DAMN! SOMEONE TAGGED ME!
LOOKS LIKE YOU WON YOUR PRIZE.
Fwoosh

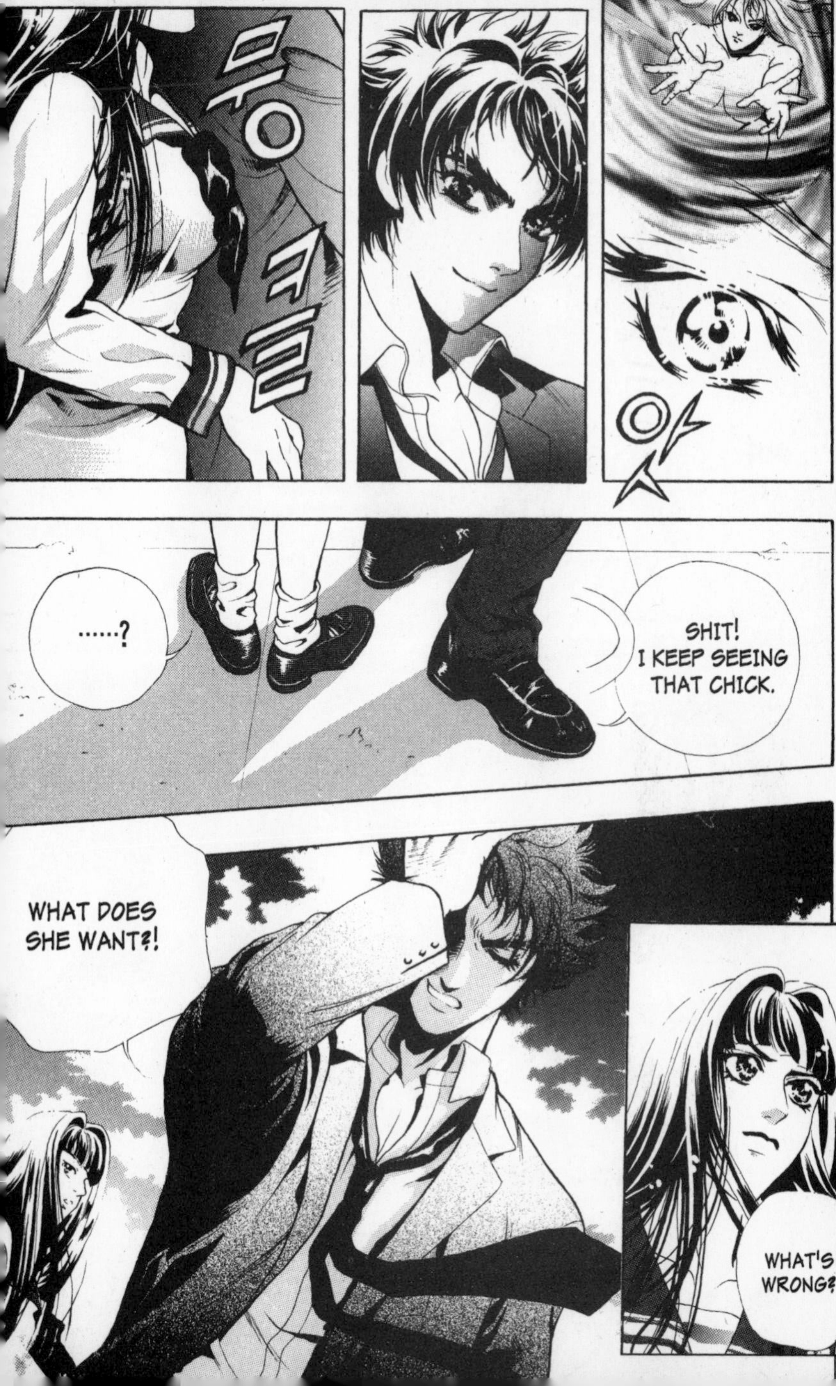
......?
SHIT! I KEEP SEEING THAT CHICK.
WHAT DOES SHE WANT?!
WHAT'S WRONG?

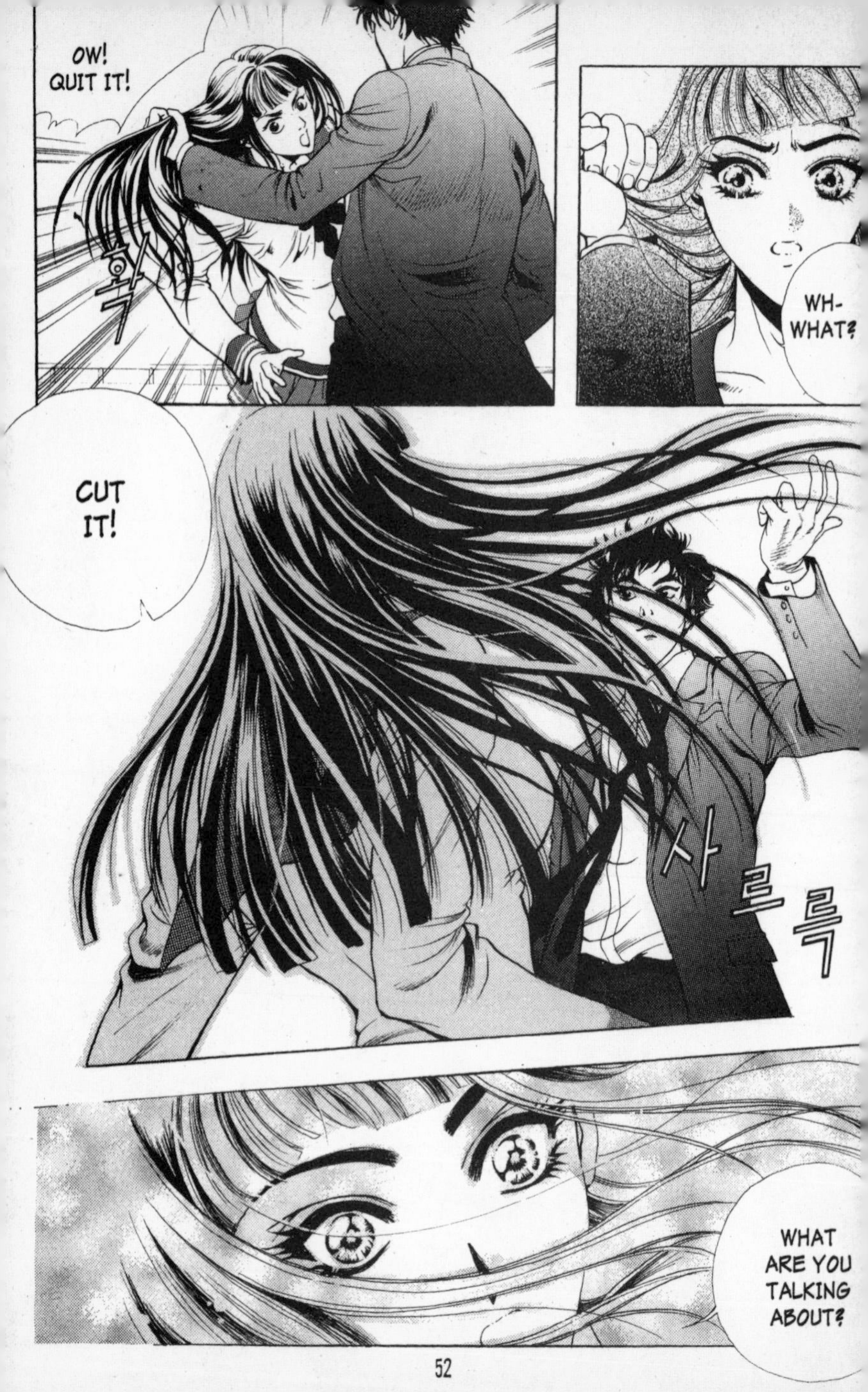
OW! QUIT IT!
WH-WHAT?
CUT IT!
사르륵
WHAT ARE YOU TALKING ABOUT?

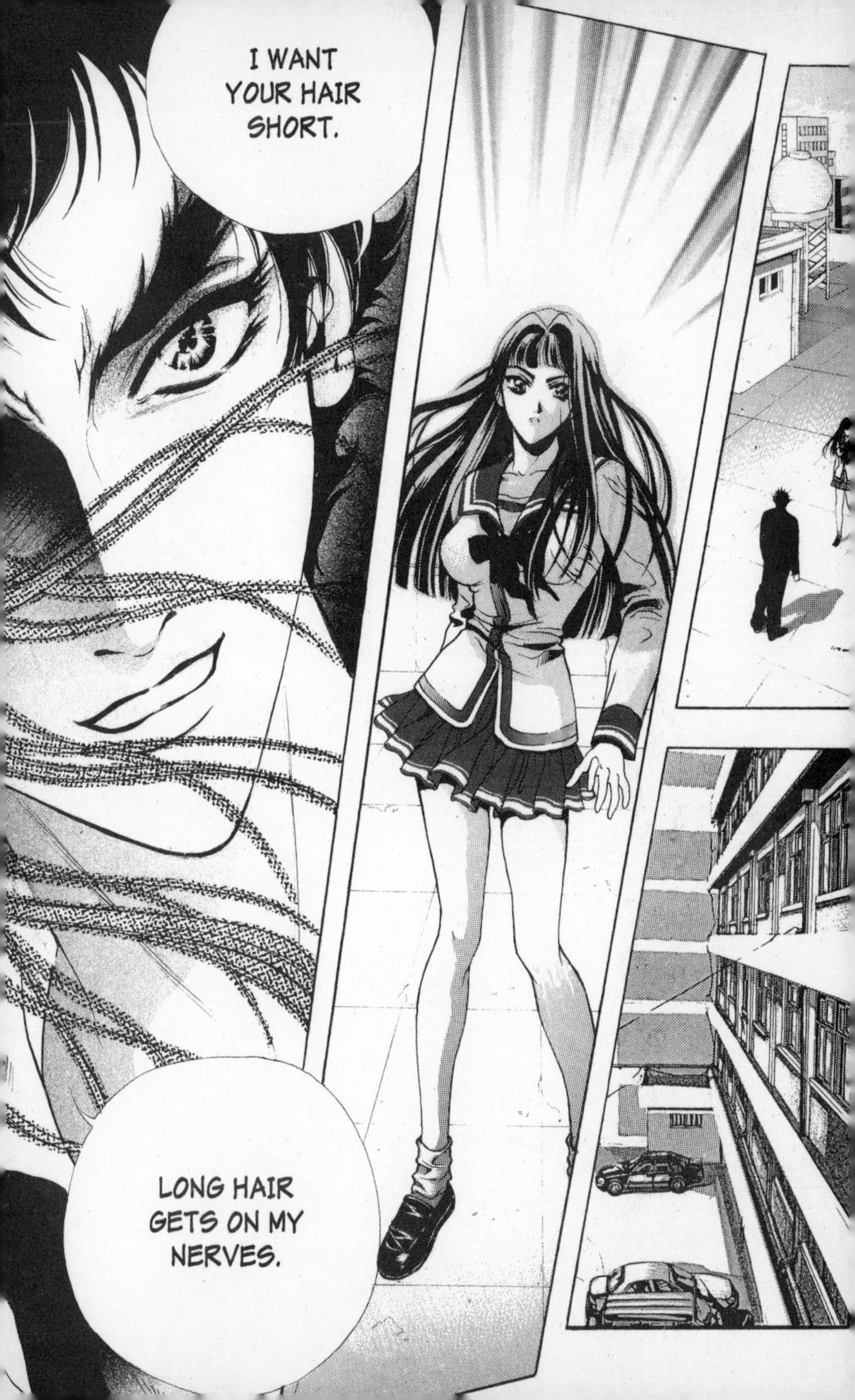
I WANT YOUR HAIR SHORT.
LONG HAIR GETS ON MY NERVES.

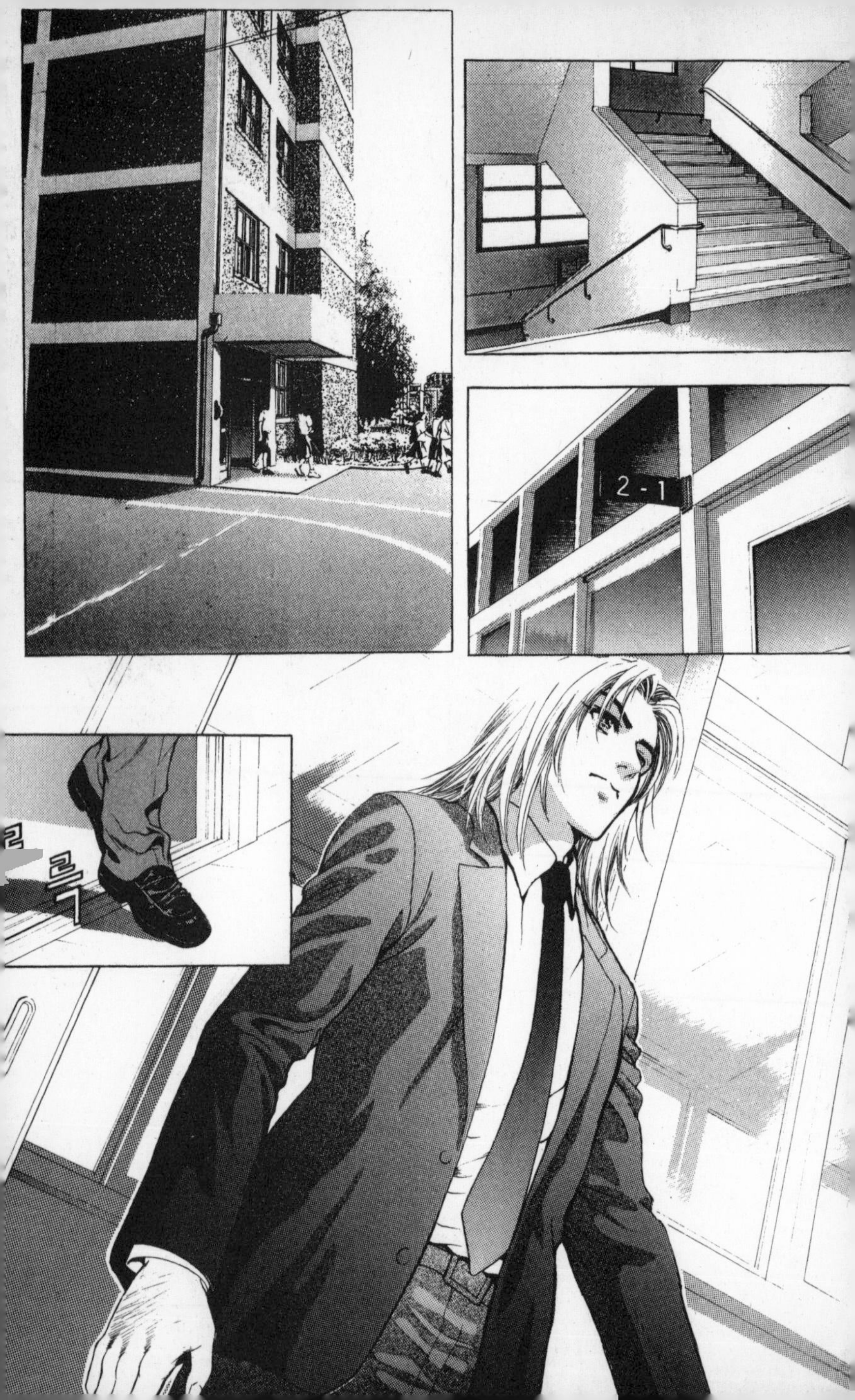
2-1
륵

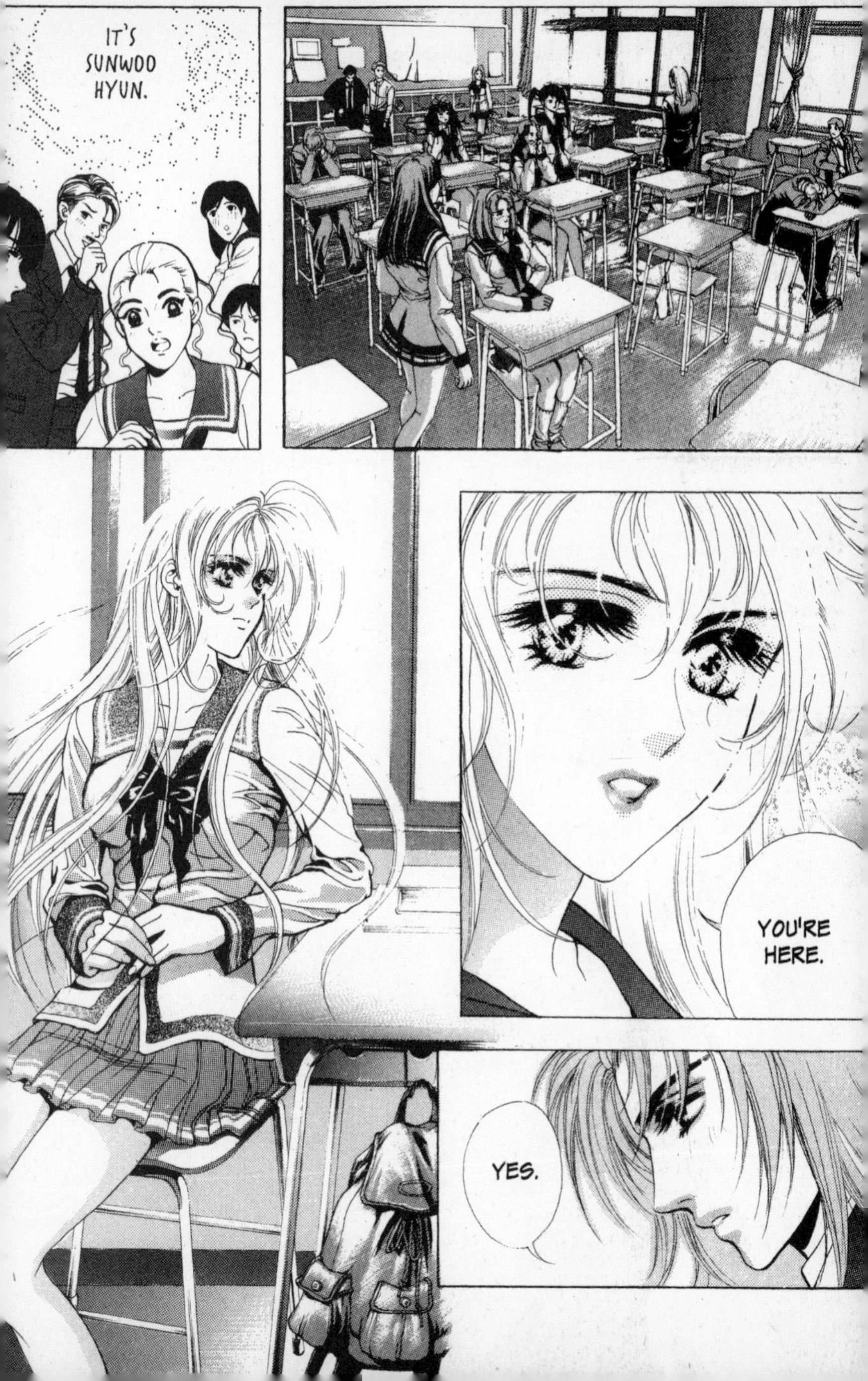
IT'S SUNWOO HYUN.
YOU'RE HERE.
YES.

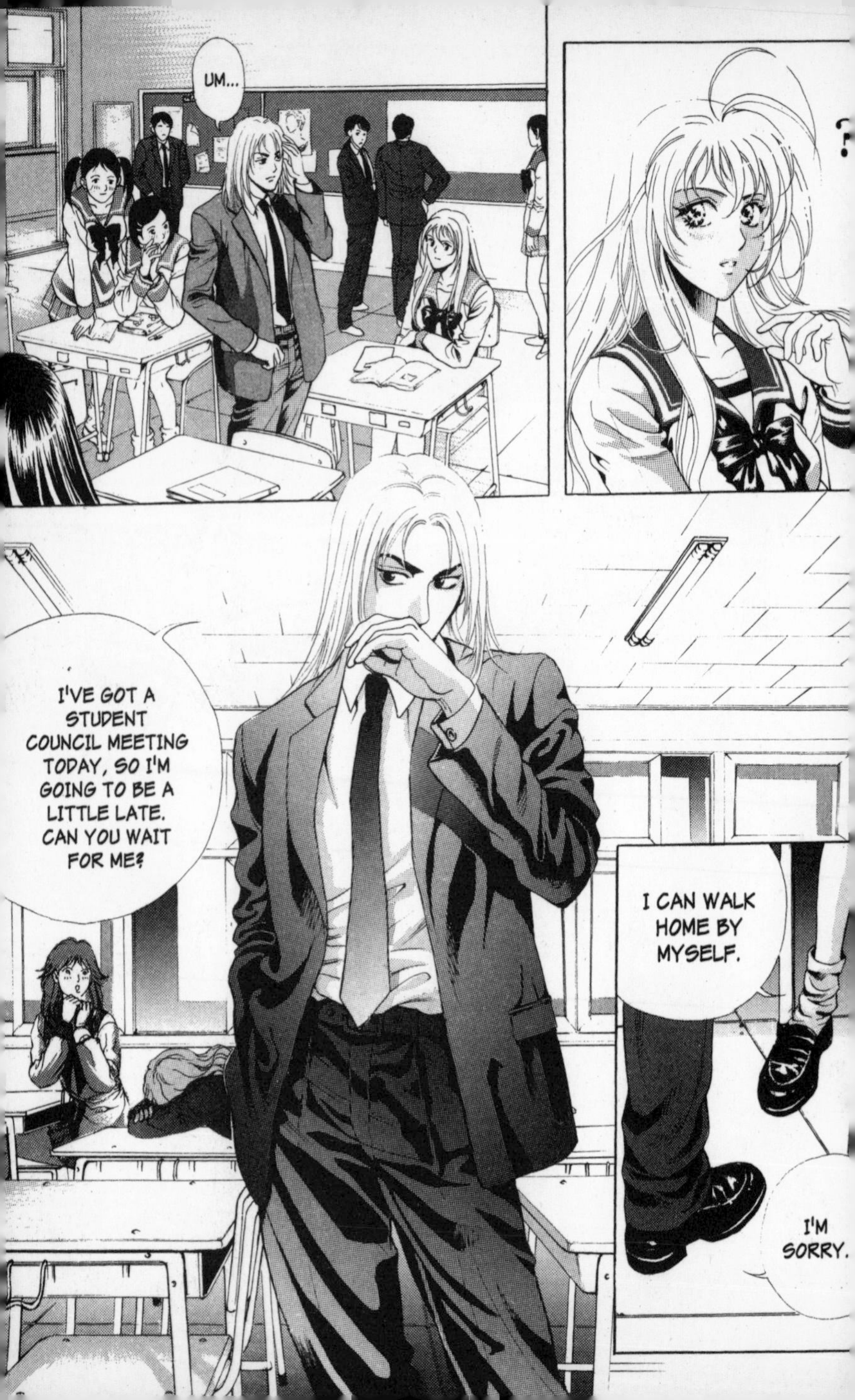
?
UM...
I'VE GOT A STUDENT COUNCIL MEETING TODAY, SO I'M GOING TO BE A LITTLE LATE. CAN YOU WAIT FOR ME?
I CAN WALK HOME BY MYSELF.
I'M SORRY.

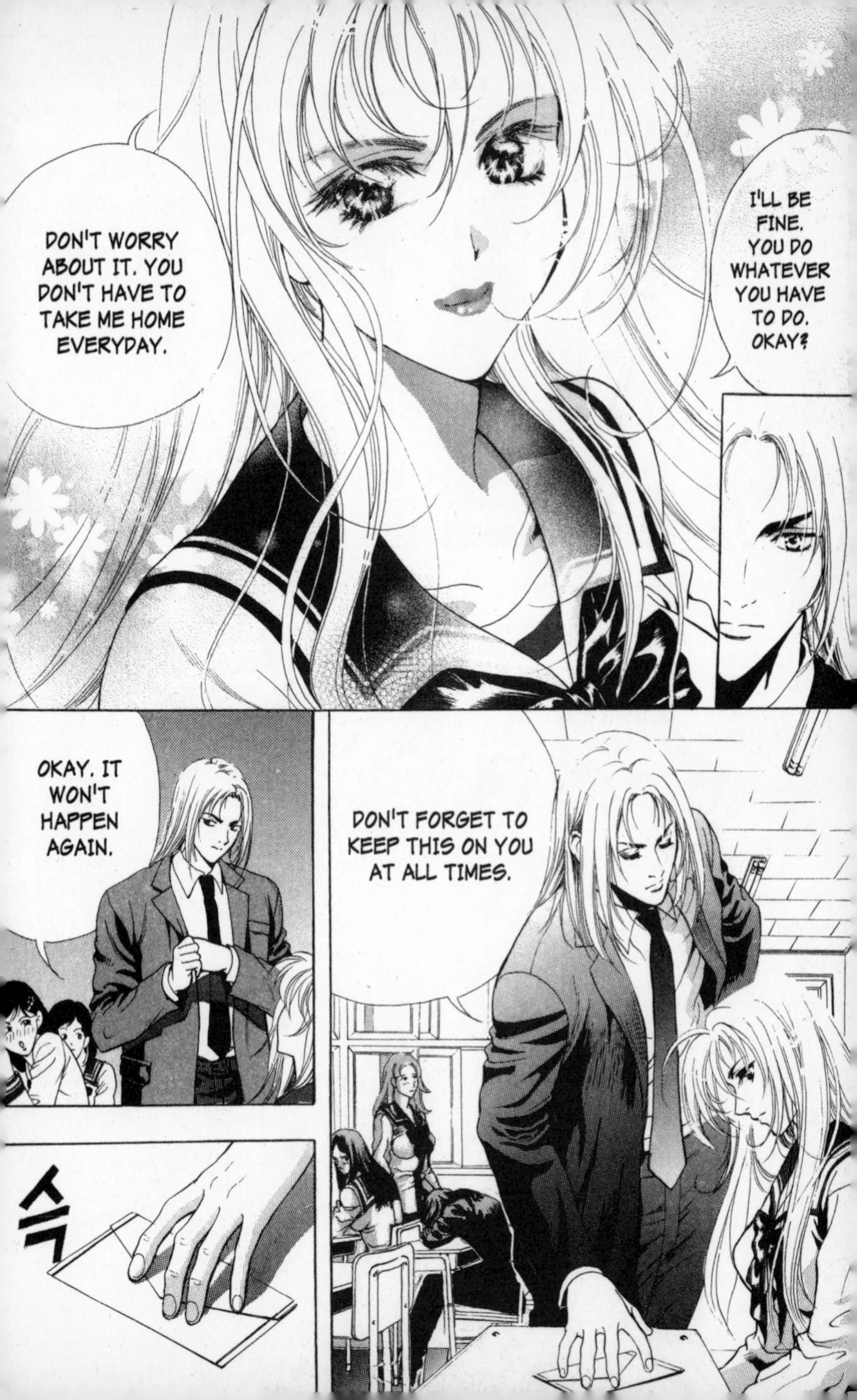
I'LL BE FINE. YOU DO WHATEVER YOU HAVE TO DO. OKAY?
DON'T WORRY ABOUT IT. YOU DON'T HAVE TO TAKE ME HOME EVERYDAY.
DON'T FORGET TO KEEP THIS ON YOU AT ALL TIMES.
OKAY. IT WON'T HAPPEN AGAIN.

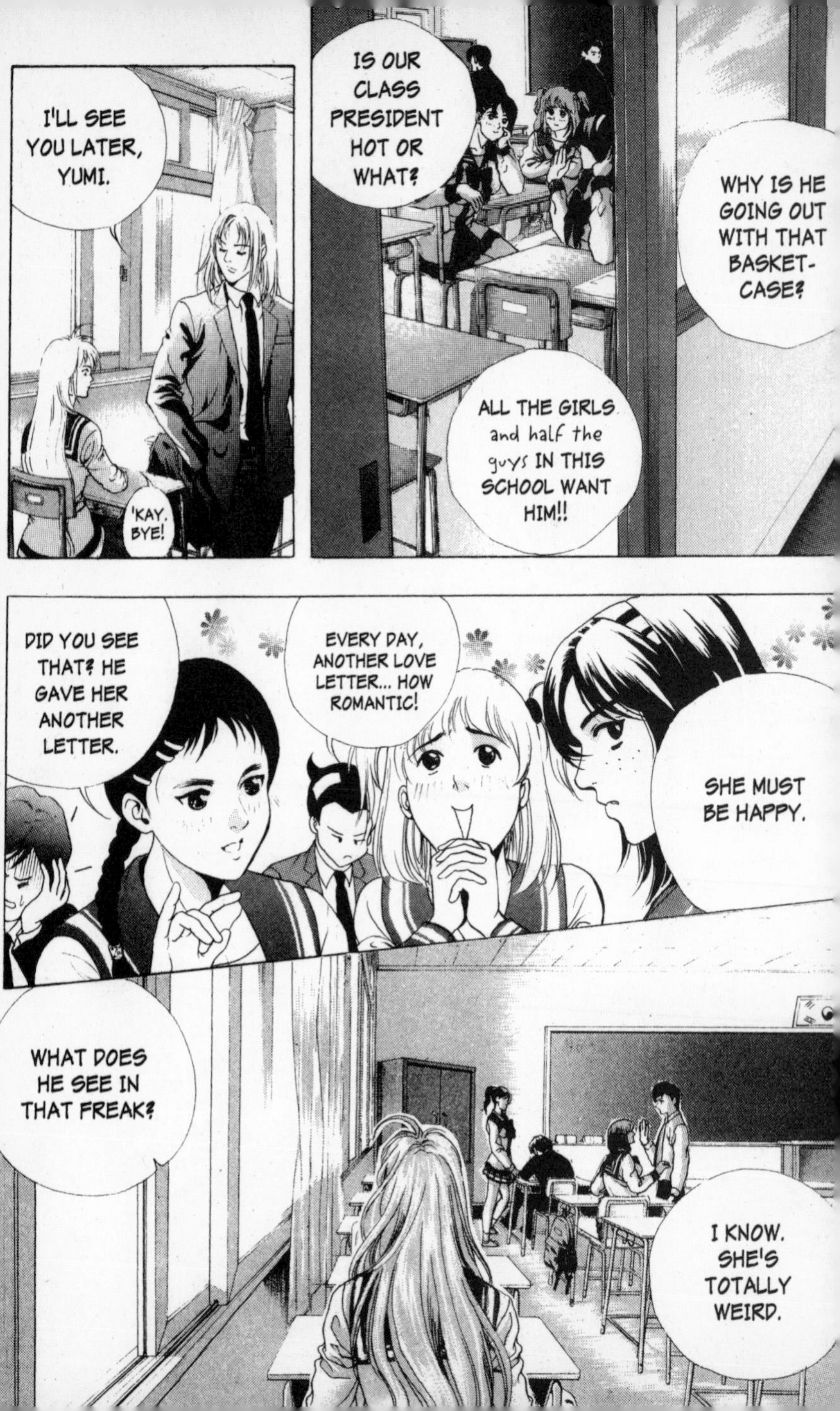

I'LL SEE YOU LATER, YUMI.
'KAY. BYE!
IS OUR CLASS PRESIDENT HOT OR WHAT?
WHY IS HE GOING OUT WITH THAT BASKET-CASE?
ALL THE GIRLS and half the guys IN THIS SCHOOL WANT HIM!!
DID YOU SEE THAT? HE GAVE HER ANOTHER LETTER.
EVERY DAY, ANOTHER LOVE LETTER... HOW ROMANTIC!
SHE MUST BE HAPPY.
WHAT DOES HE SEE IN THAT FREAK?
I KNOW. SHE'S TOTALLY WEIRD.

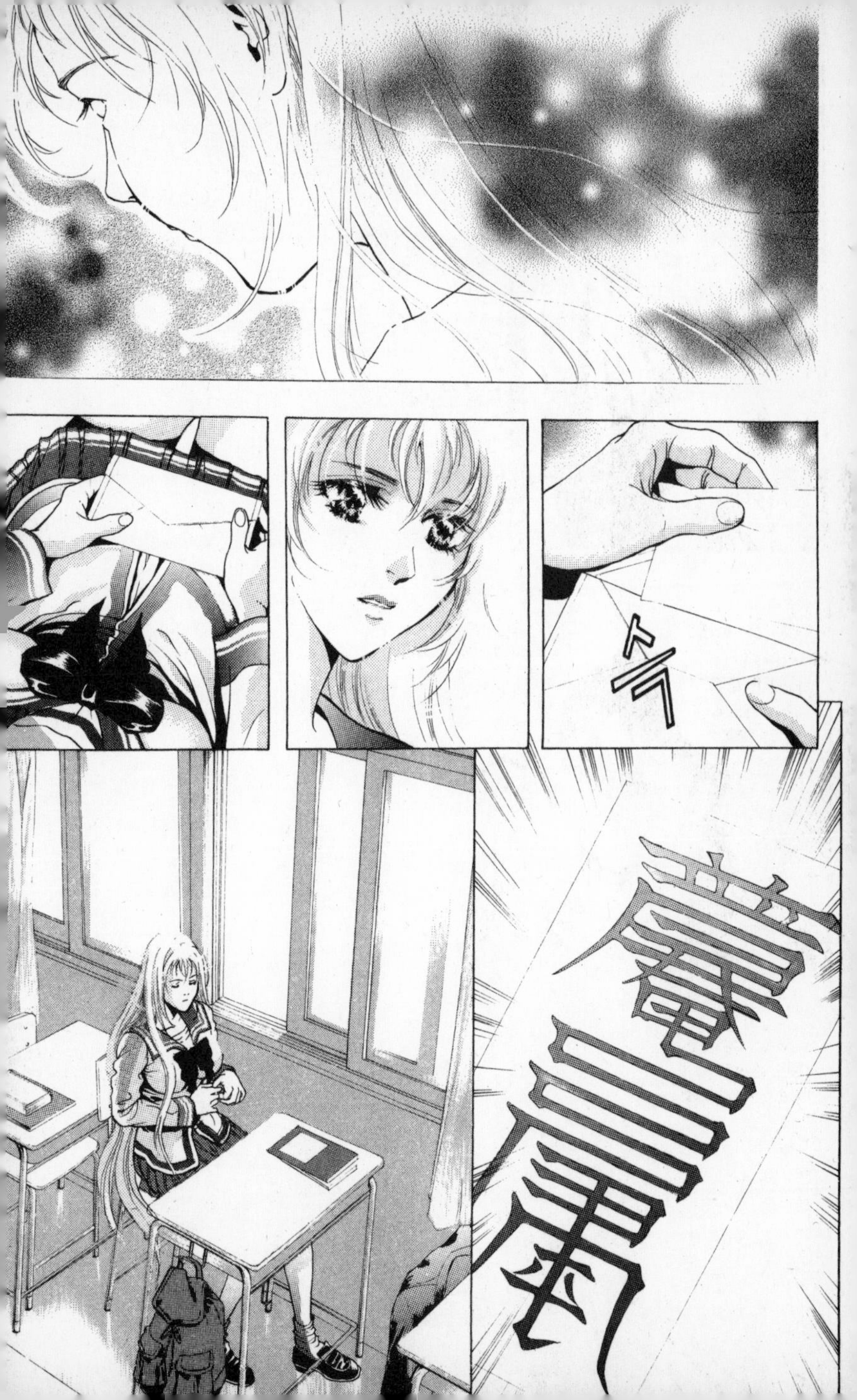

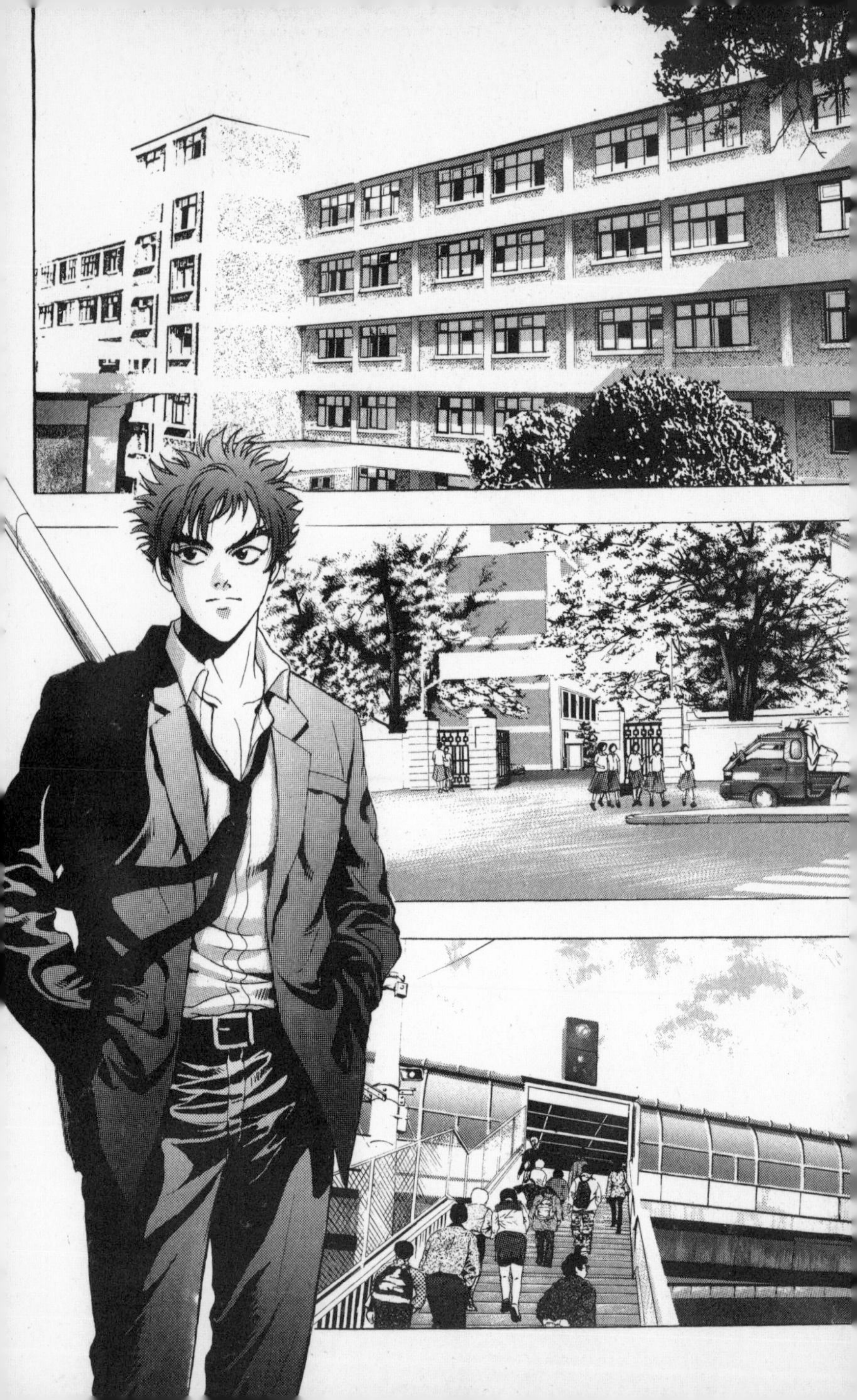

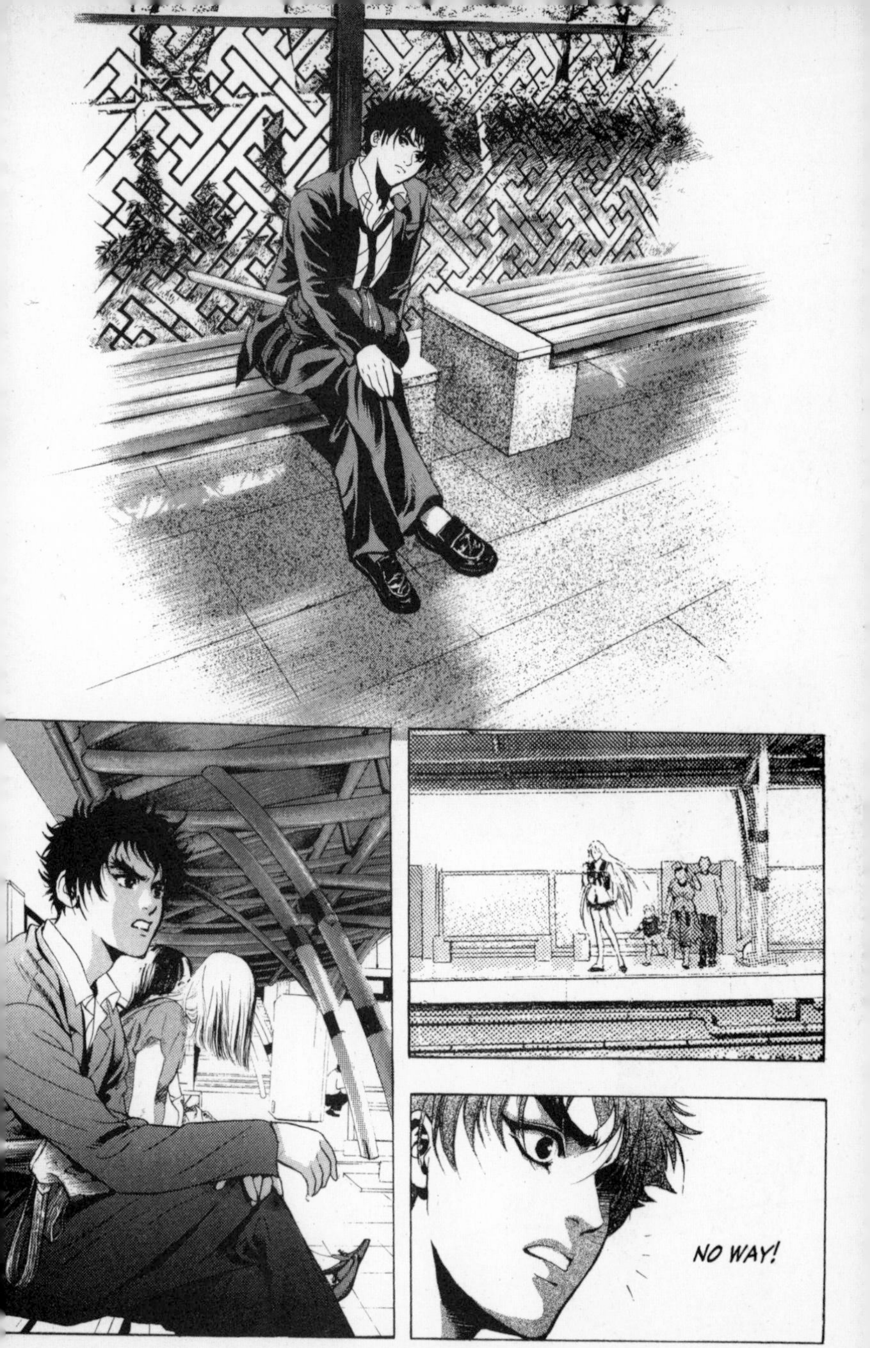
NO WAY!

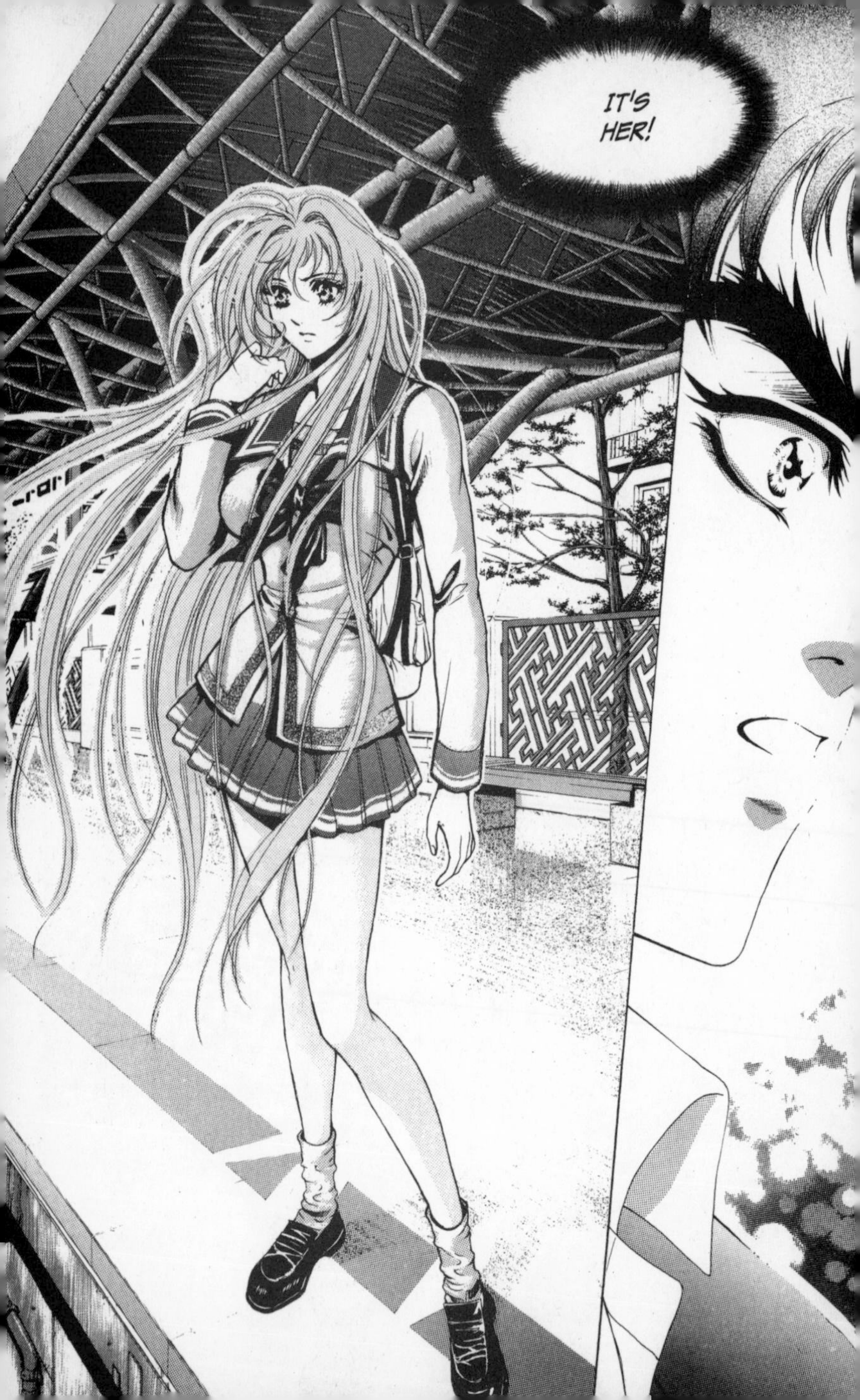
IT'S
HER!

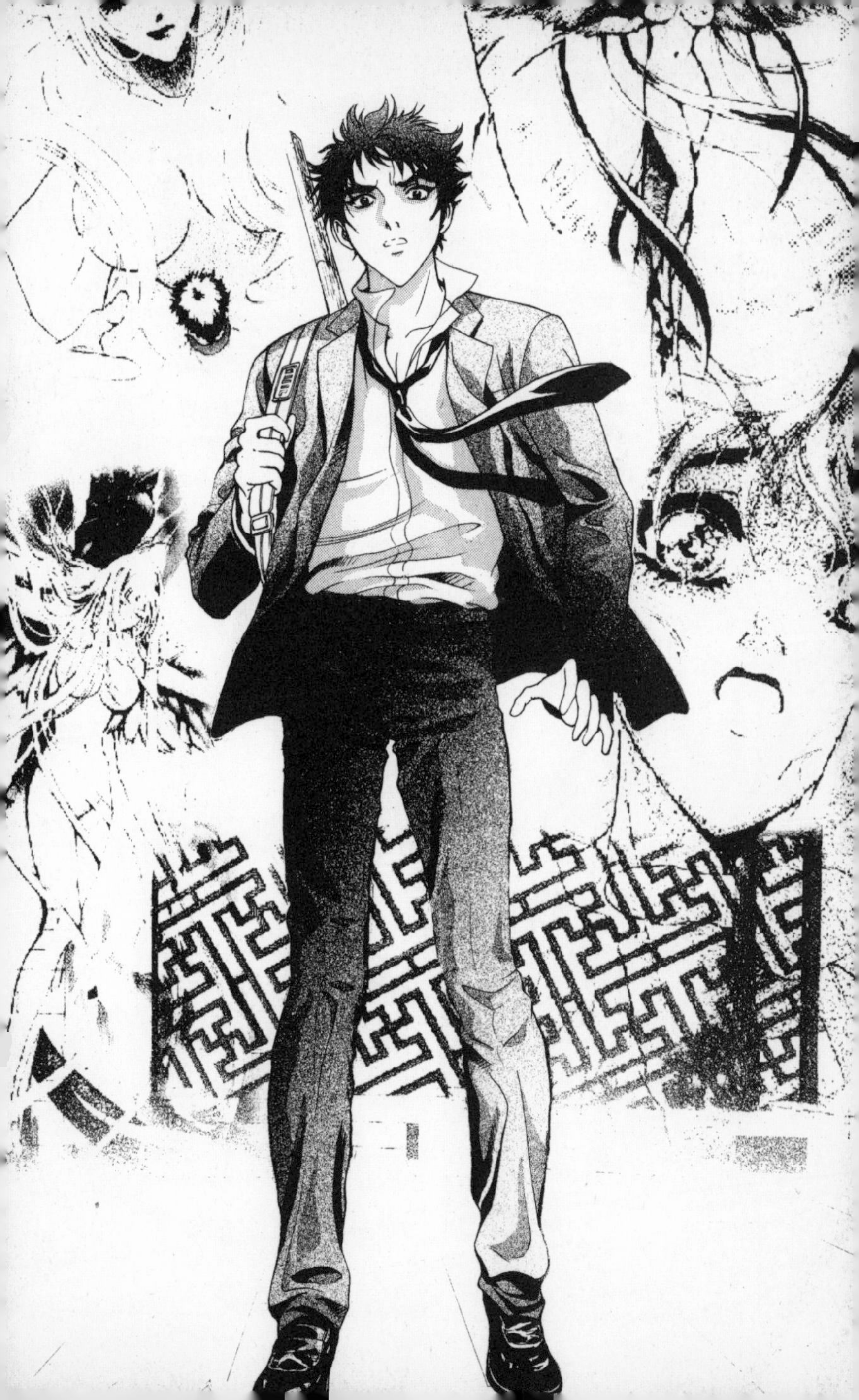

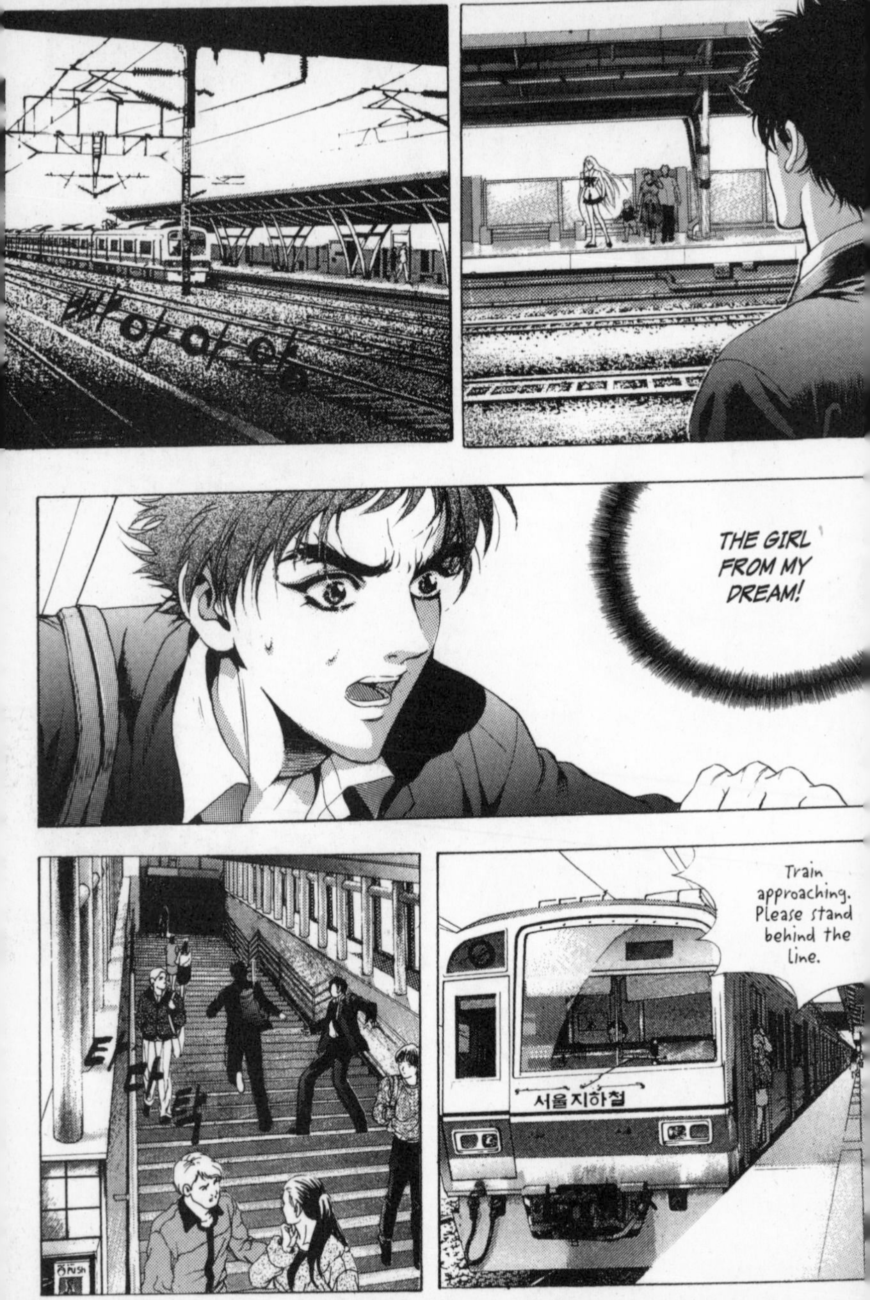
빠아아앙
THE GIRL FROM MY DREAM!
타다닥
PUSH
서울지하철
Train approaching. Please stand behind the line.

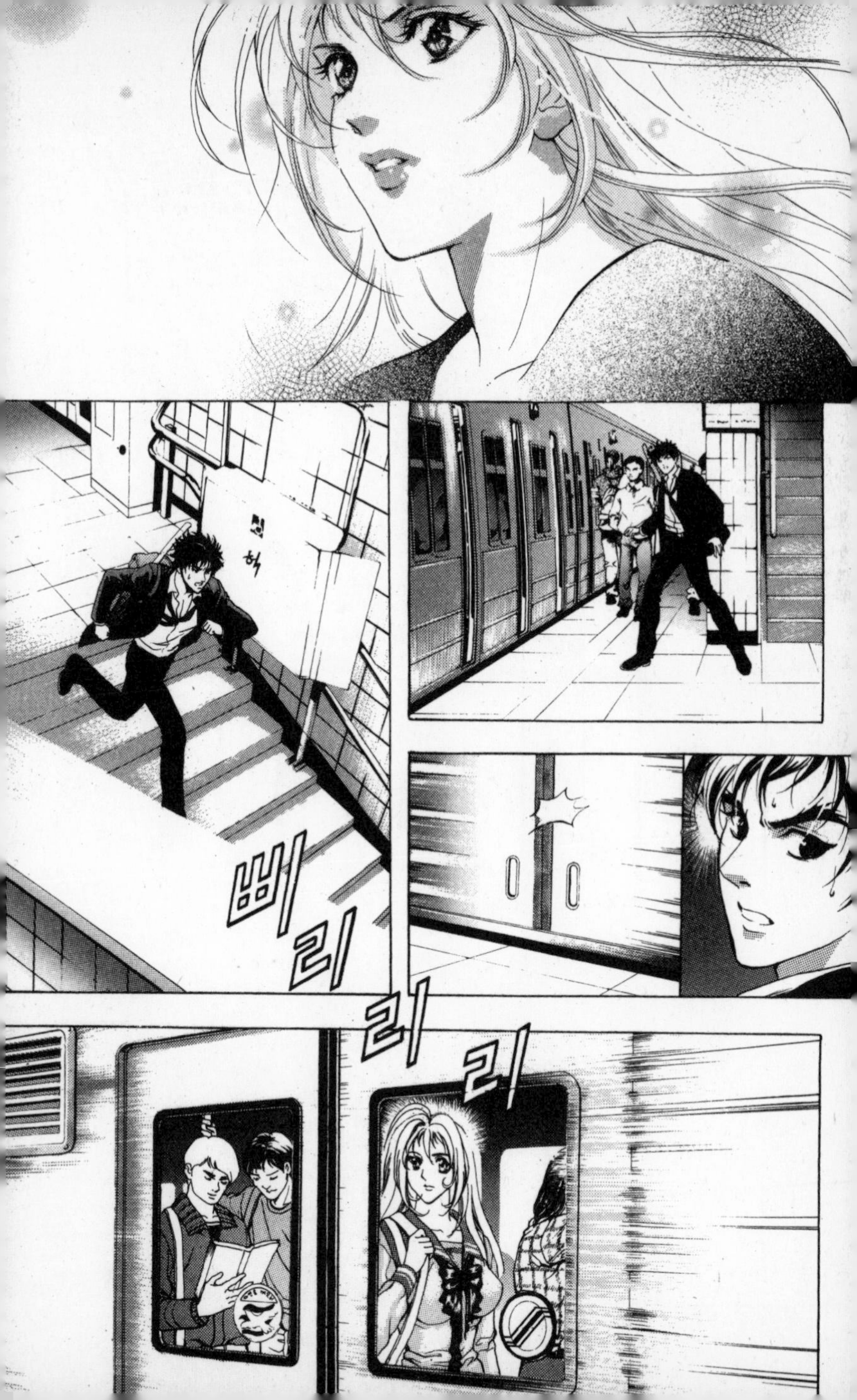
헉
삐리리리

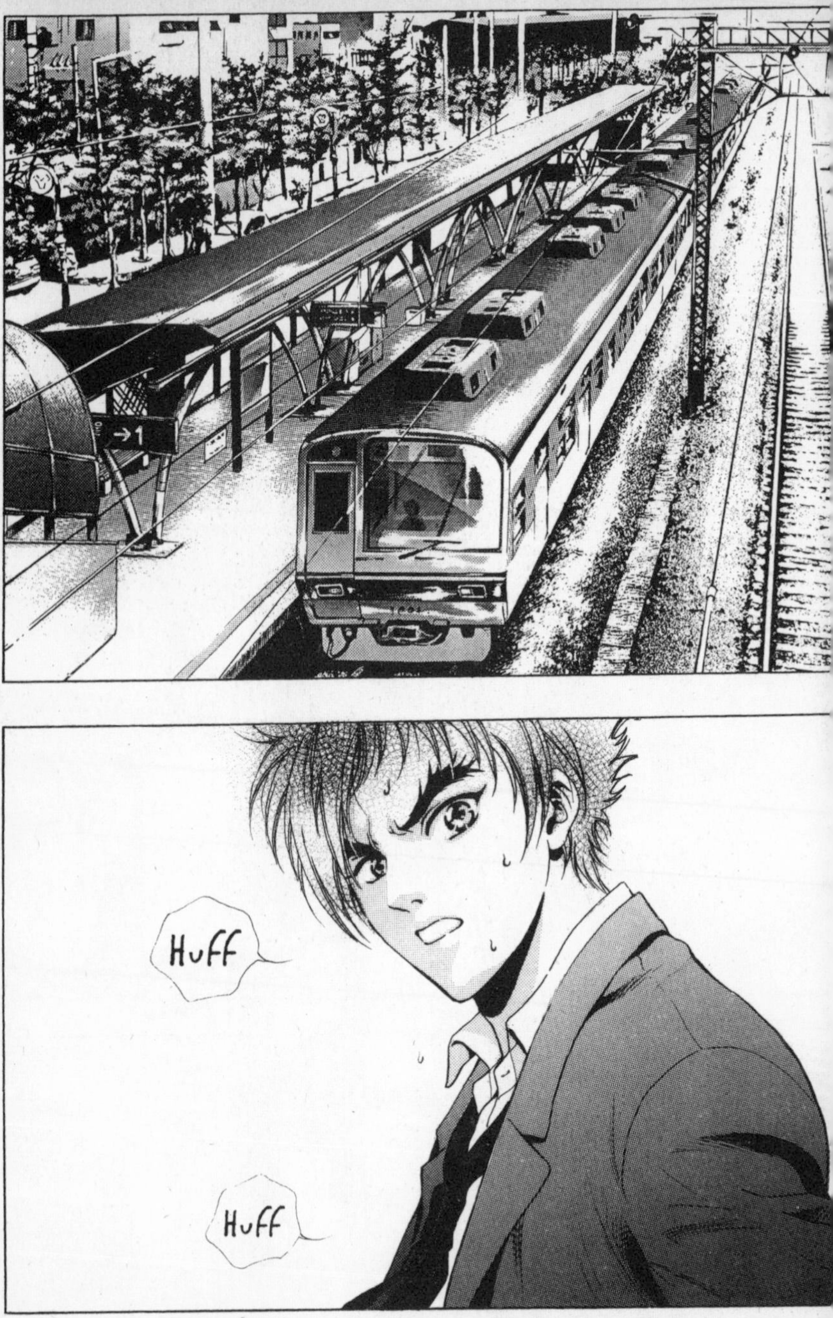
→1
Huff
Huff

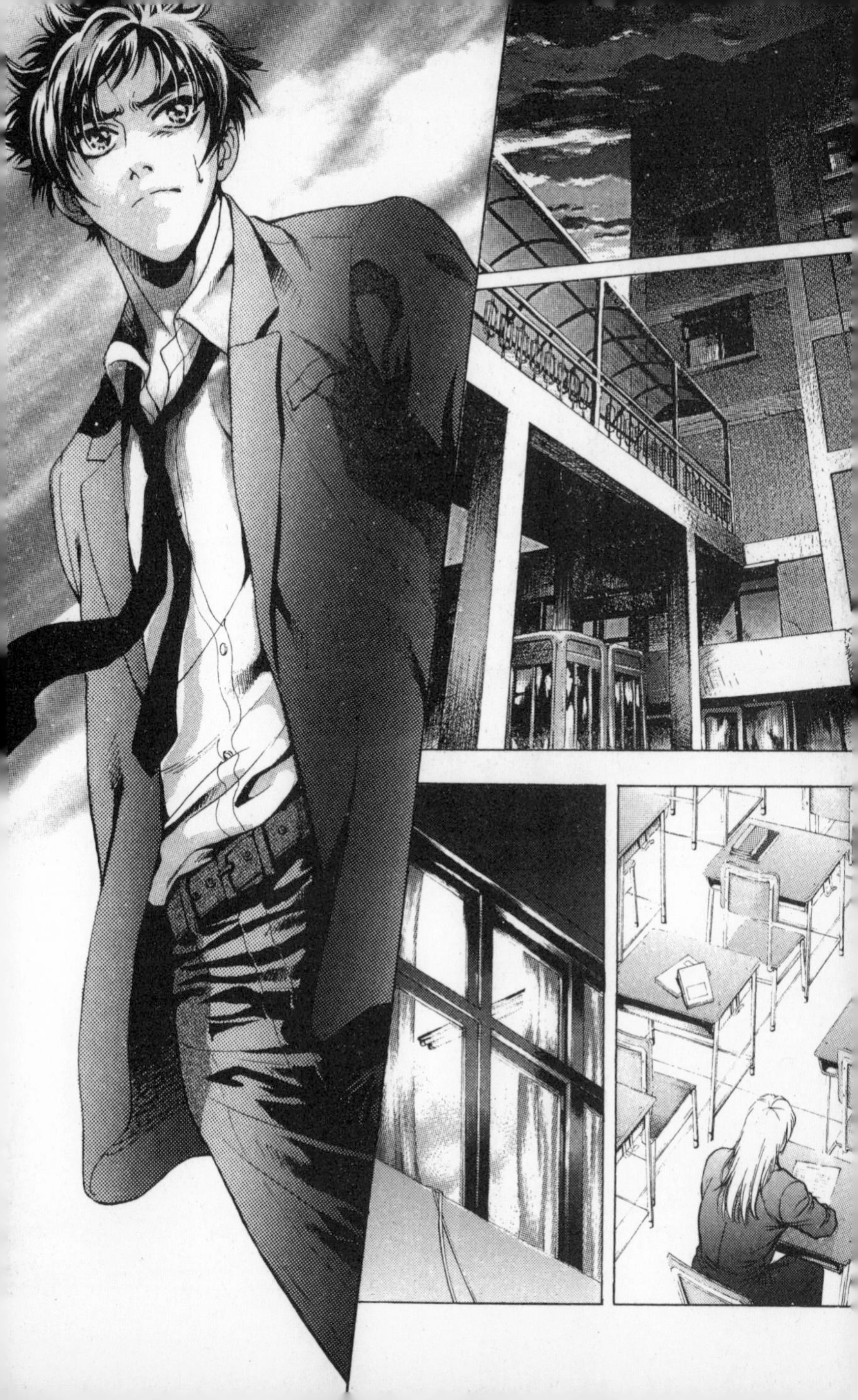

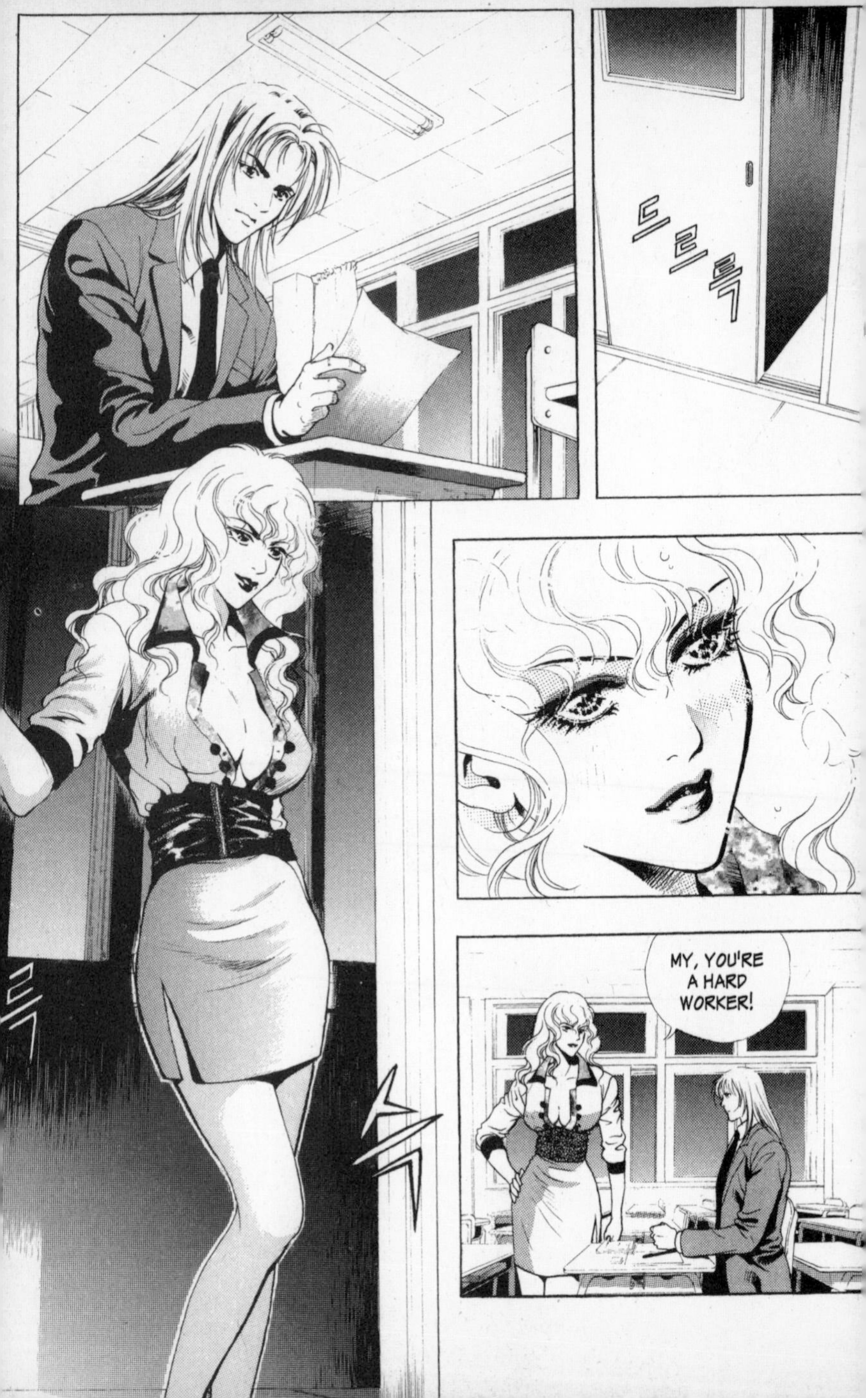
드르륵
MY, YOU'RE A HARD WORKER!

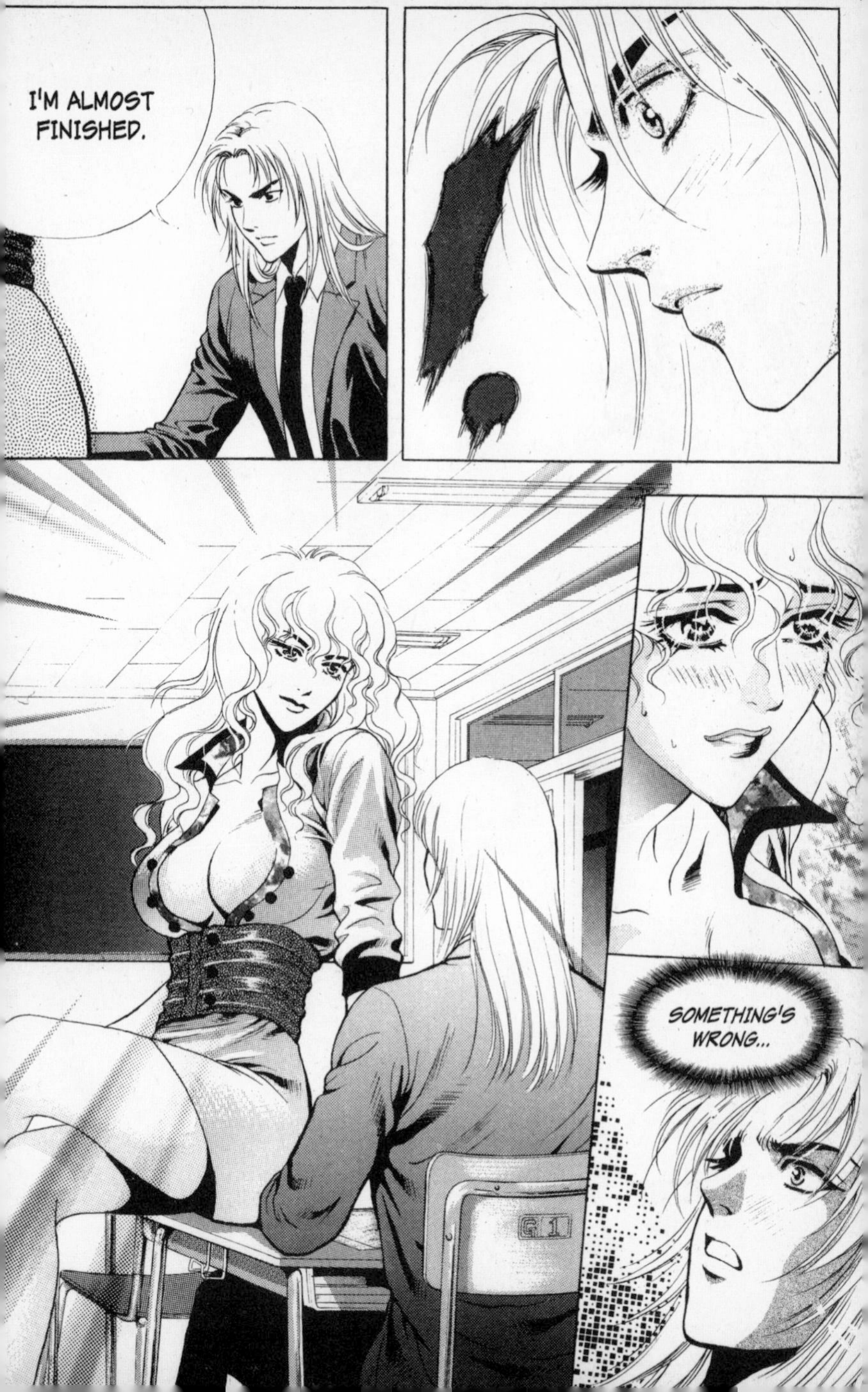
I'M ALMOST FINISHED.
SOMETHING'S WRONG...

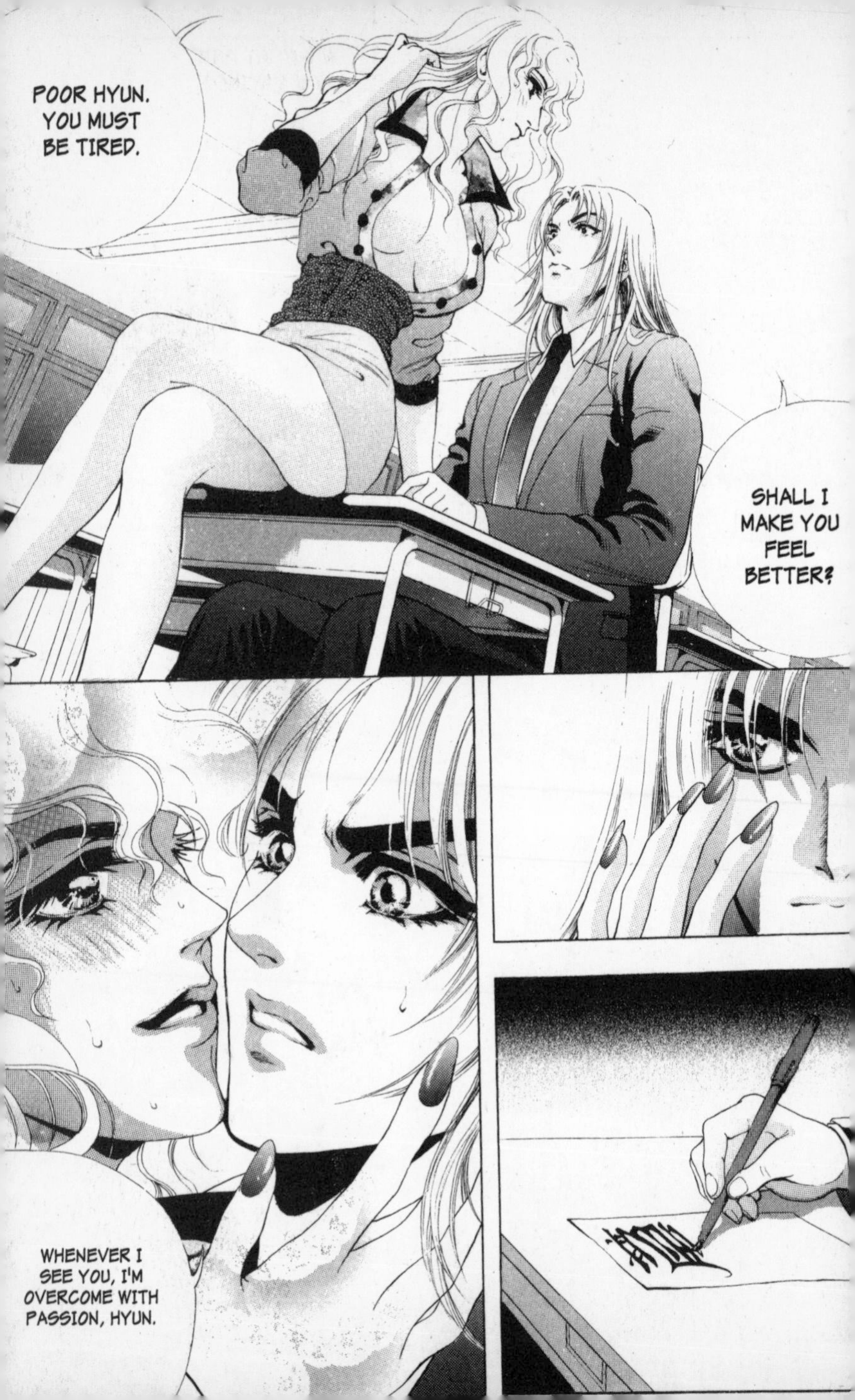
POOR HYUN. YOU MUST BE TIRED.
SHALL I MAKE YOU FEEL BETTER?
WHENEVER I SEE YOU, I'M OVERCOME WITH PASSION, HYUN.

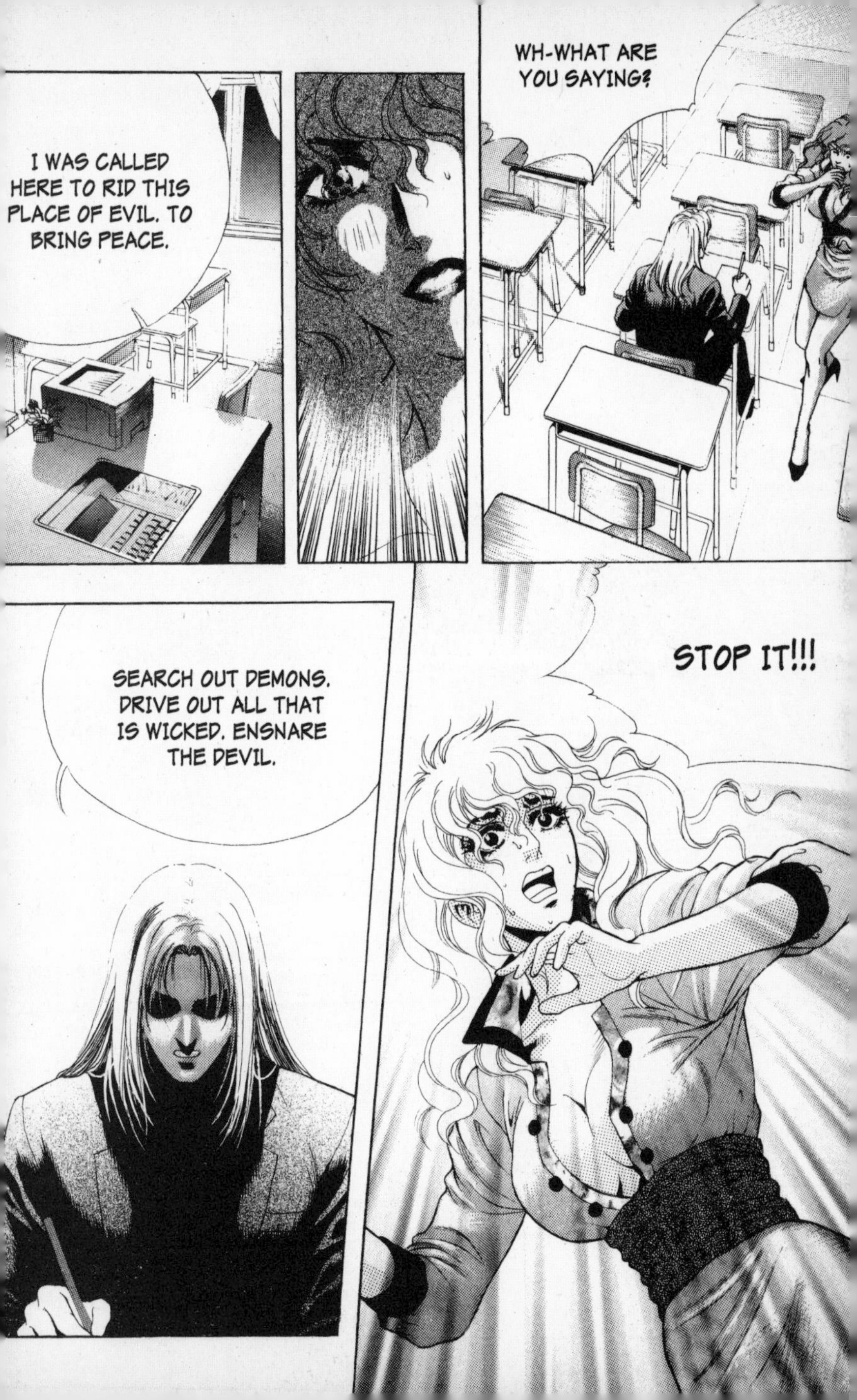
I WAS CALLED HERE TO RID THIS PLACE OF EVIL. TO BRING PEACE.
WH-WHAT ARE YOU SAYING?
SEARCH OUT DEMONS. DRIVE OUT ALL THAT IS WICKED. ENSNARE THE DEVIL.
STOP IT!!!

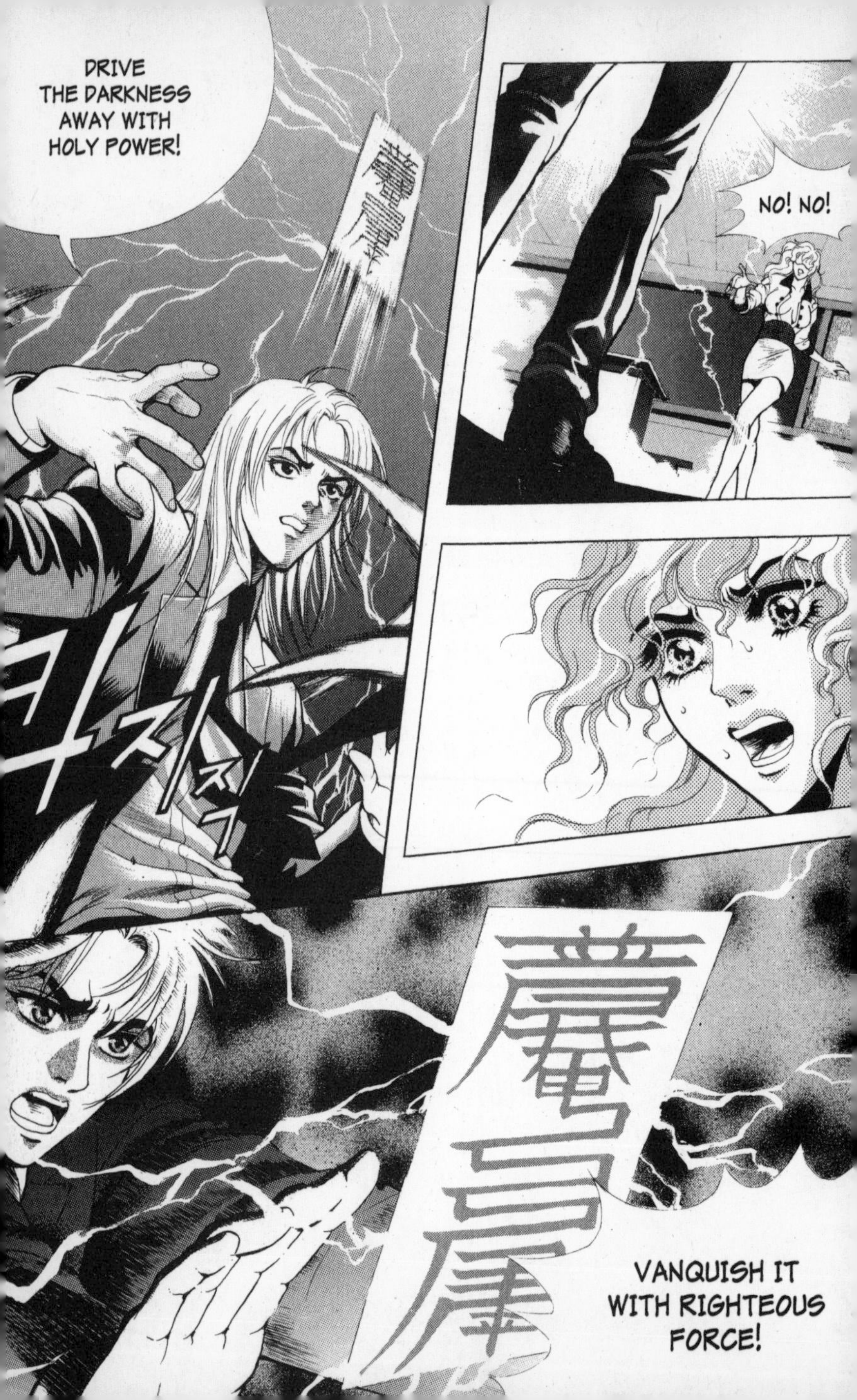
DRIVE THE DARKNESS AWAY WITH HOLY POWER!
NO! NO!
VANQUISH IT WITH RIGHTEOUS FORCE!

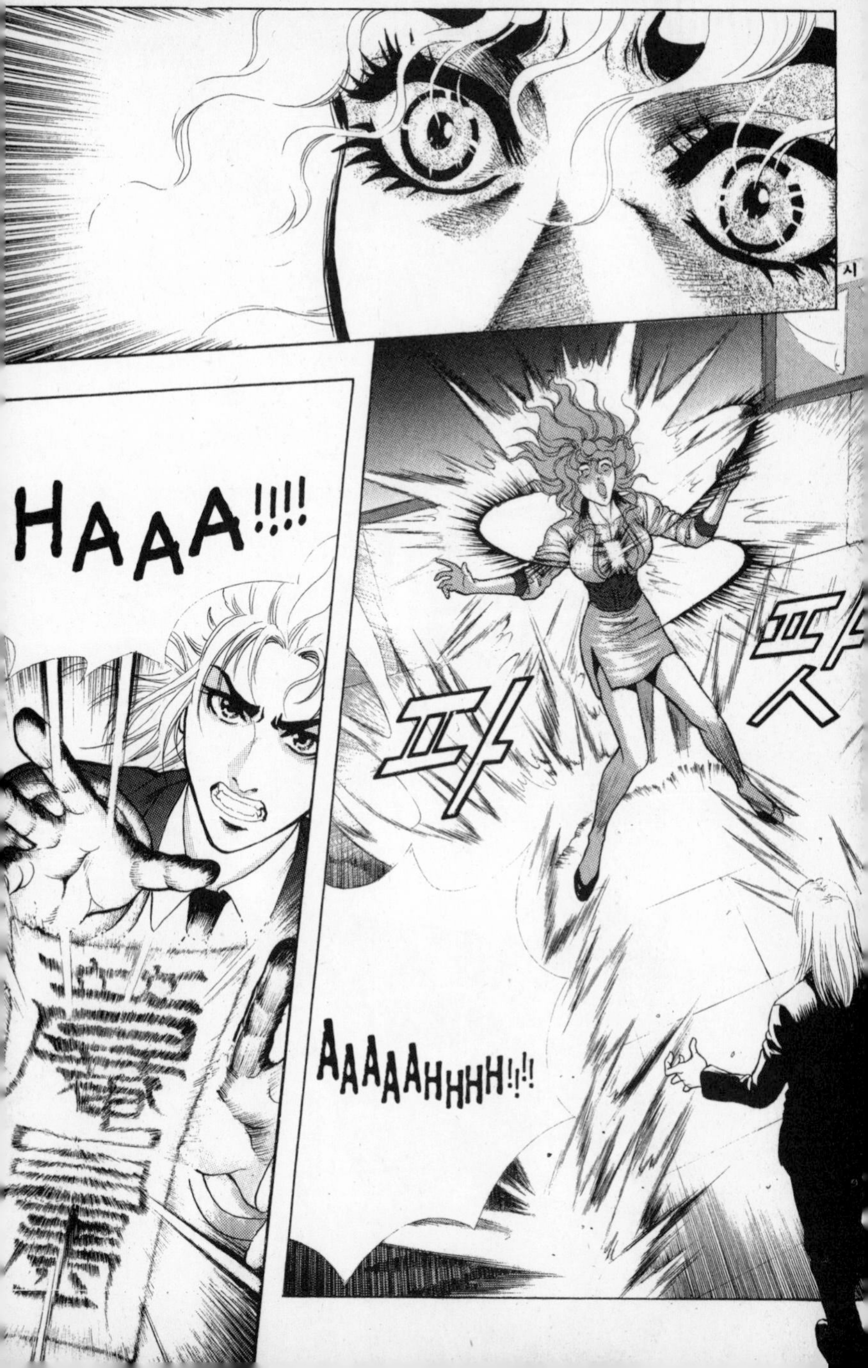
HAAA!!!!
팟
파
AAAAAHHHH!!!!

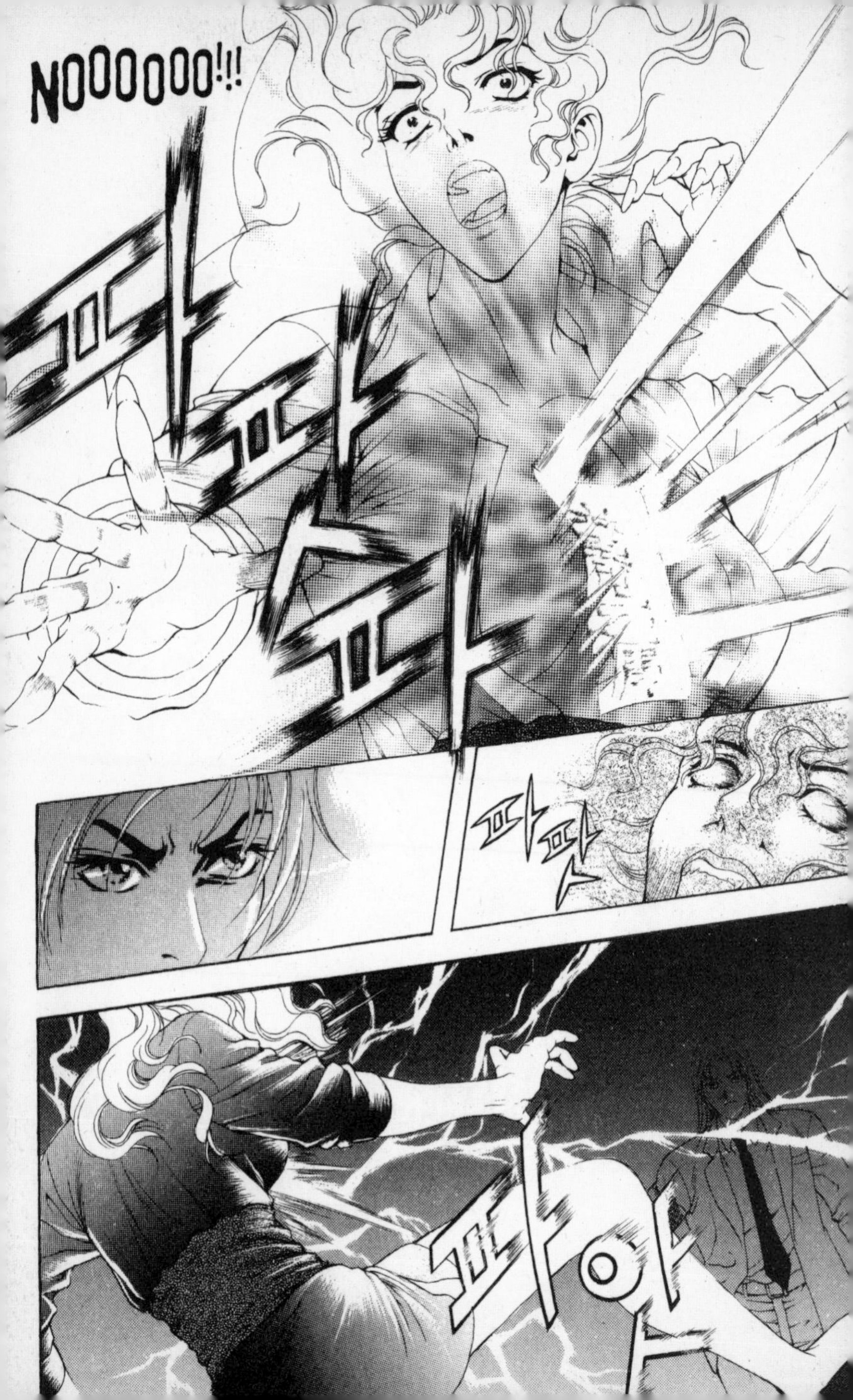
NOOOOOO!!!

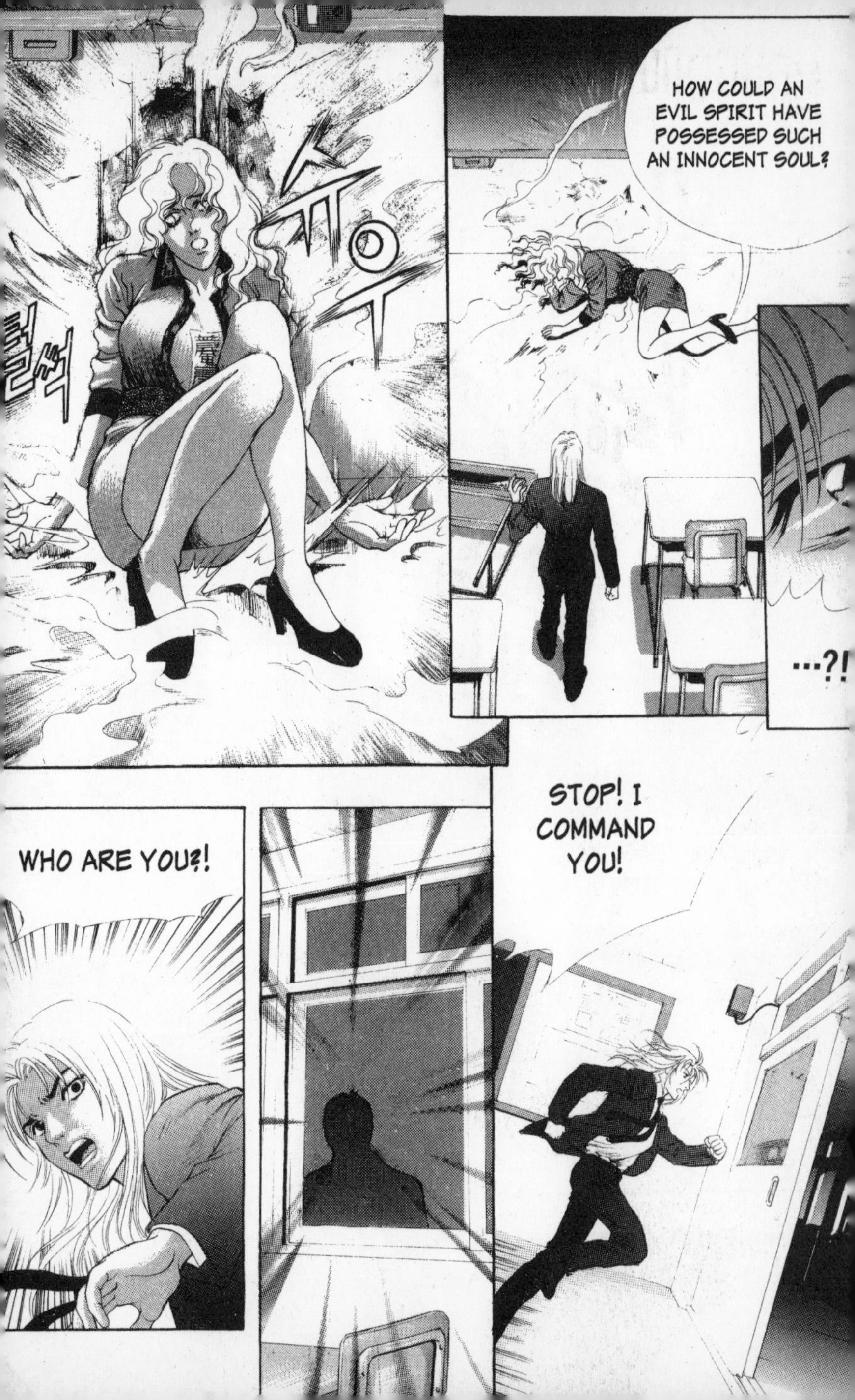
HOW COULD AN EVIL SPIRIT HAVE POSSESSED SUCH AN INNOCENT SOUL?
...?!
WHO ARE YOU?!
STOP! I COMMAND YOU!

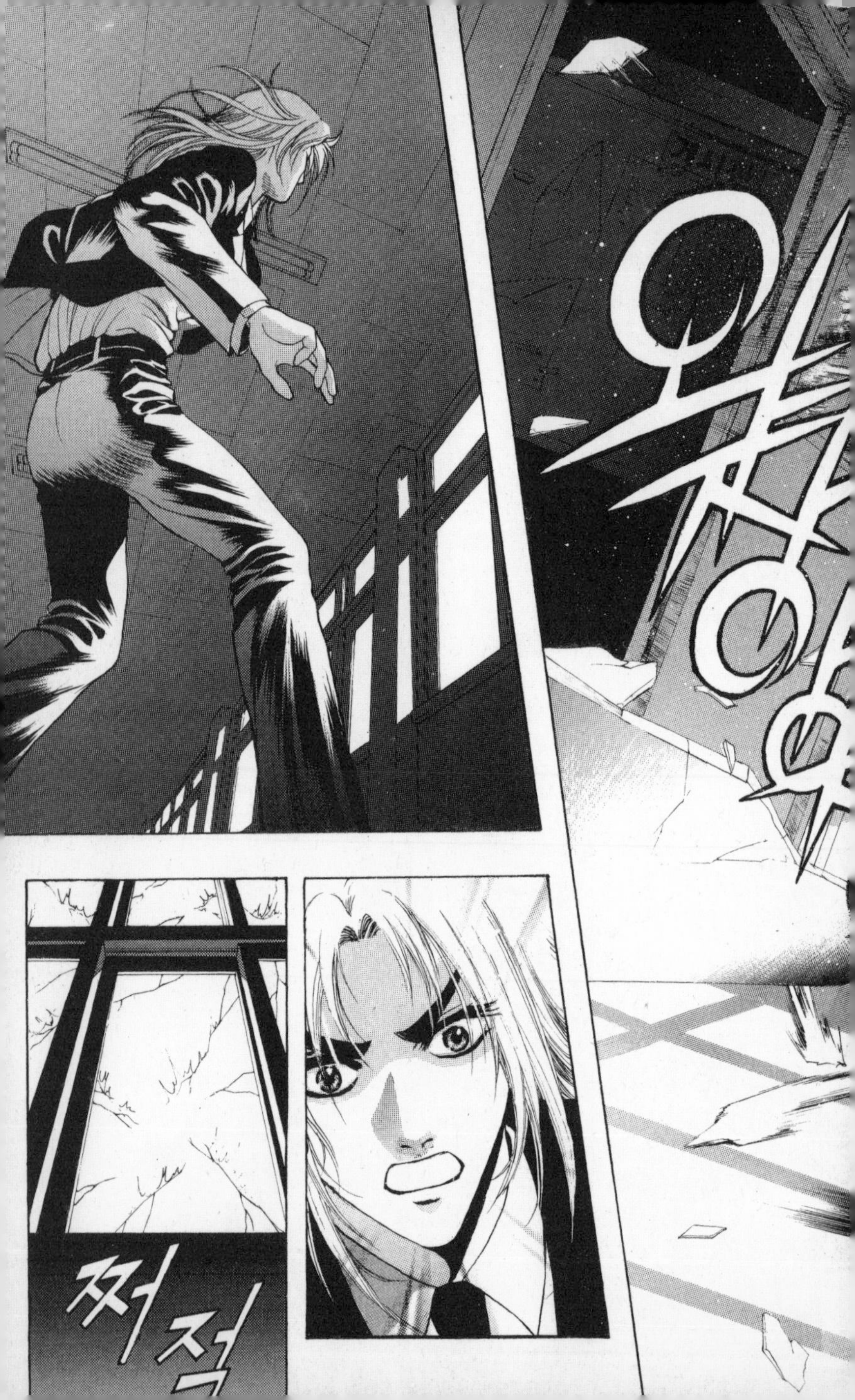
쩌적

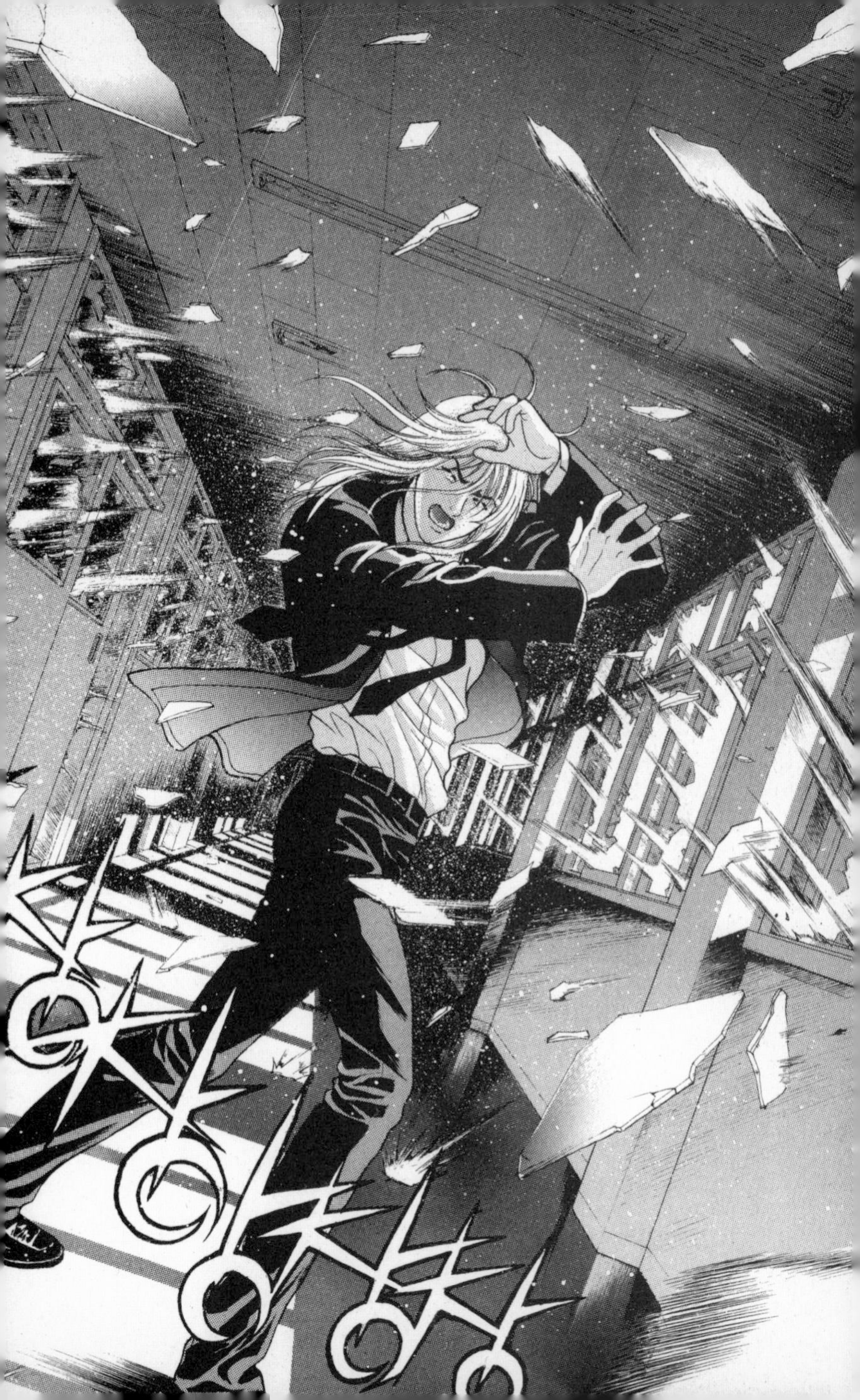

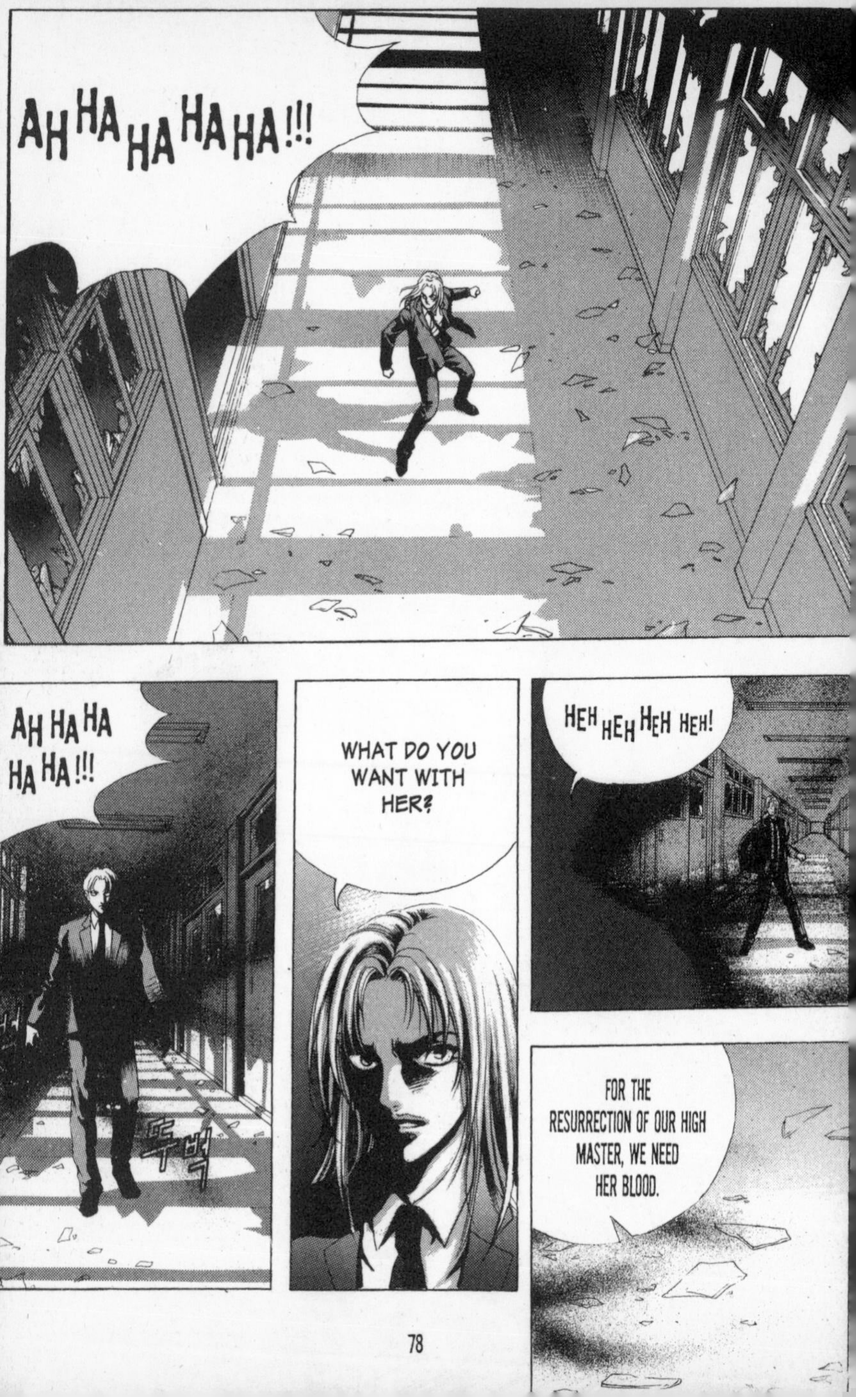
AH HA HA HA HA HA!!!
AH HA HA HA HA!!!
뚜벅
WHAT DO YOU WANT WITH HER?
HEH HEH HEH HEH!
FOR THE RESURRECTION OF OUR HIGH MASTER, WE NEED HER BLOOD.

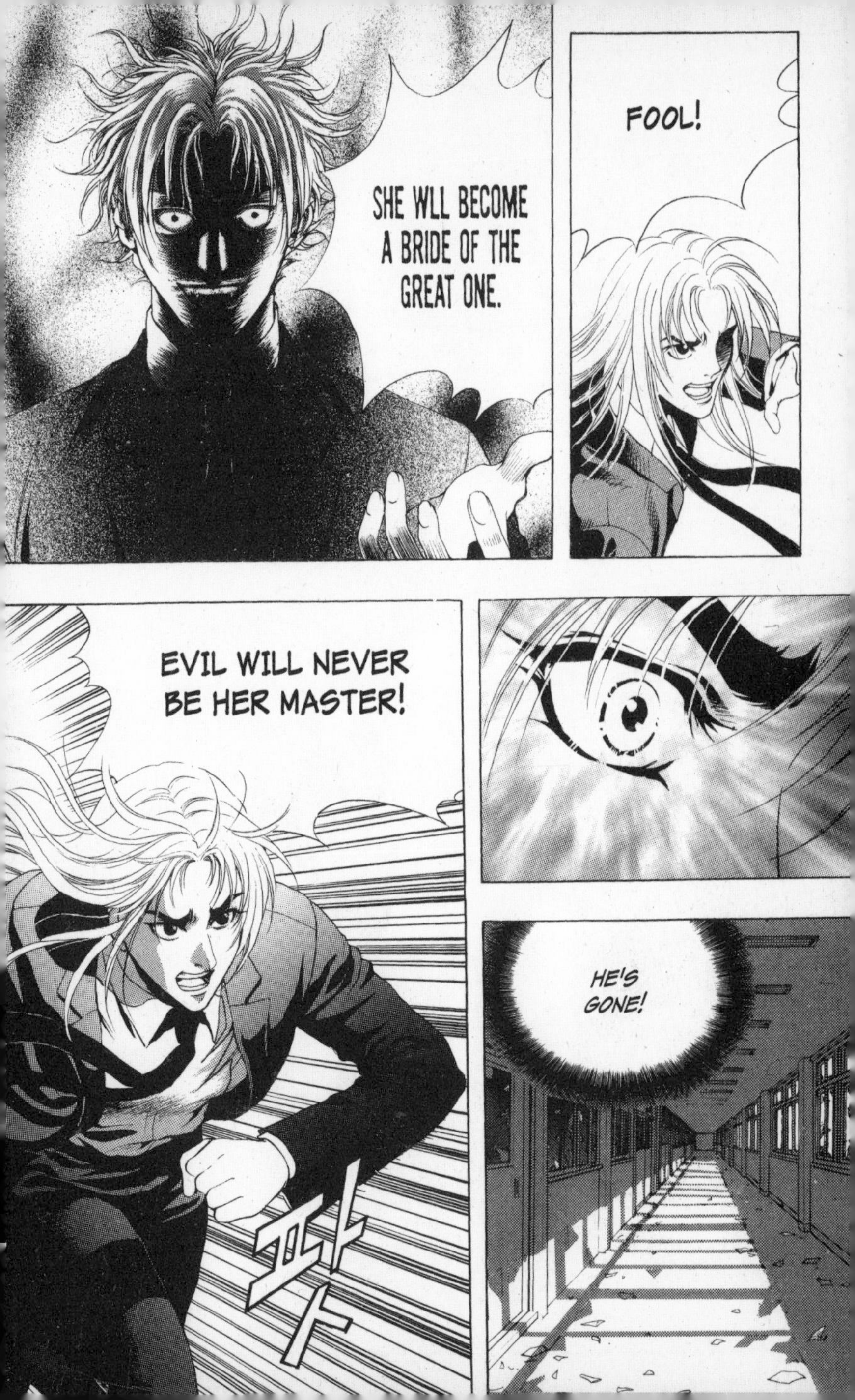
SHE WLL BECOME A BRIDE OF THE GREAT ONE.
FOOL!
EVIL WILL NEVER BE HER MASTER!
HE'S GONE!

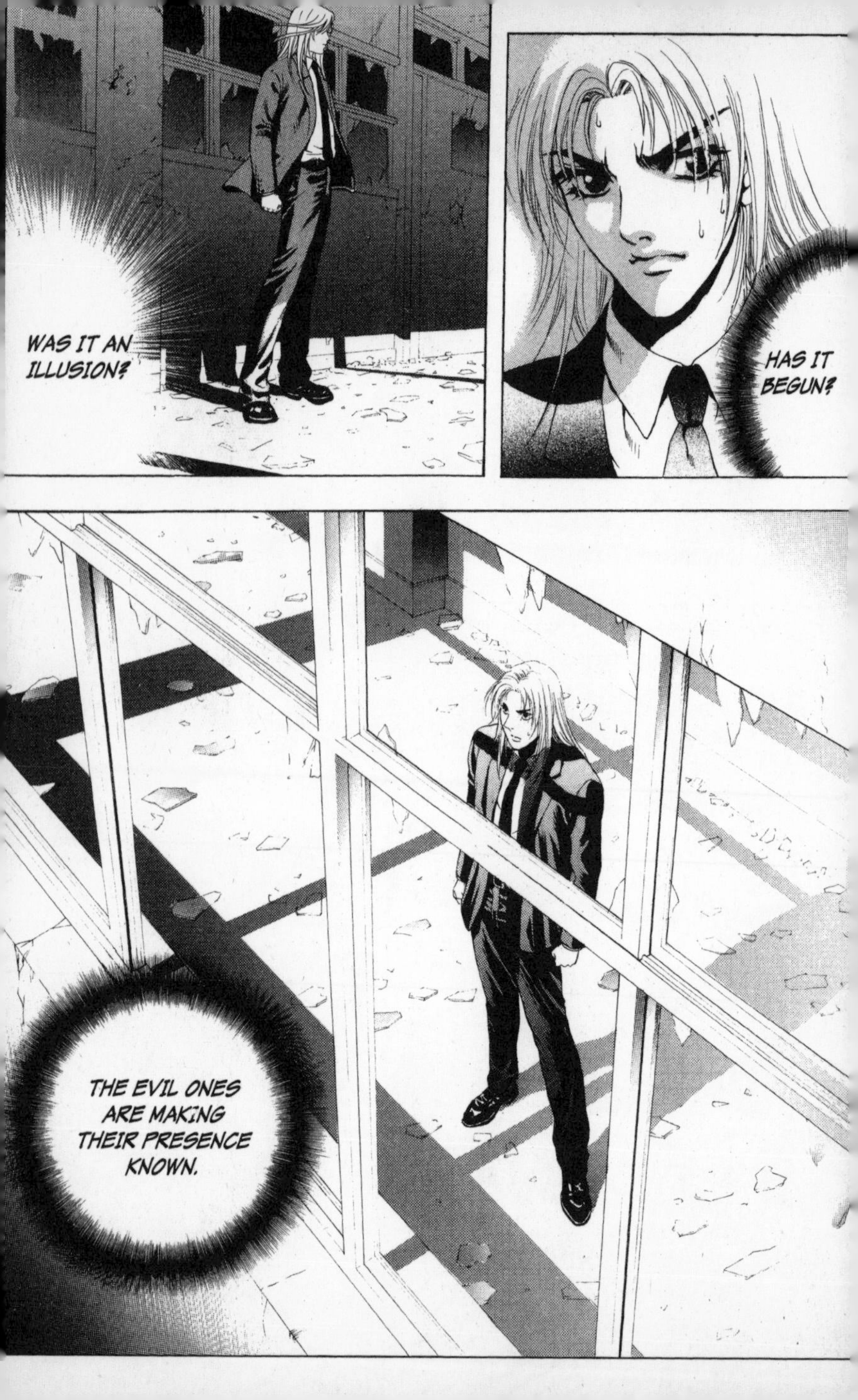
WAS IT AN ILLUSION?
HAS IT BEGUN?
THE EVIL ONES ARE MAKING THEIR PRESENCE KNOWN.

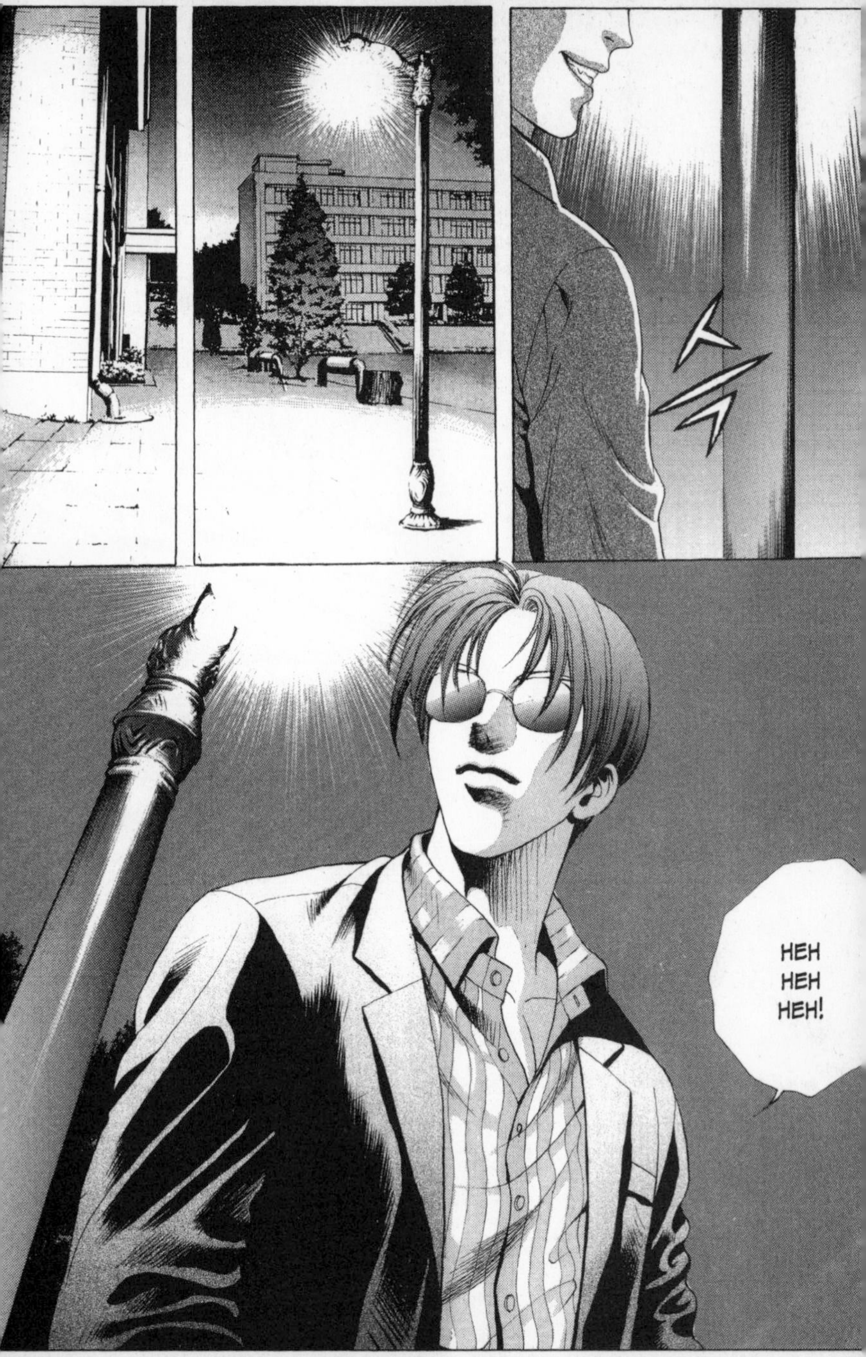
HEH
HEH
HEH!

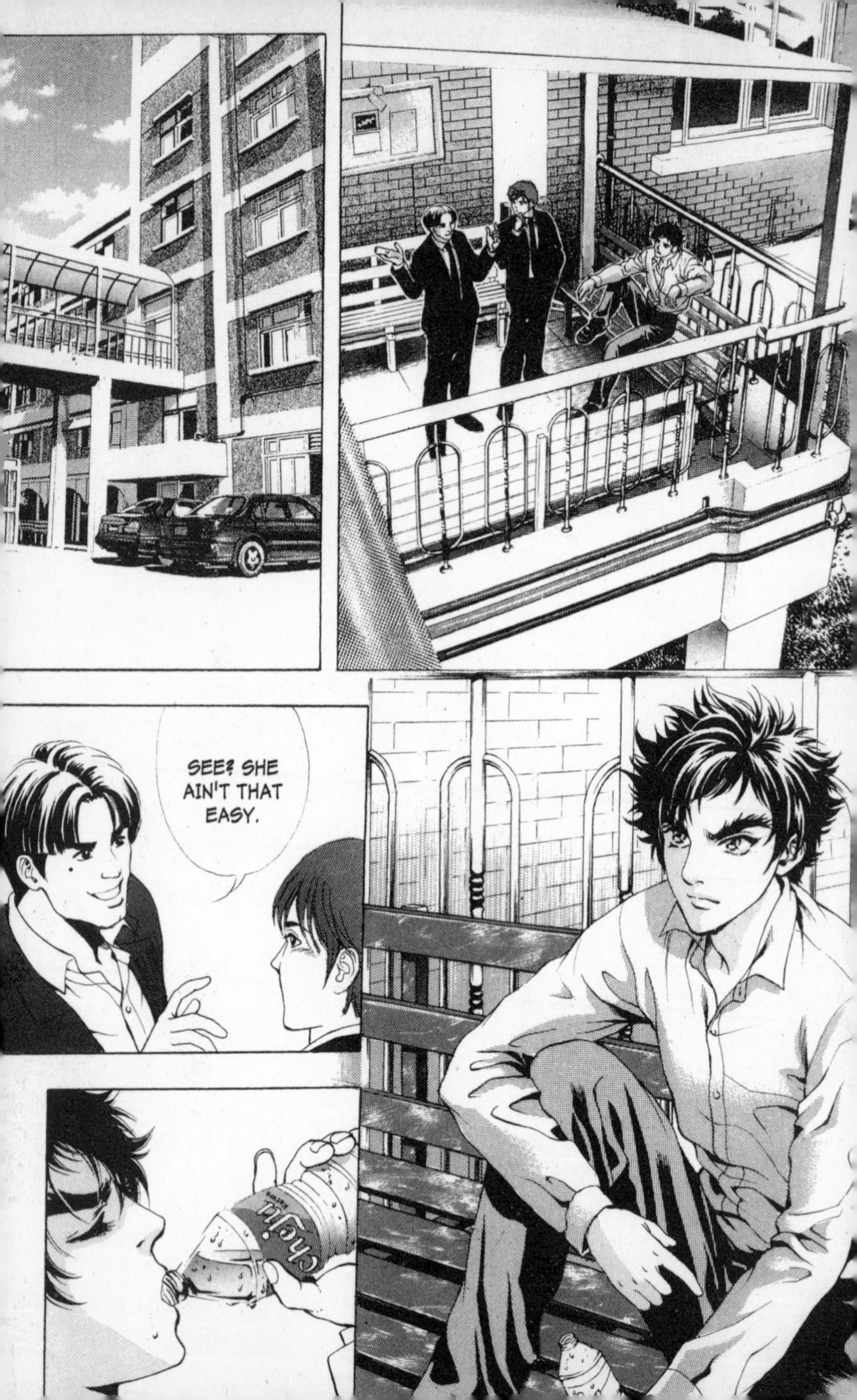
SEE? SHE AIN'T THAT EASY.

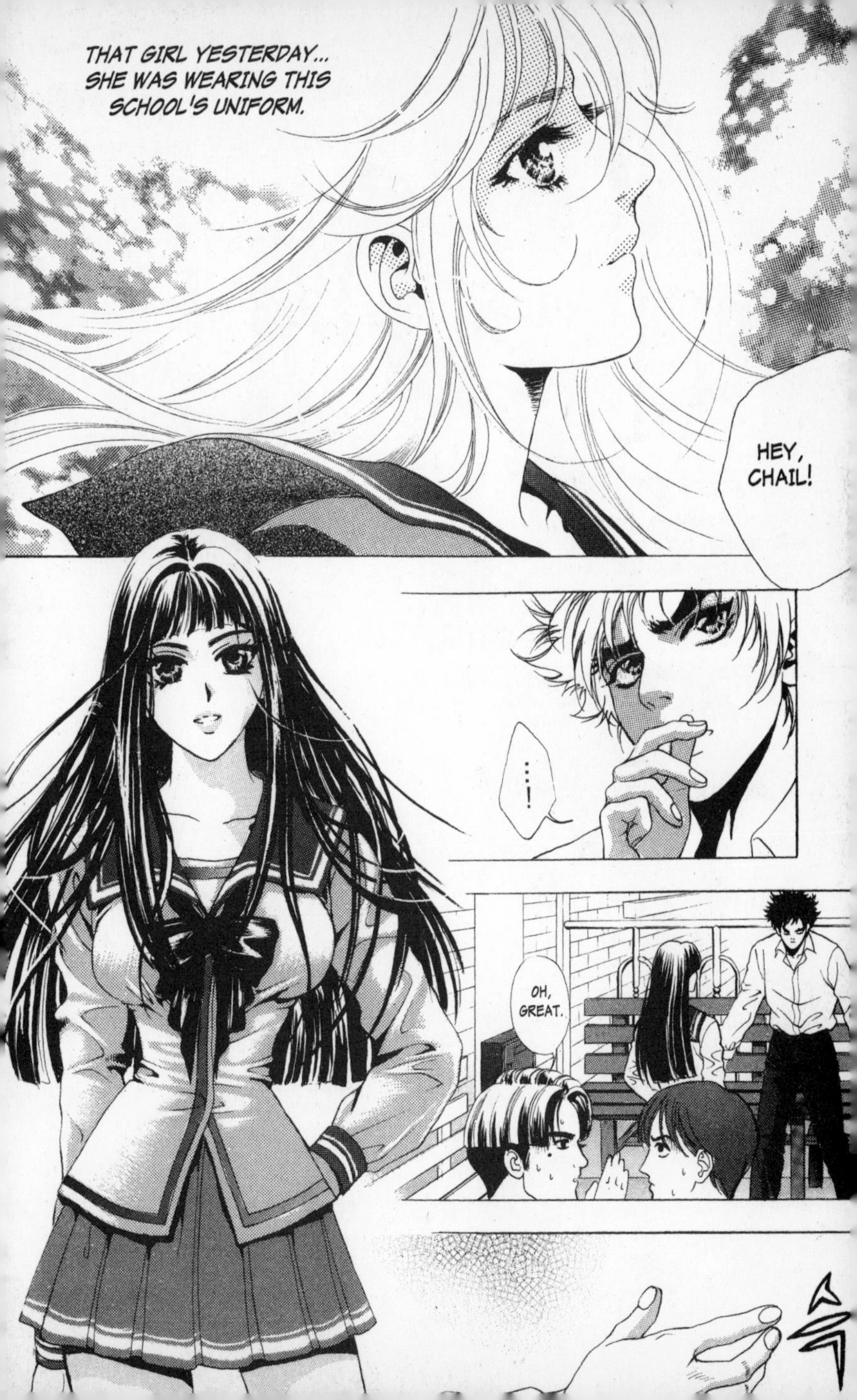
THAT GIRL YESTERDAY... SHE WAS WEARING THIS SCHOOL'S UNIFORM.
HEY, CHAIL!
...!
OH, GREAT.

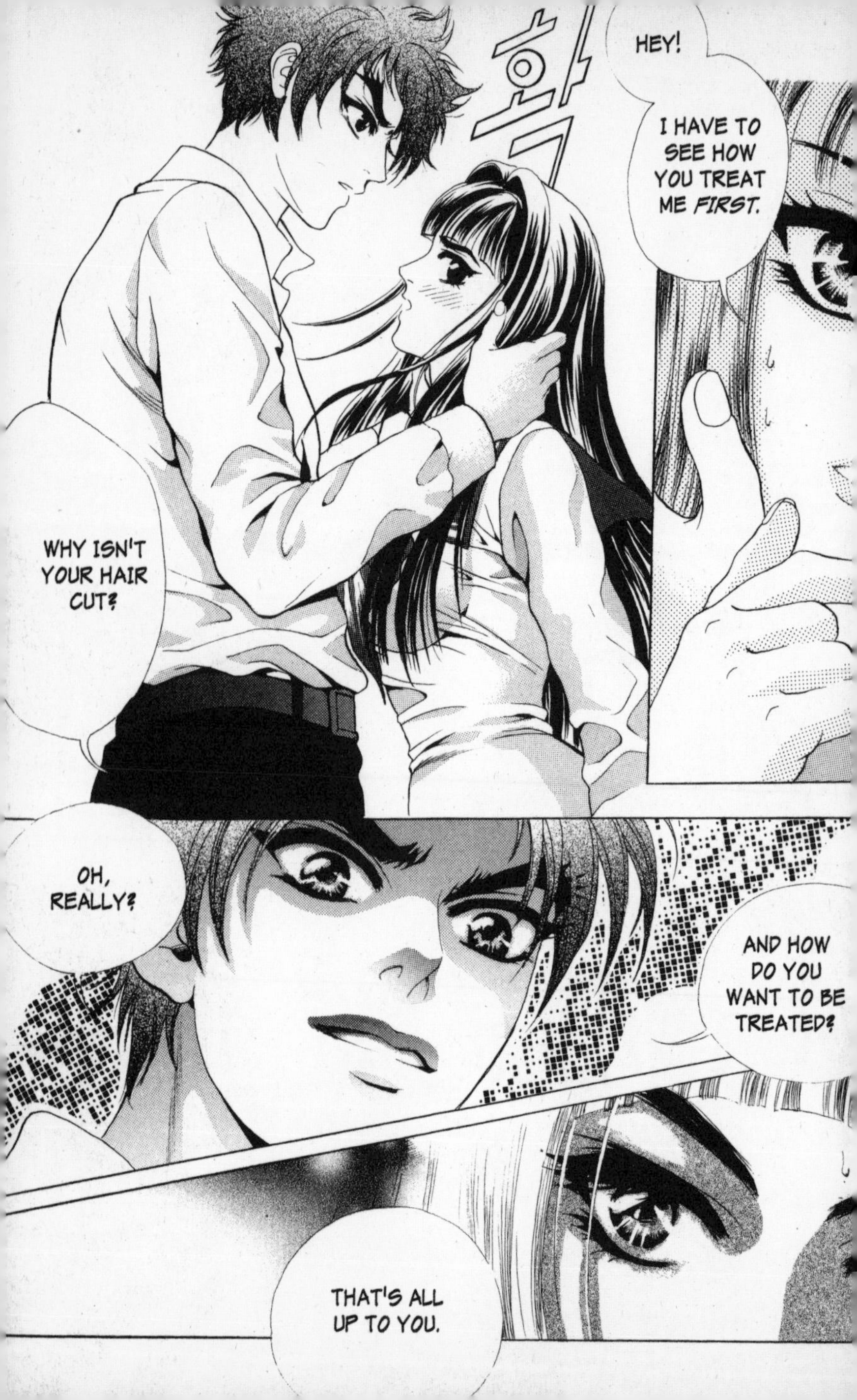
WHY ISN'T YOUR HAIR CUT?
HEY!
I HAVE TO SEE HOW YOU TREAT ME *FIRST*.
OH, REALLY?
AND HOW DO YOU WANT TO BE TREATED?
THAT'S ALL UP TO YOU.

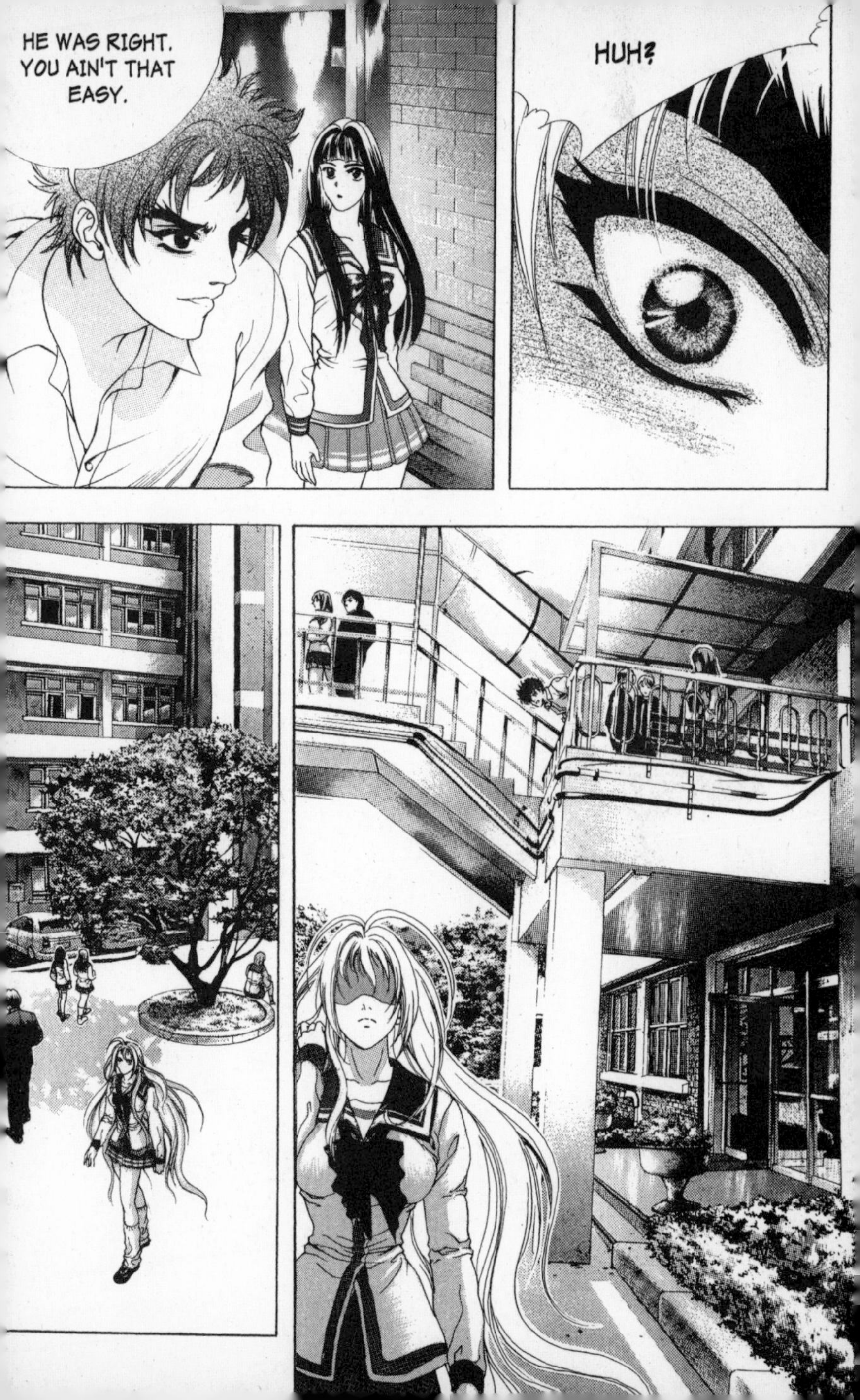
HUH?
HE WAS RIGHT. YOU AIN'T THAT EASY.

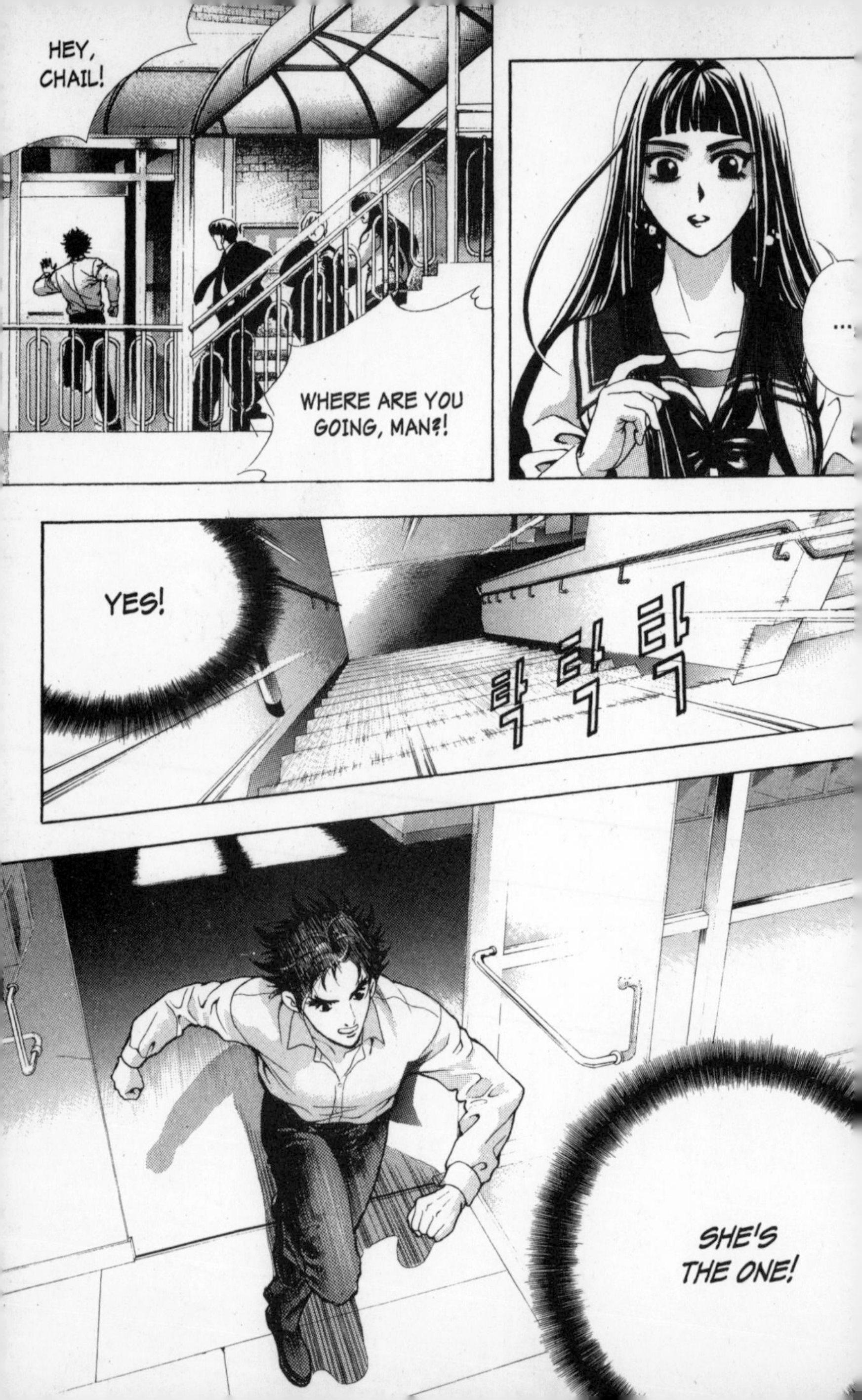
HEY, CHAIL!
WHERE ARE YOU GOING, MAN?!
...
YES!
탁 탁 탁
SHE'S THE ONE!

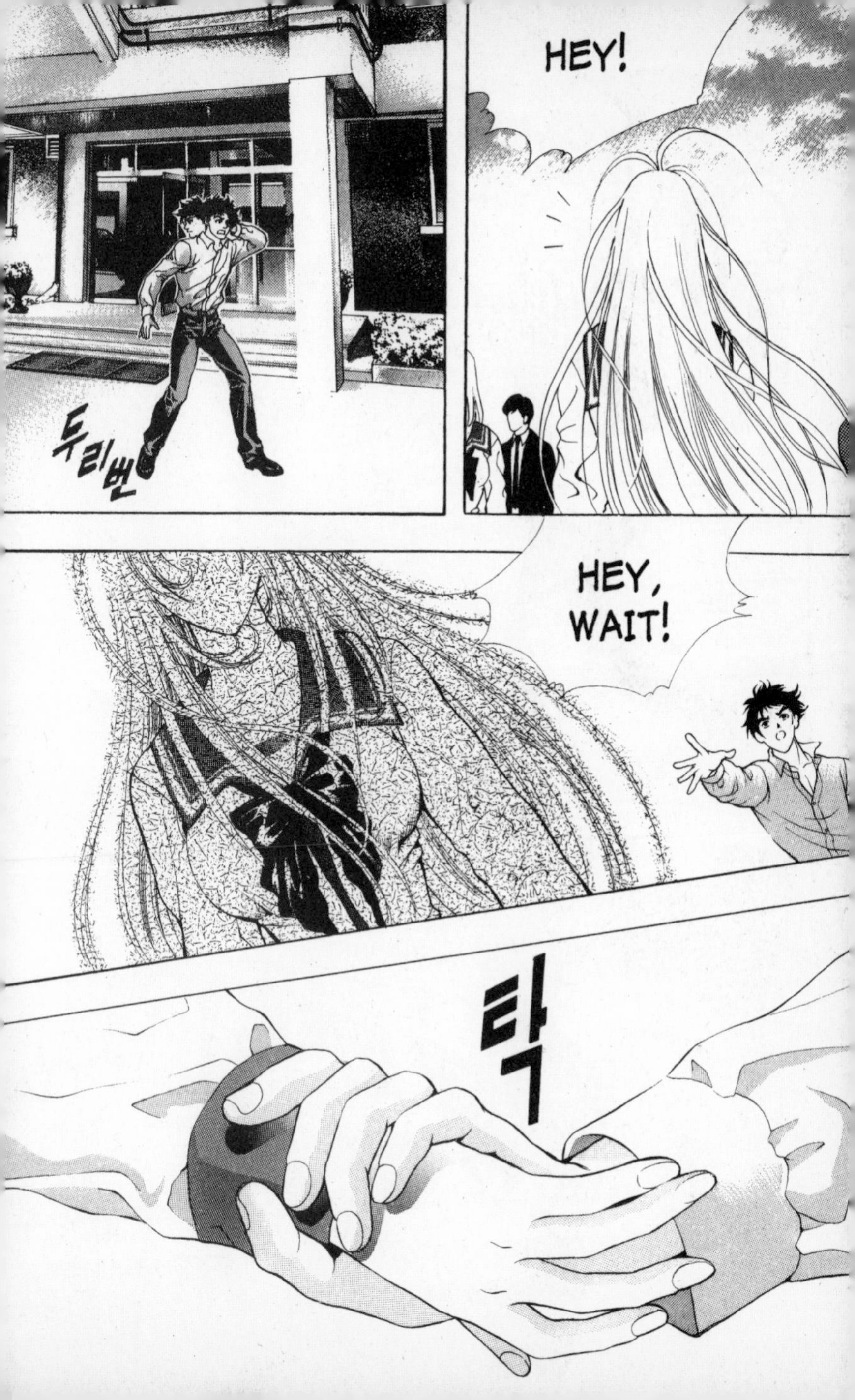
두리번
HEY!
HEY, WAIT!
탁

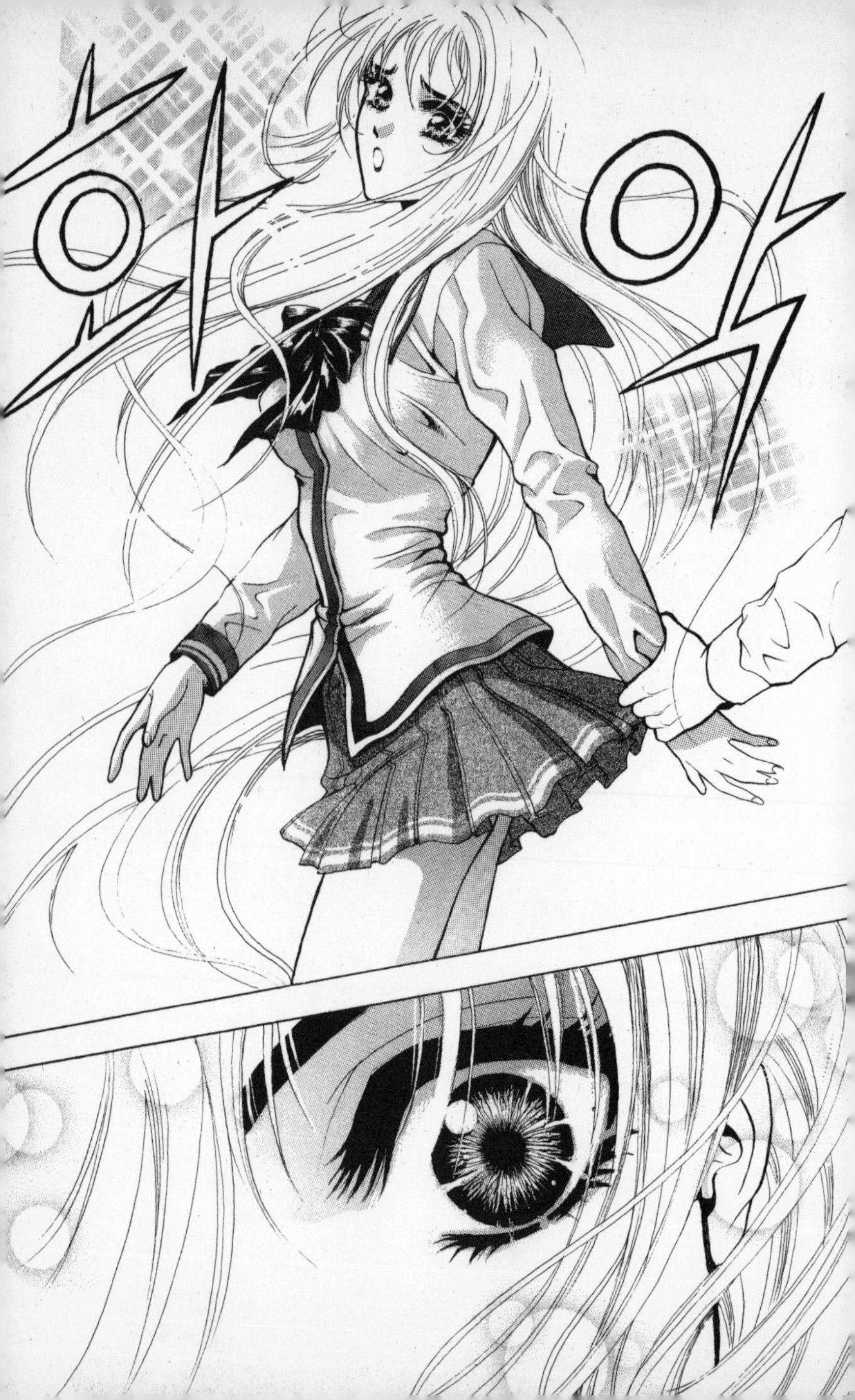

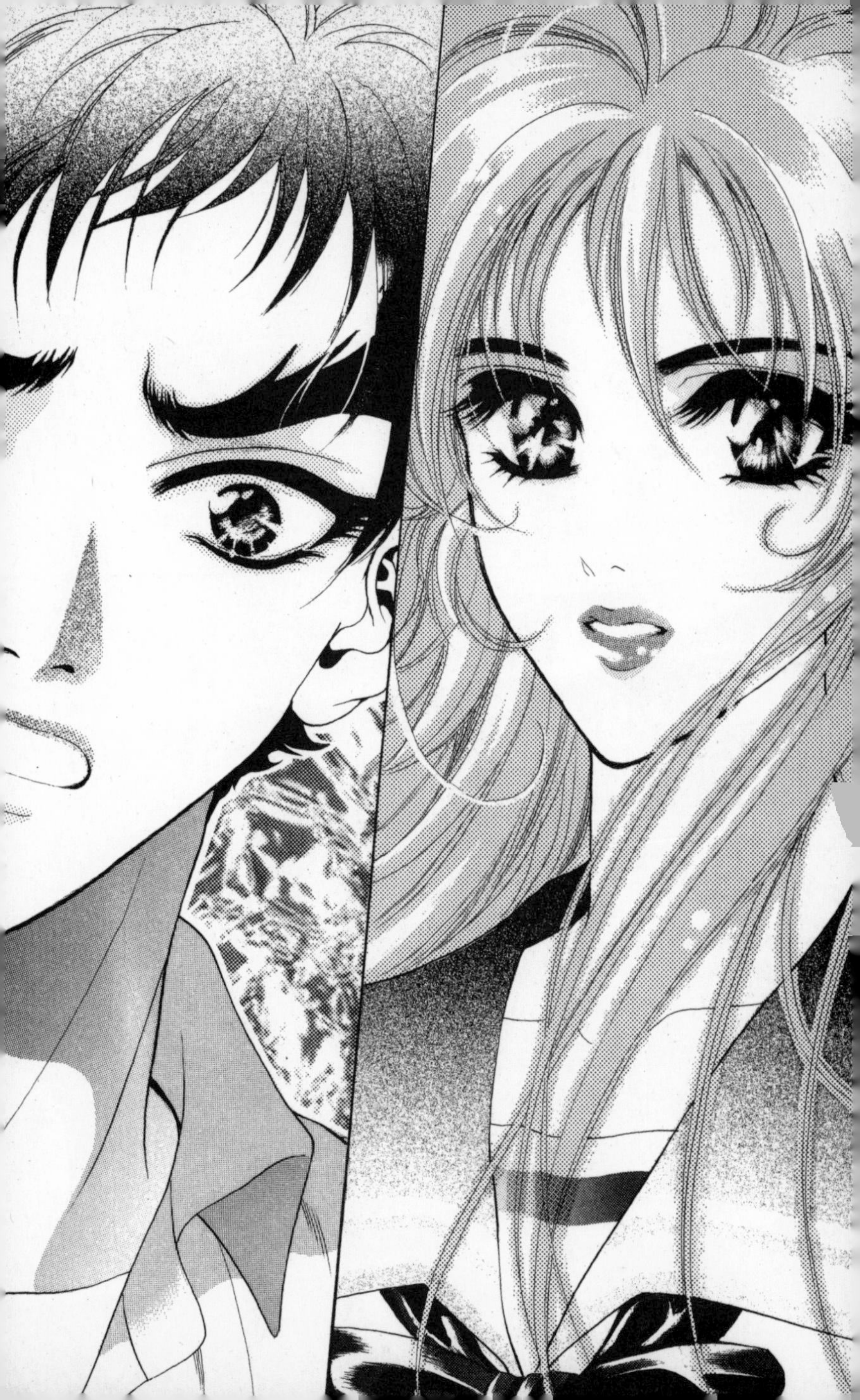

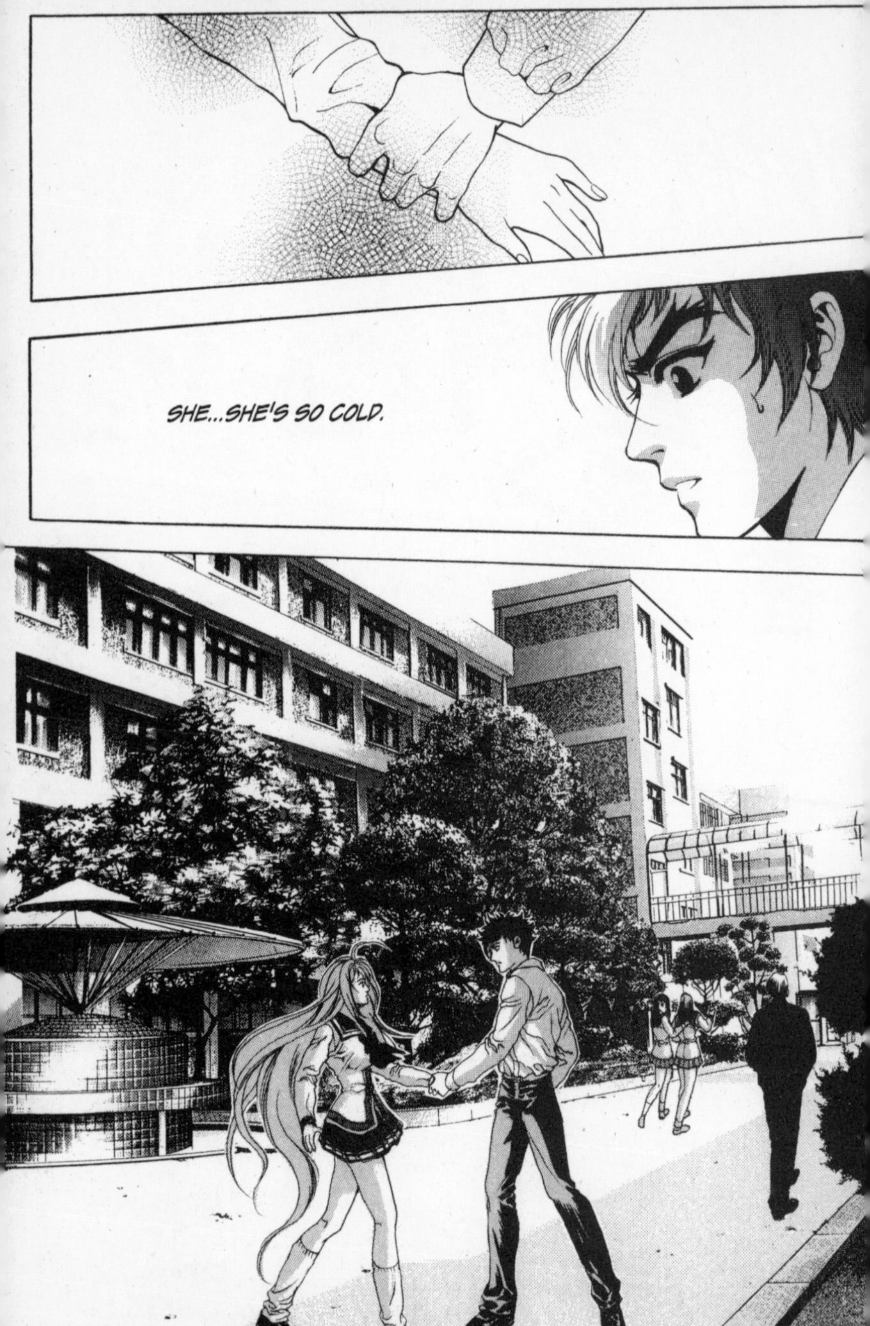
SHE...SHE'S SO COLD.

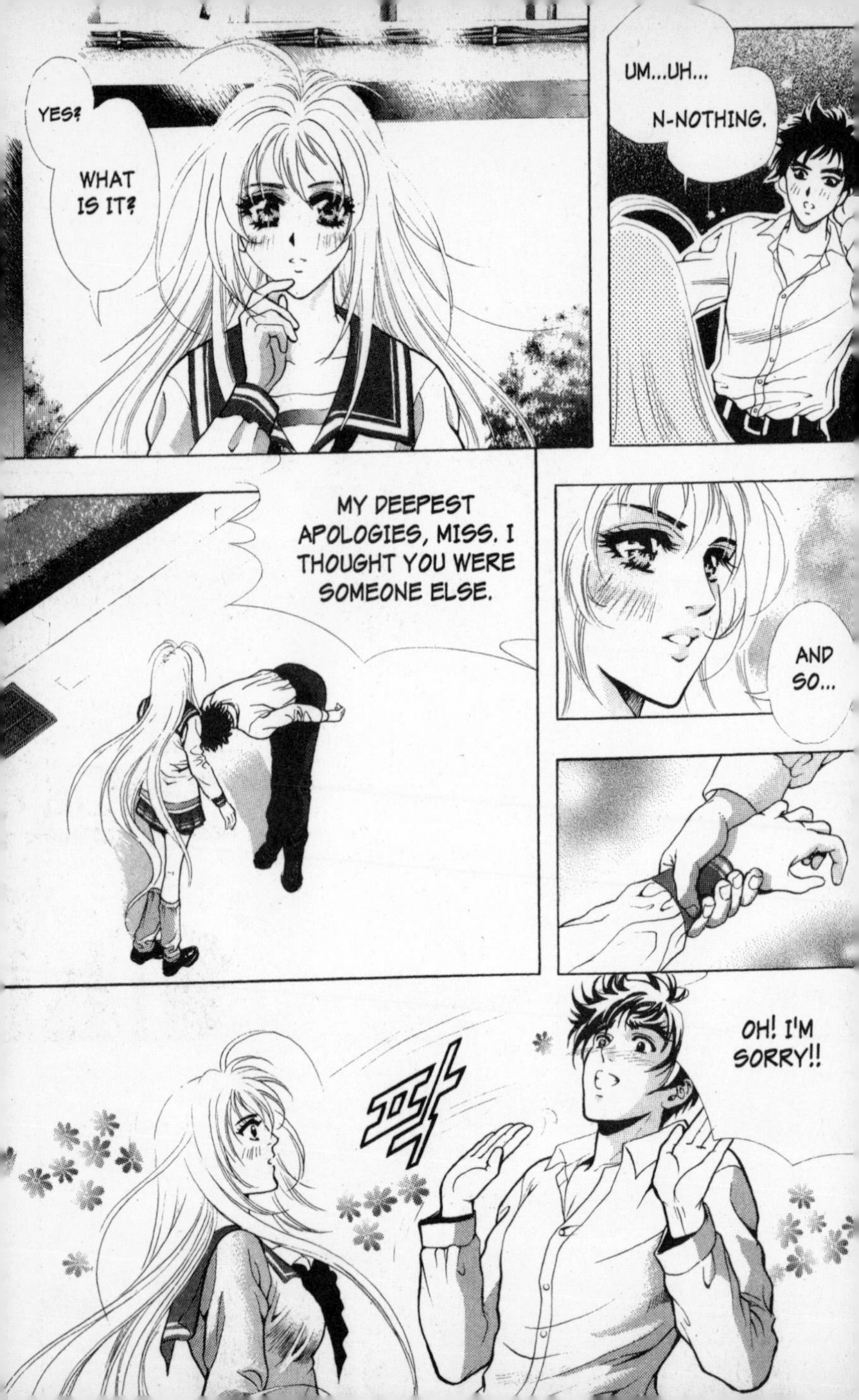
YES? WHAT IS IT?
UM...UH... N-NOTHING.
MY DEEPEST APOLOGIES, MISS. I THOUGHT YOU WERE SOMEONE ELSE.
AND SO...
OH! I'M SORRY!!

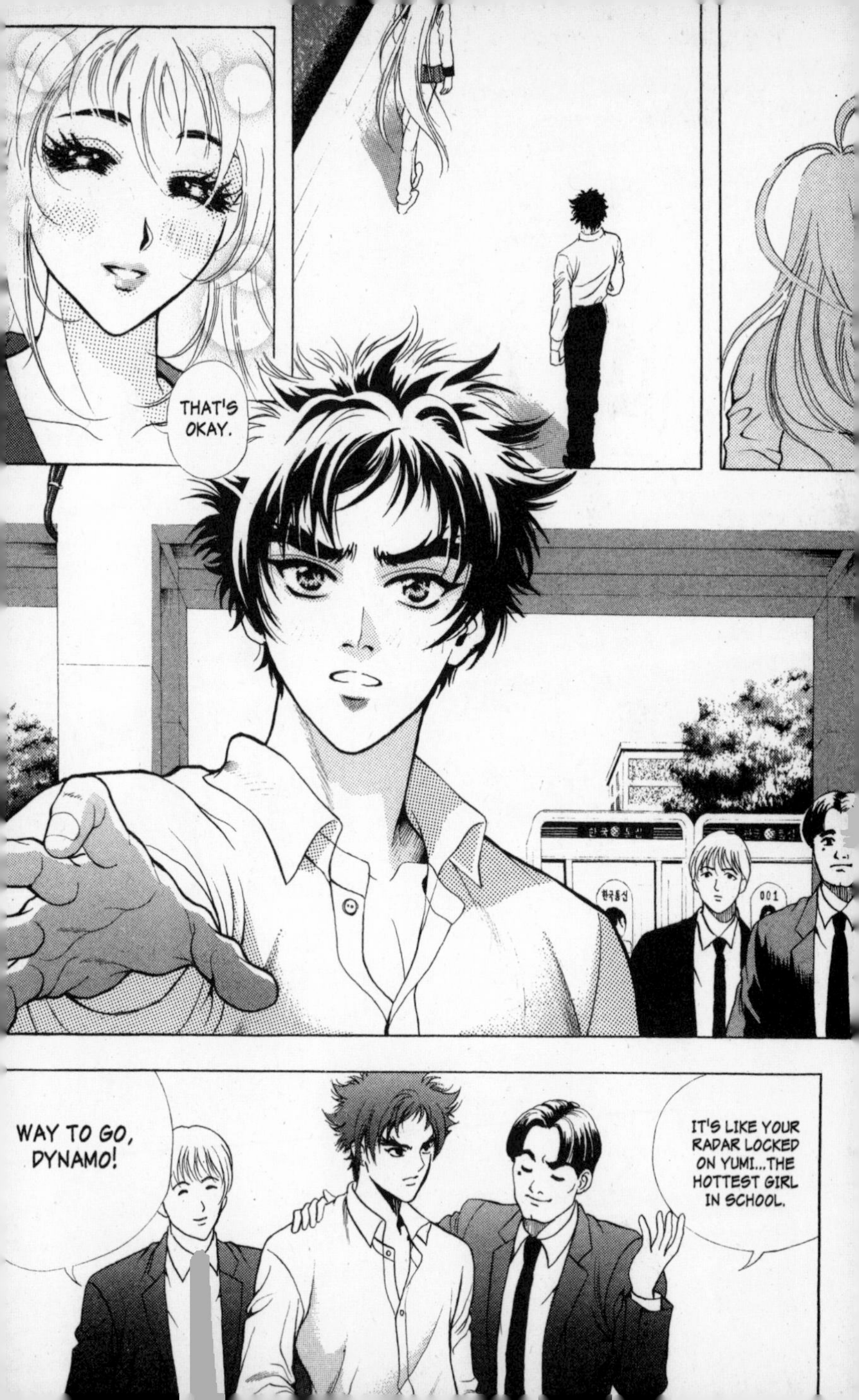
THAT'S OKAY.
WAY TO GO, DYNAMO!
IT'S LIKE YOUR RADAR LOCKED ON YUMI...THE HOTTEST GIRL IN SCHOOL.

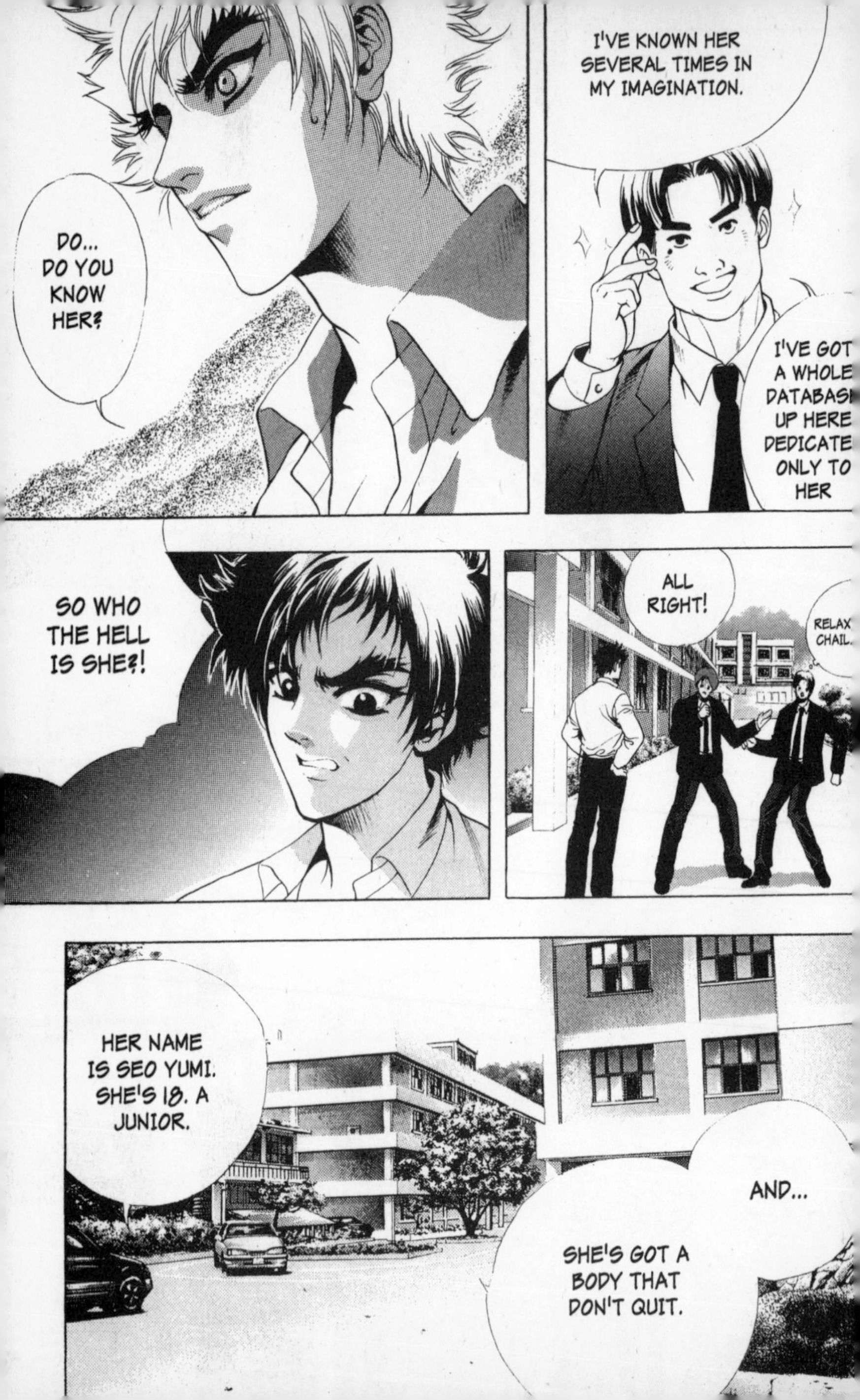
DO... DO YOU KNOW HER?
I'VE KNOWN HER SEVERAL TIMES IN MY IMAGINATION.
I'VE GOT A WHOLE DATABAS UP HERE DEDICATE ONLY TO HER
SO WHO THE HELL IS SHE?!
ALL RIGHT!
RELAX CHAIL.
HER NAME IS SEO YUMI. SHE'S 18. A JUNIOR.
AND...
SHE'S GOT A BODY THAT DON'T QUIT.

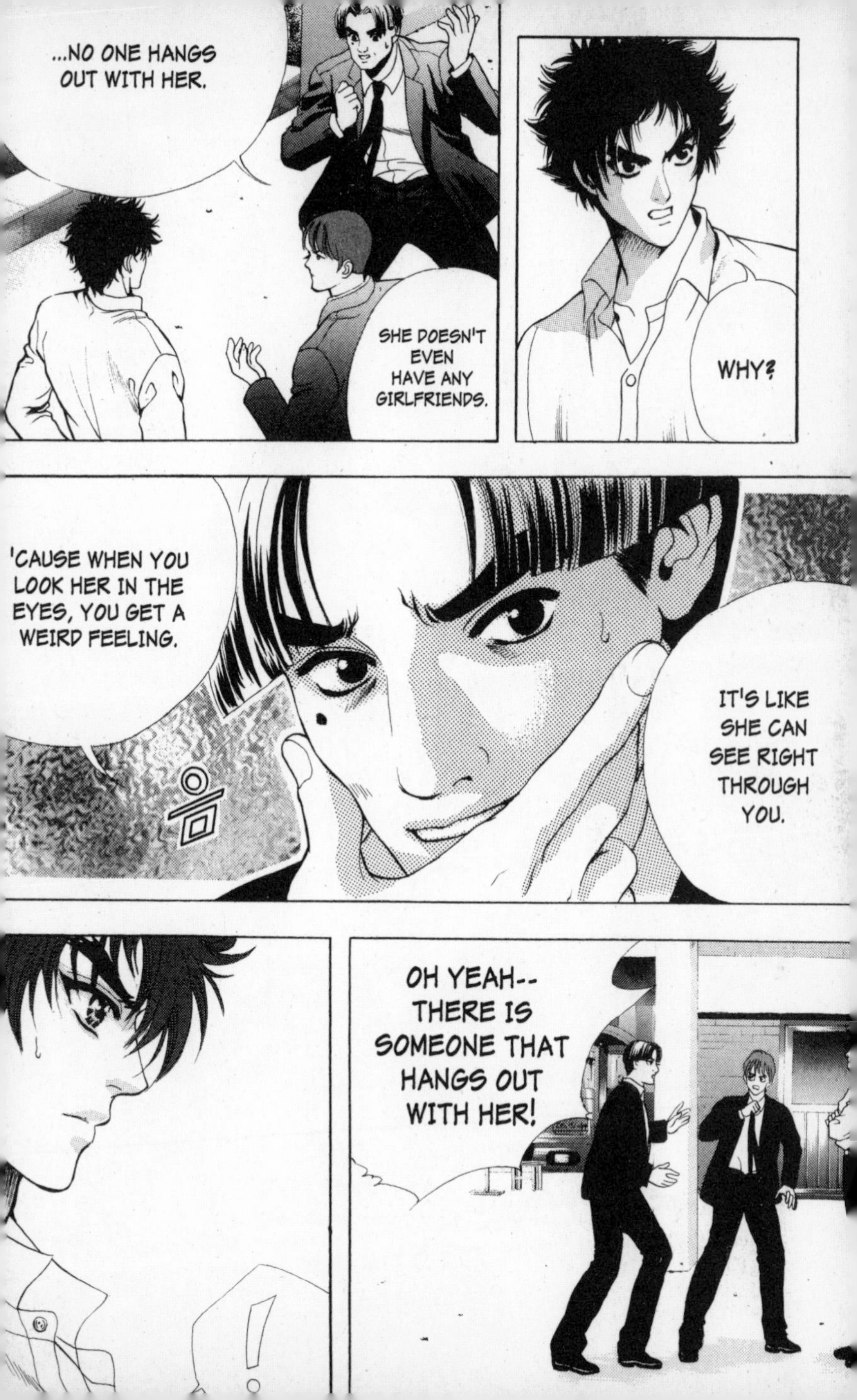
...NO ONE HANGS OUT WITH HER.
SHE DOESN'T EVEN HAVE ANY GIRLFRIENDS.
WHY?
'CAUSE WHEN YOU LOOK HER IN THE EYES, YOU GET A WEIRD FEELING.
음
IT'S LIKE SHE CAN SEE RIGHT THROUGH YOU.
!
OH YEAH-- THERE IS SOMEONE THAT HANGS OUT WITH HER!

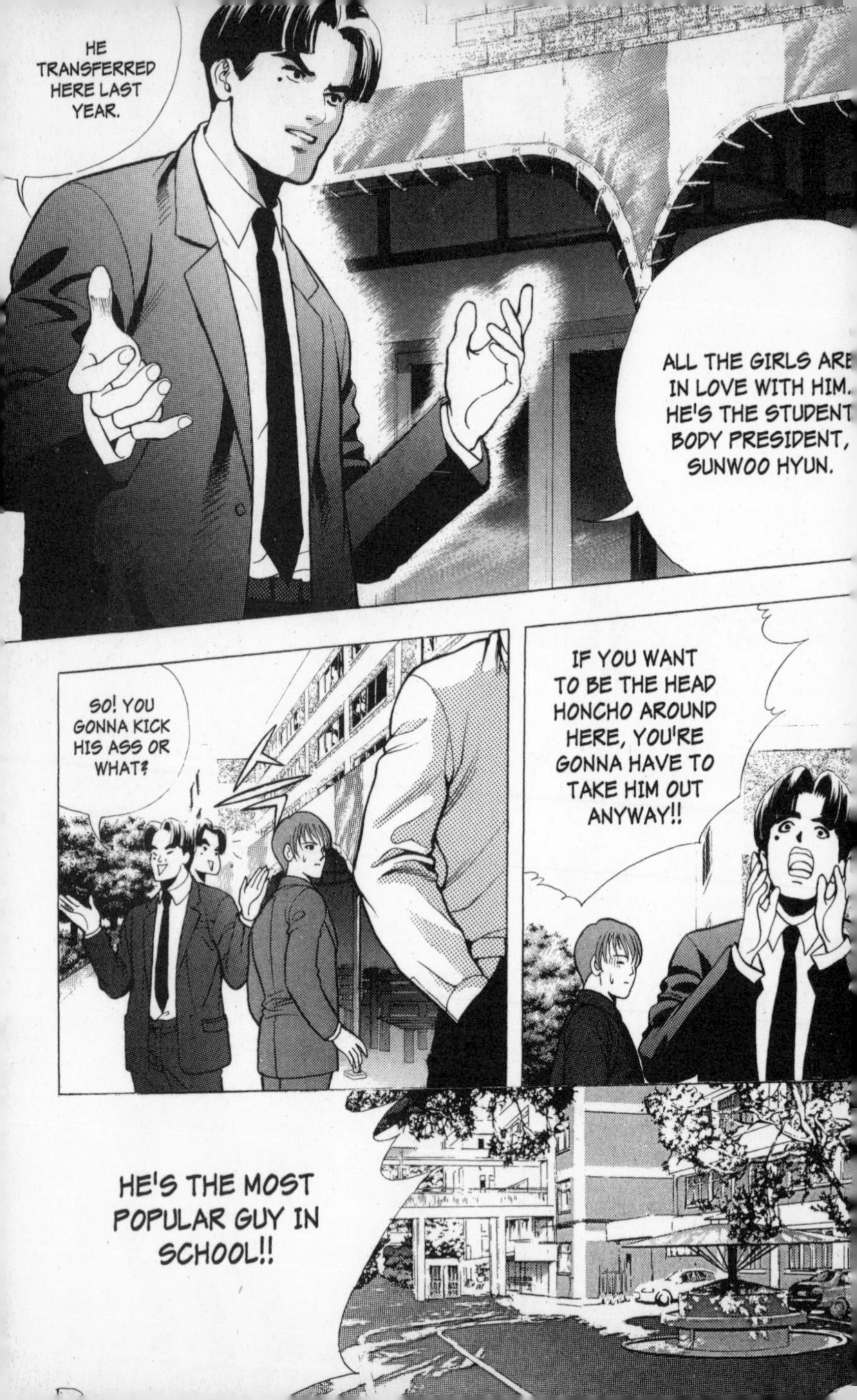
HE TRANSFERRED HERE LAST YEAR.
ALL THE GIRLS ARE IN LOVE WITH HIM. HE'S THE STUDENT BODY PRESIDENT, SUNWOO HYUN.
SO! YOU GONNA KICK HIS ASS OR WHAT?
IF YOU WANT TO BE THE HEAD HONCHO AROUND HERE, YOU'RE GONNA HAVE TO TAKE HIM OUT ANYWAY!!
HE'S THE MOST POPULAR GUY IN SCHOOL!!

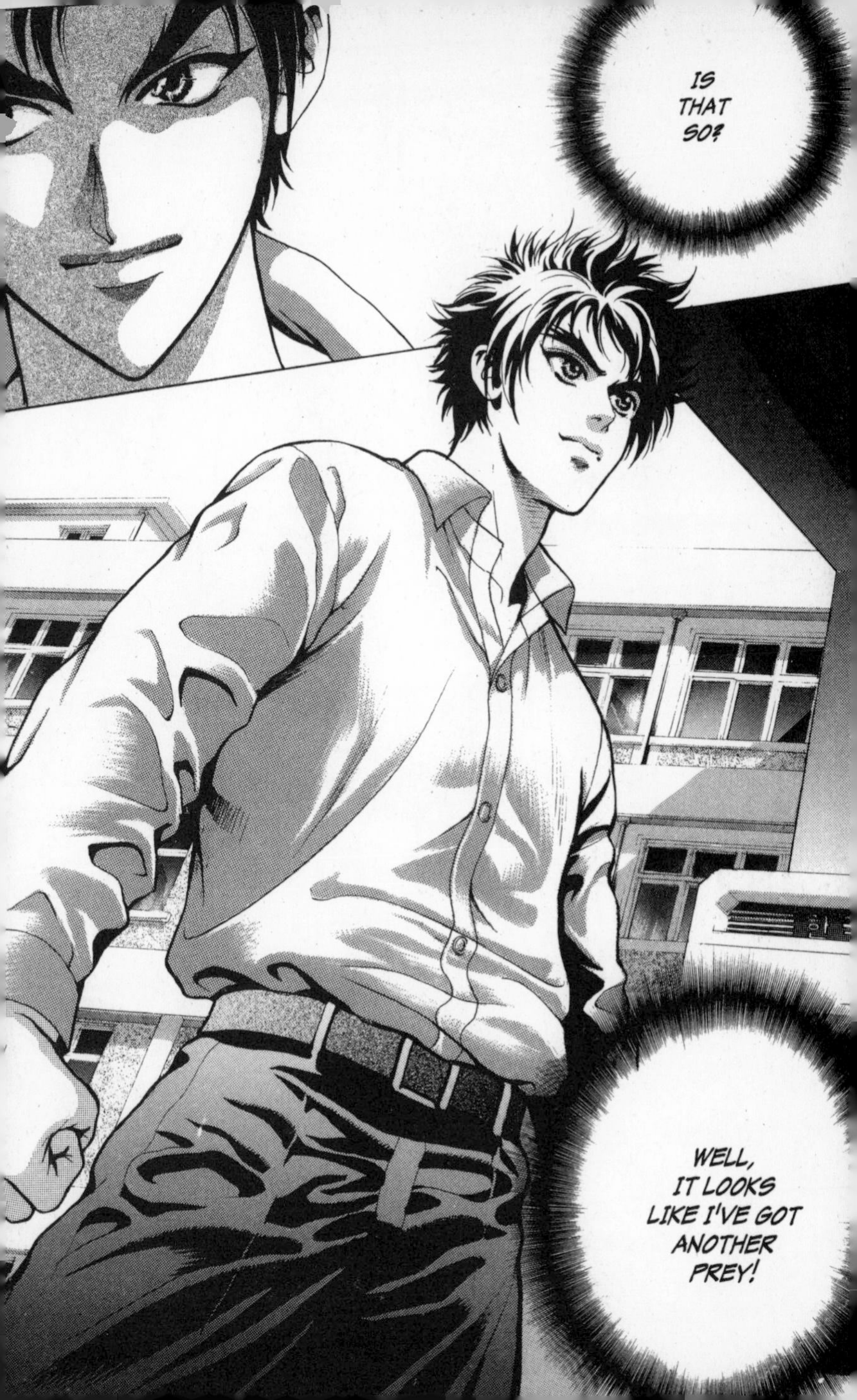
IS THAT SO?
WELL, IT LOOKS LIKE I'VE GOT ANOTHER PREY!

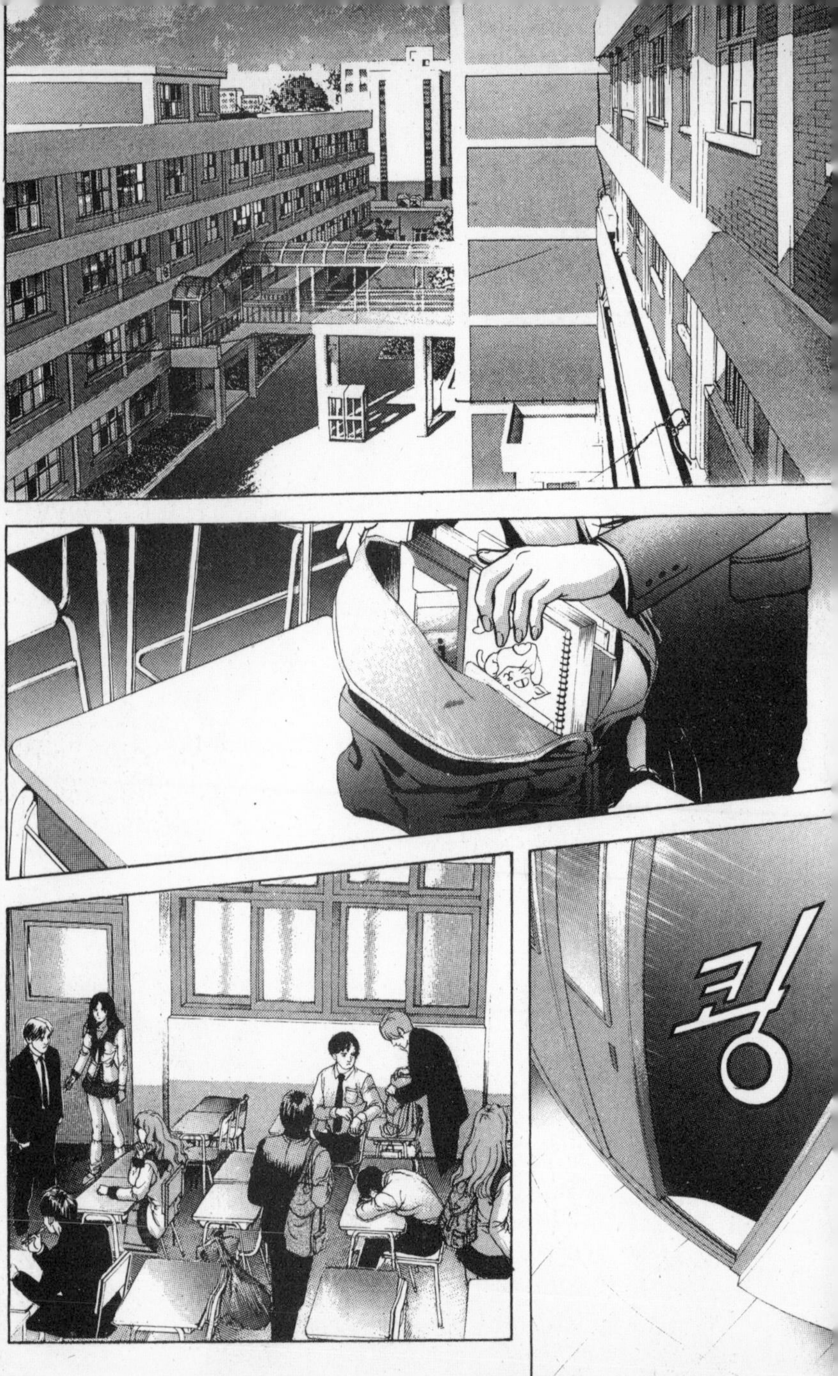
쾅

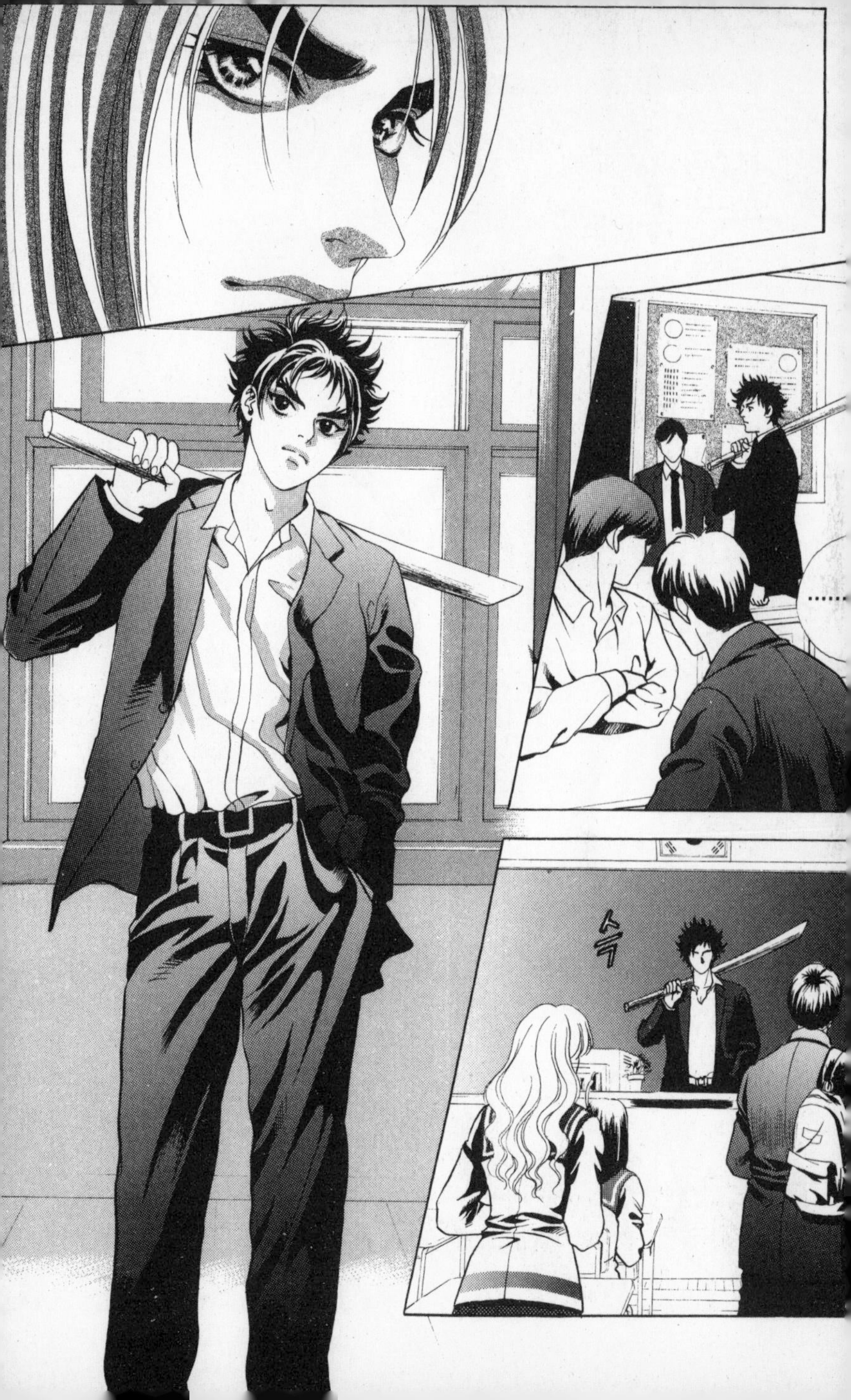
슥

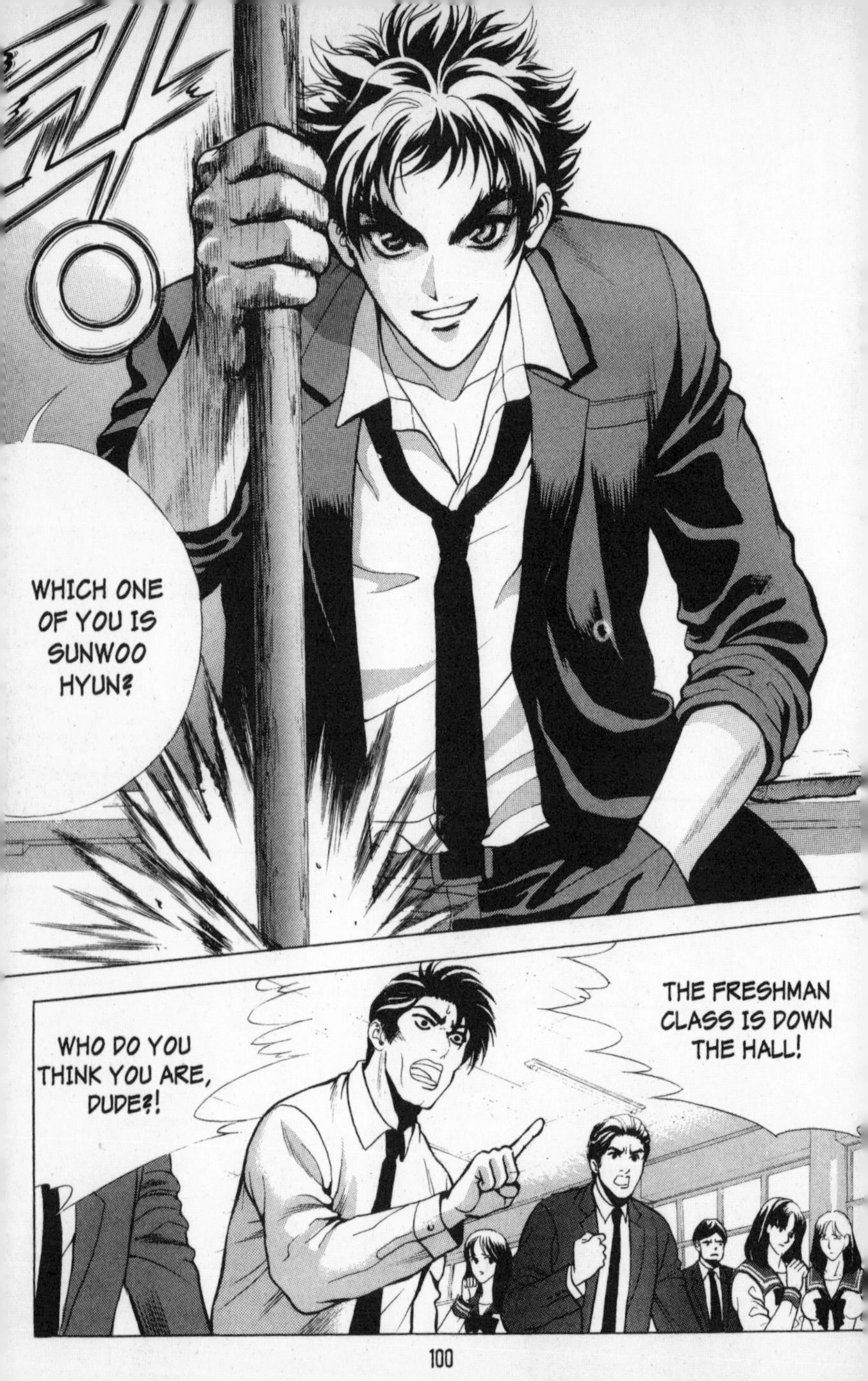
WHICH ONE OF YOU IS SUNWOO HYUN?
THE FRESHMAN CLASS IS DOWN THE HALL!
WHO DO YOU THINK YOU ARE, DUDE?!

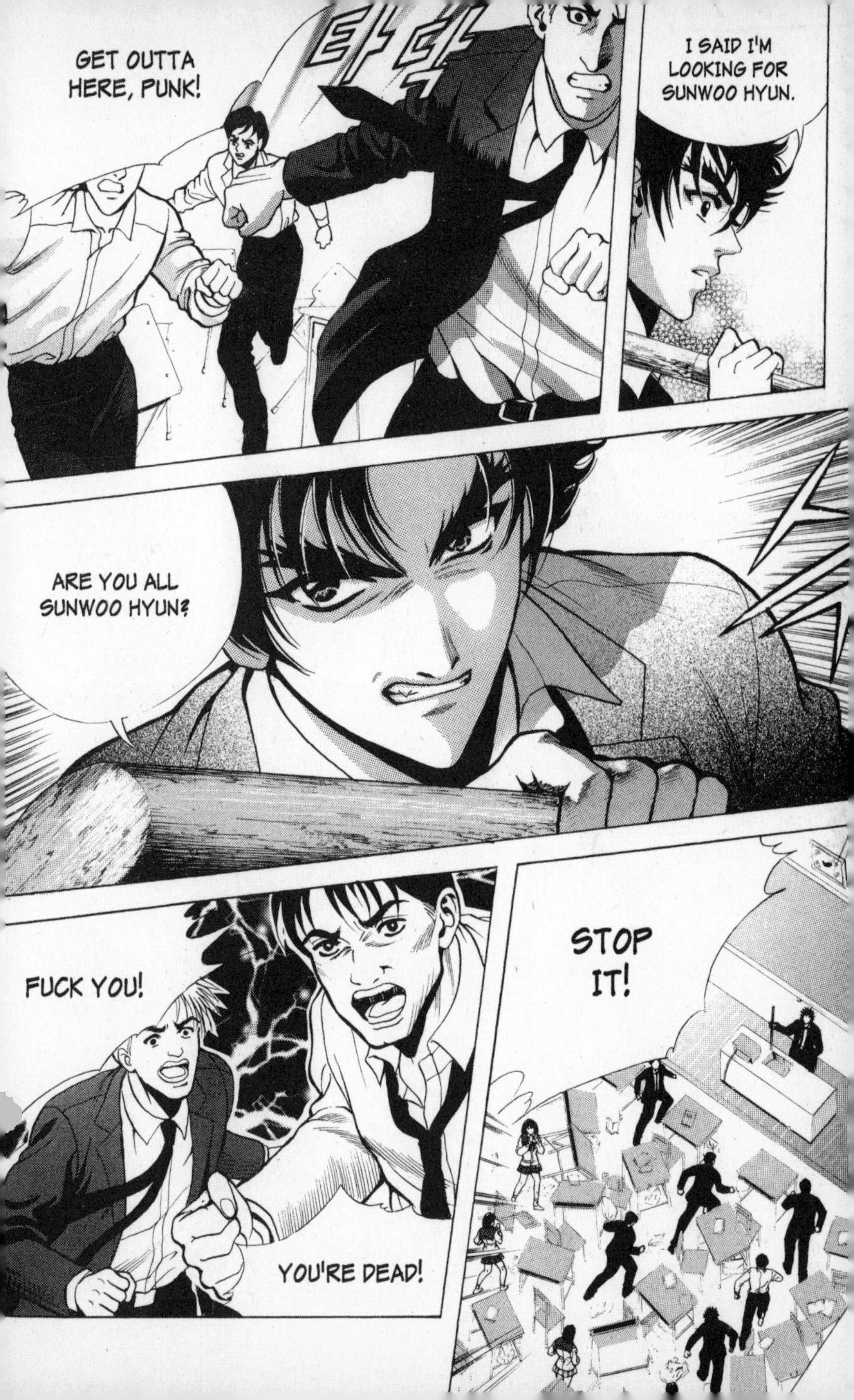
GET OUTTA HERE, PUNK!
타닥
I SAID I'M LOOKING FOR SUNWOO HYUN.
ARE YOU ALL SUNWOO HYUN?
FUCK YOU!
YOU'RE DEAD!
STOP IT!

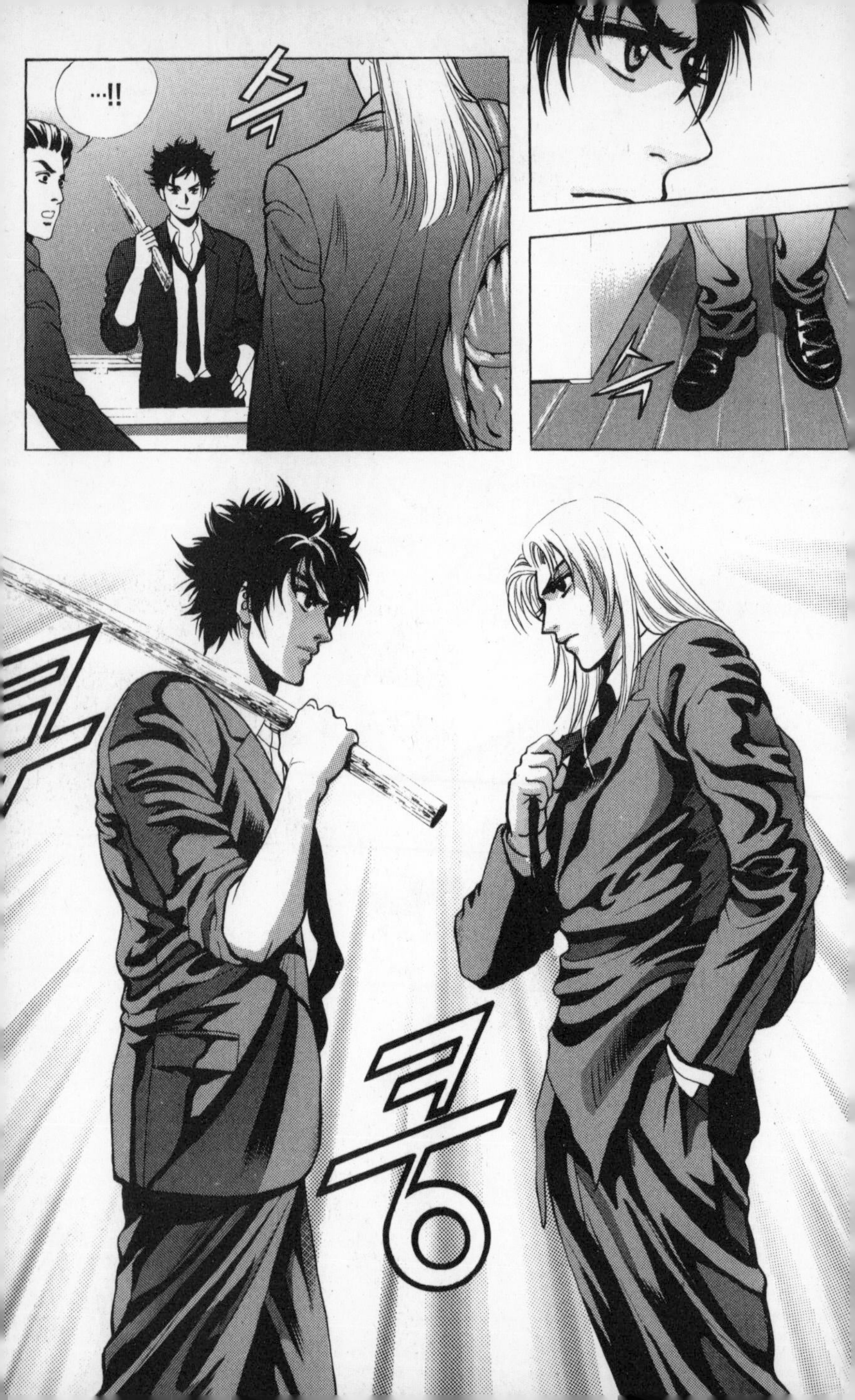
...!!

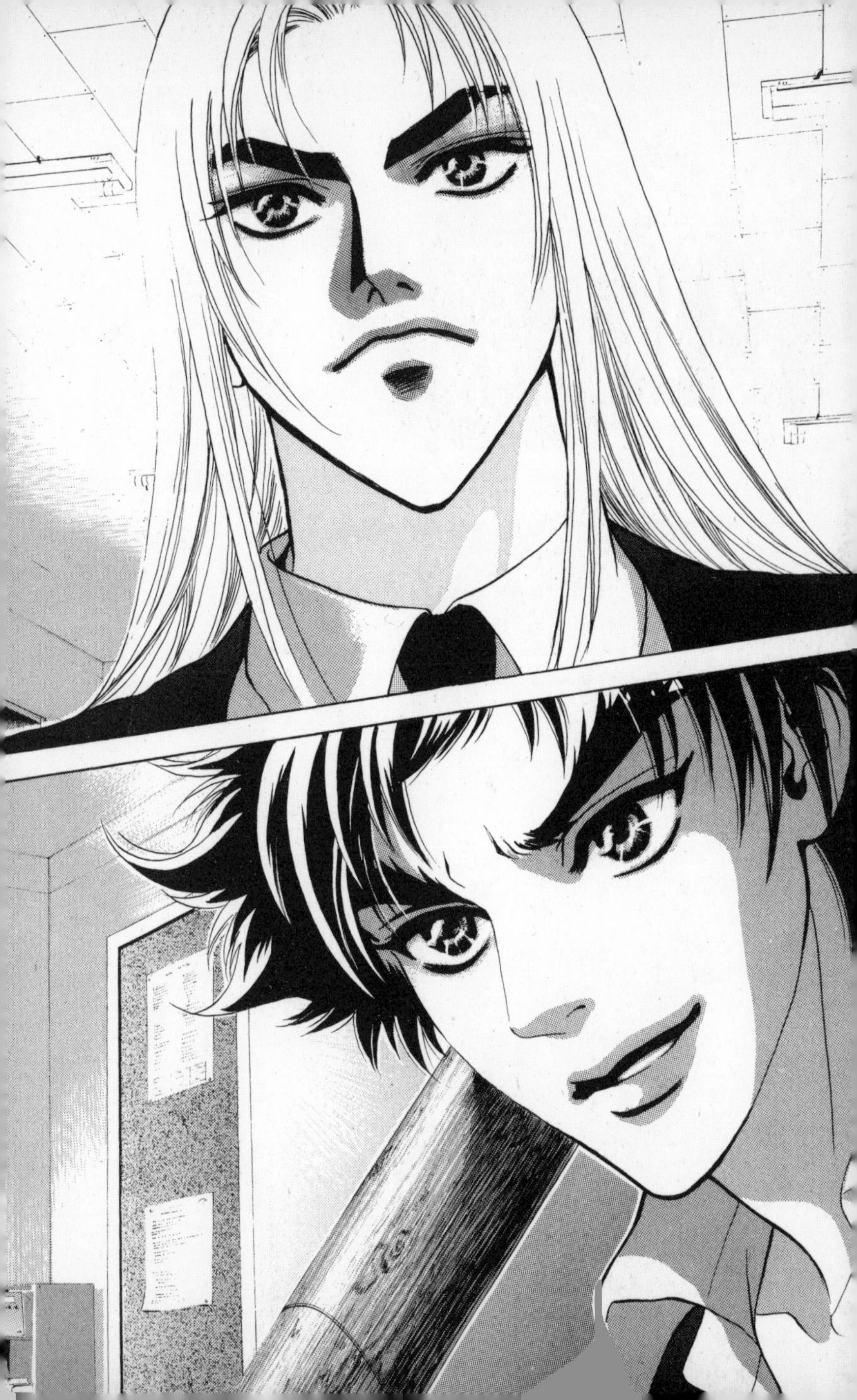

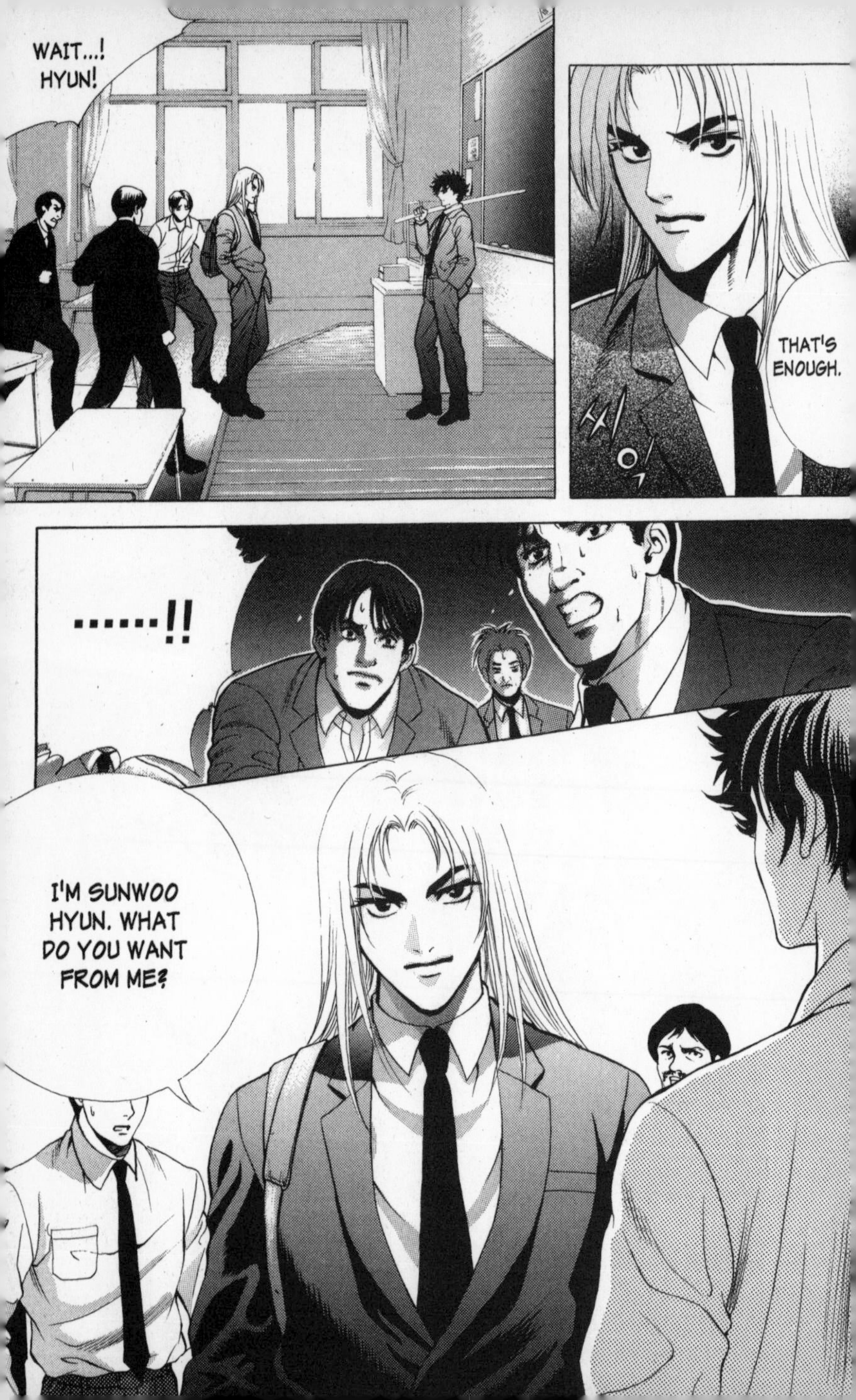
WAIT...! HYUN!
THAT'S ENOUGH.
......!!
I'M SUNWOO HYUN. WHAT DO YOU WANT FROM ME?

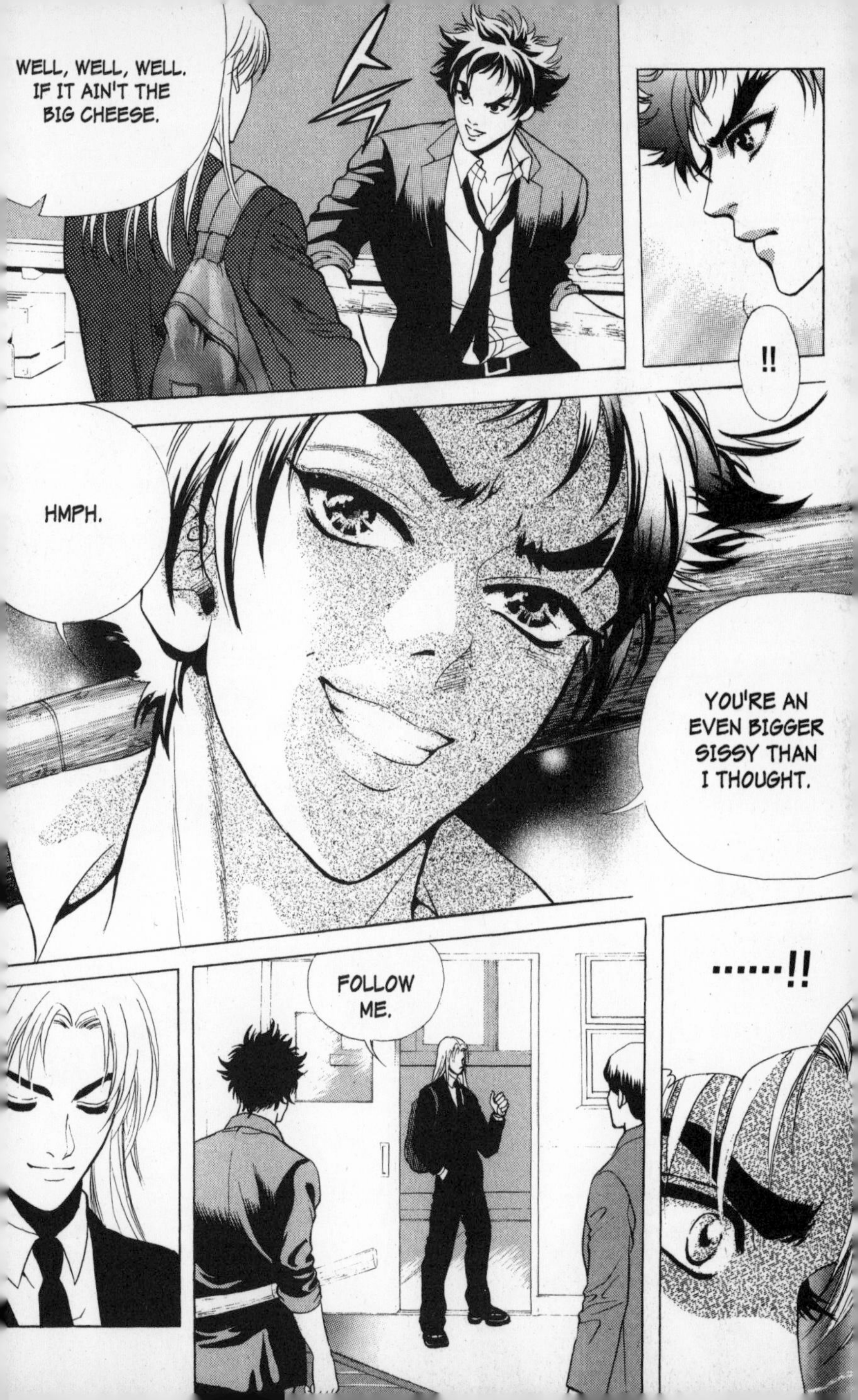
!!
WELL, WELL, WELL. IF IT AIN'T THE BIG CHEESE.
YOU'RE AN EVEN BIGGER SISSY THAN I THOUGHT.
HMPH.
......!!
FOLLOW ME.

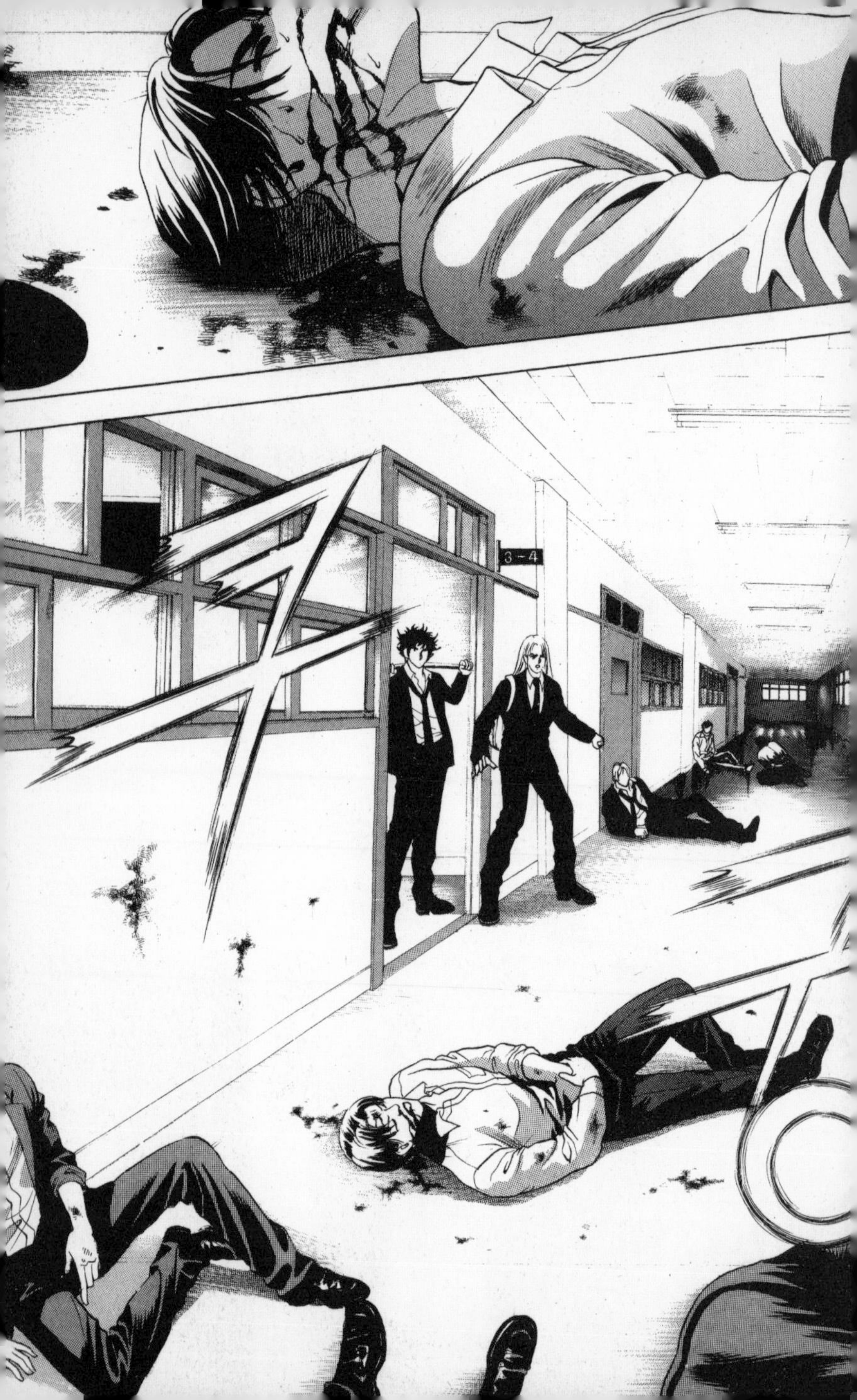
3-4

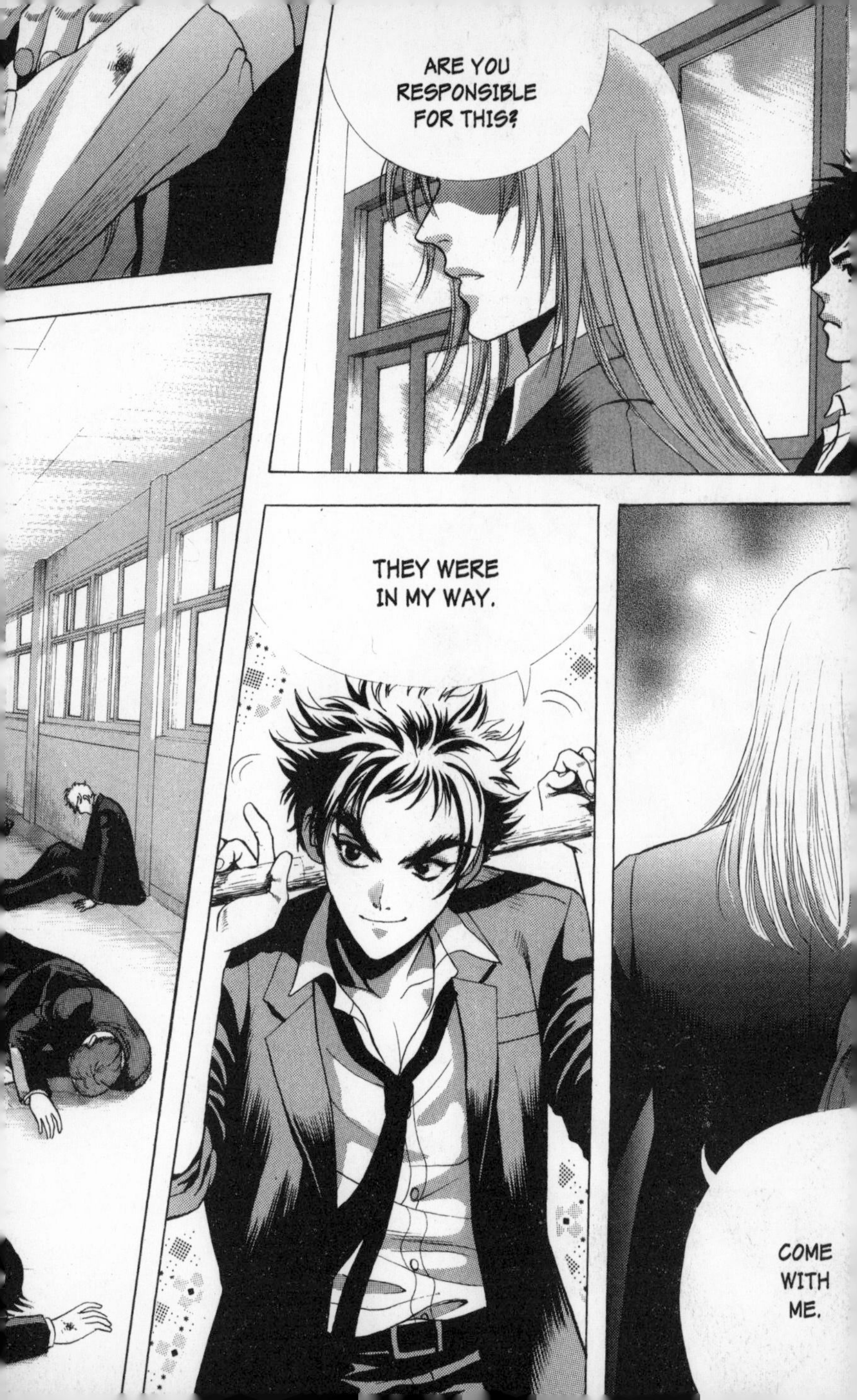
ARE YOU RESPONSIBLE FOR THIS?
THEY WERE IN MY WAY.
COME WITH ME.

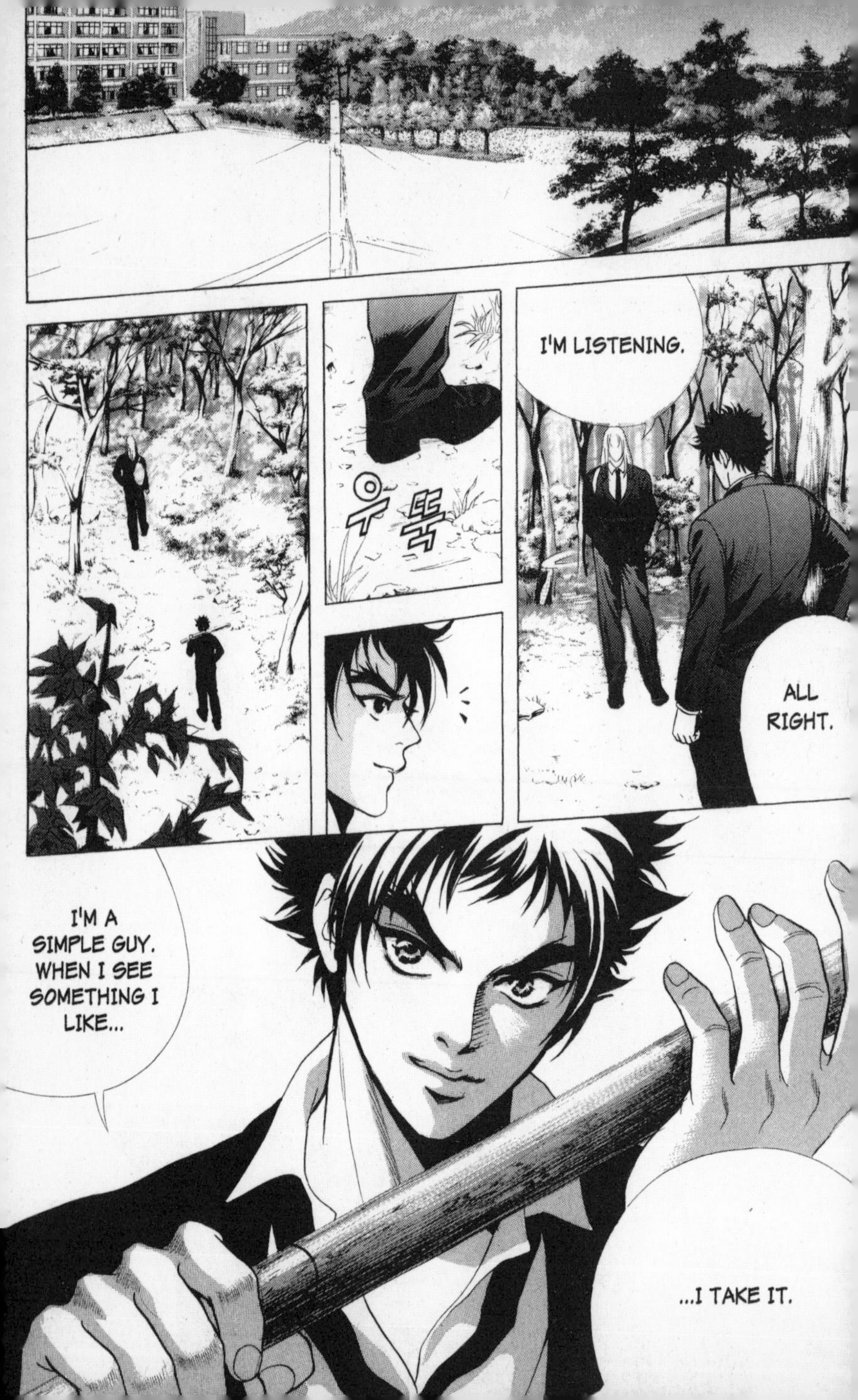
우뚝
I'M LISTENING.
ALL RIGHT.
I'M A SIMPLE GUY. WHEN I SEE SOMETHING I LIKE...
...I TAKE IT.

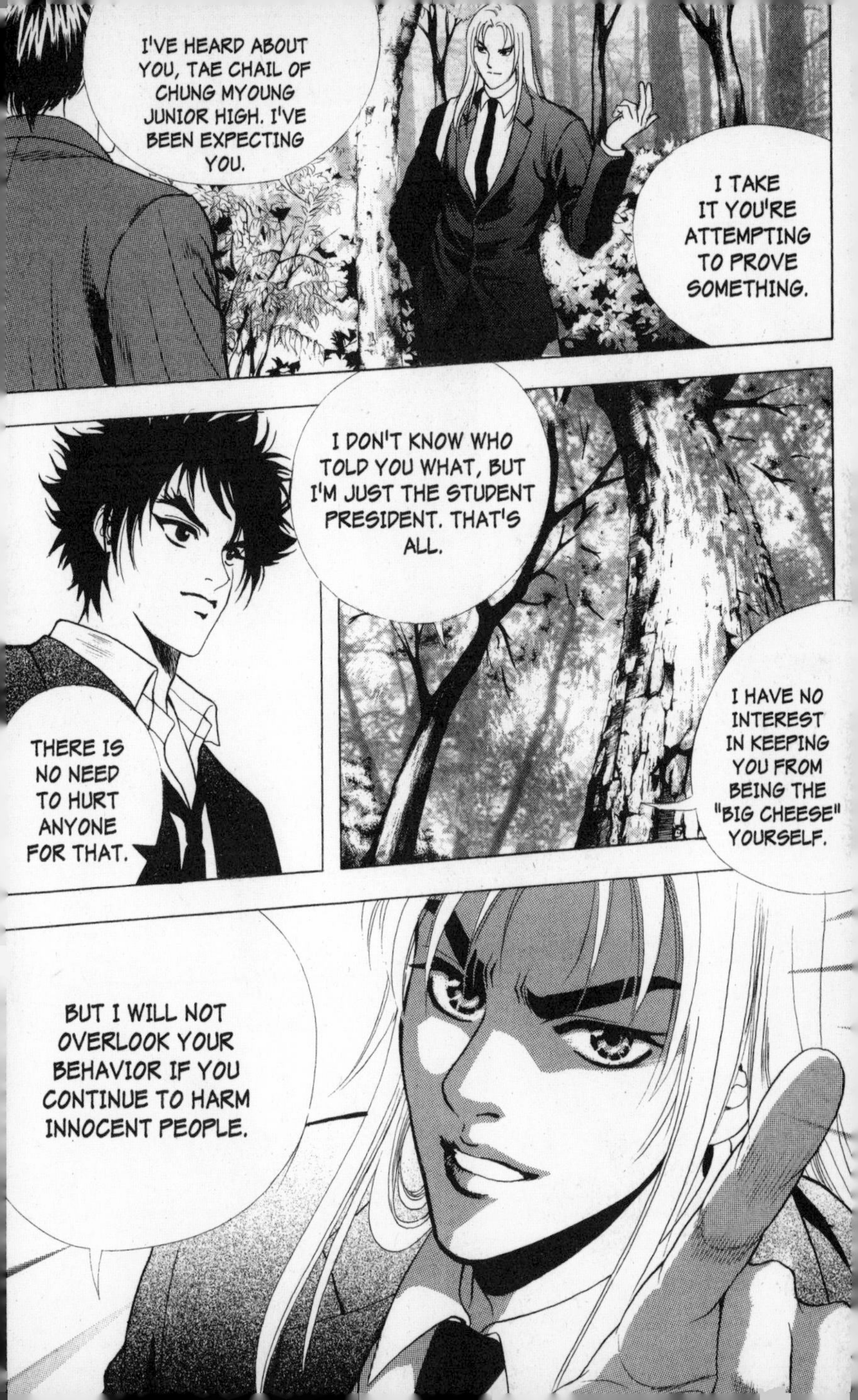
I'VE HEARD ABOUT YOU, TAE CHAIL OF CHUNG MYOUNG JUNIOR HIGH. I'VE BEEN EXPECTING YOU.
I TAKE IT YOU'RE ATTEMPTING TO PROVE SOMETHING.
I DON'T KNOW WHO TOLD YOU WHAT, BUT I'M JUST THE STUDENT PRESIDENT. THAT'S ALL.
THERE IS NO NEED TO HURT ANYONE FOR THAT.
I HAVE NO INTEREST IN KEEPING YOU FROM BEING THE "BIG CHEESE" YOURSELF.
BUT I WILL NOT OVERLOOK YOUR BEHAVIOR IF YOU CONTINUE TO HARM INNOCENT PEOPLE.

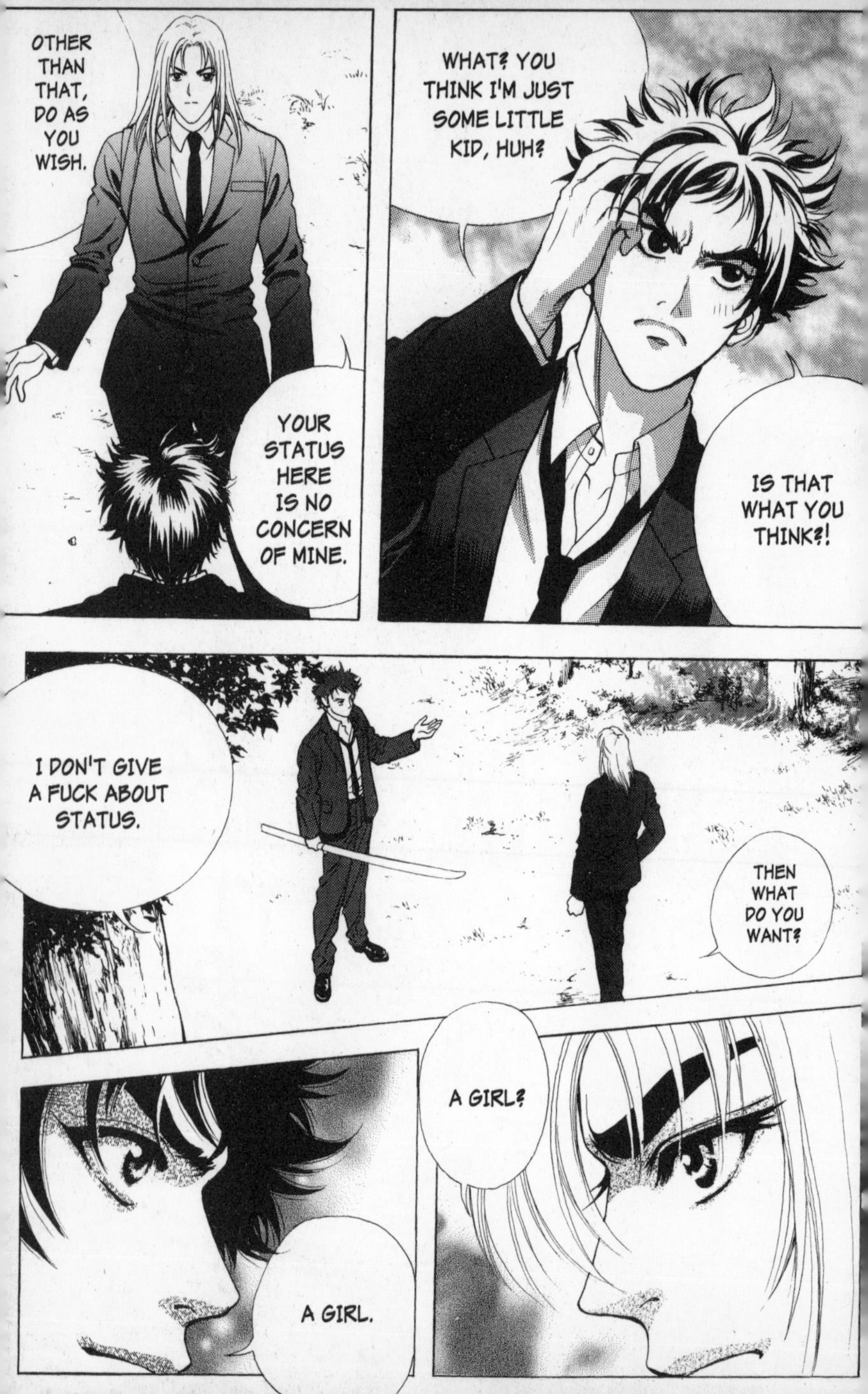
YOUR STATUS HERE IS NO CONCERN OF MINE.
OTHER THAN THAT, DO AS YOU WISH.
WHAT? YOU THINK I'M JUST SOME LITTLE KID, HUH?
IS THAT WHAT YOU THINK?!
I DON'T GIVE A FUCK ABOUT STATUS.
THEN WHAT DO YOU WANT?
A GIRL.
A GIRL?

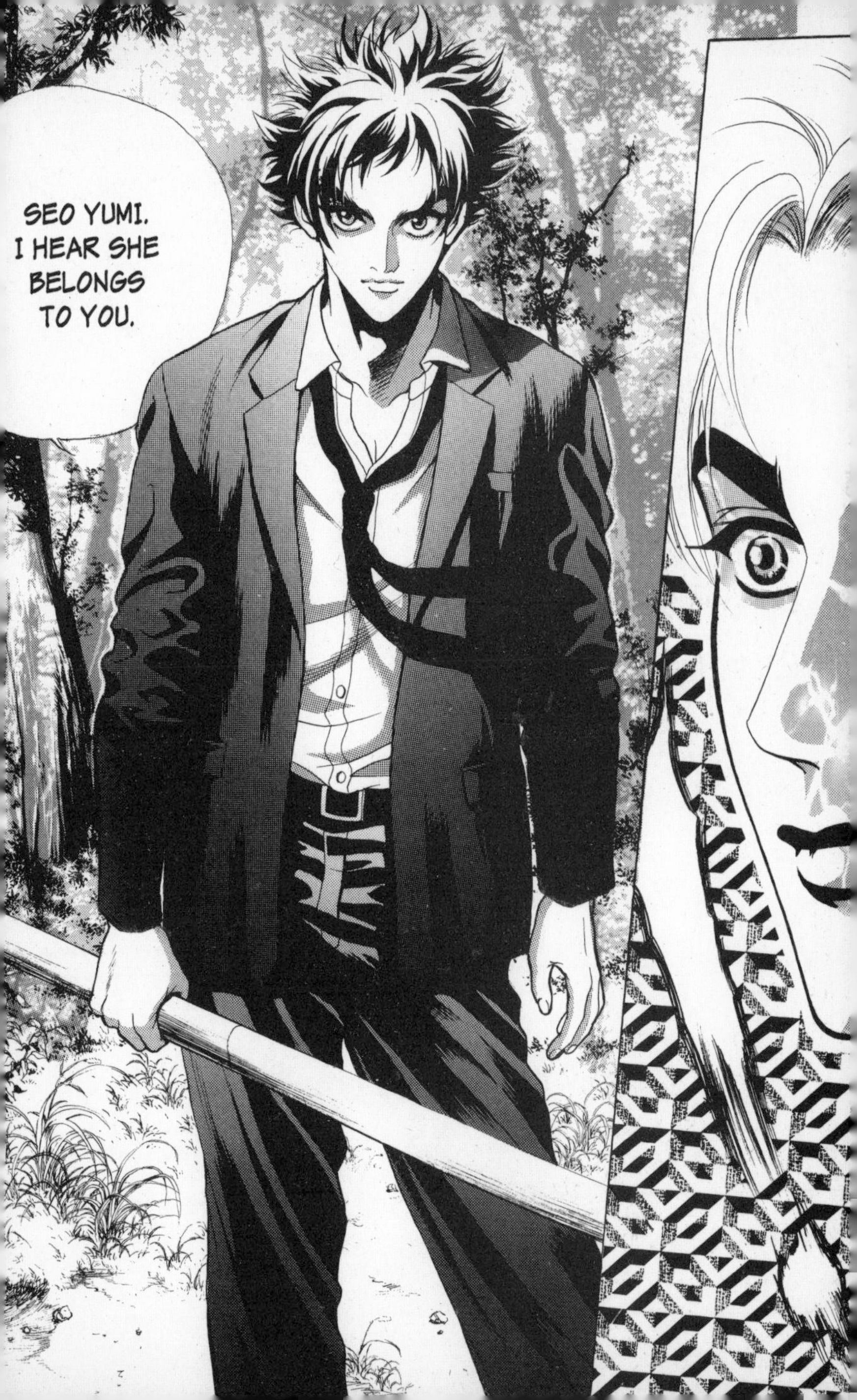
SEO YUMI. I HEAR SHE BELONGS TO YOU.

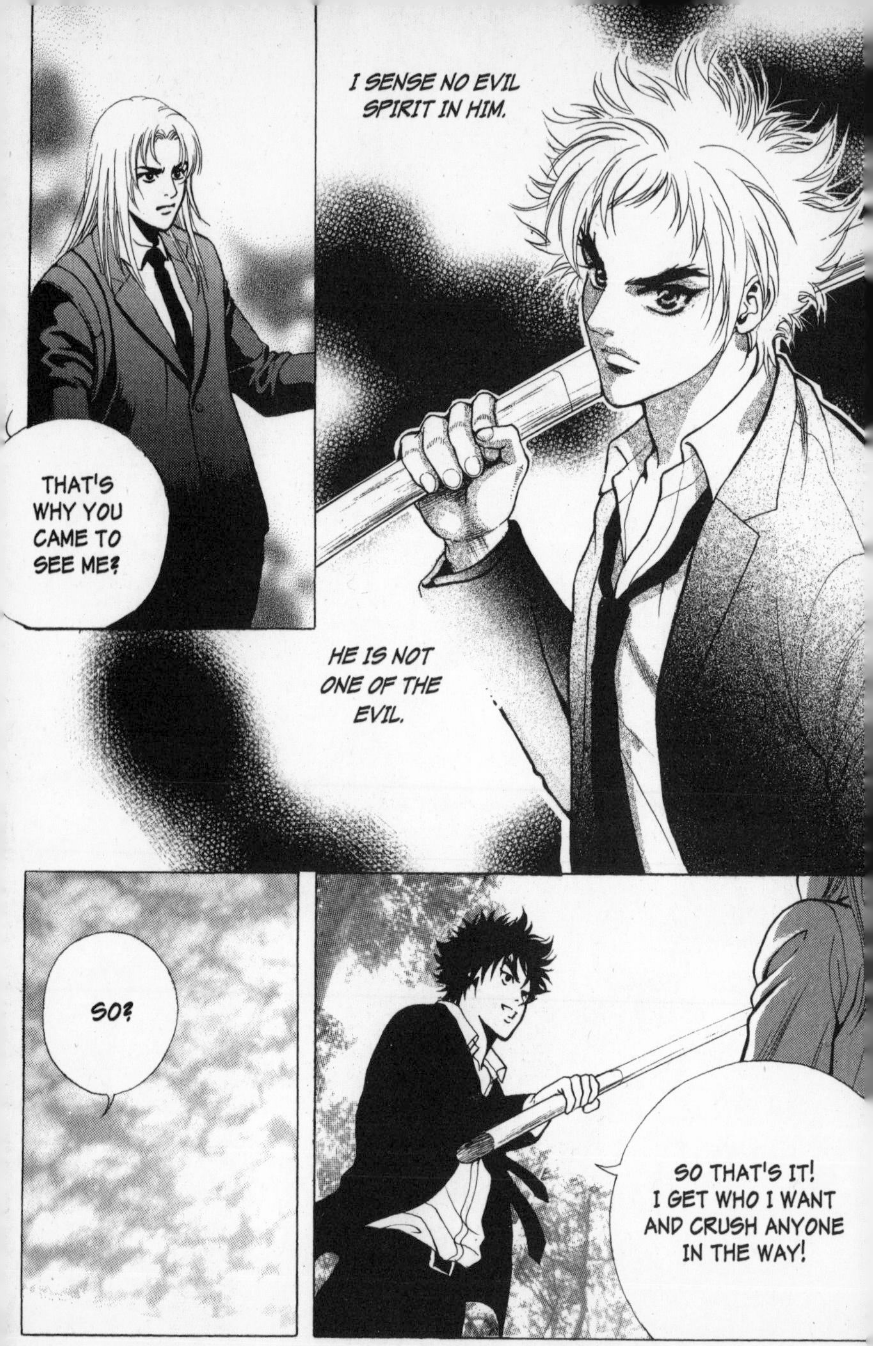
THAT'S WHY YOU CAME TO SEE ME?
I SENSE NO EVIL SPIRIT IN HIM.
HE IS NOT ONE OF THE EVIL.
SO?
SO THAT'S IT! I GET WHO I WANT AND CRUSH ANYONE IN THE WAY!

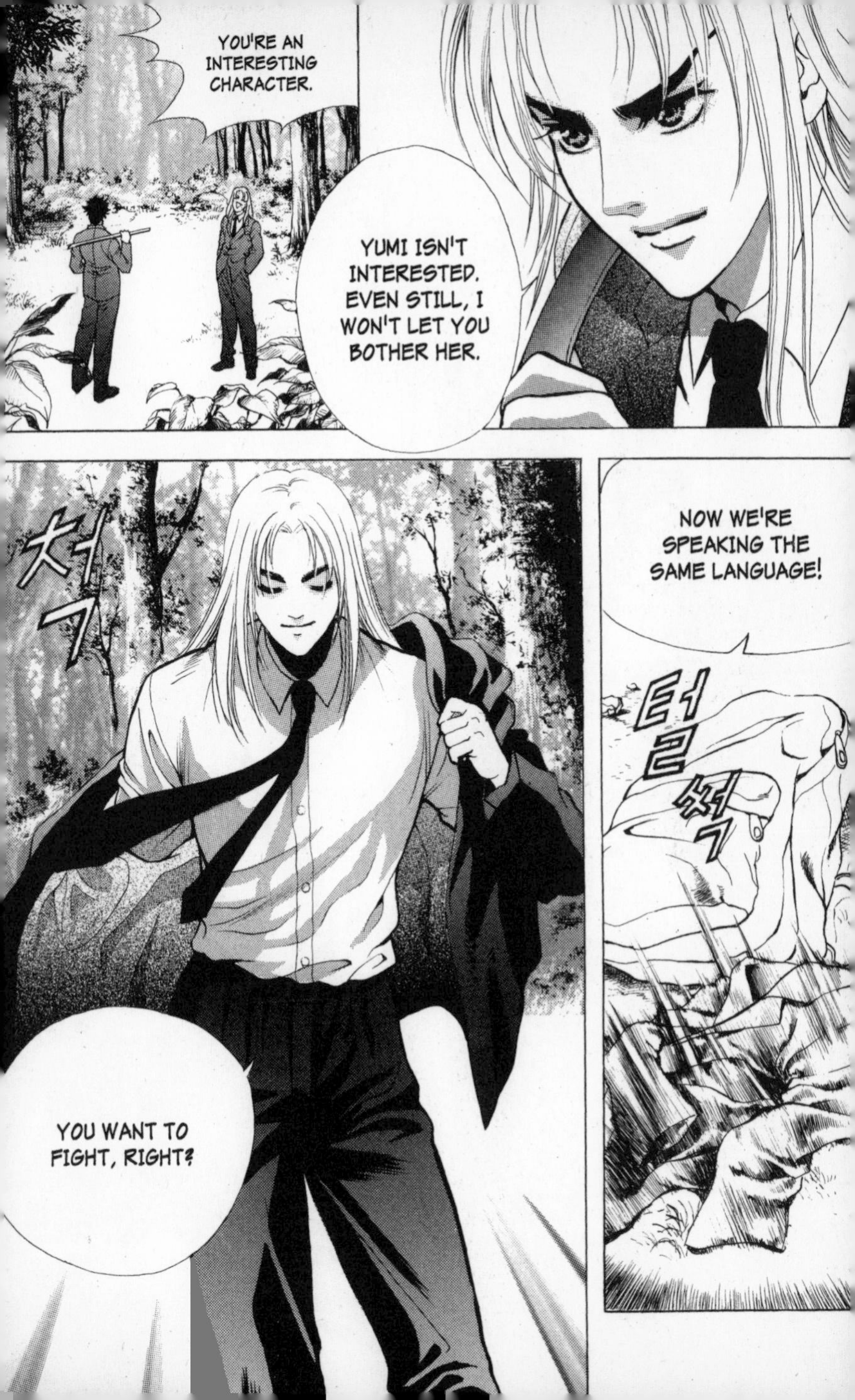
YOU'RE AN INTERESTING CHARACTER.
YUMI ISN'T INTERESTED. EVEN STILL, I WON'T LET YOU BOTHER HER.
척
YOU WANT TO FIGHT, RIGHT?
NOW WE'RE SPEAKING THE SAME LANGUAGE!
털썩

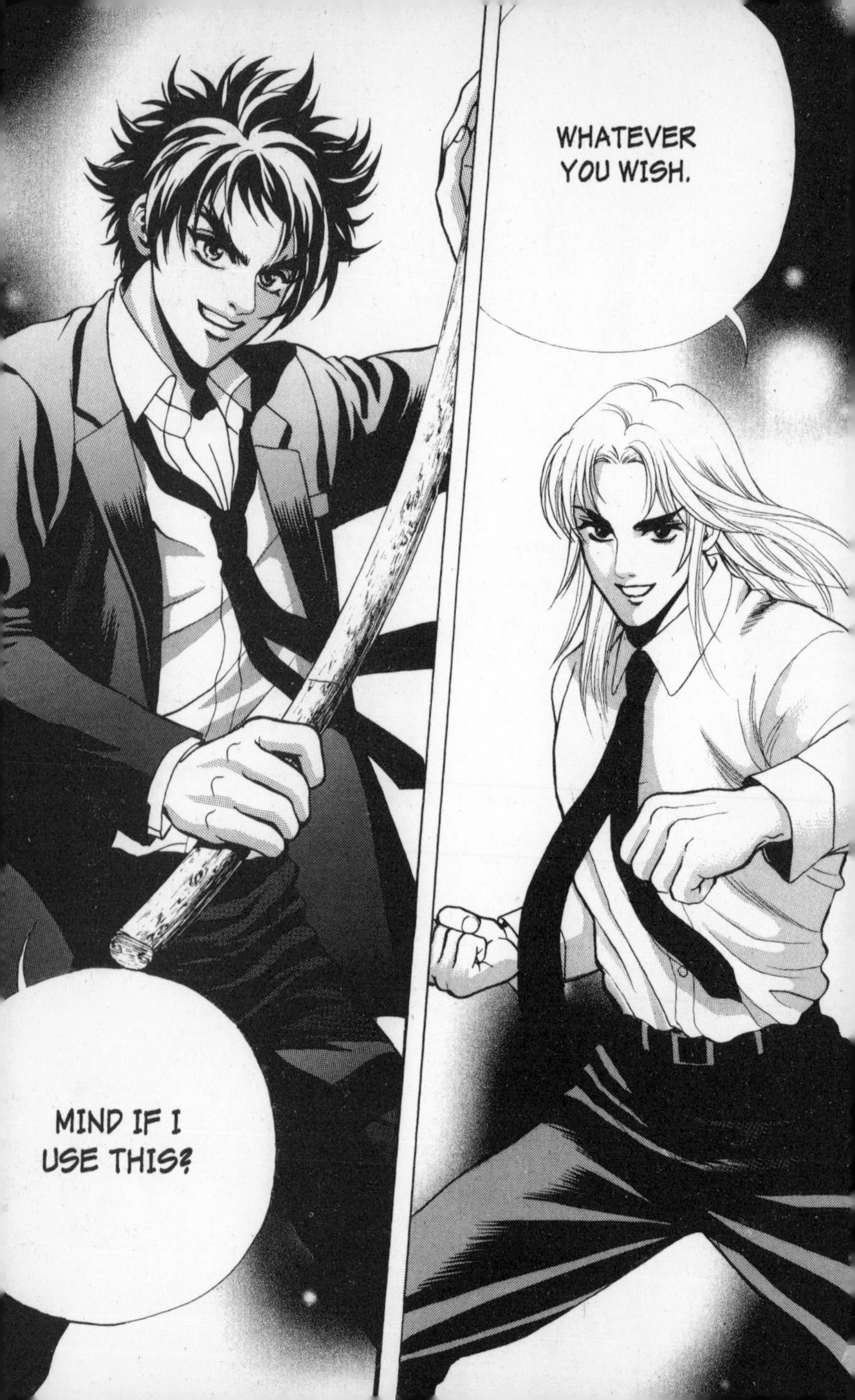
MIND IF I USE THIS?
WHATEVER YOU WISH.

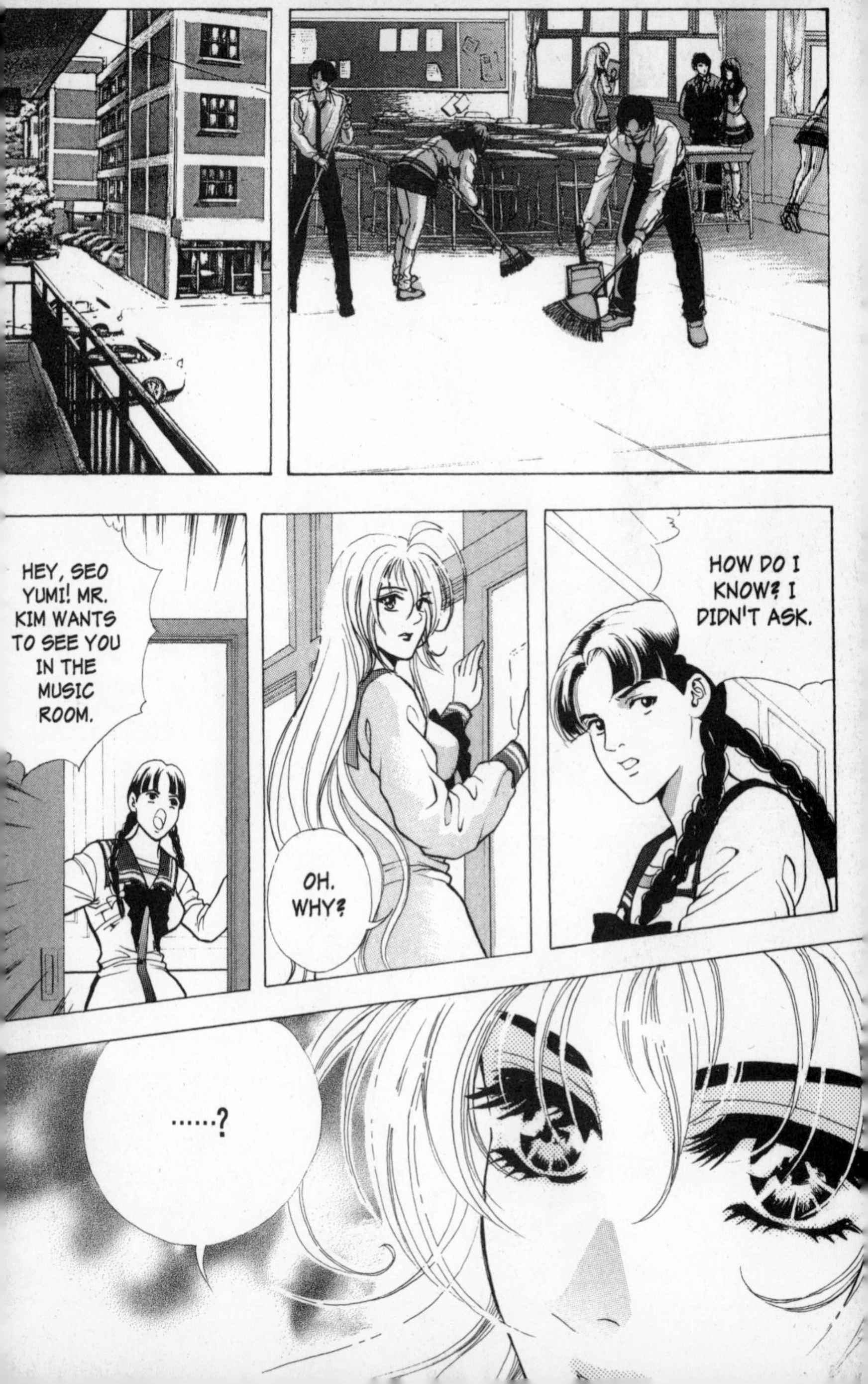
HEY, SEO YUMI! MR. KIM WANTS TO SEE YOU IN THE MUSIC ROOM.
OH. WHY?
HOW DO I KNOW? I DIDN'T ASK.
......?

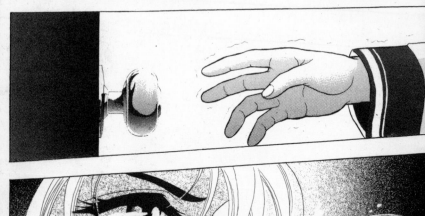

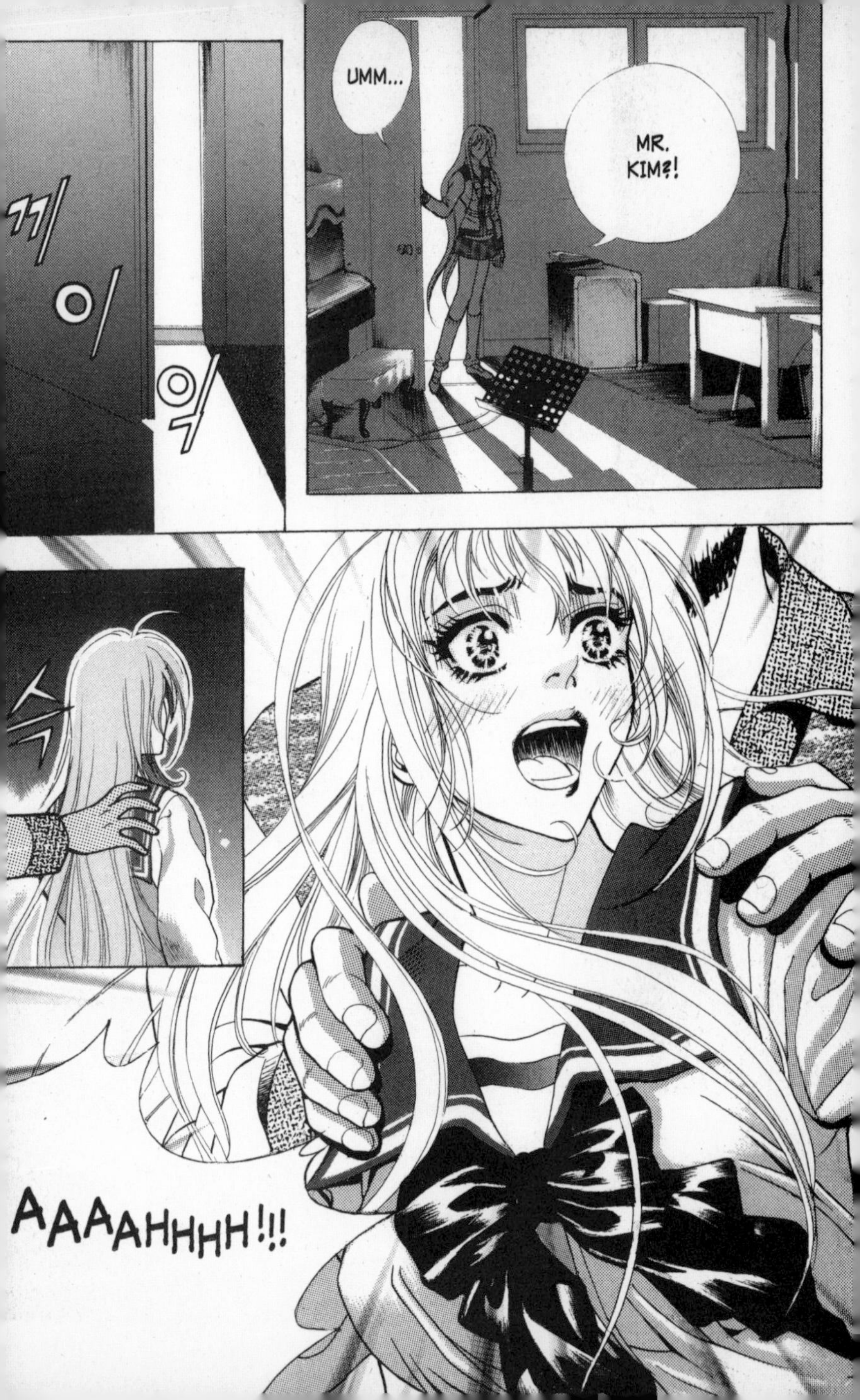
UMM...
MR. KIM?!
AAAAHHHH!!!

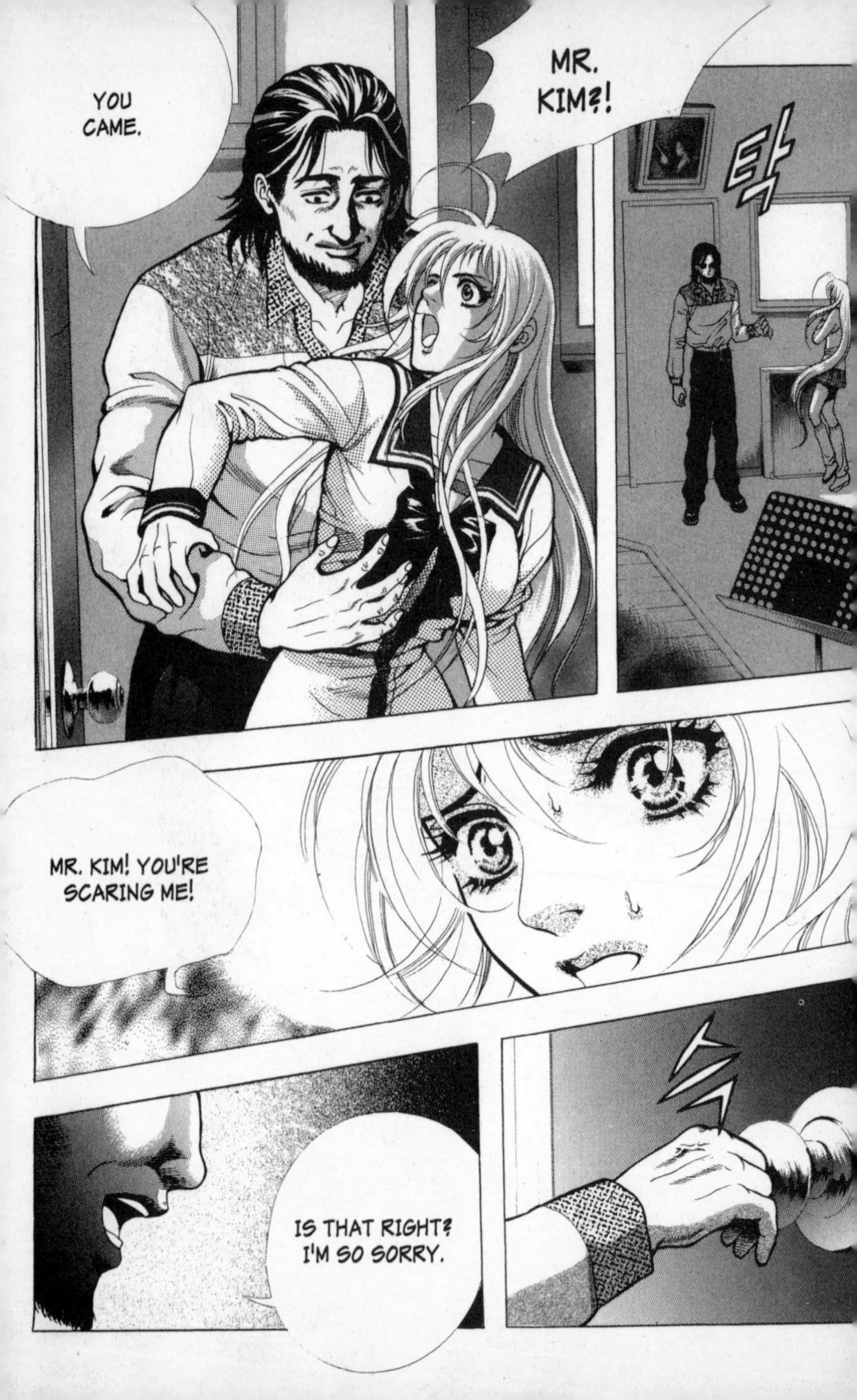
YOU CAME.
MR. KIM?!
탁
MR. KIM! YOU'RE SCARING ME!
IS THAT RIGHT? I'M SO SORRY.

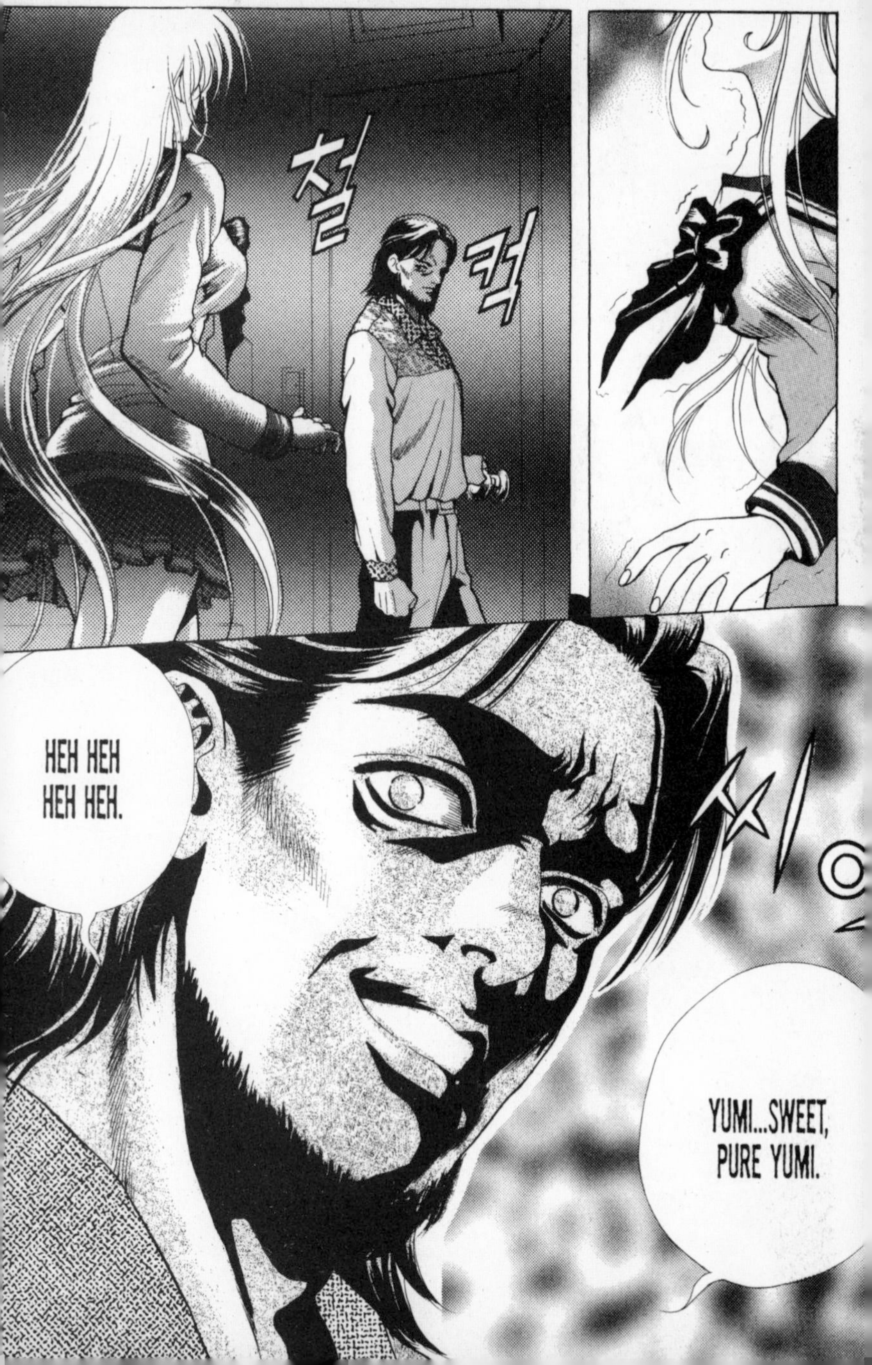
철컥
HEH HEH HEH HEH.
YUMI...SWEET, PURE YUMI.

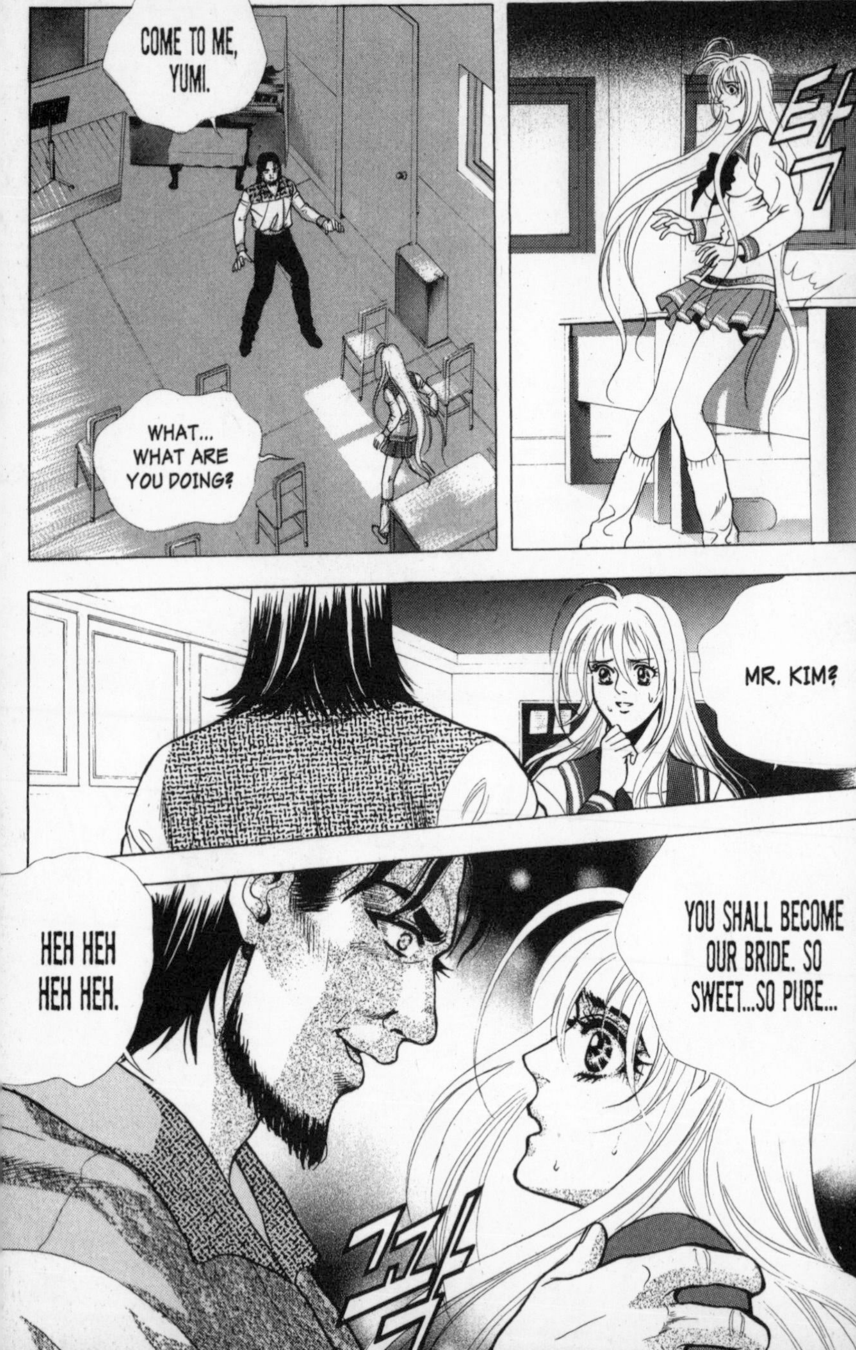
COME TO ME, YUMI.
WHAT... WHAT ARE YOU DOING?
탁
MR. KIM?
HEH HEH HEH HEH.
YOU SHALL BECOME OUR BRIDE. SO SWEET...SO PURE...

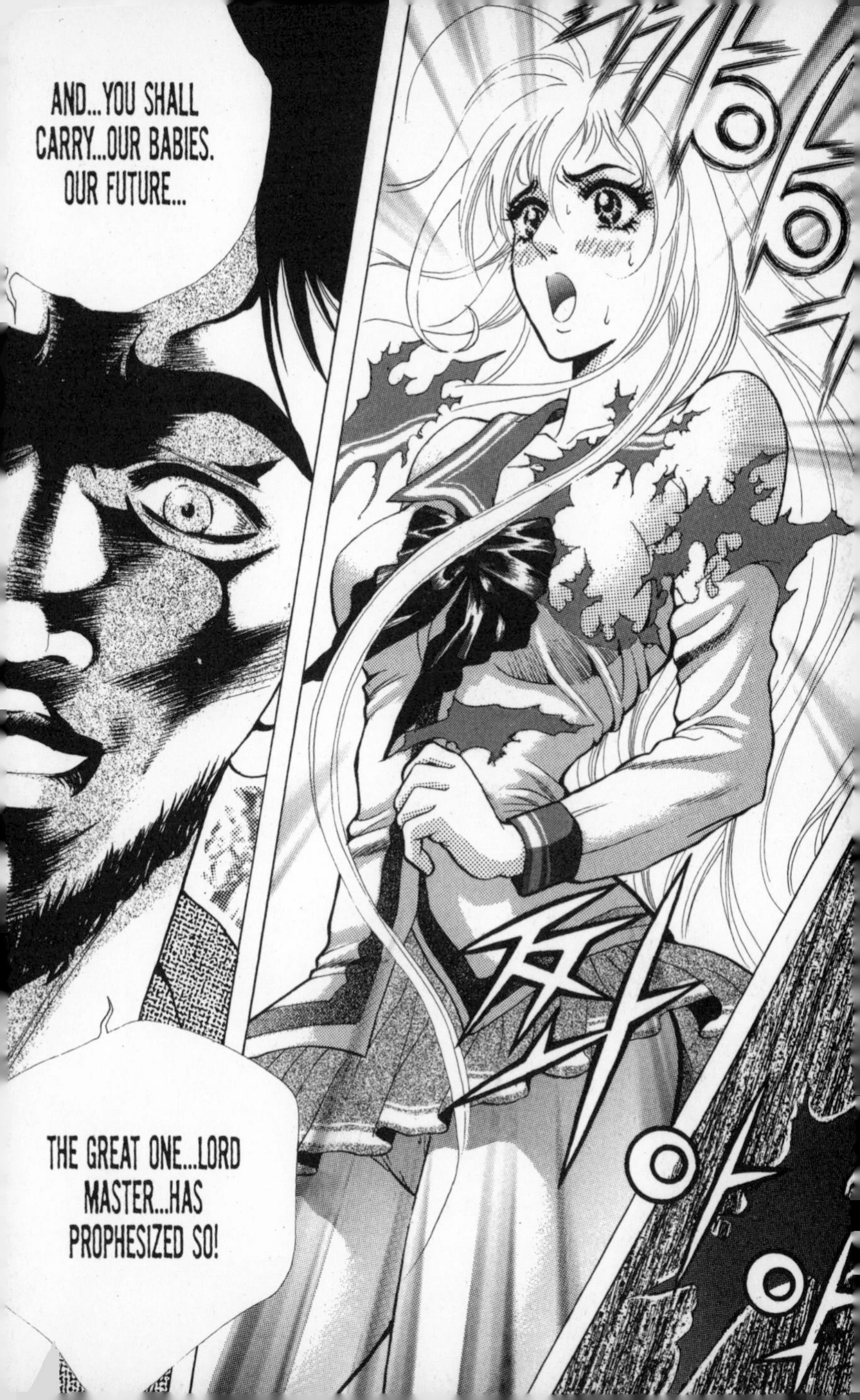
AND...YOU SHALL CARRY...OUR BABIES. OUR FUTURE...
THE GREAT ONE...LORD MASTER...HAS PROPHESIZED SO!

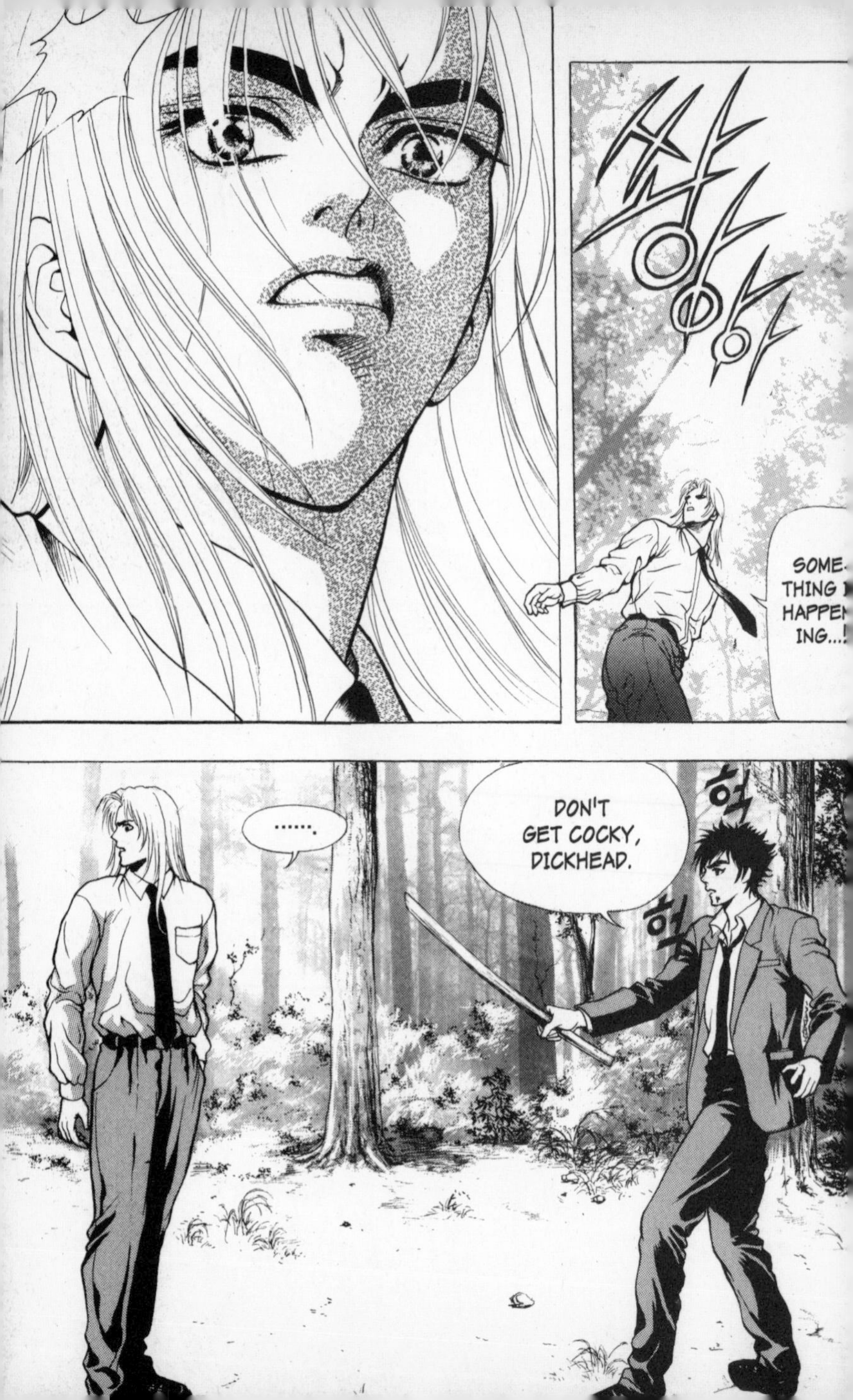
SOME-
THING
HAPPEN
ING...!
DON'T GET COCKY, DICKHEAD.
헉 헉
....

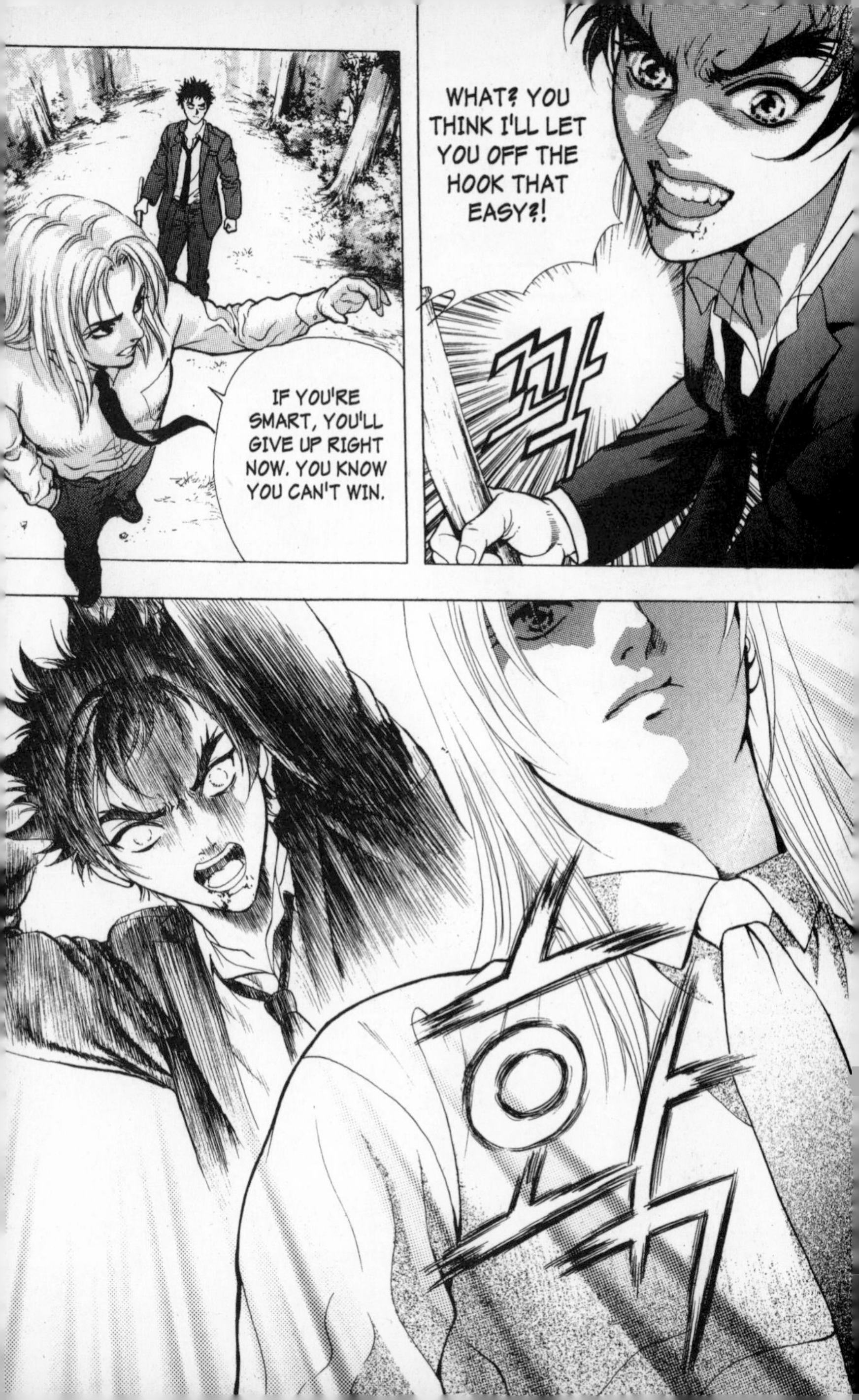
IF YOU'RE SMART, YOU'LL GIVE UP RIGHT NOW. YOU KNOW YOU CAN'T WIN.
WHAT? YOU THINK I'LL LET YOU OFF THE HOOK THAT EASY?!

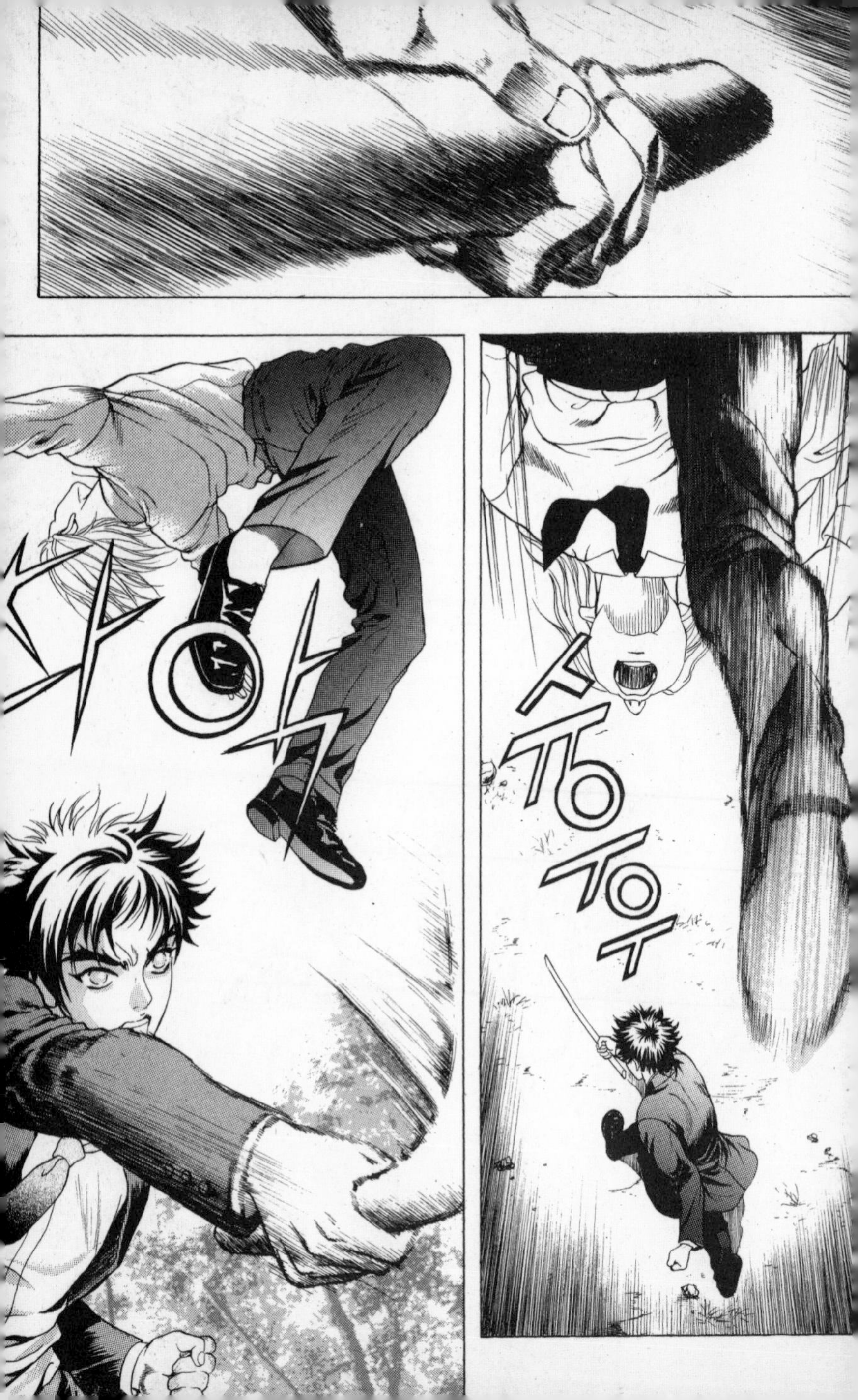

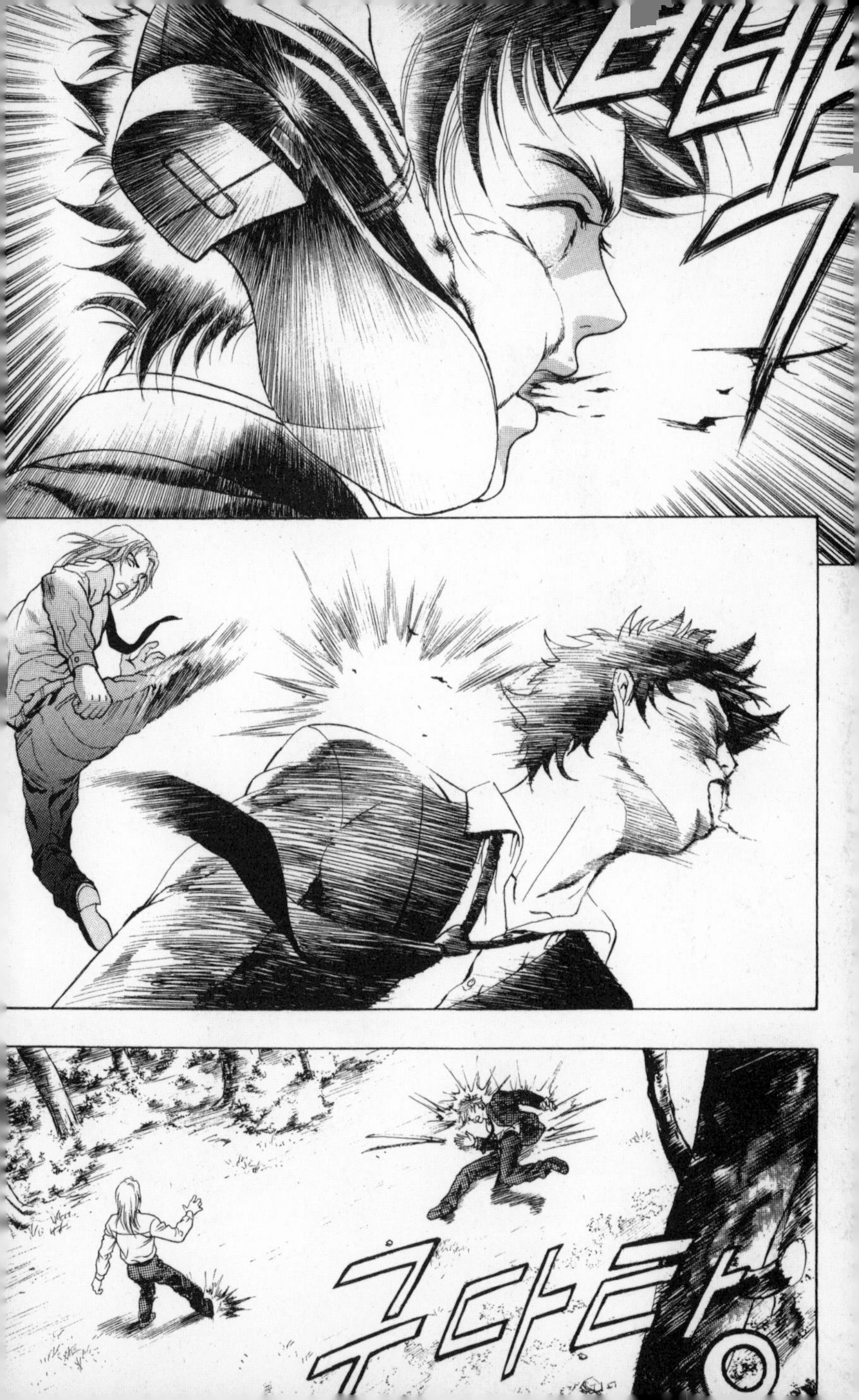

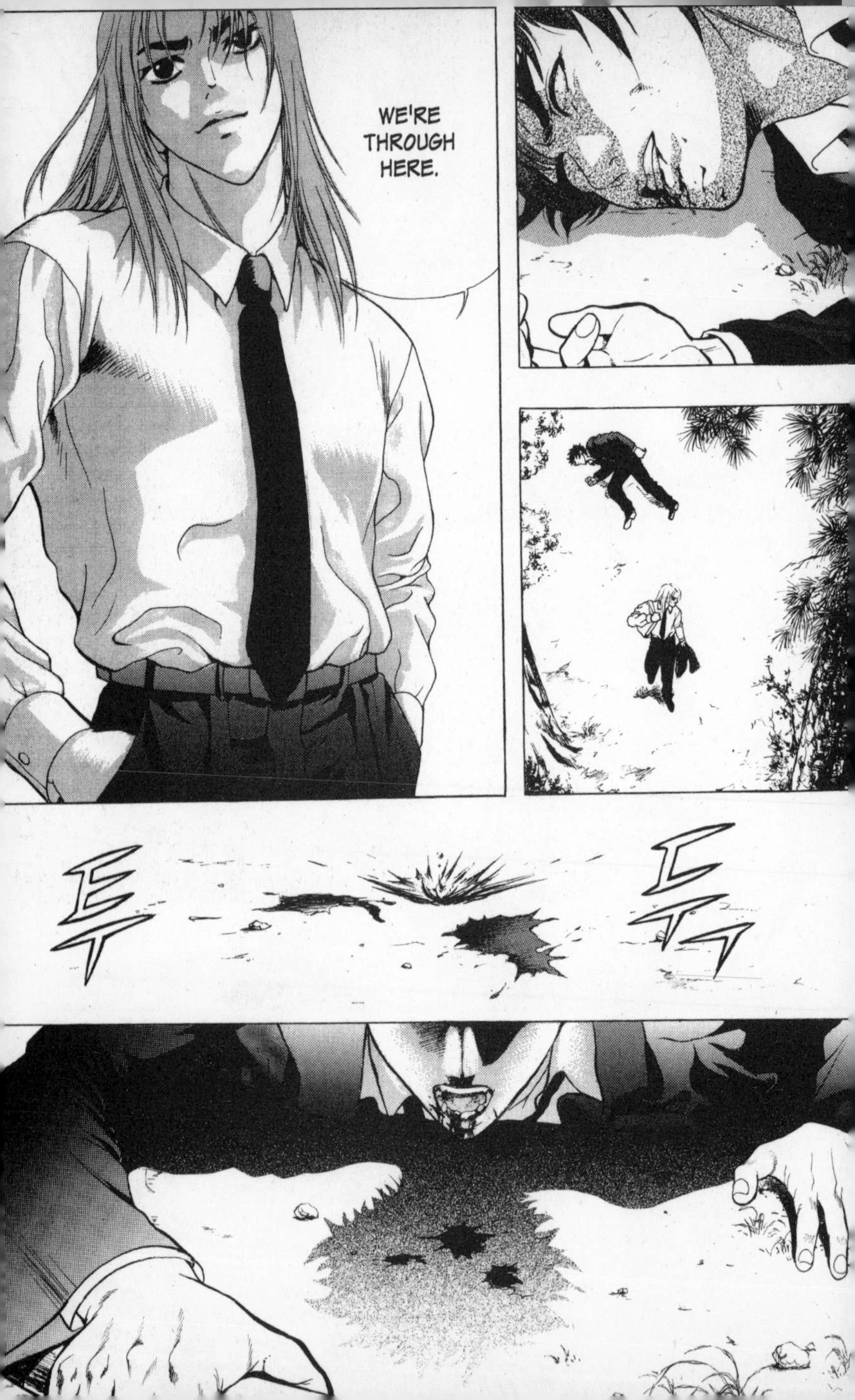
WE'RE THROUGH HERE.

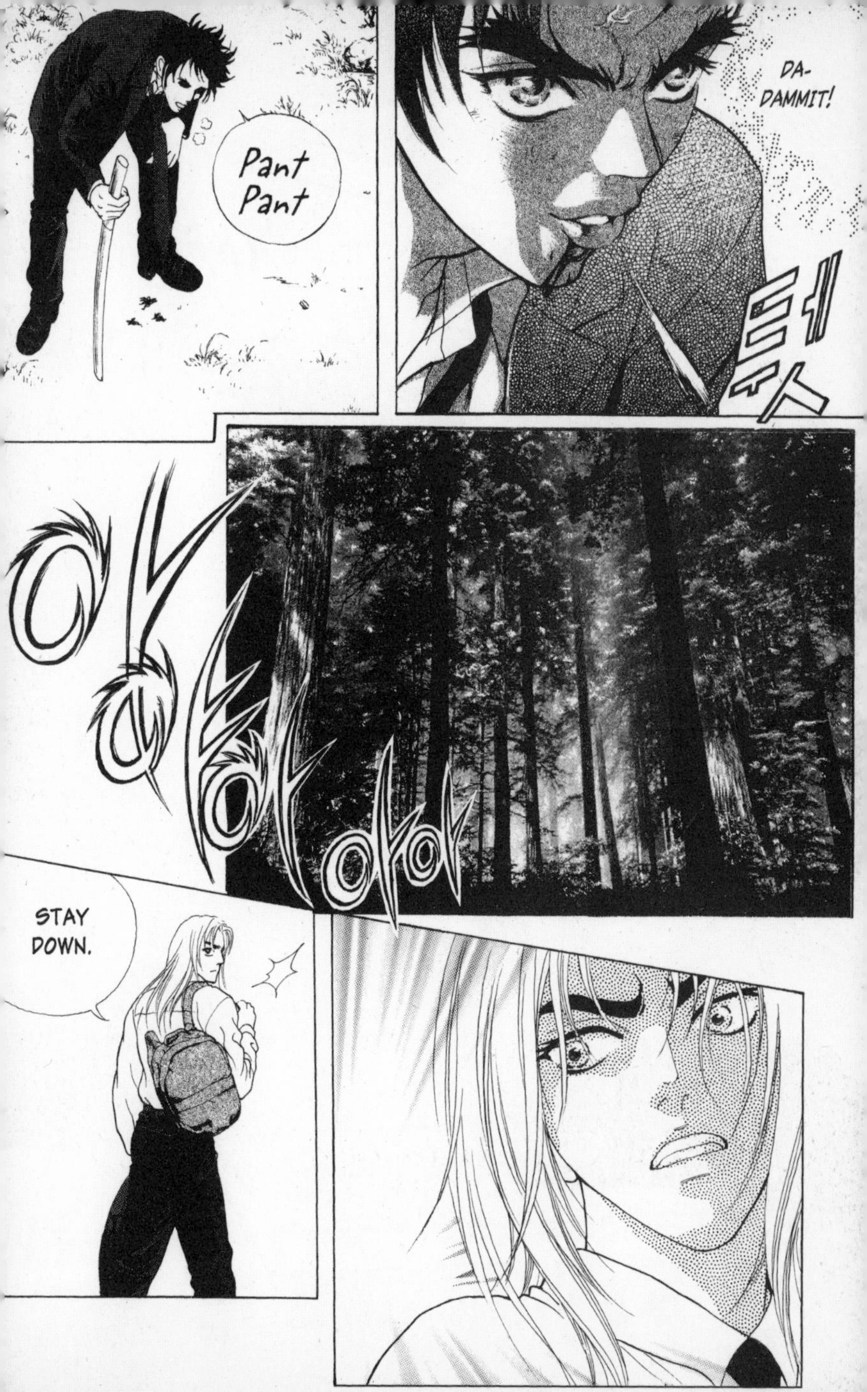
Pant
Pant
DA-
DAMMIT!
STAY
DOWN.

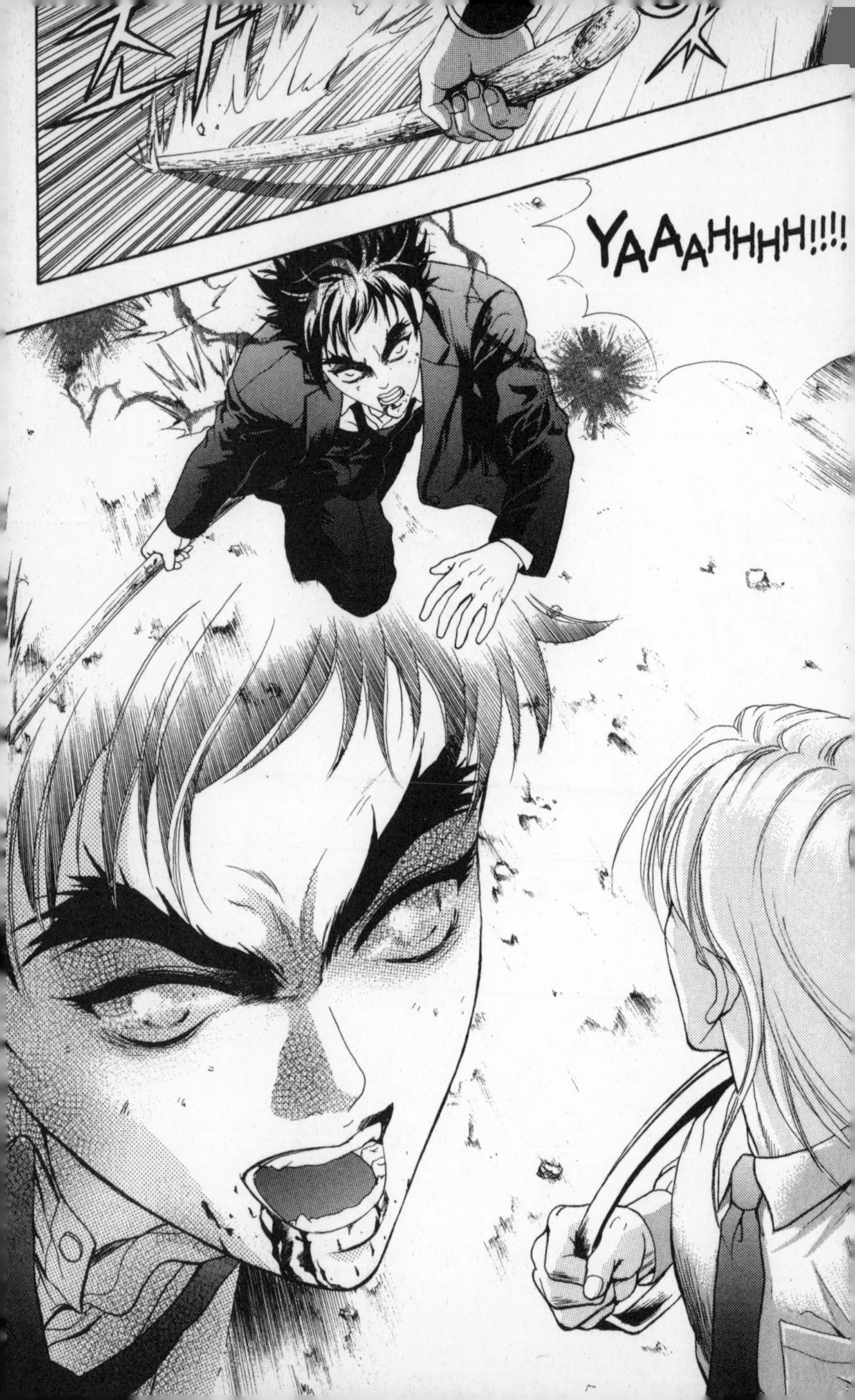
YAAAHHHH!!!!

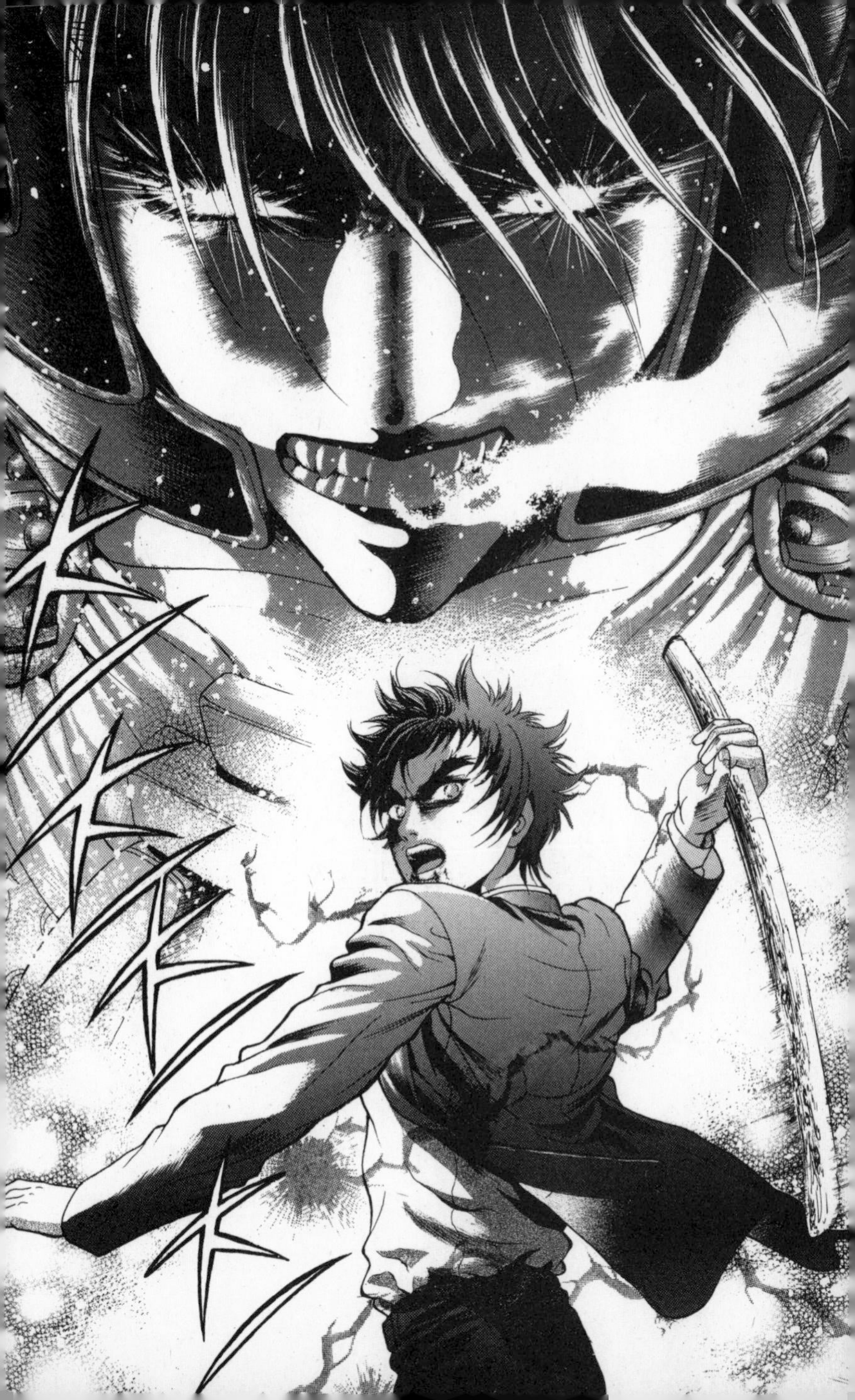

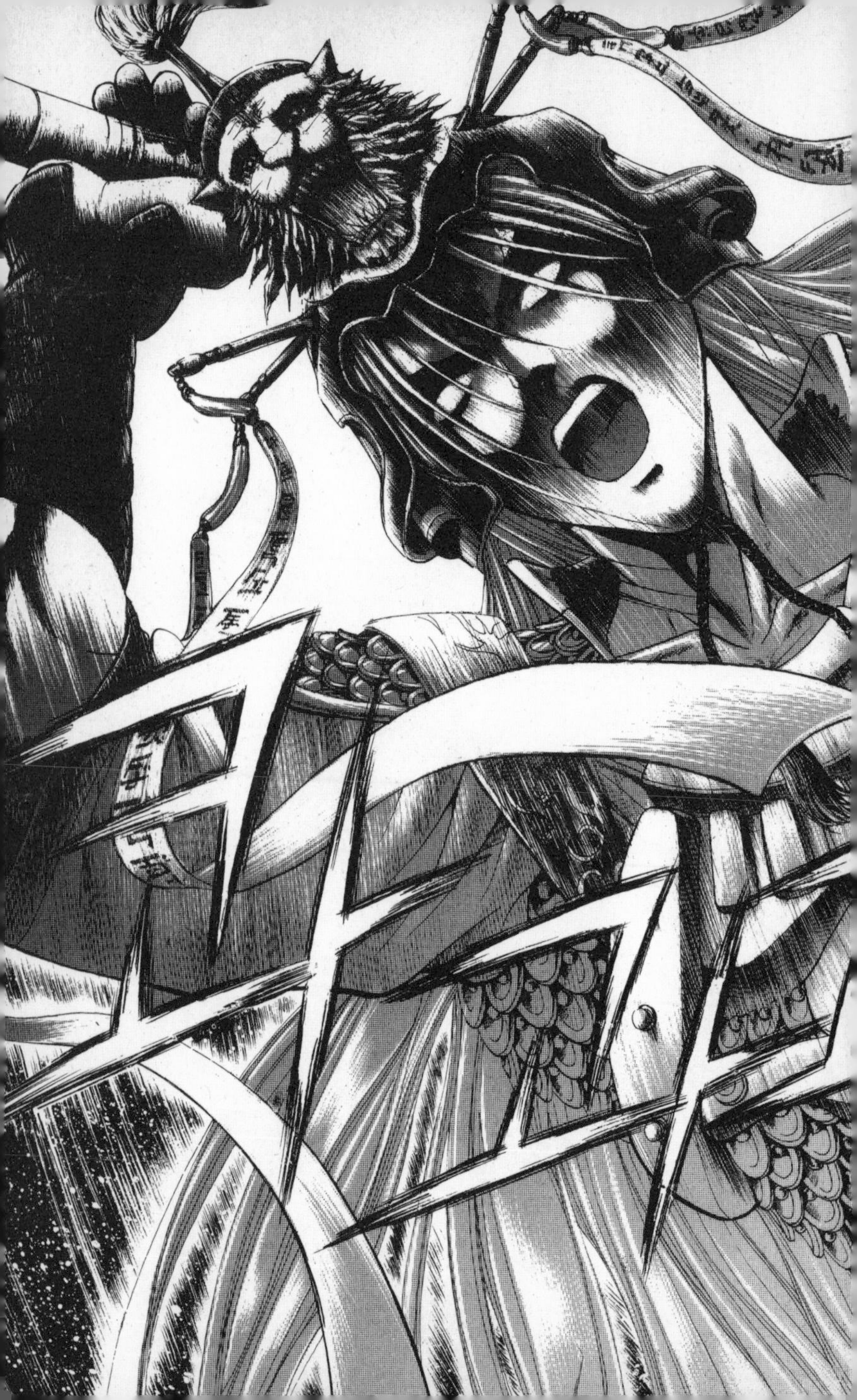

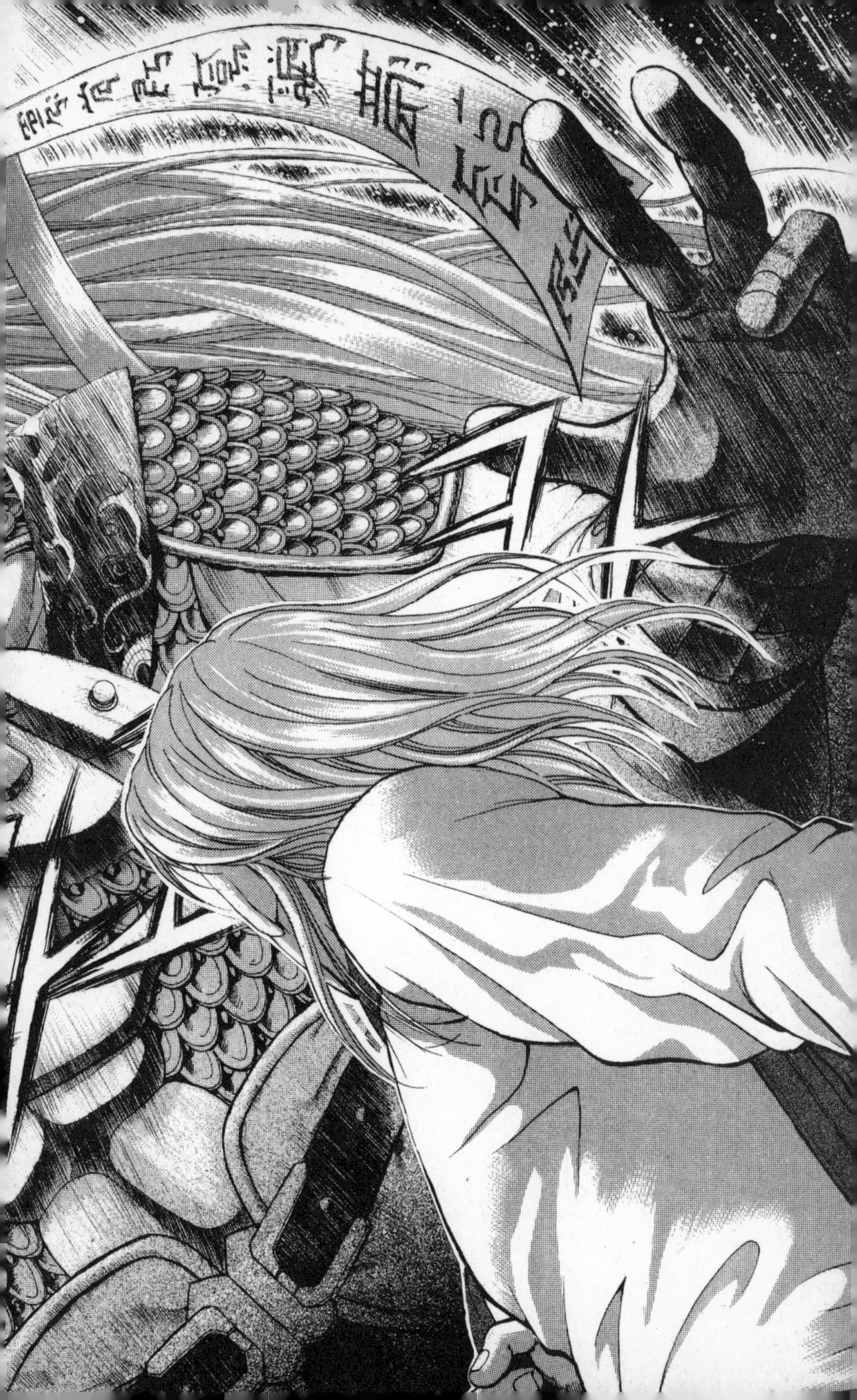

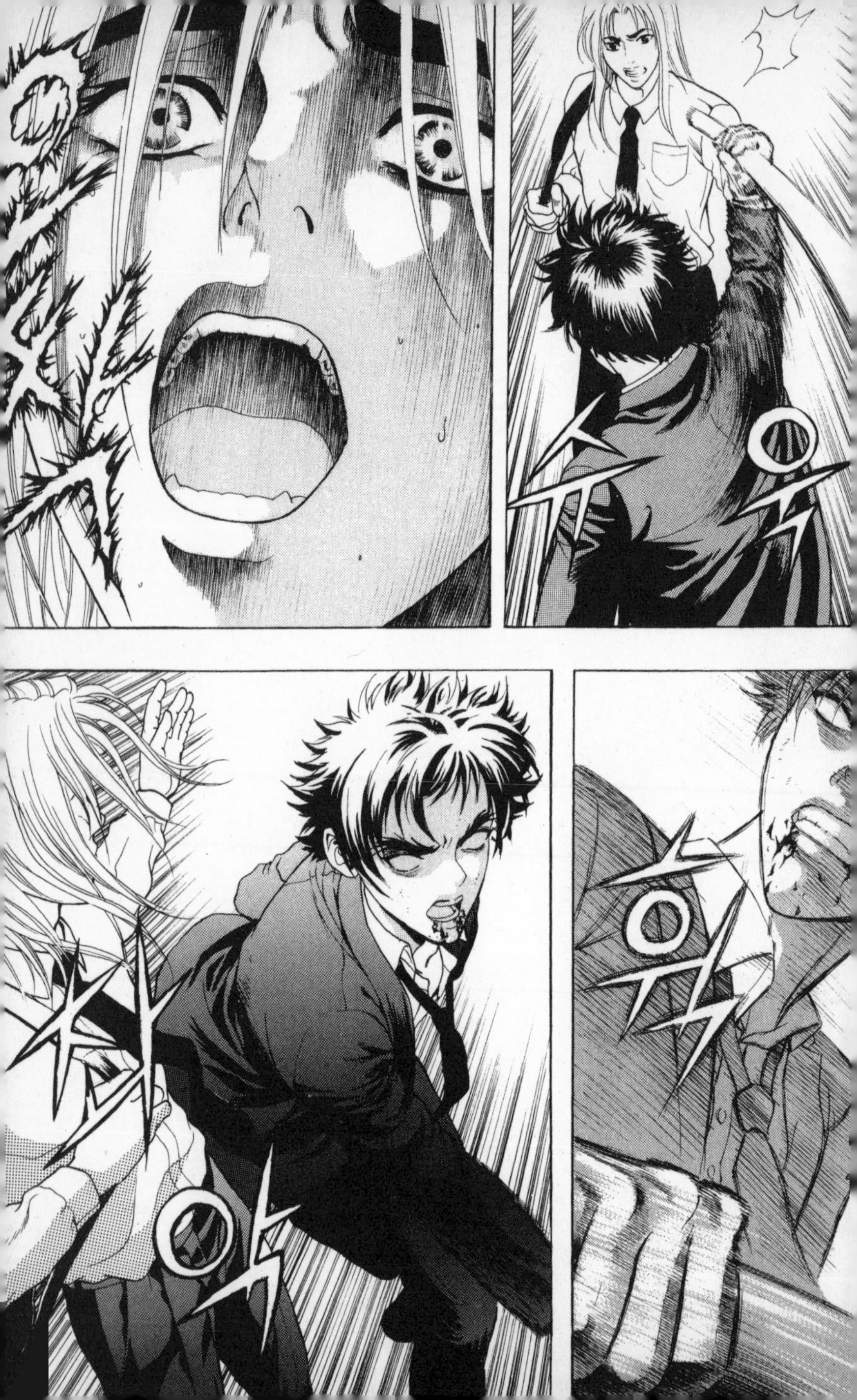

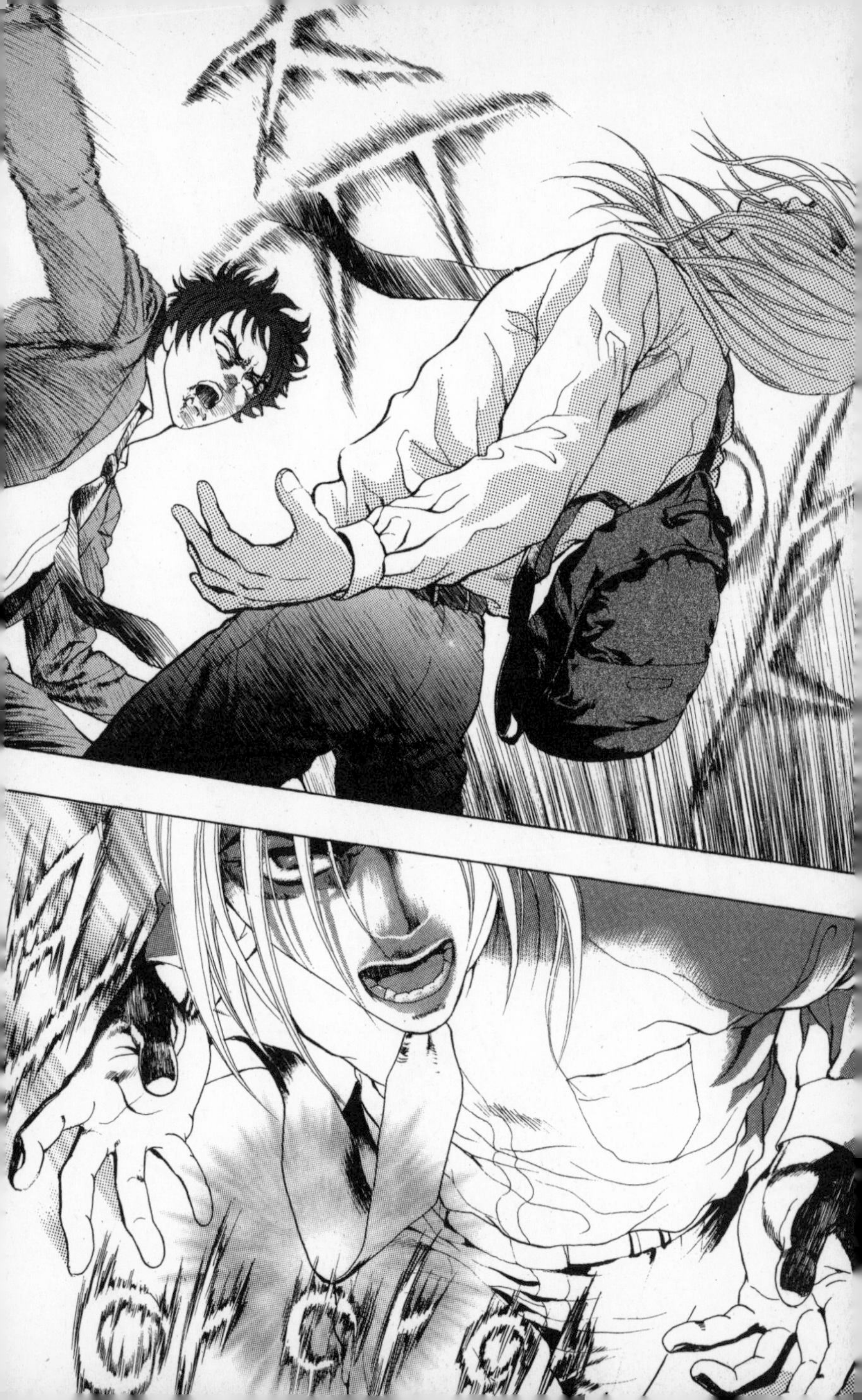

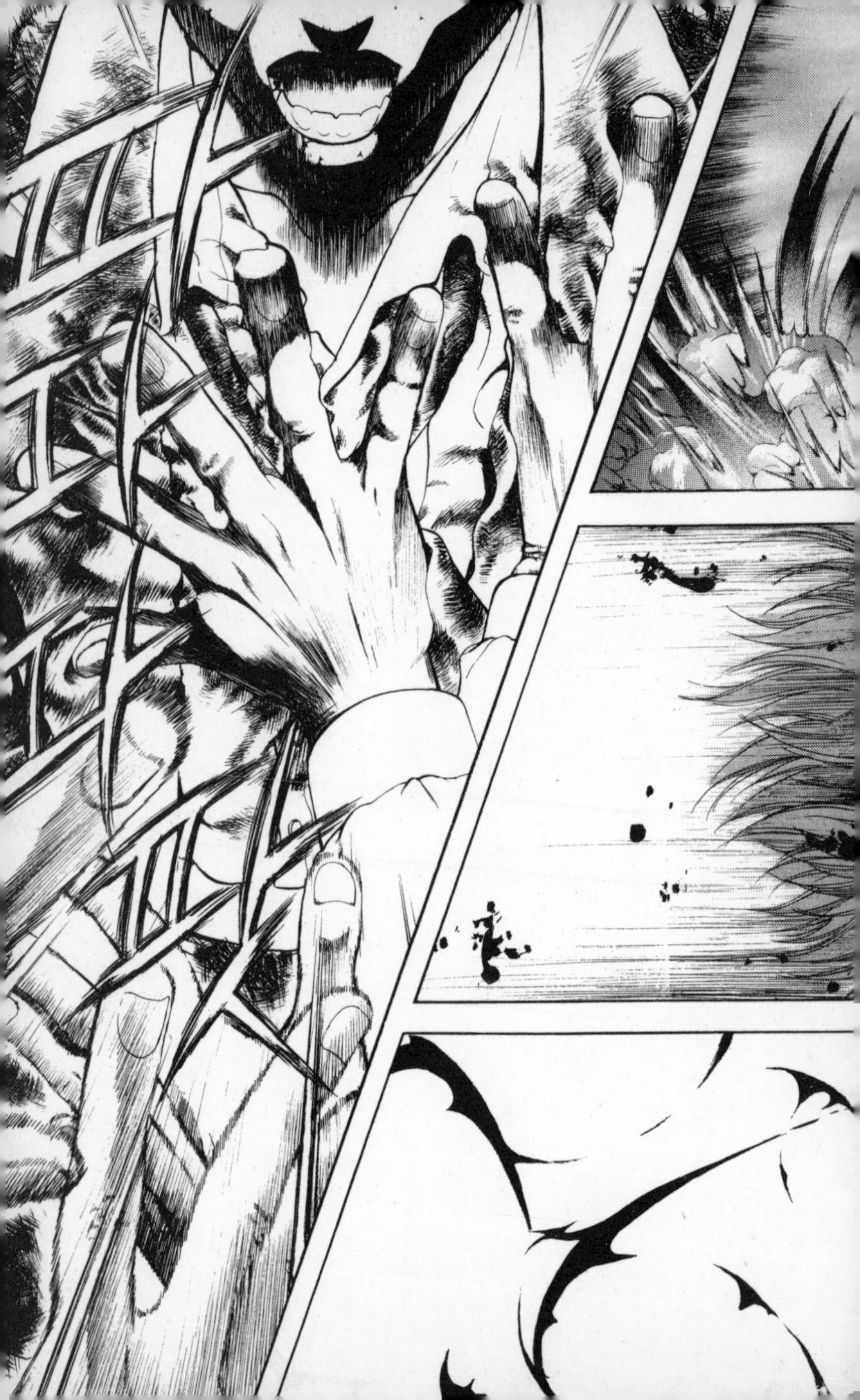

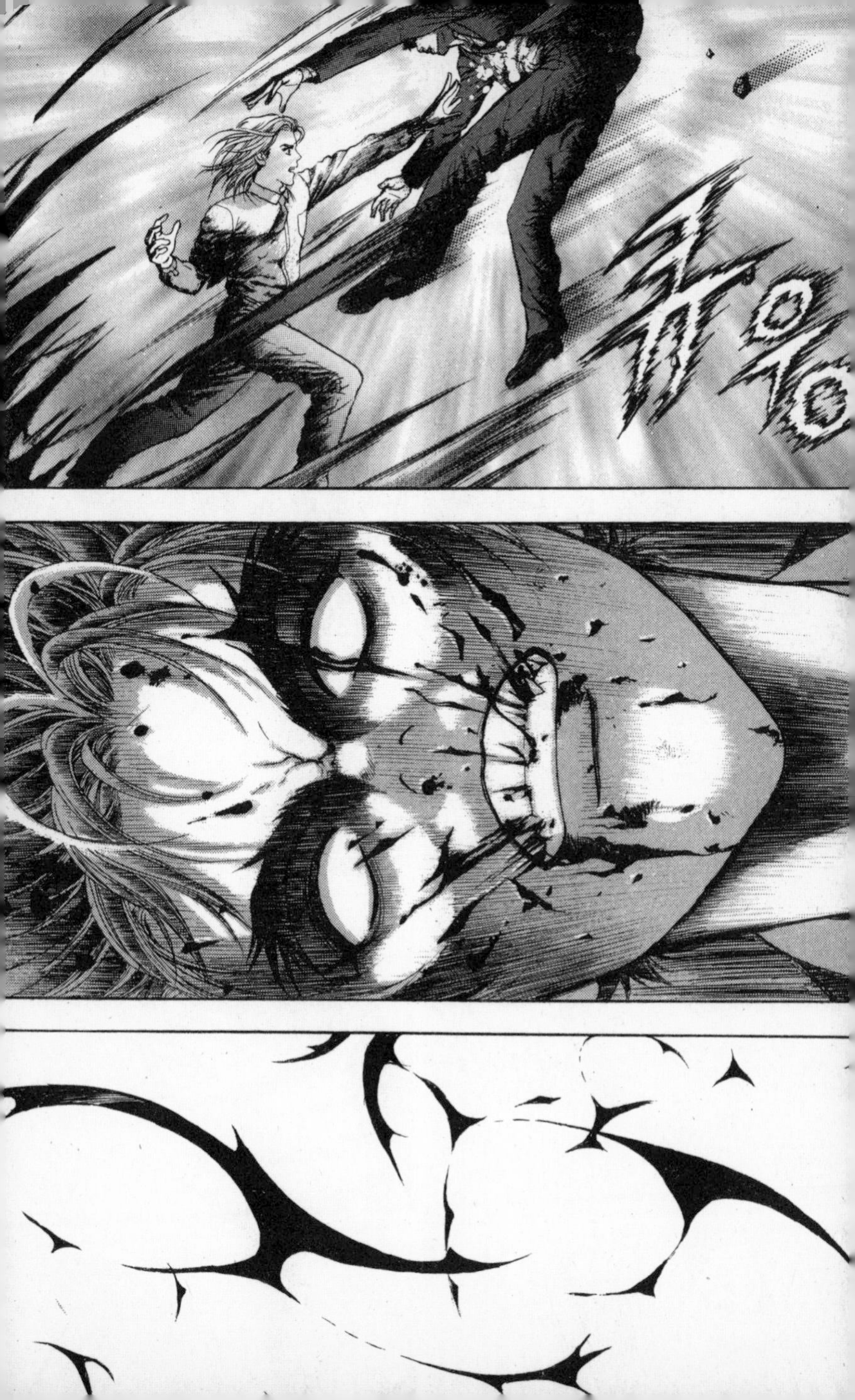
콰앙

I'M SORRY I USED SO MUCH POWER. YOU CAUGHT ME OFF GUARD.

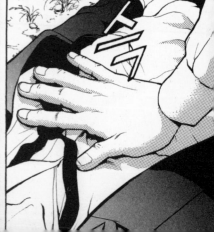

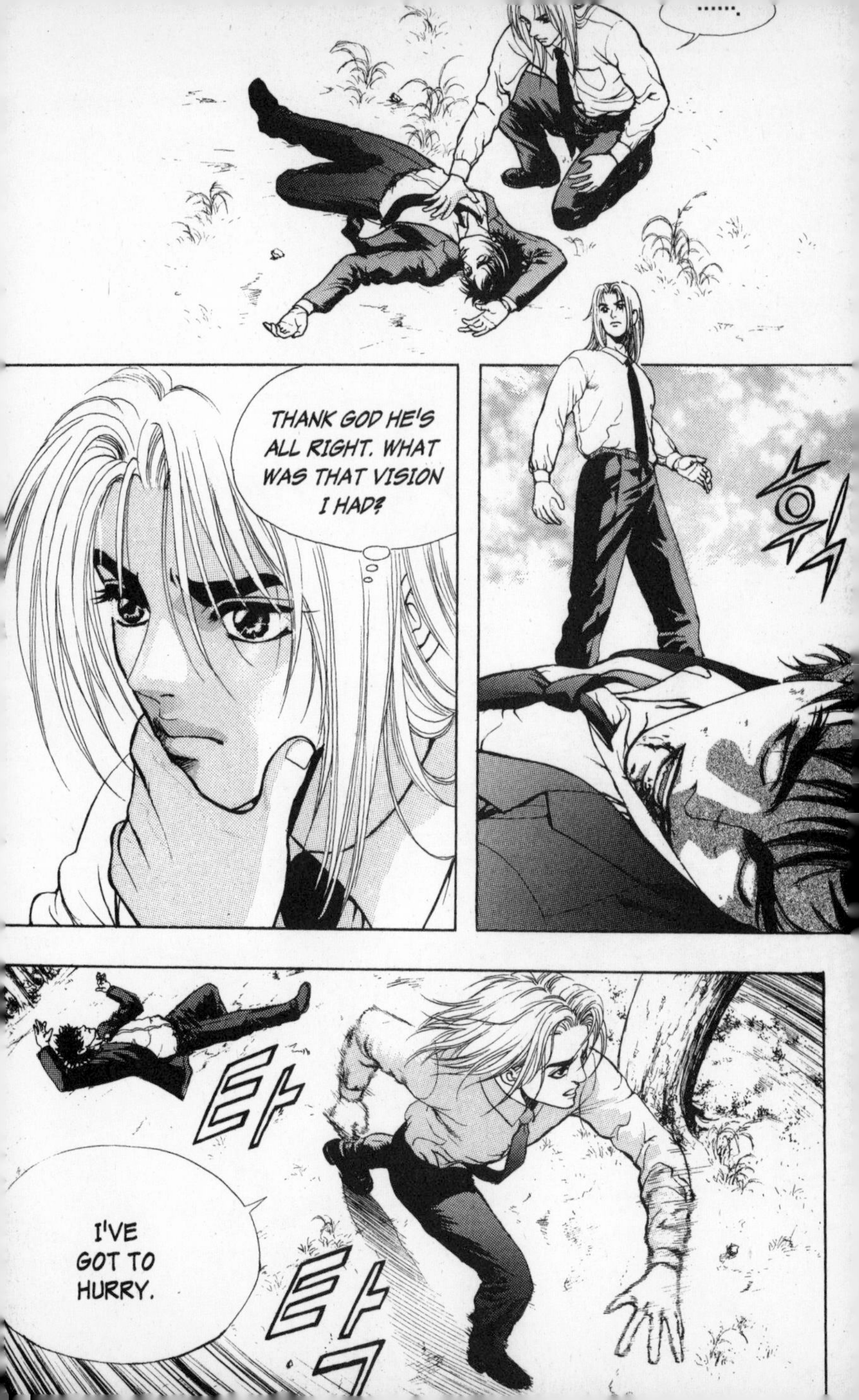
......
THANK GOD HE'S ALL RIGHT. WHAT WAS THAT VISION I HAD?
I'VE GOT TO HURRY.

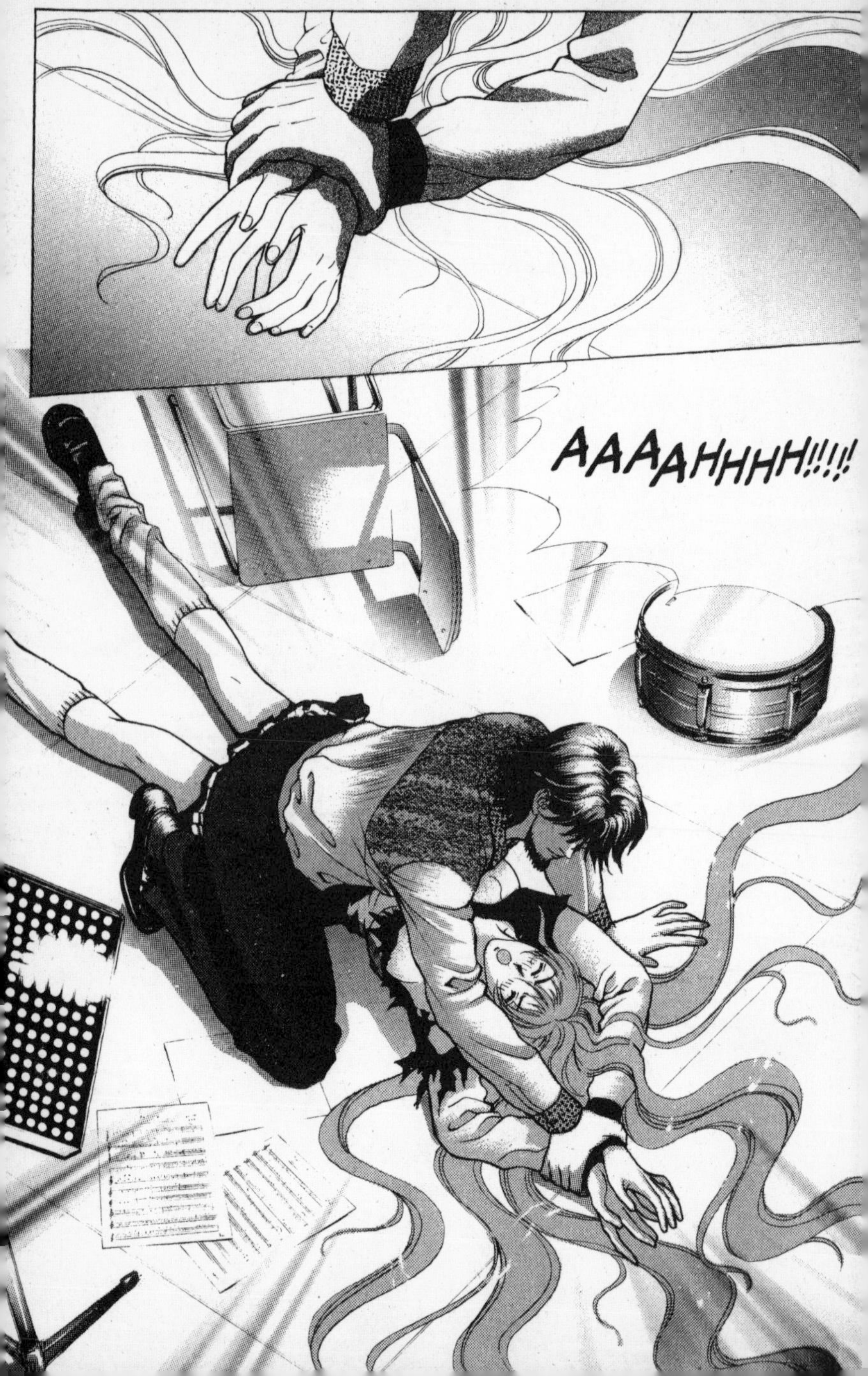
AAAAHHHH!!!!!

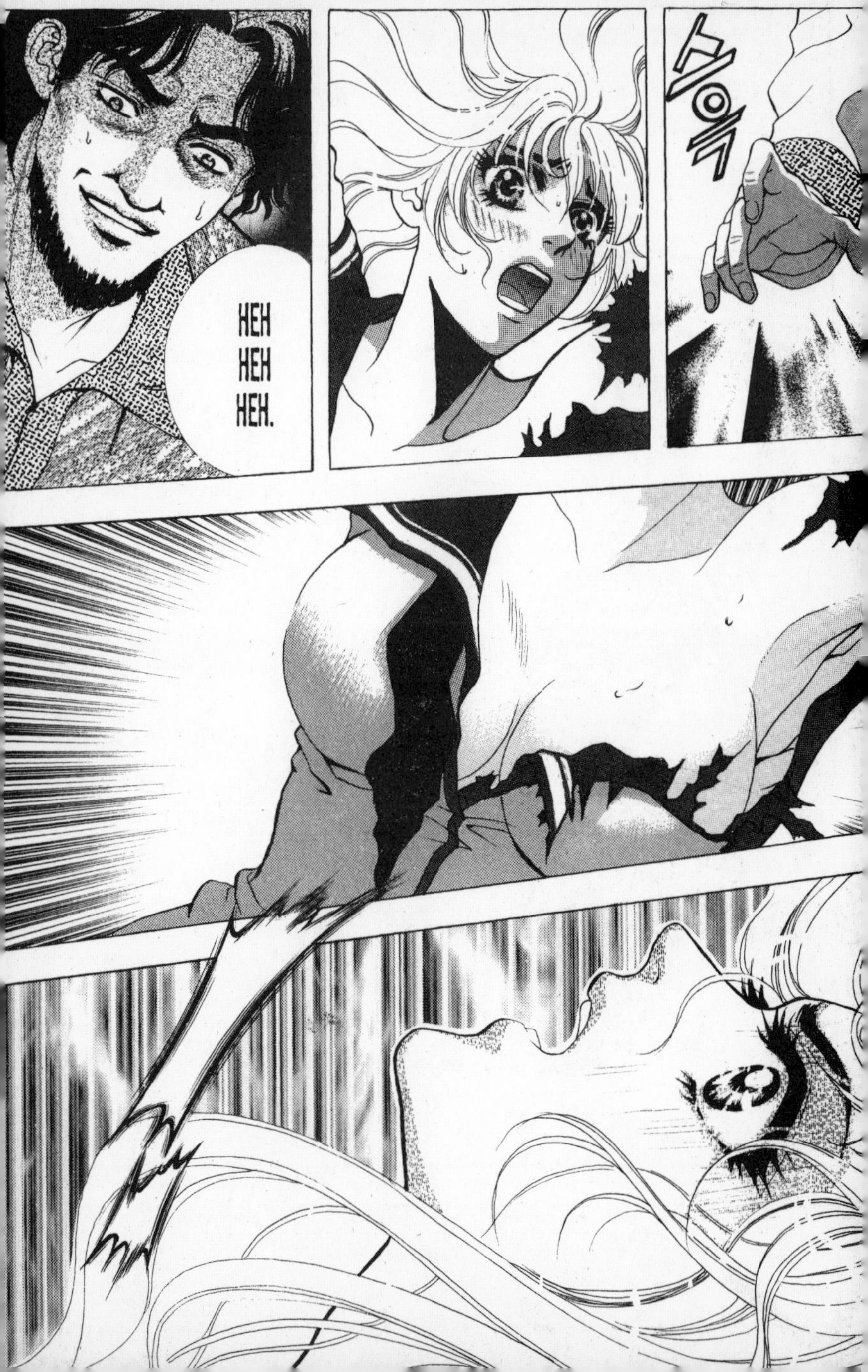
HEH
HEH
HEH.

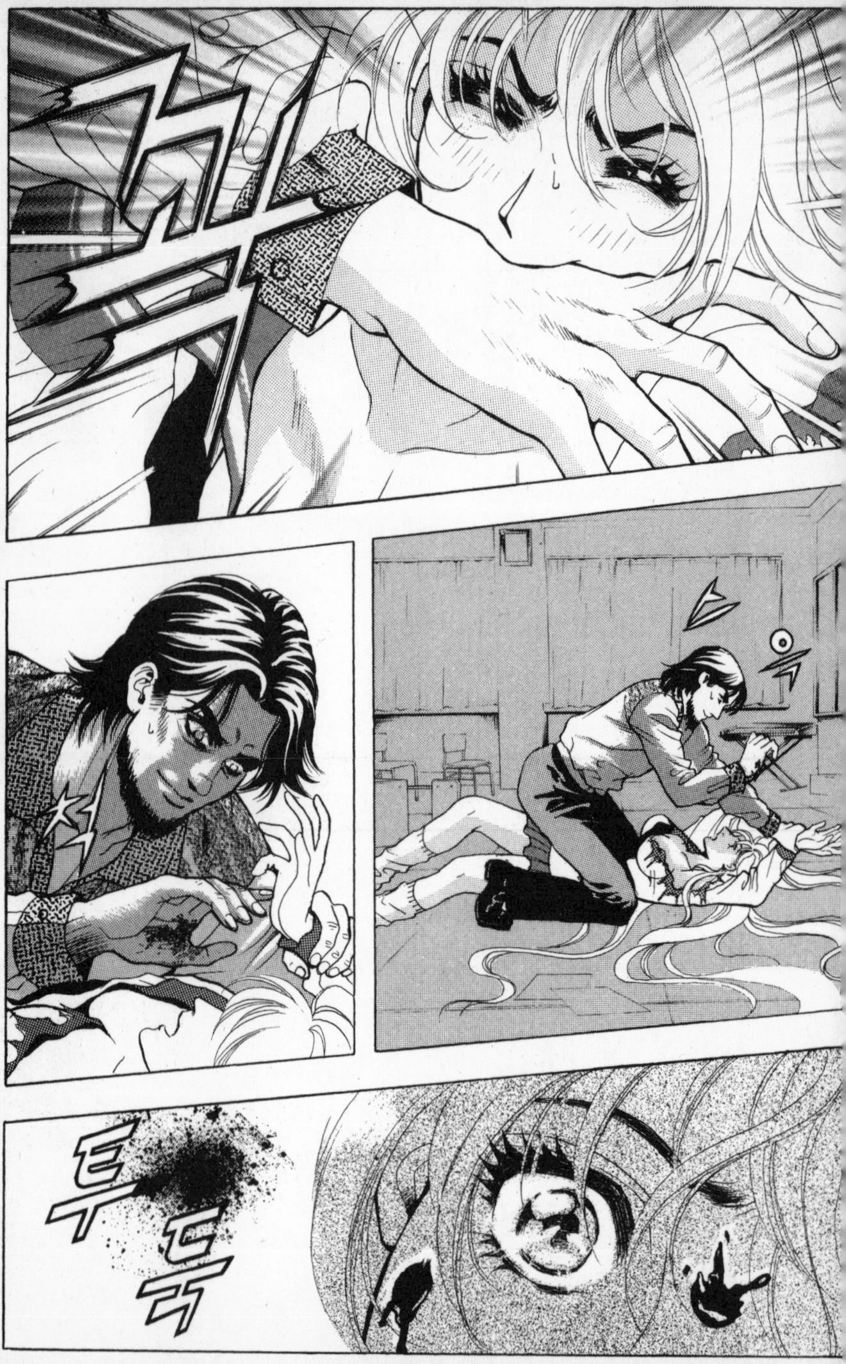

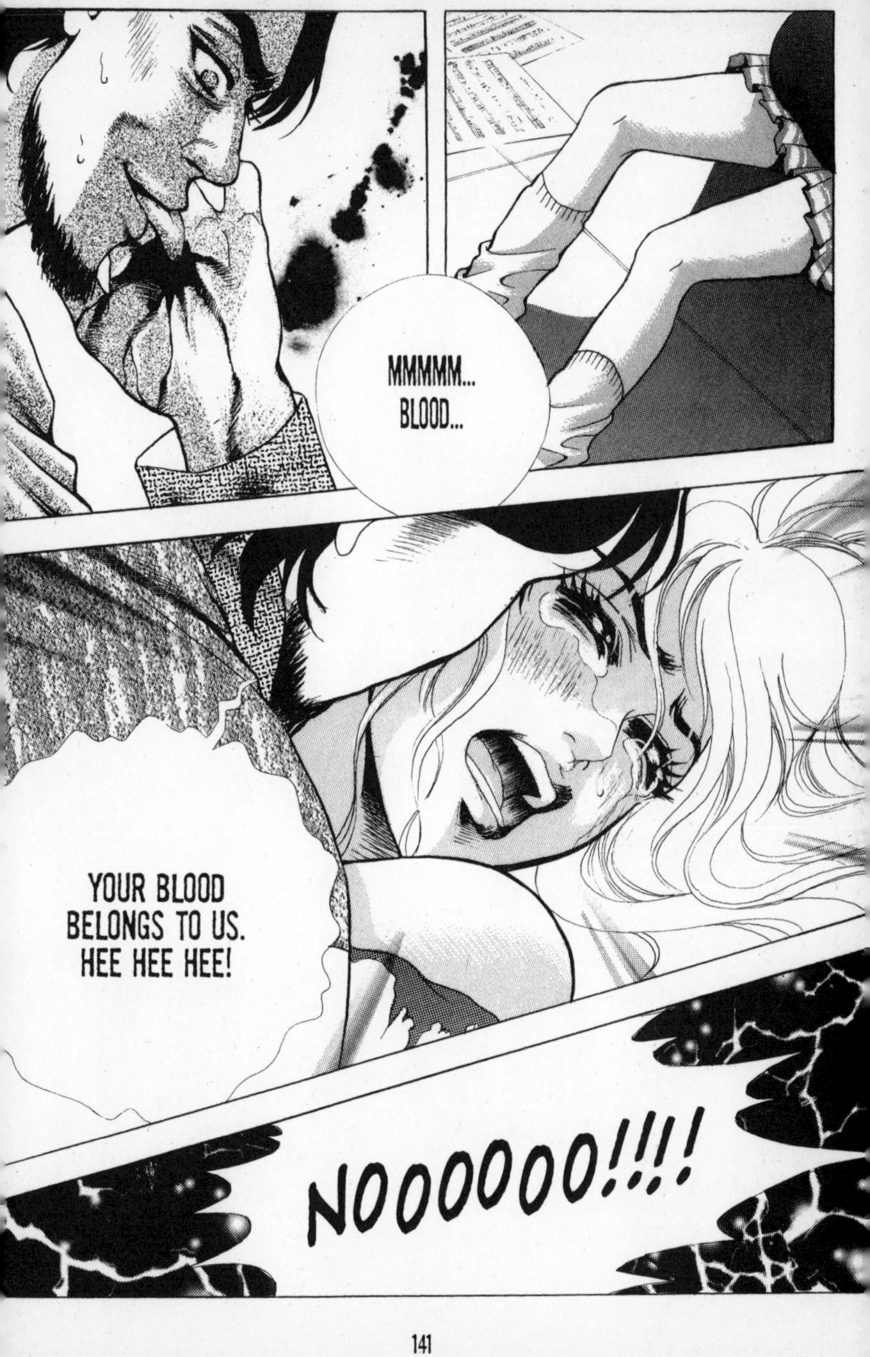
MMMMM...
BLOOD...
YOUR BLOOD BELONGS TO US. HEE HEE HEE!
NOOOOOO!!!!

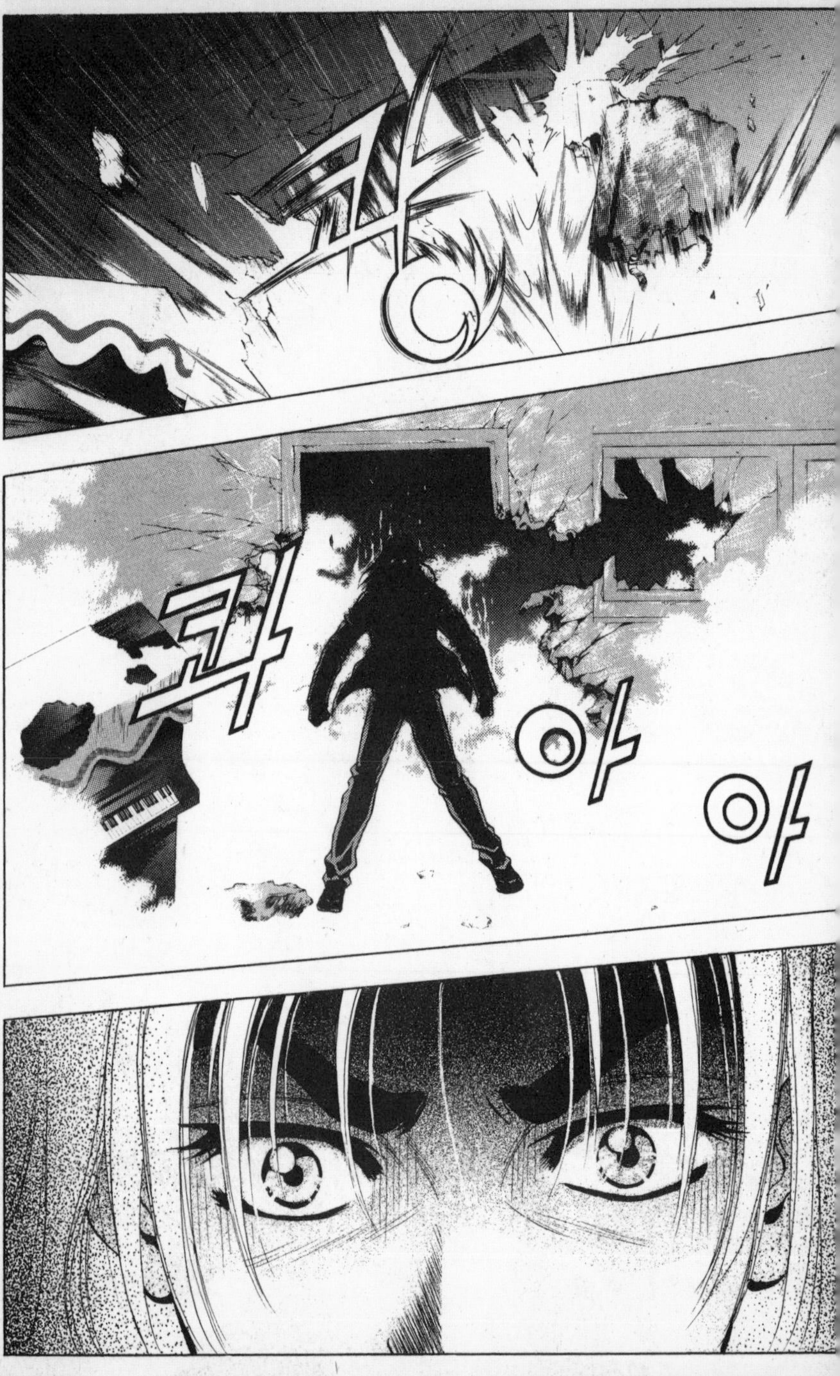
쾅
콰아아

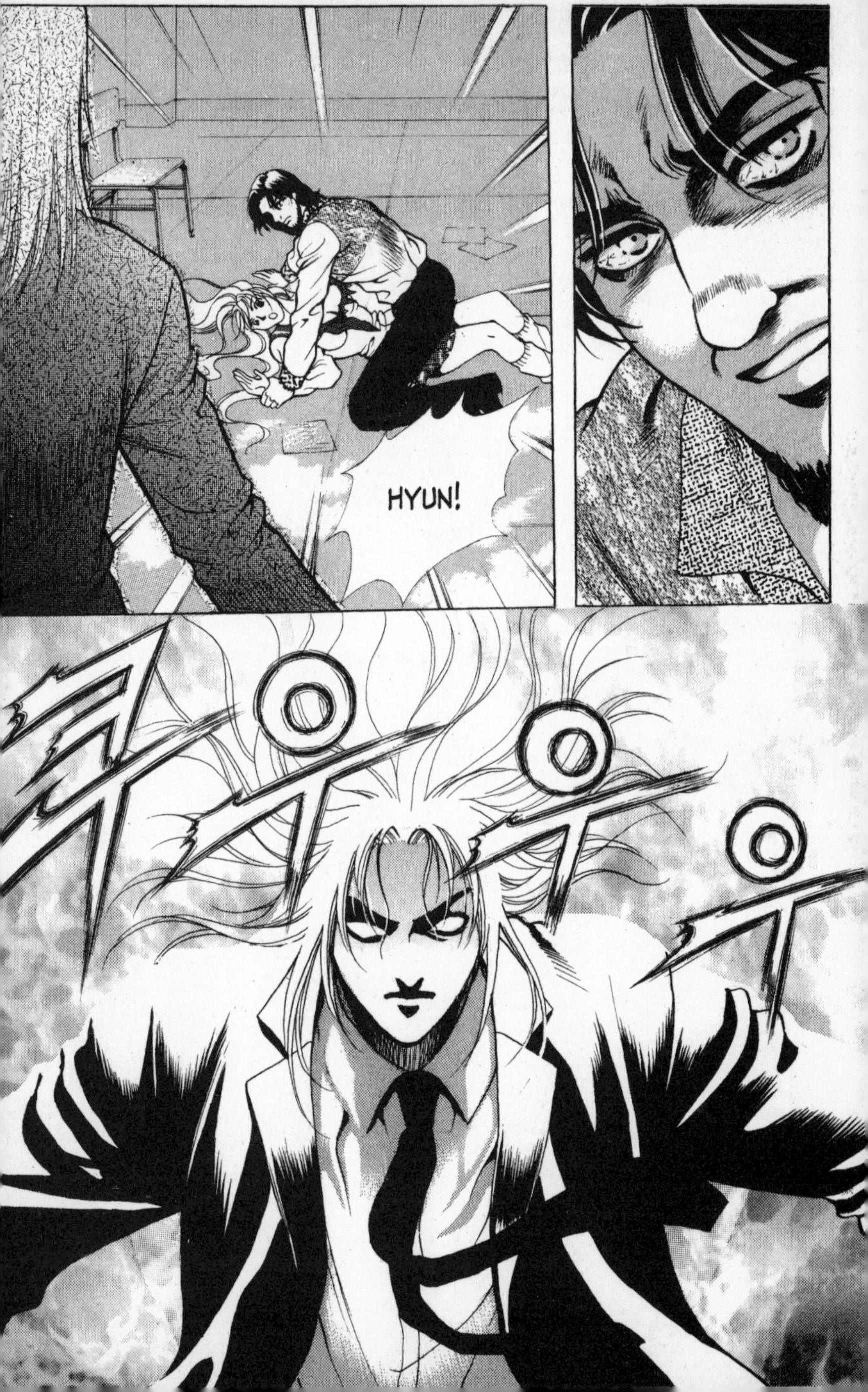
HYUN!

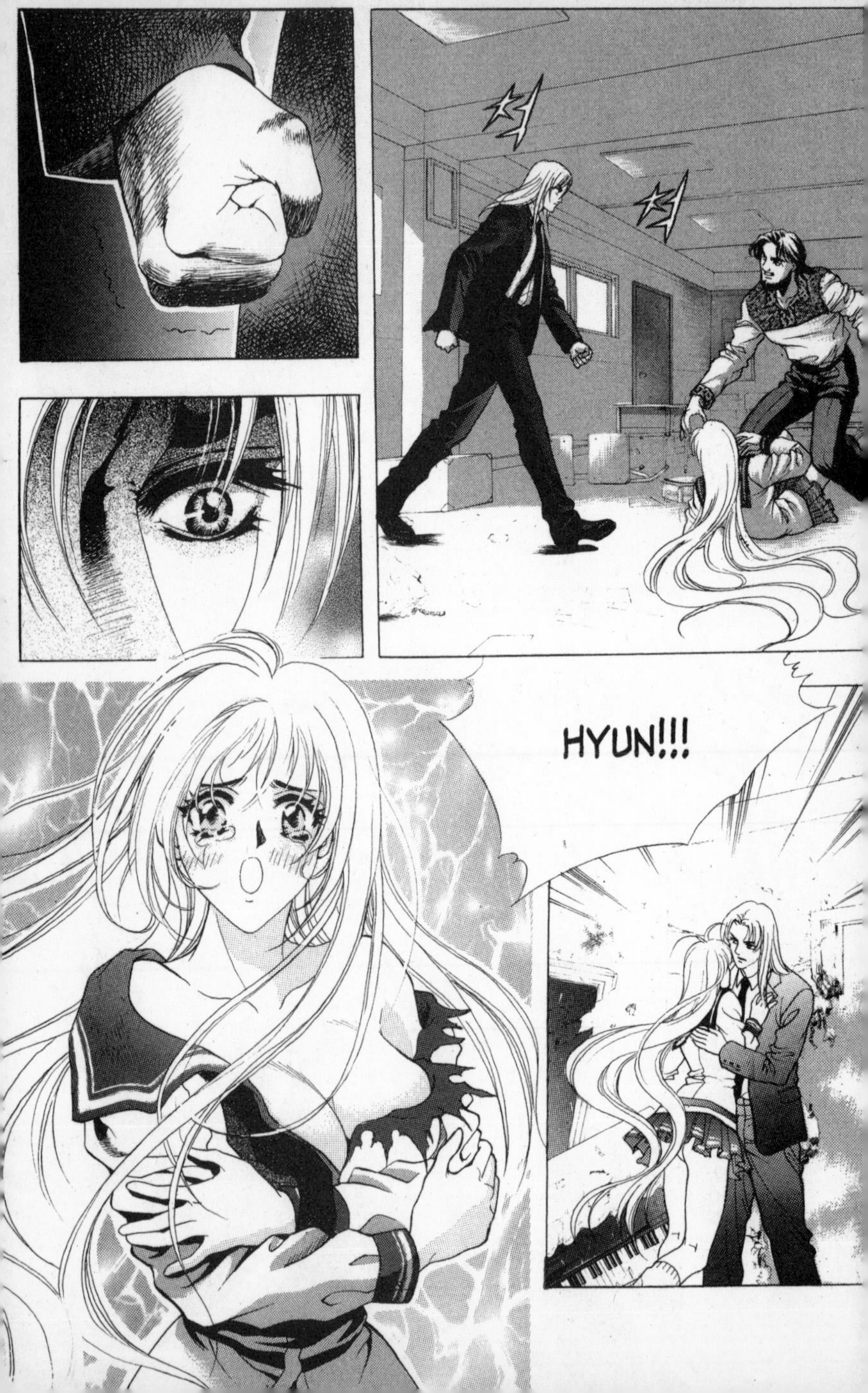
HYUN!!!

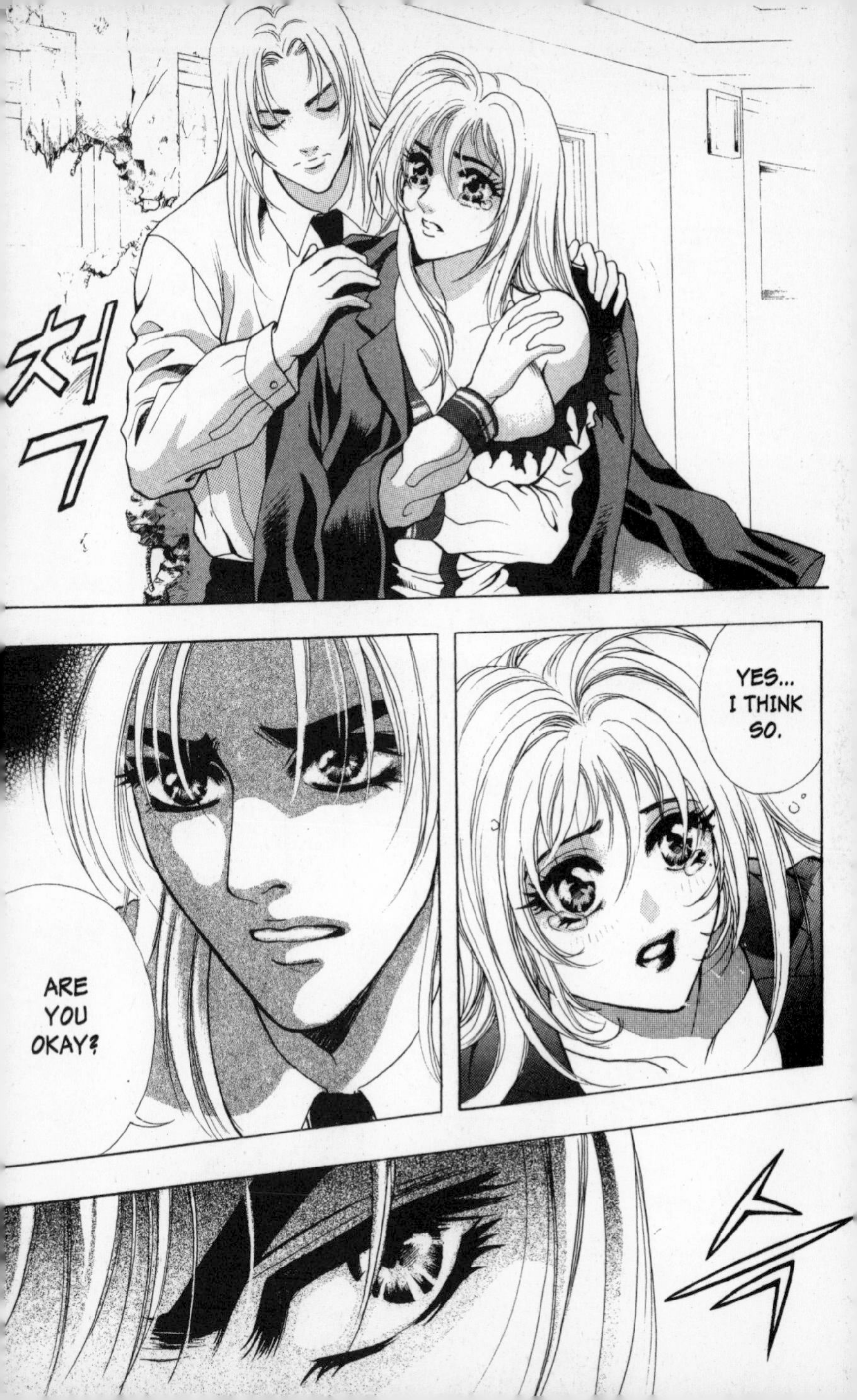
척
ARE YOU OKAY?
YES... I THINK SO.

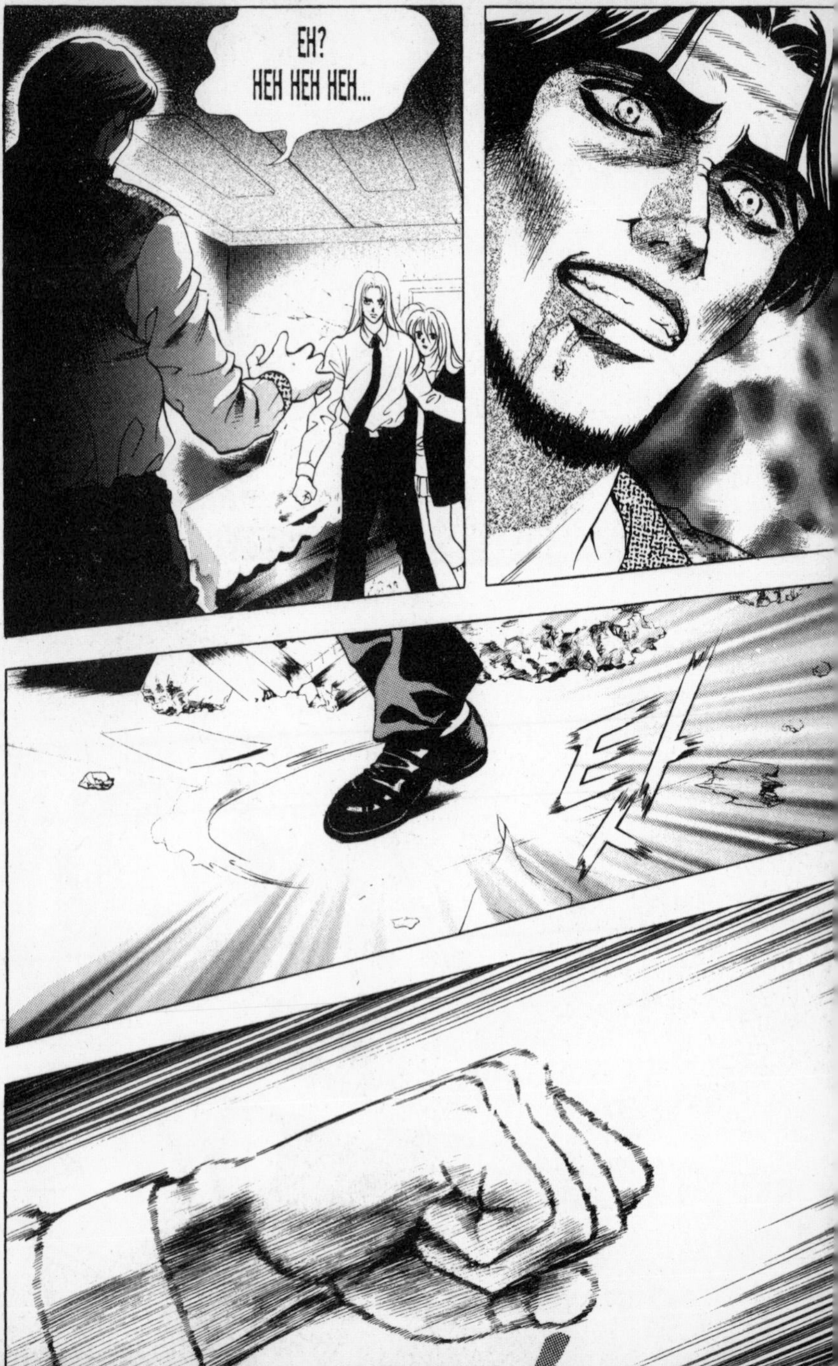
EH?
HEH HEH HEH...

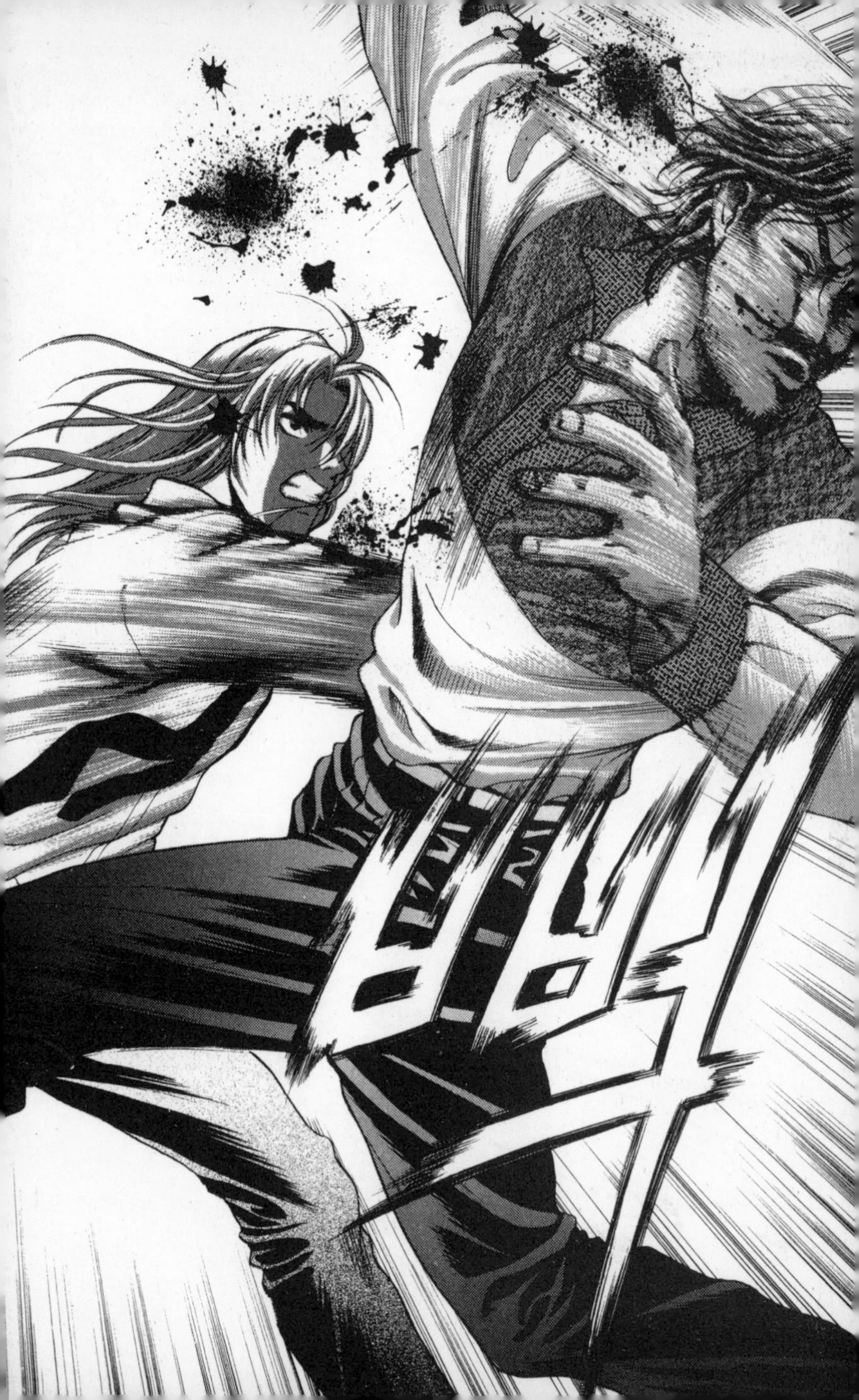
빡

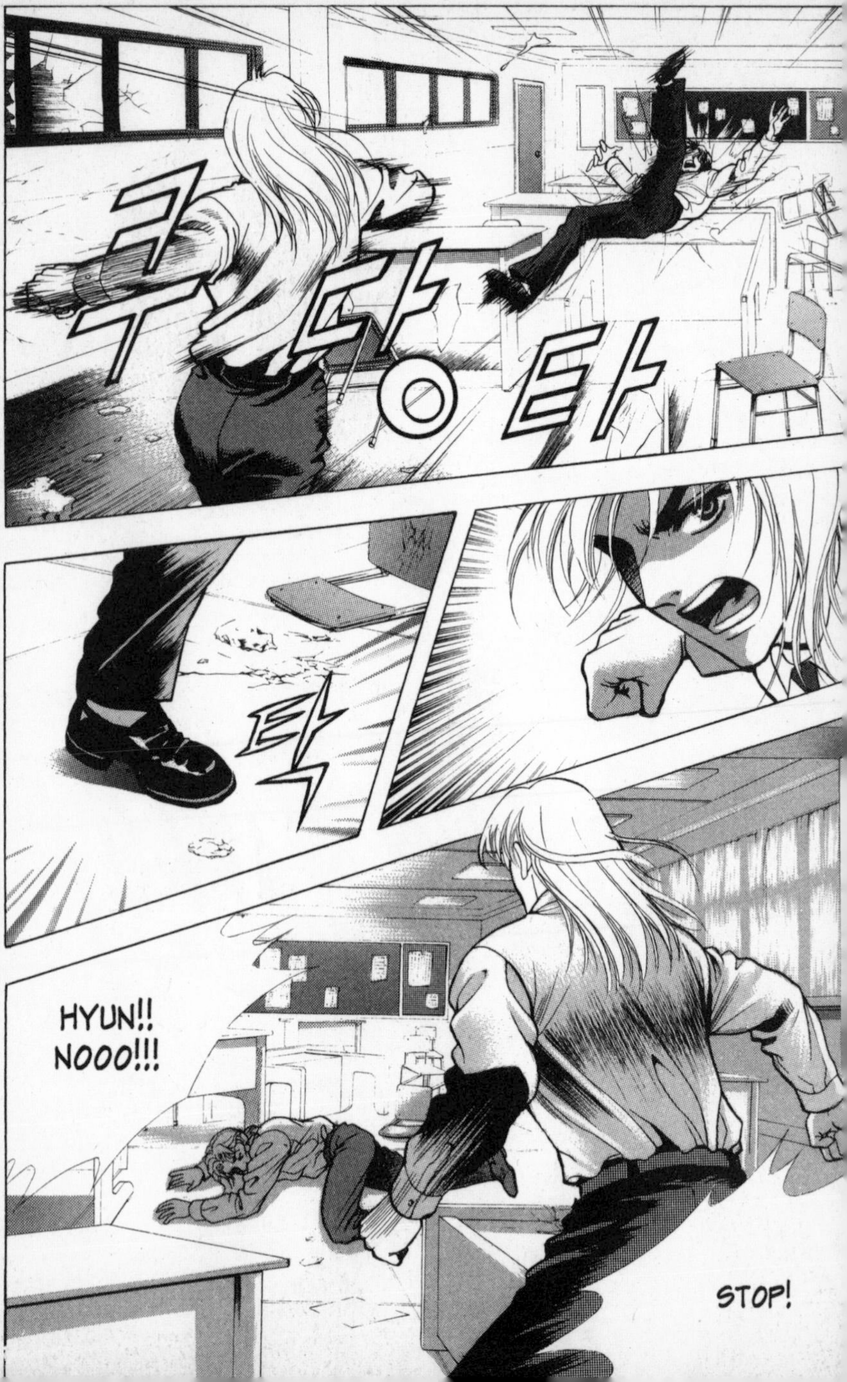

쿠당타
타
HYUN!!
NOOO!!!
STOP!

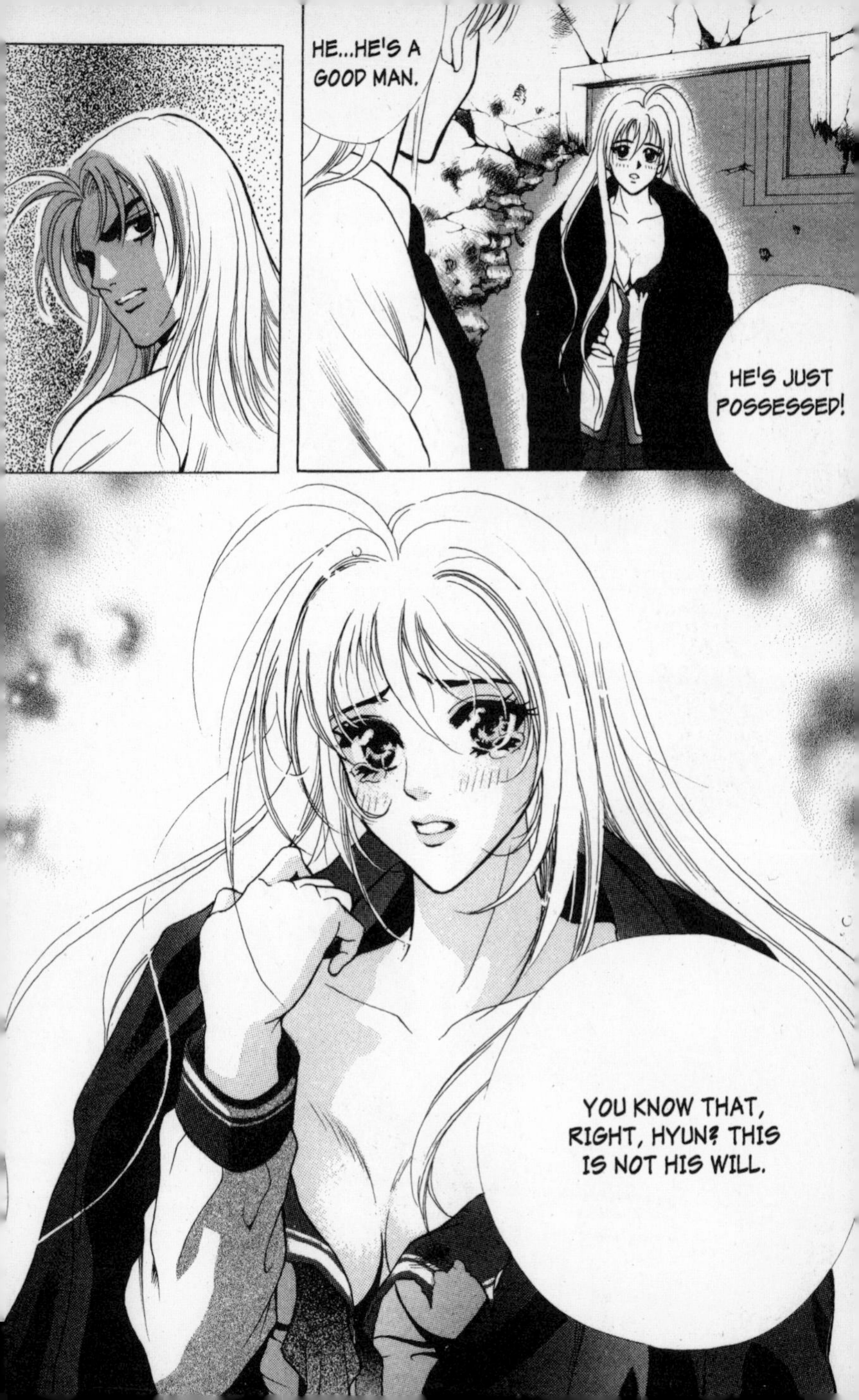
HE...HE'S A GOOD MAN.
HE'S JUST POSSESSED!
YOU KNOW THAT, RIGHT, HYUN? THIS IS NOT HIS WILL.

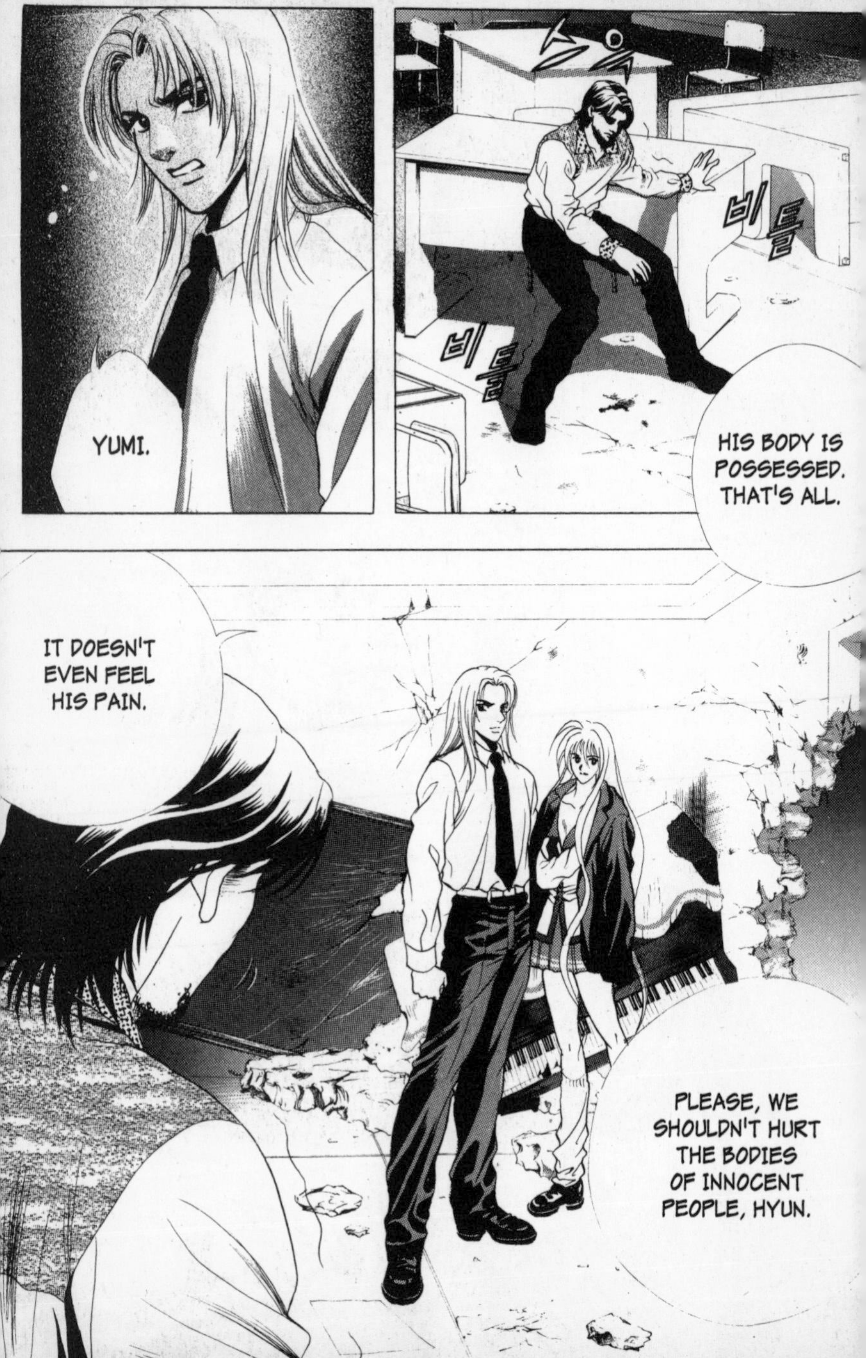
YUMI.
비틀
비틀
HIS BODY IS POSSESSED. THAT'S ALL.
IT DOESN'T EVEN FEEL HIS PAIN.
PLEASE, WE SHOULDN'T HURT THE BODIES OF INNOCENT PEOPLE, HYUN.

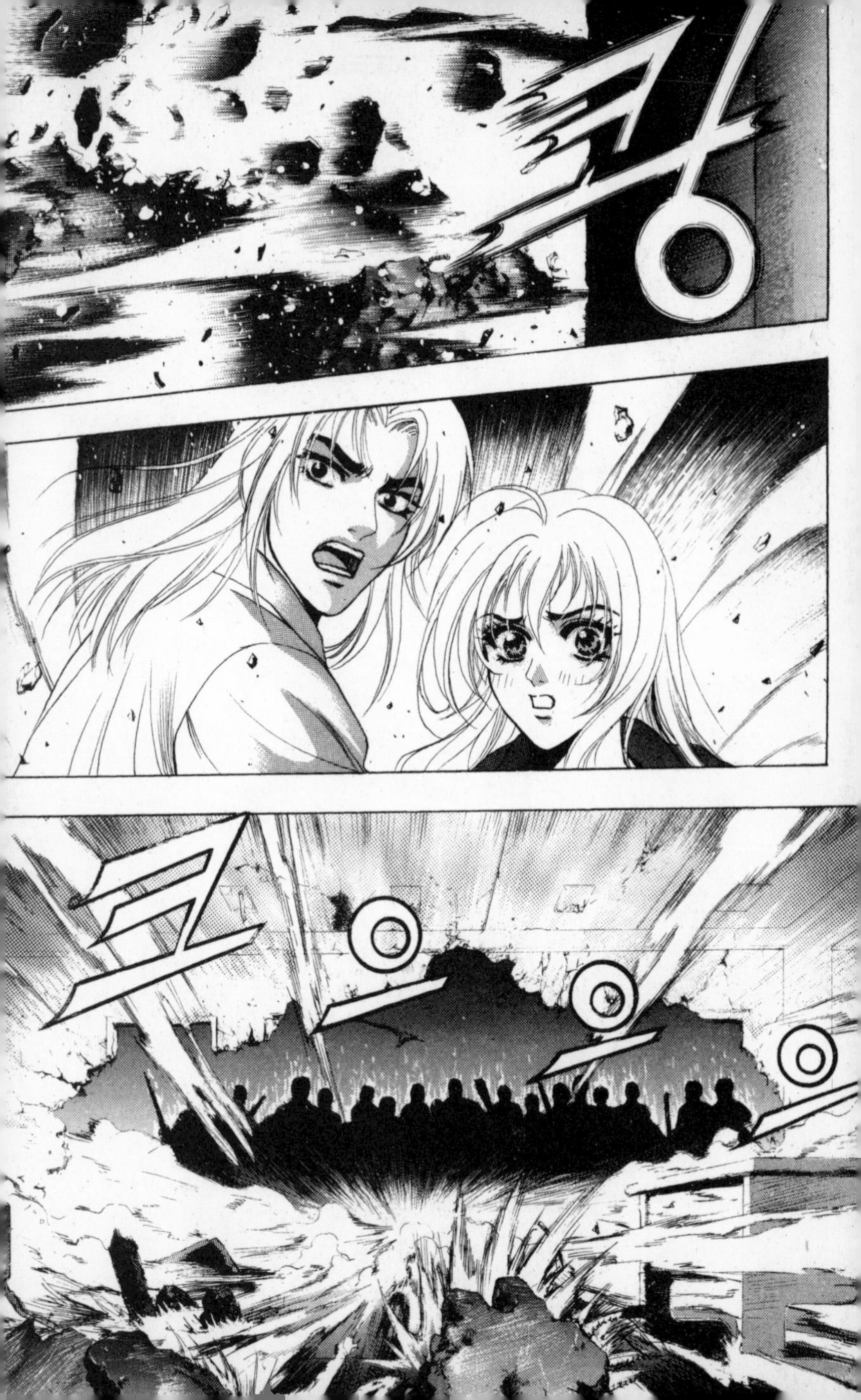

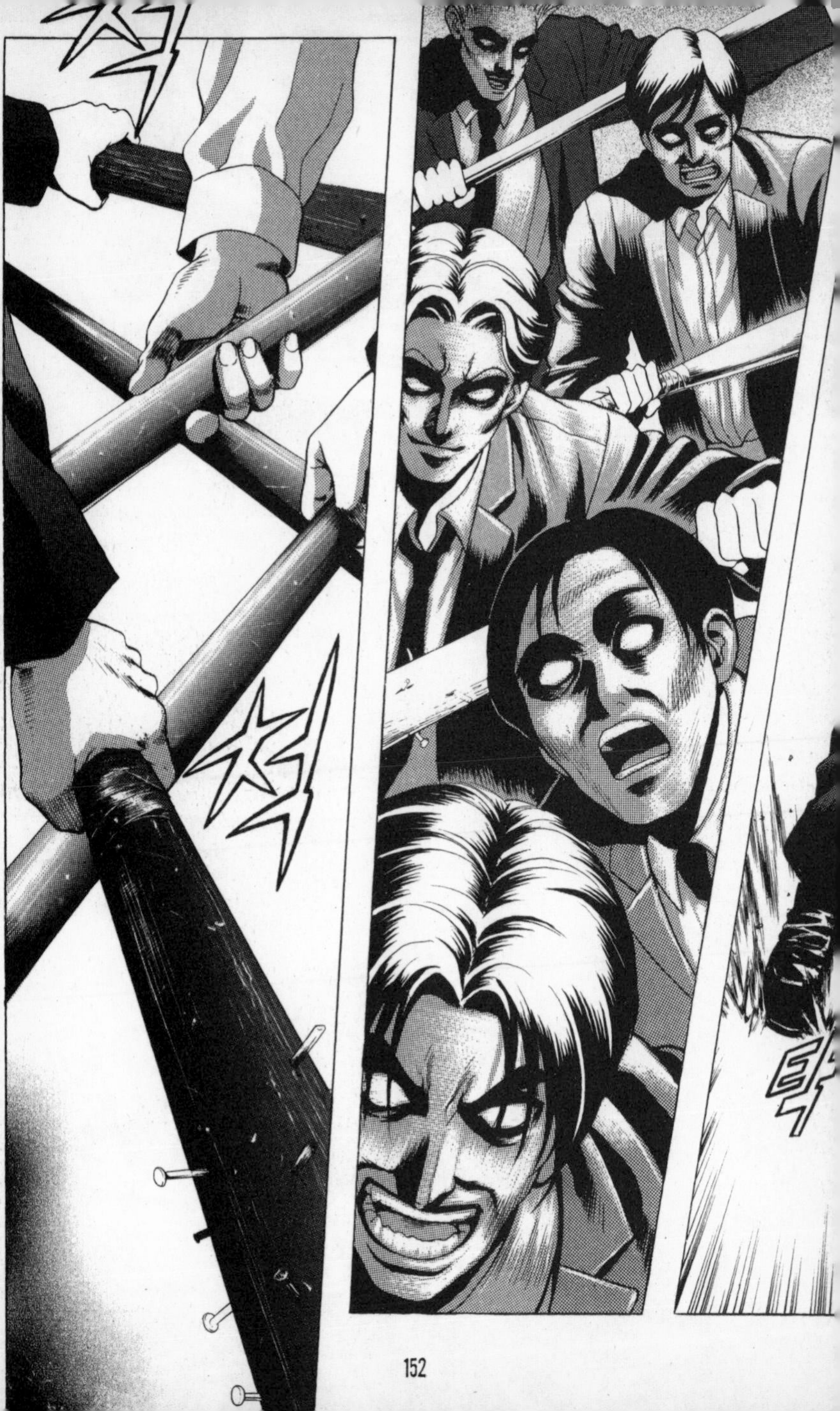

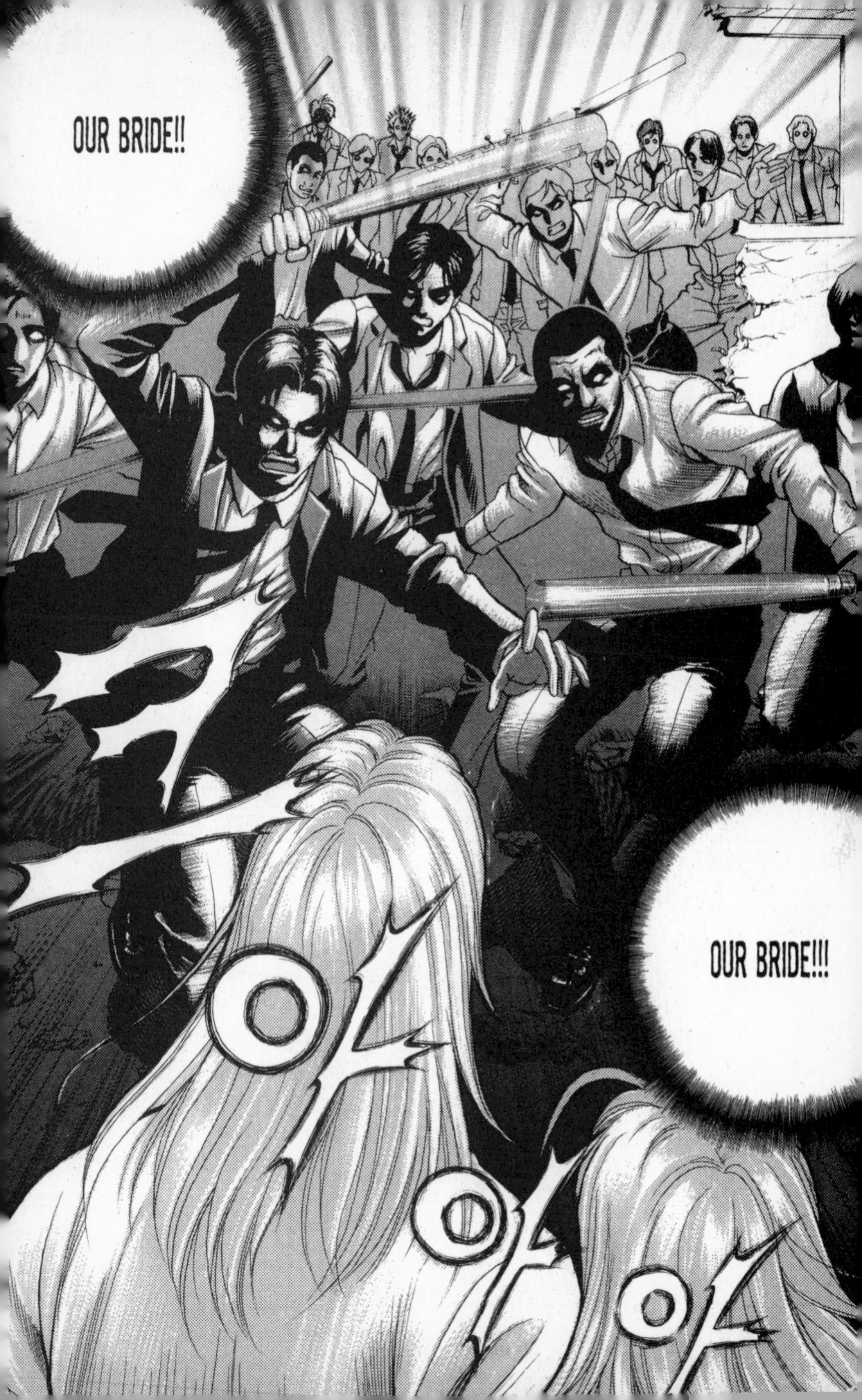
OUR BRIDE!!
OUR BRIDE!!!

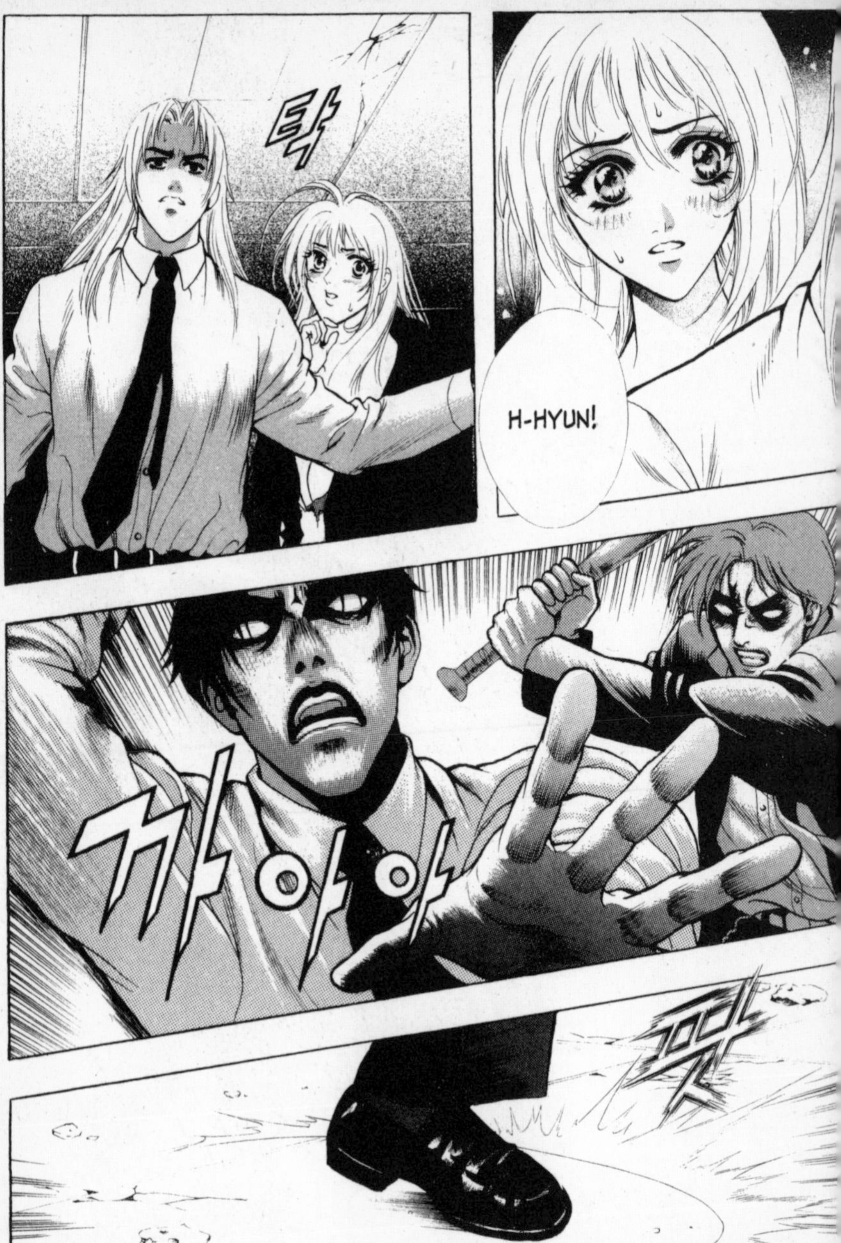
탁
H-HYUN!

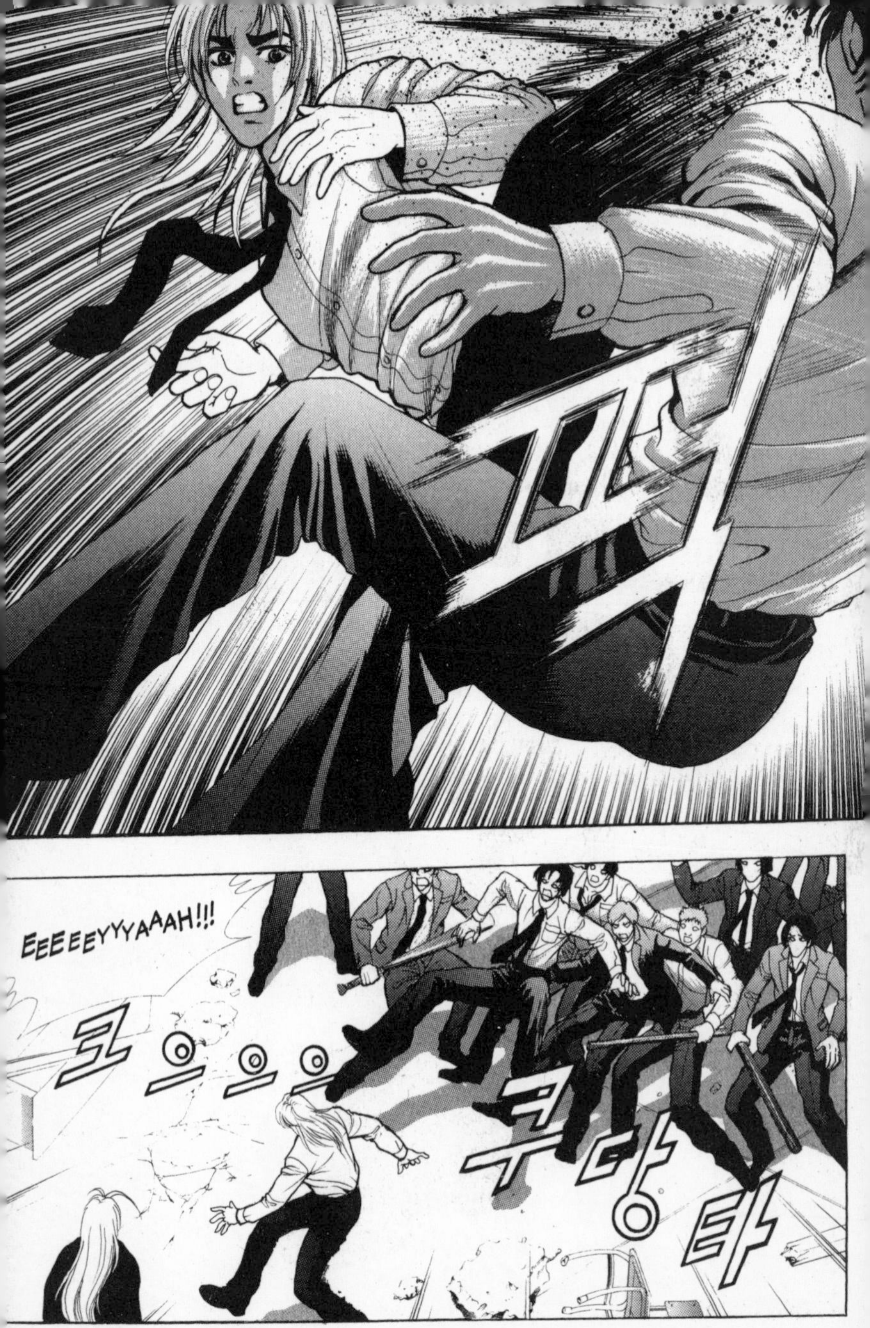
EEEEEYYYAAAH!!!
크으으으

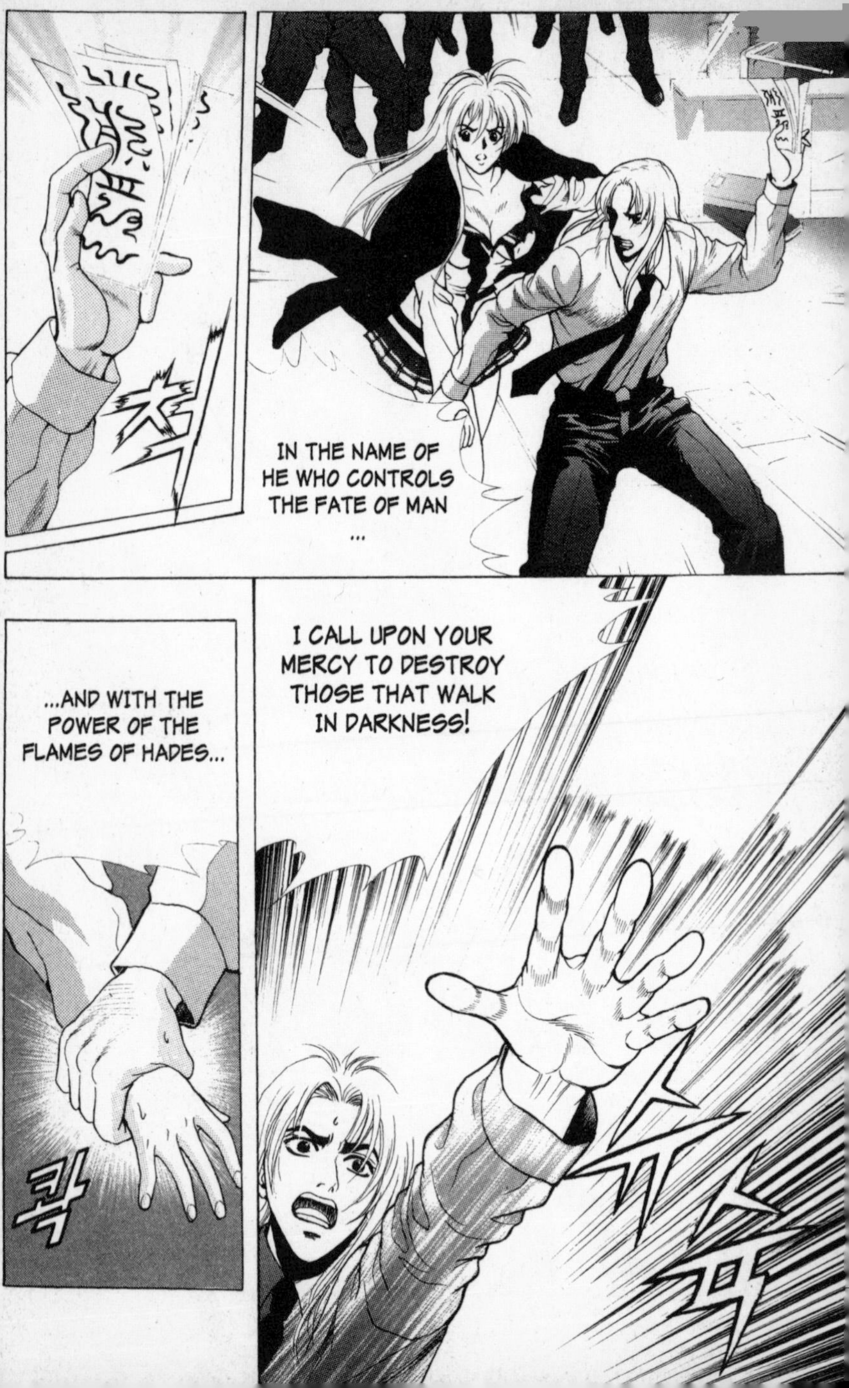
IN THE NAME OF HE WHO CONTROLS THE FATE OF MAN ...
...AND WITH THE POWER OF THE FLAMES OF HADES...
I CALL UPON YOUR MERCY TO DESTROY THOSE THAT WALK IN DARKNESS!

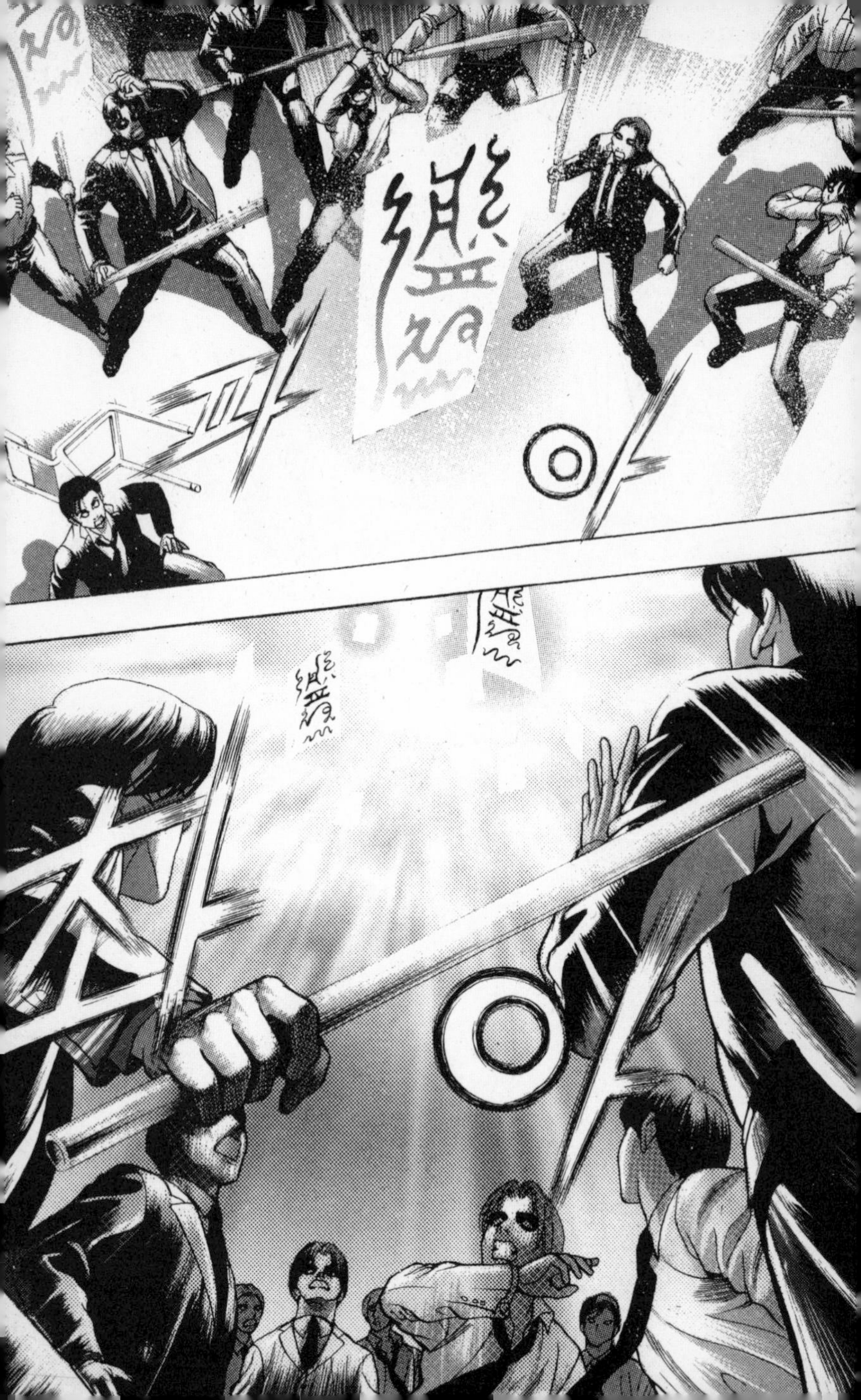

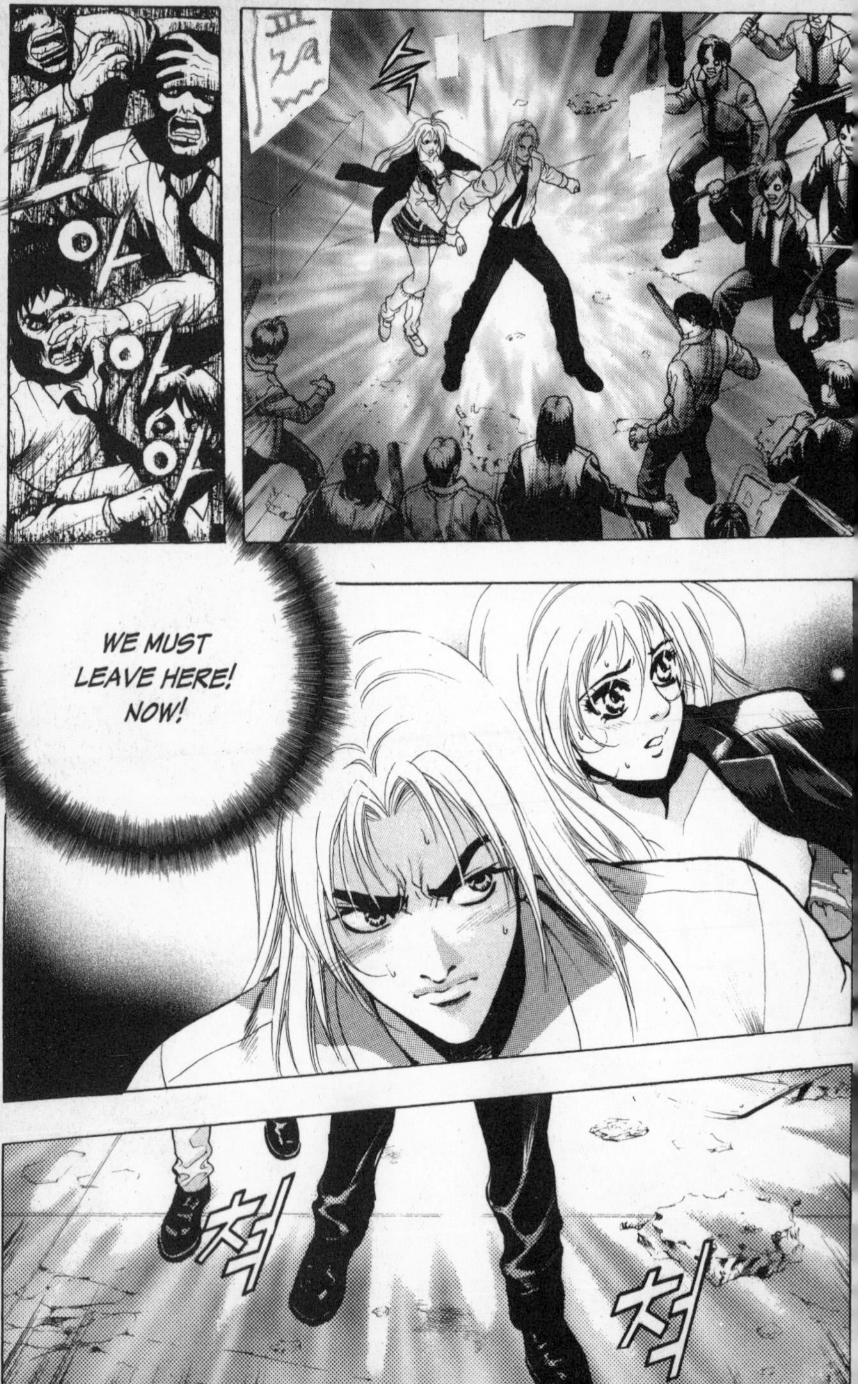
WE MUST LEAVE HERE! NOW!

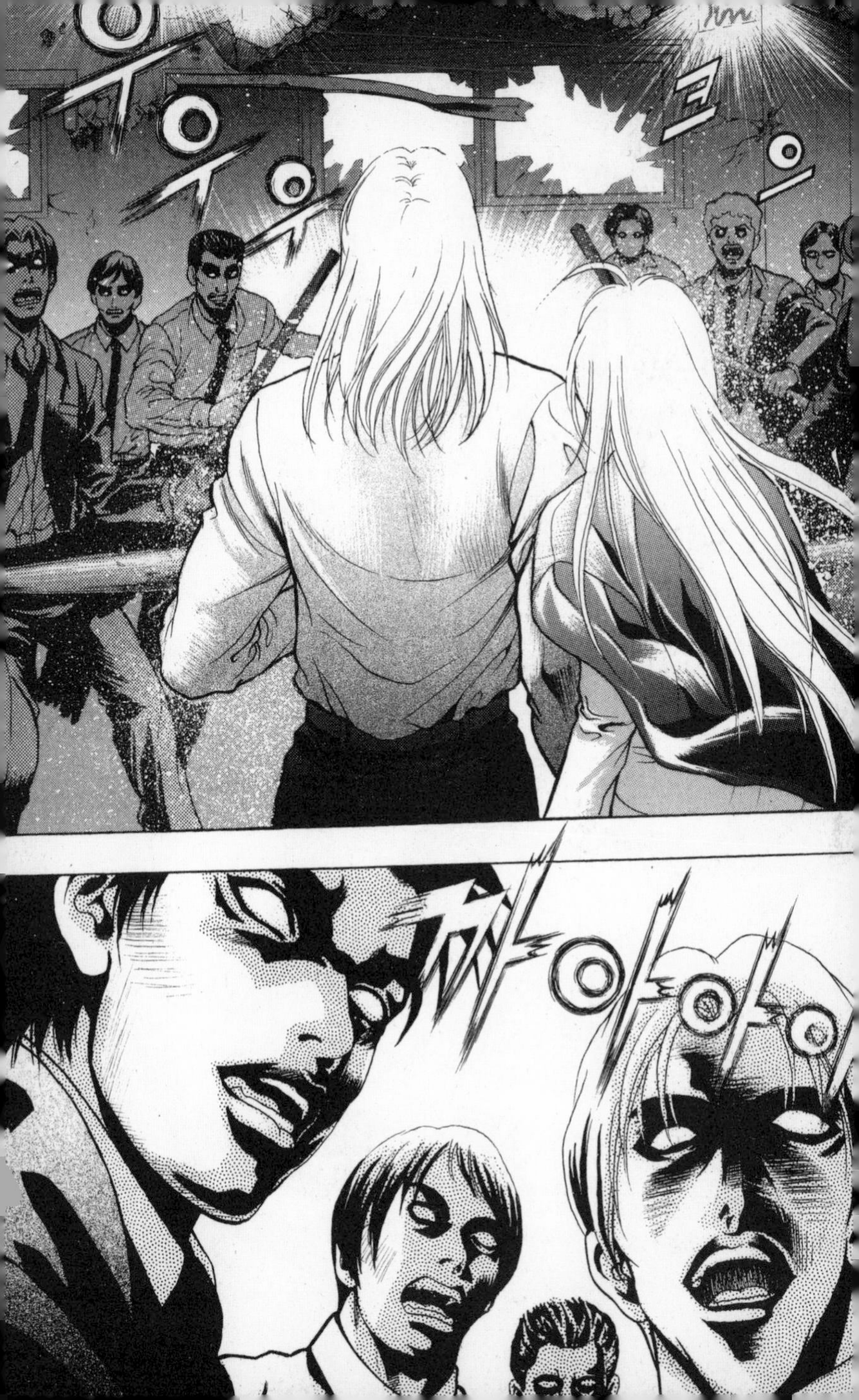
우우우
크으
꺄아아아

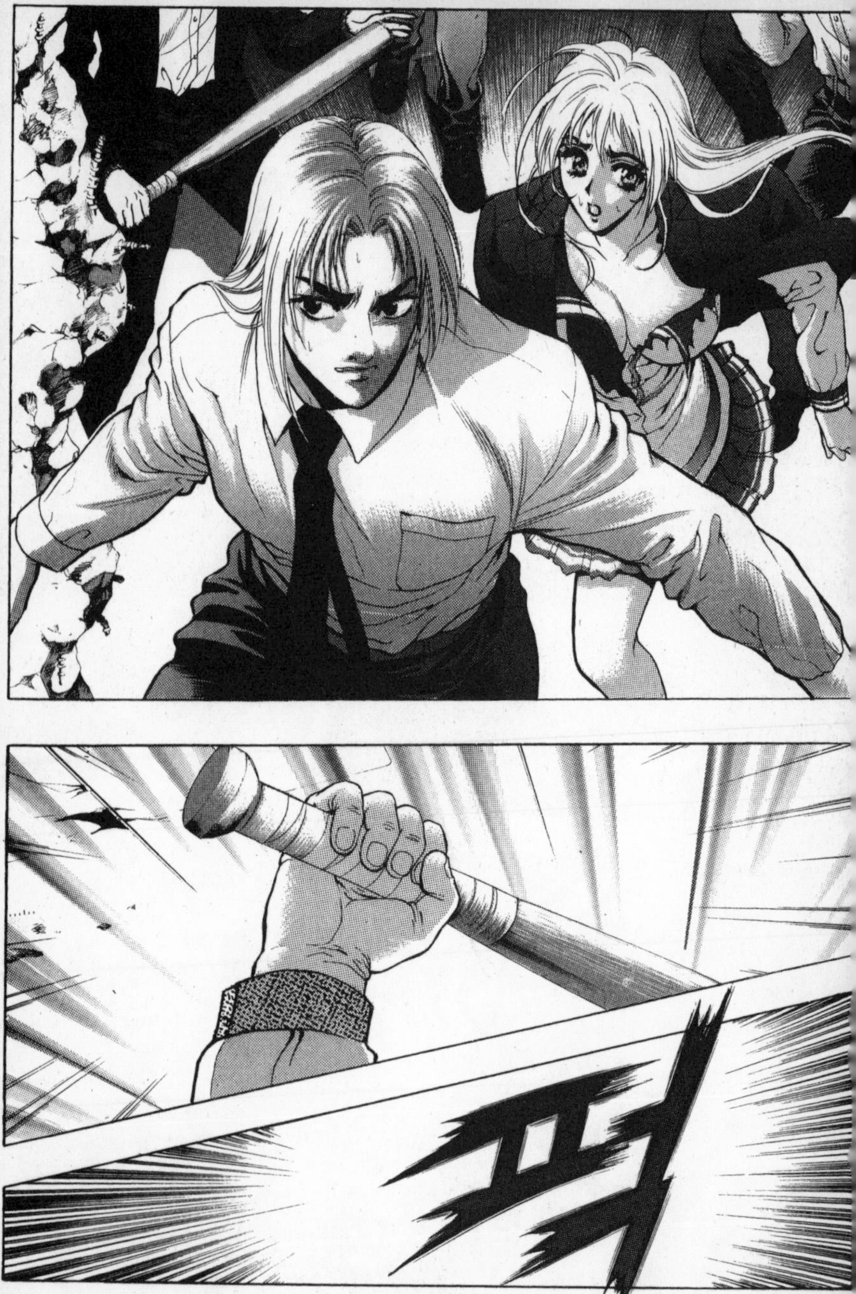

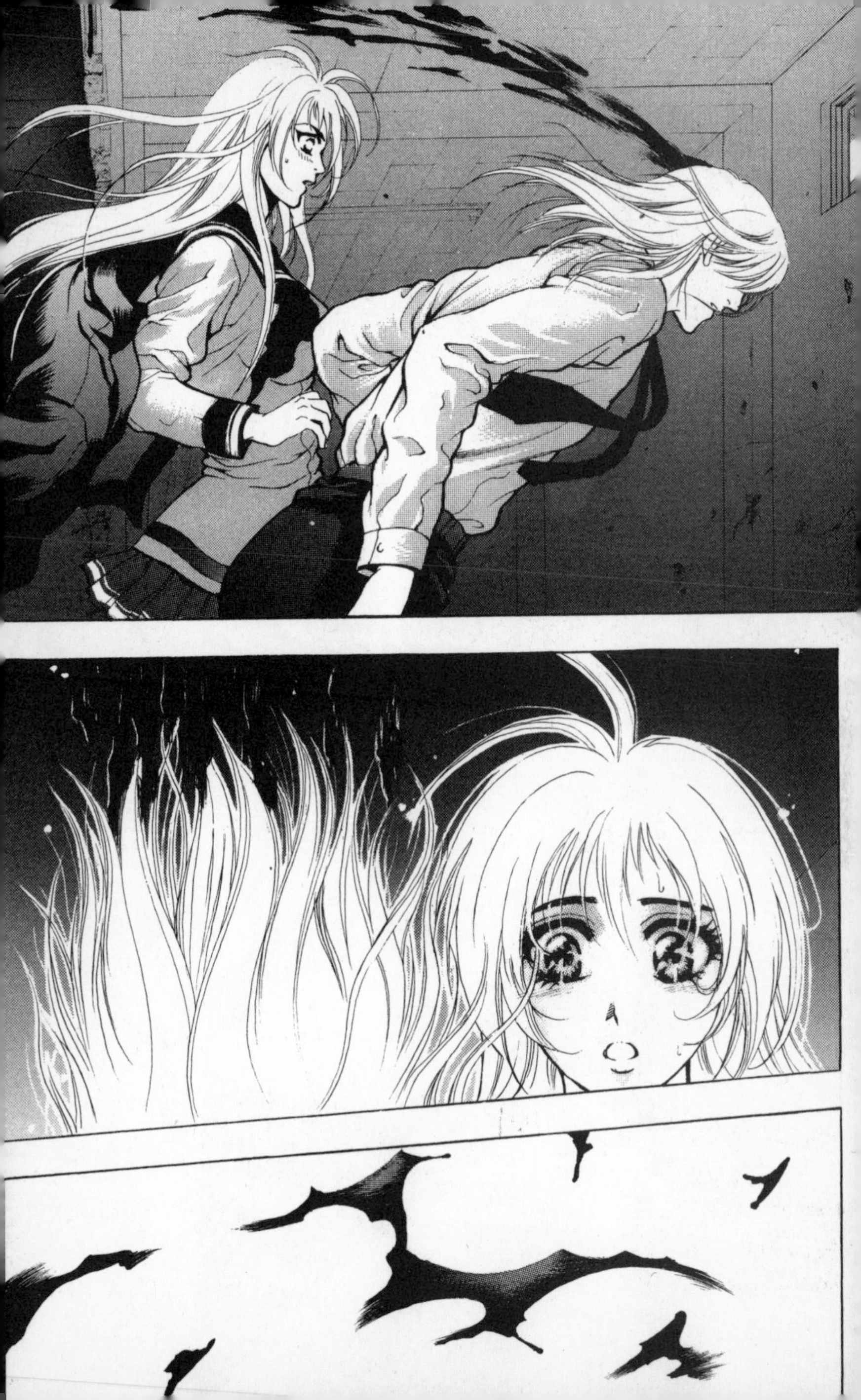

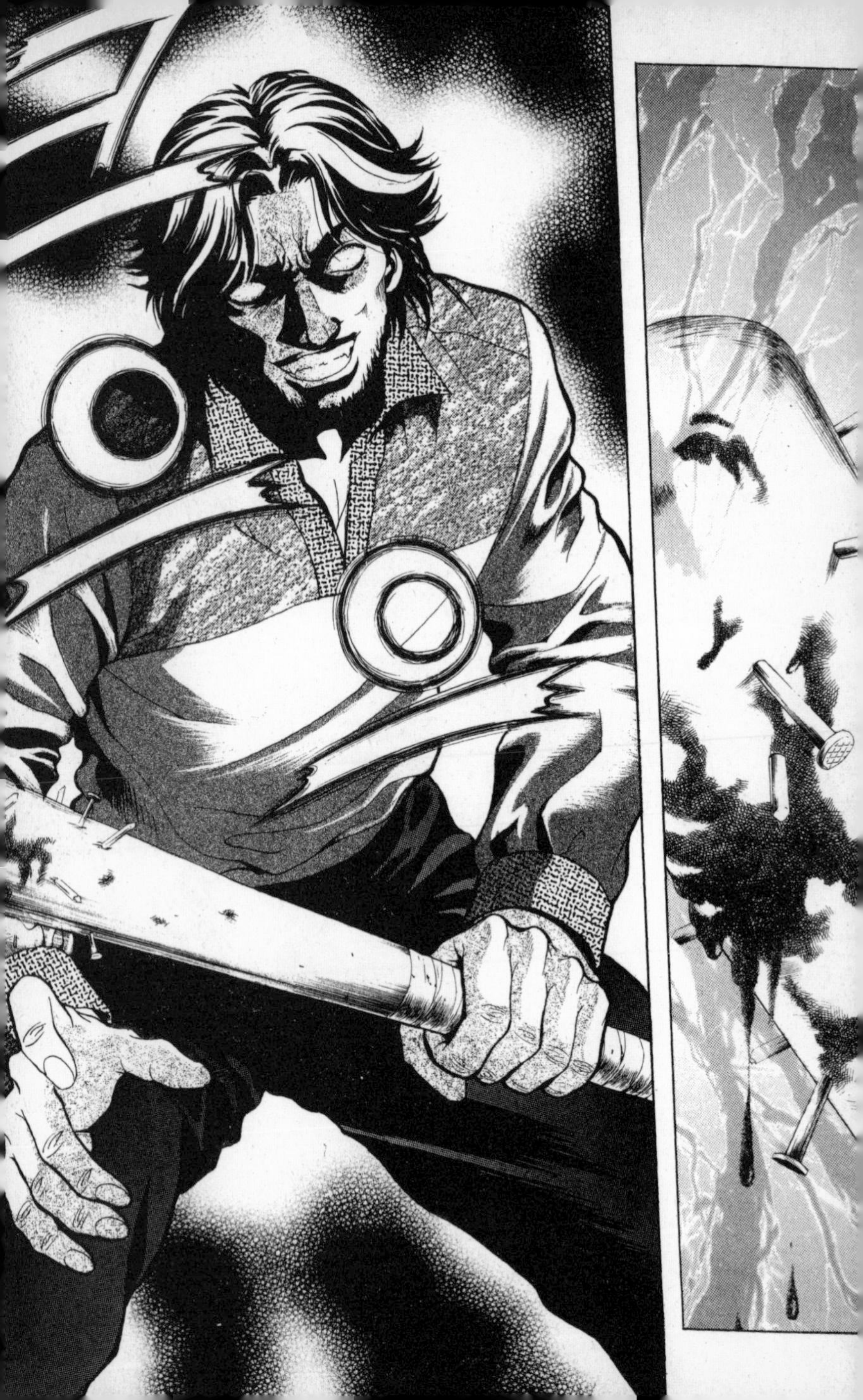

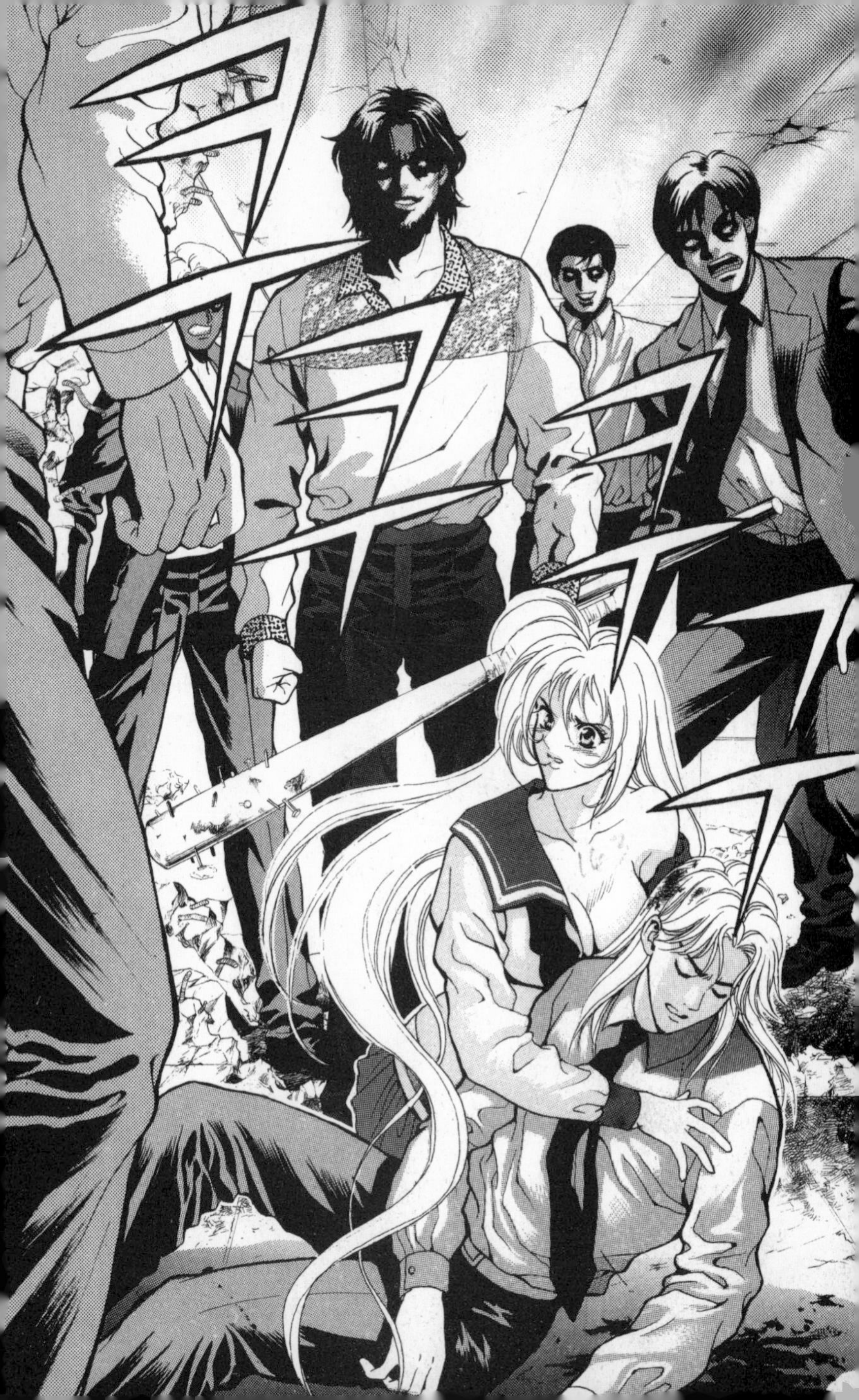

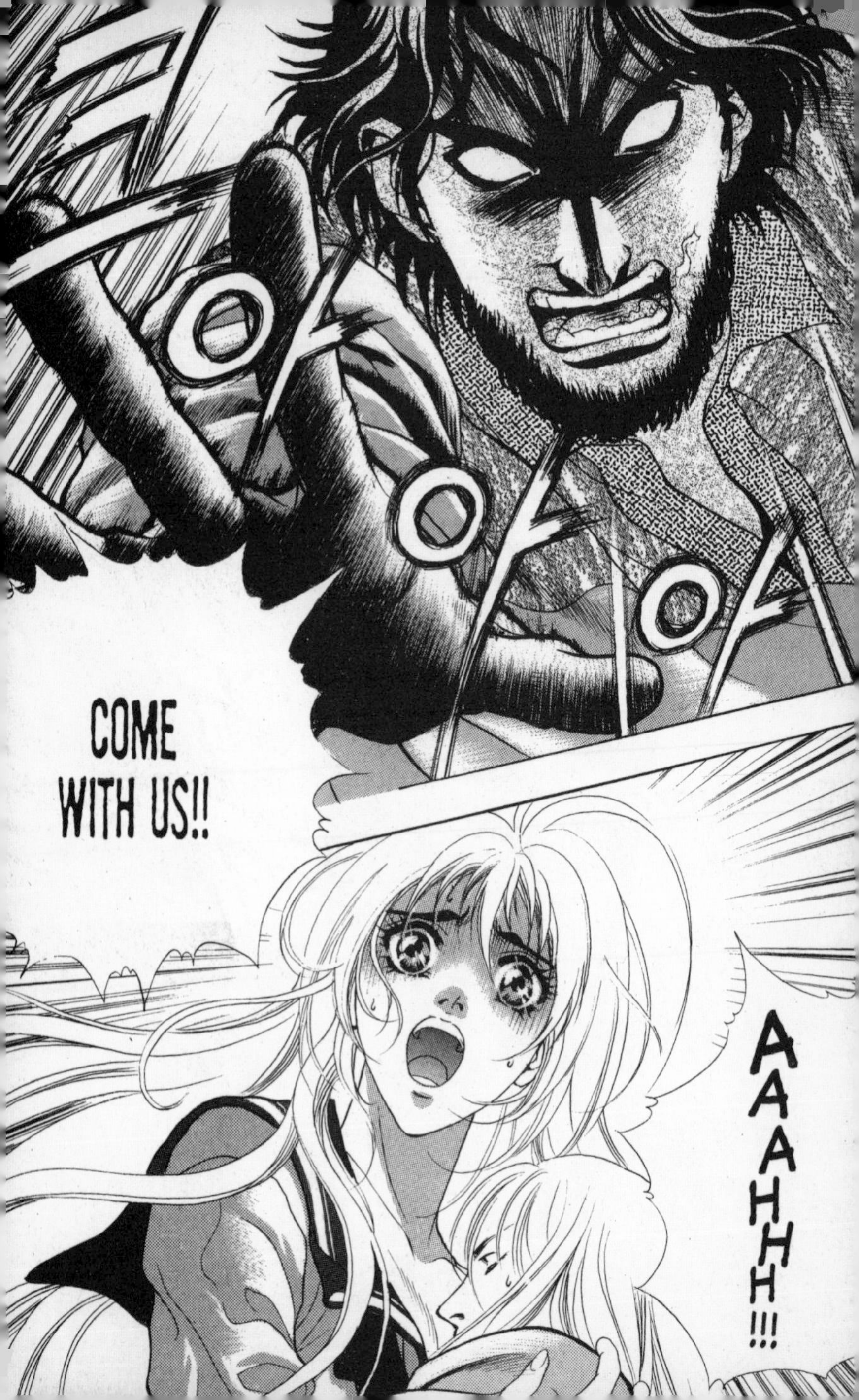
COME WITH US!!
AAAHHH!!!

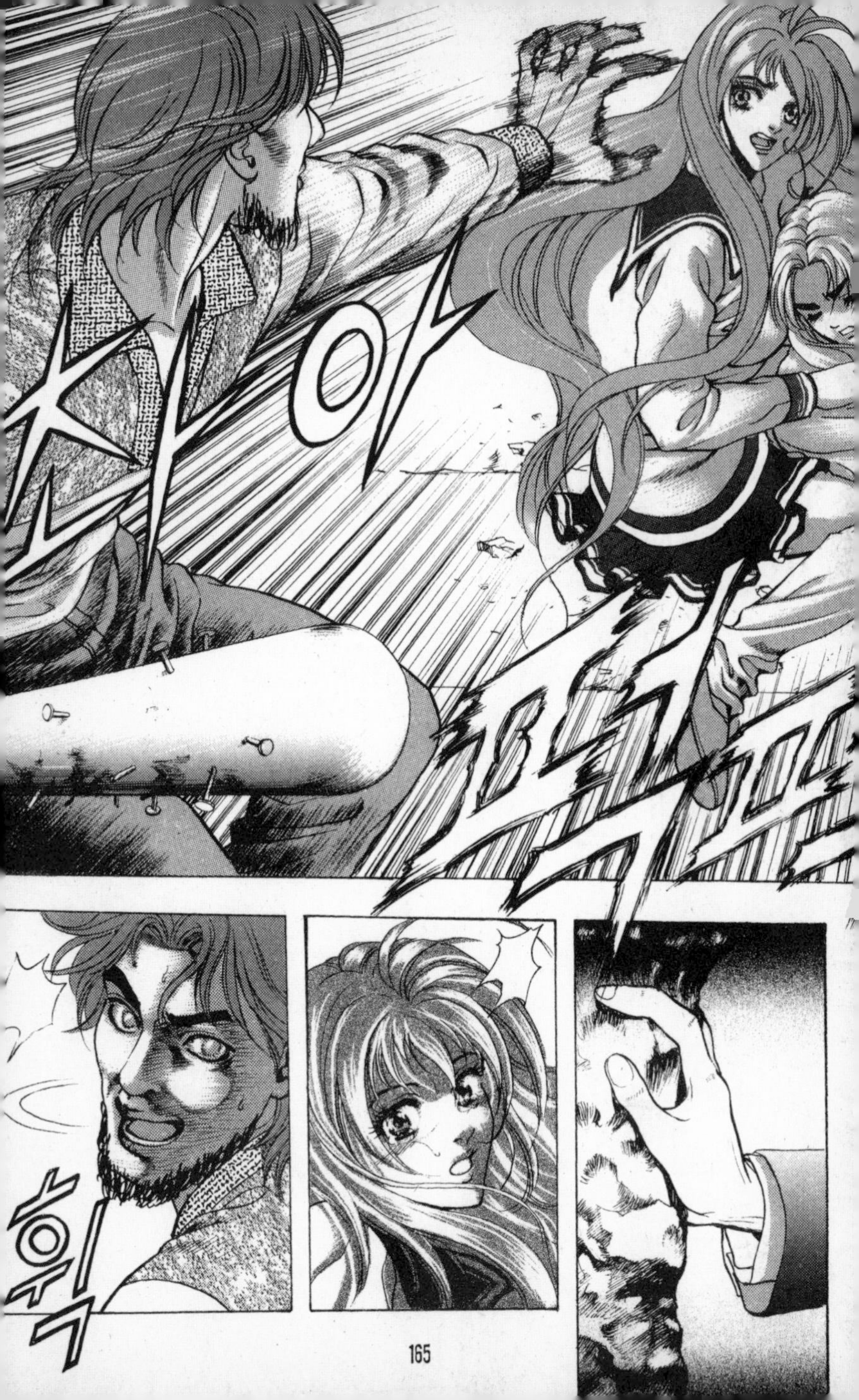

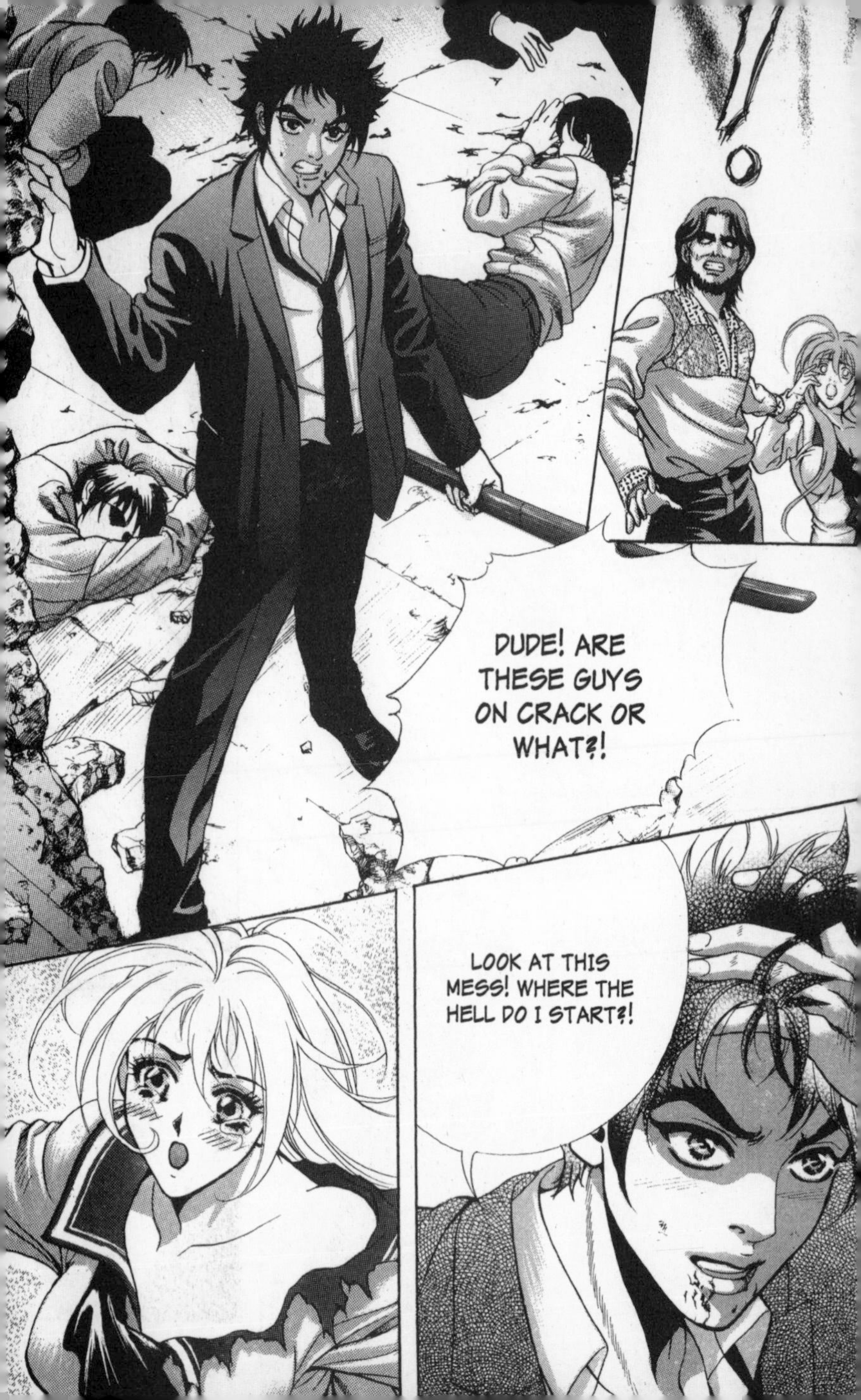
!
DUDE! ARE THESE GUYS ON CRACK OR WHAT?!
LOOK AT THIS MESS! WHERE THE HELL DO I START?!

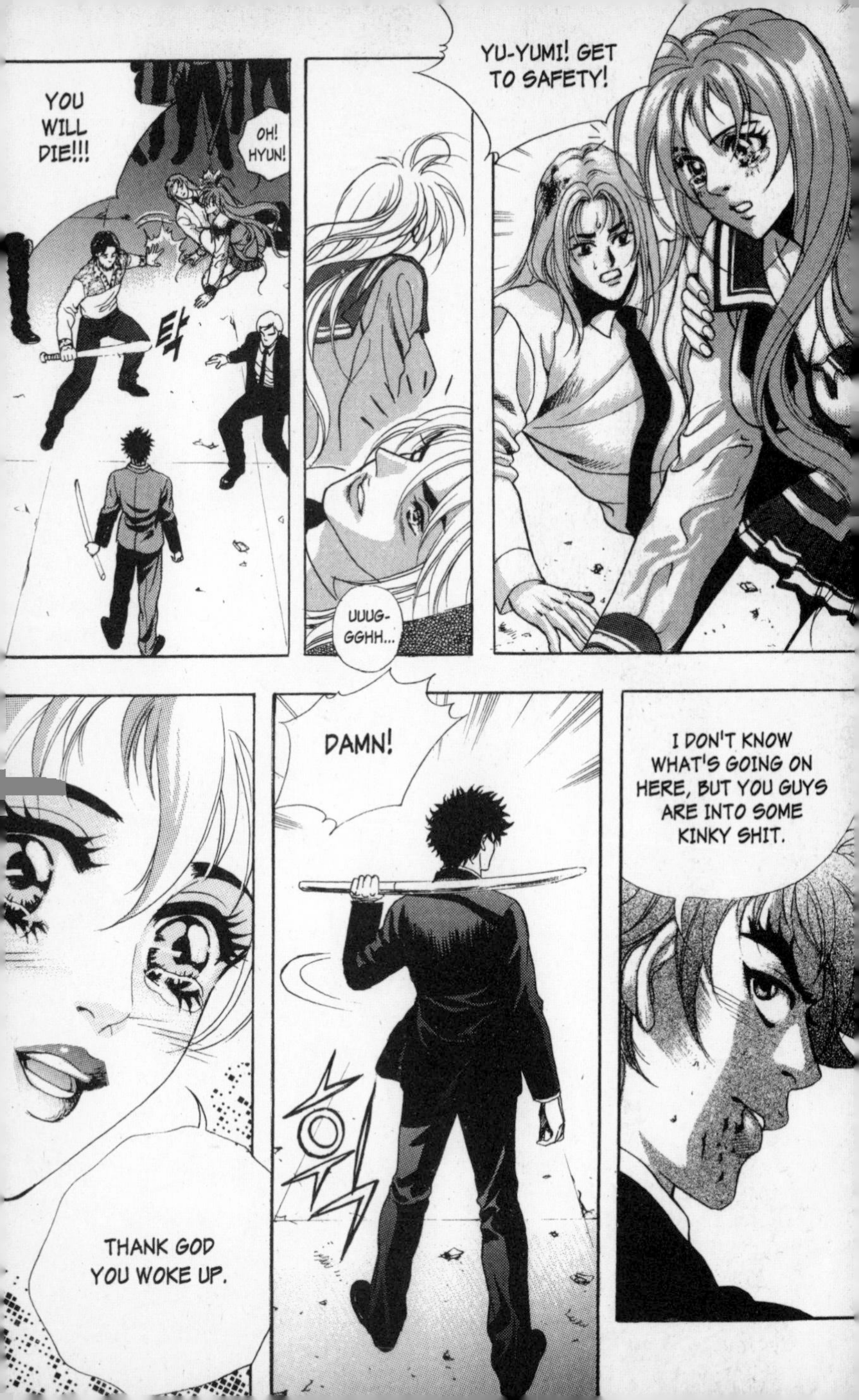
YOU WILL DIE!!!
OH! HYUN!
YU-YUMI! GET TO SAFETY!
UUUG-GGHH...
THANK GOD YOU WOKE UP.
DAMN!
I DON'T KNOW WHAT'S GOING ON HERE, BUT YOU GUYS ARE INTO SOME KINKY SHIT.

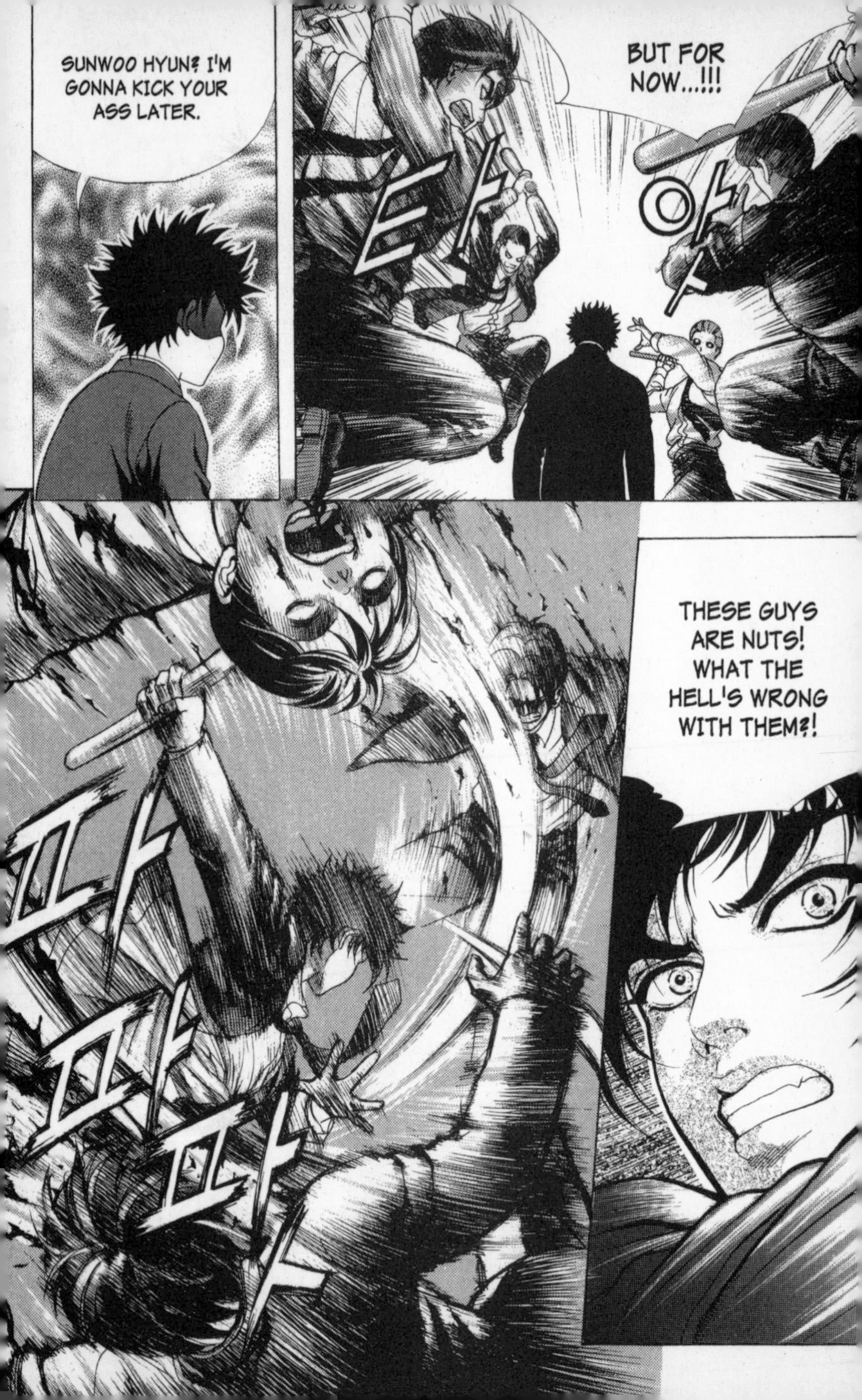
SUNWOO HYUN? I'M GONNA KICK YOUR ASS LATER.
BUT FOR NOW...!!!
THESE GUYS ARE NUTS! WHAT THE HELL'S WRONG WITH THEM?!

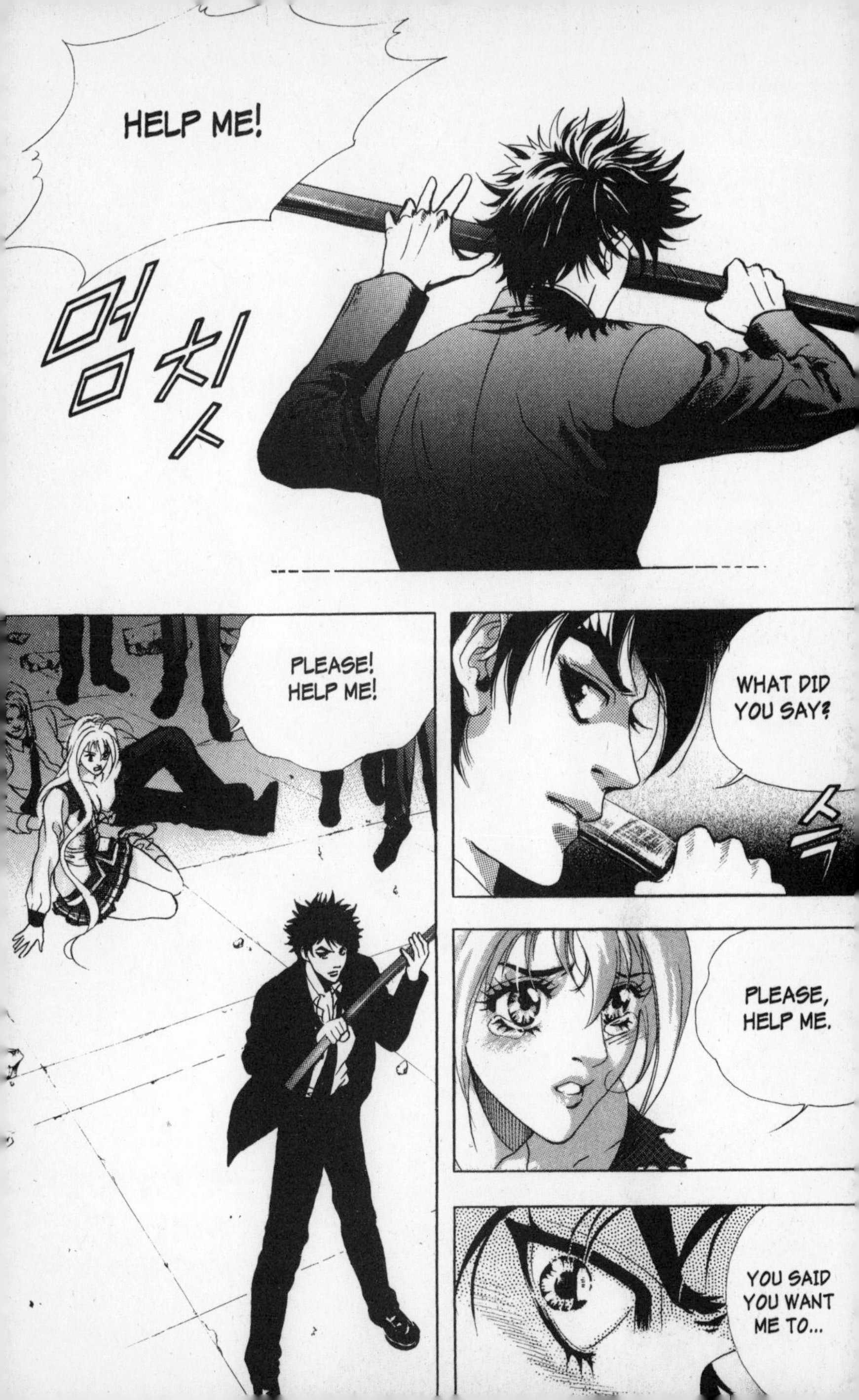
HELP ME!
멈칫
PLEASE! HELP ME!
WHAT DID YOU SAY?
PLEASE, HELP ME.
YOU SAID YOU WANT ME TO...

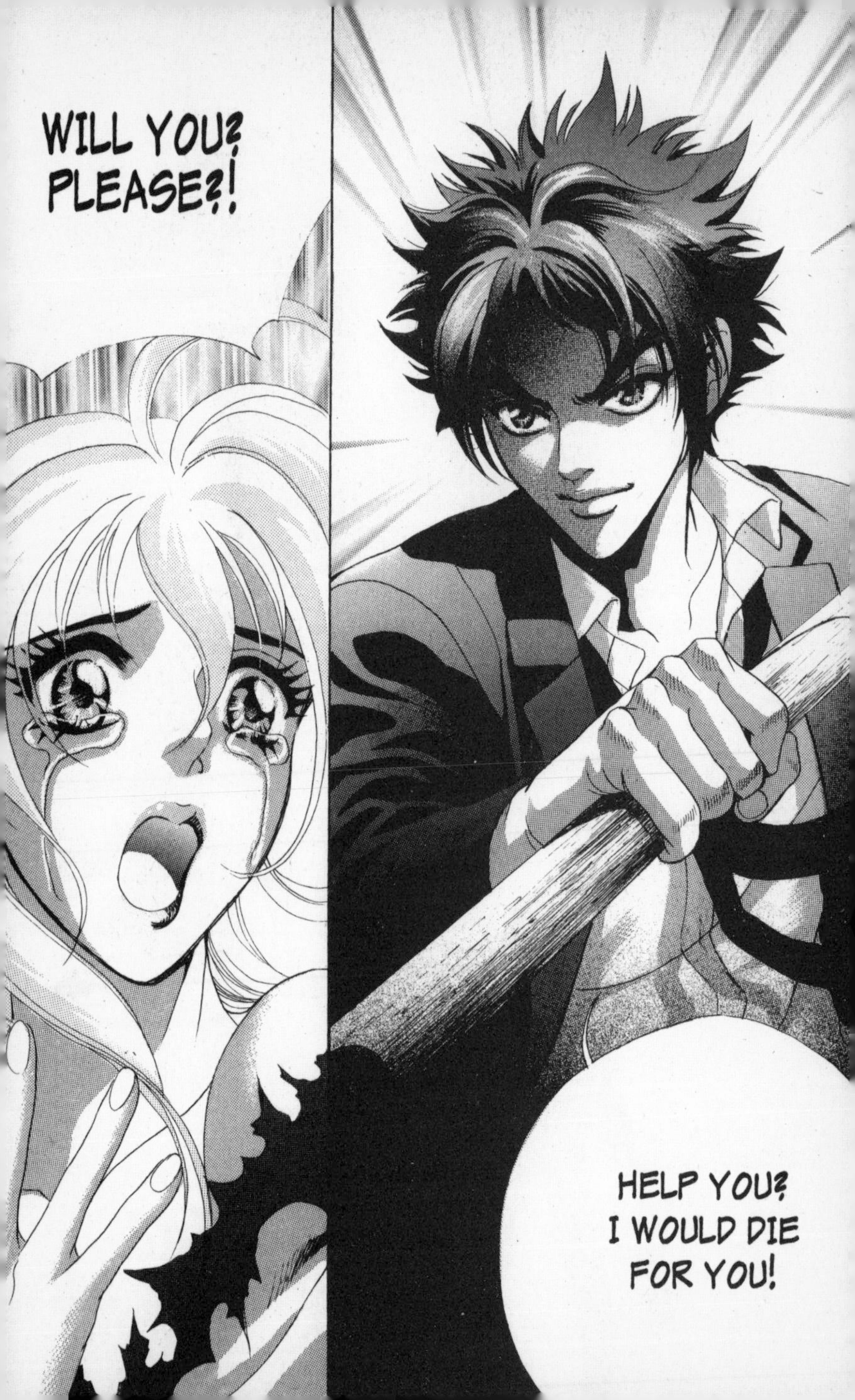
HELP YOU? I WOULD DIE FOR YOU!
WILL YOU? PLEASE?!

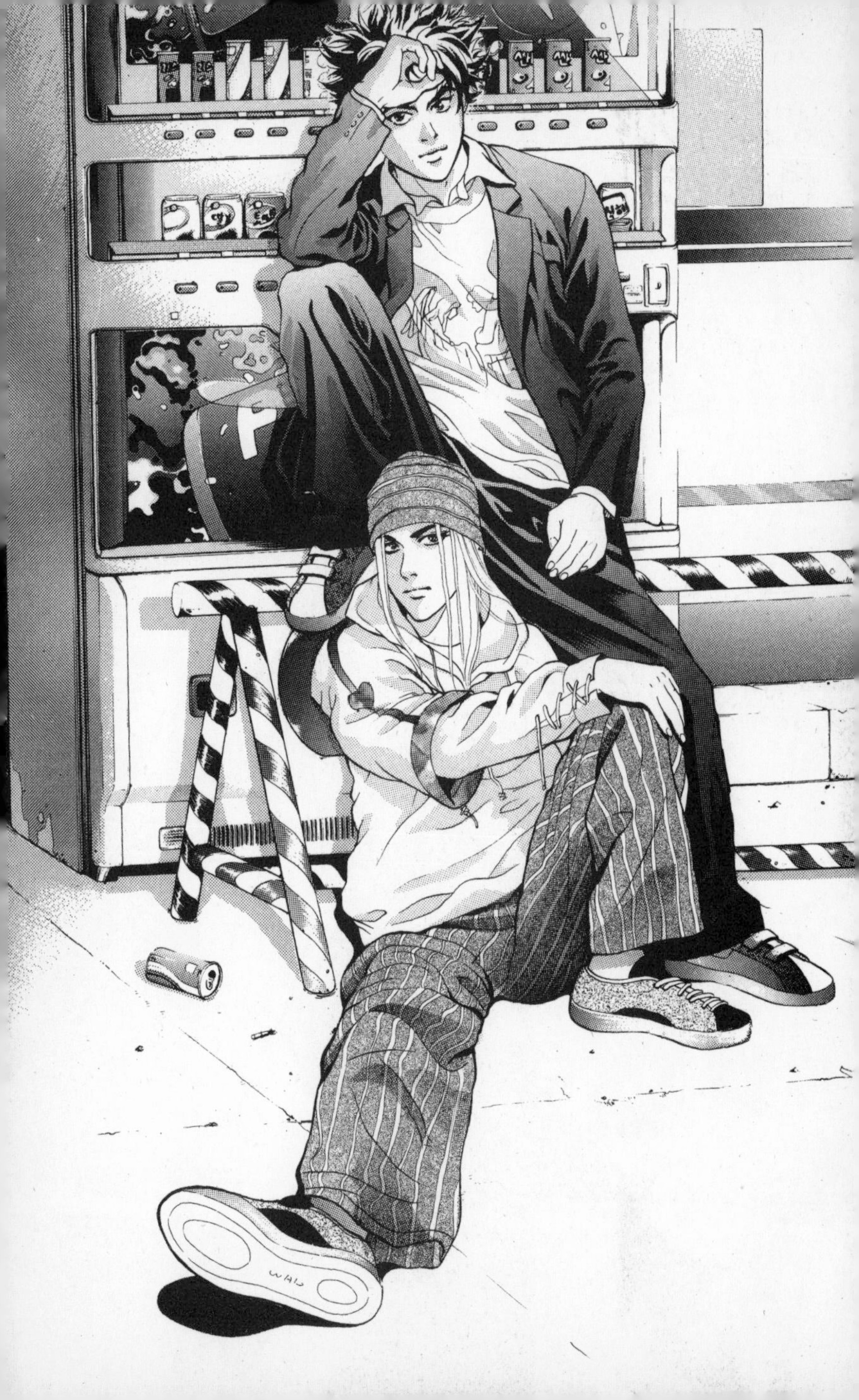

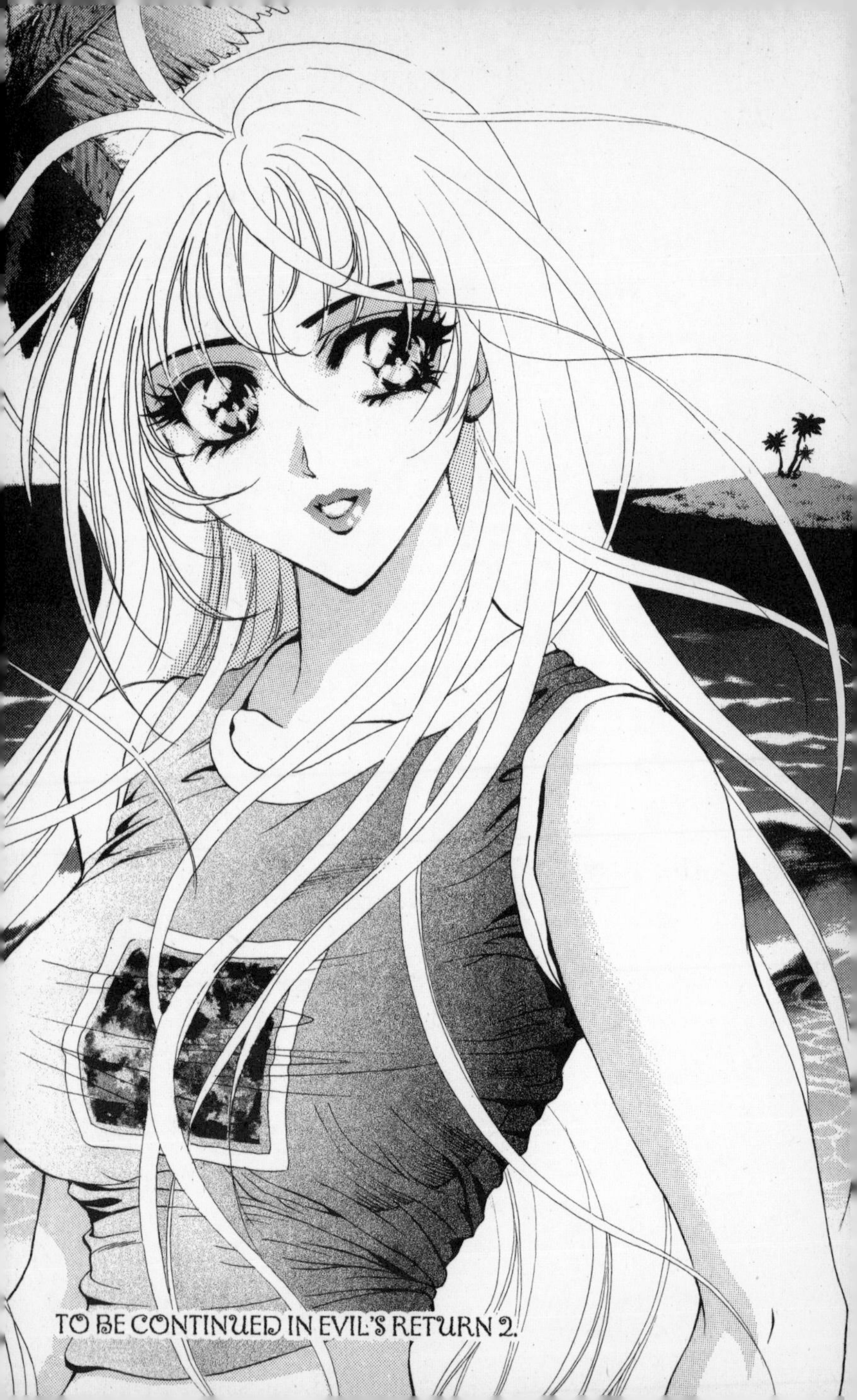
TO BE CONTINUED IN EVIL'S RETURN 2.

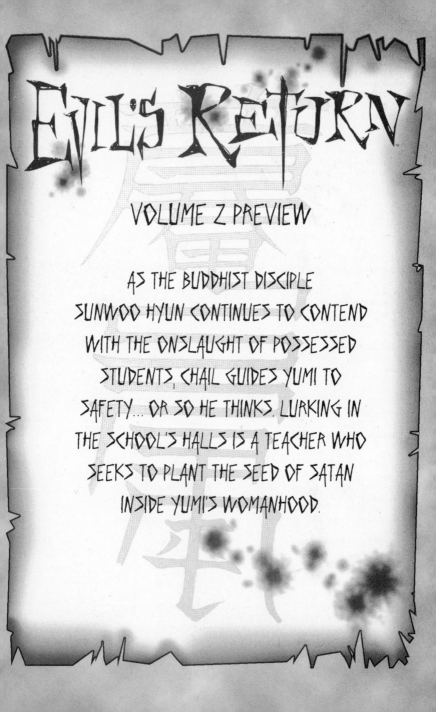

EVIL'S RETURN

VOLUME Z PREVIEW

AS THE BUDDHIST DISCIPLE
SUNWOO HYUN CONTINUES TO CONTEND
WITH THE ONSLAUGHT OF POSSESSED
STUDENTS, CHAIL GUIDES YUMI TO
SAFETY... OR SO HE THINKS. LURKING IN
THE SCHOOL'S HALLS IS A TEACHER WHO
SEEKS TO PLANT THE SEED OF SATAN
INSIDE YUMI'S WOMANHOOD.

MANGA

.HACK//LEGEND OF THE TWILIGHT
@LARGE
ABENOBASHI: MAGICAL SHOPPING ARCADE
A.I. LOVE YOU
AI YORI AOSHI
ANGELIC LAYER
ARM OF KANNON
BABY BIRTH
BATTLE ROYALE
BATTLE VIXENS
BRAIN POWERED
BRIGADOON
B'TX
CANDIDATE FOR GODDESS, THE
CARDCAPTOR SAKURA
CARDCAPTOR SAKURA - MASTER OF THE CLOW
CHOBITS
CHRONICLES OF THE CURSED SWORD
CLAMP SCHOOL DETECTIVES
CLOVER
COMIC PARTY
CONFIDENTIAL CONFESSIONS
CORRECTOR YUI
COWBOY BEBOP
COWBOY BEBOP: SHOOTING STAR
CRAZY LOVE STORY
CRESCENT MOON
CROSS
CULDCEPT
CYBORG 009
D•N•ANGEL
DEMON DIARY
DEMON ORORON, THE
DEUS VITAE
DIABOLO
DIGIMON
DIGIMON TAMERS
DIGIMON ZERO TWO
DOLL
DRAGON HUNTER
DRAGON KNIGHTS
DRAGON VOICE
DREAM SAGA
DUKLYON: CLAMP SCHOOL DEFENDERS
EERIE QUEERIE!
ERICA SAKURAZAWA: COLLECTED WORKS
ET CETERA
ETERNITY
EVIL'S RETURN
FAERIES' LANDING
FAKE
FLCL
FLOWER OF THE DEEP SLEEP
FORBIDDEN DANCE
FRUITS BASKET
G GUNDAM

GATEKEEPERS
GETBACKERS
GIRL GOT GAME
GIRLS' EDUCATIONAL CHARTER
GRAVITATION
GTO
GUNDAM BLUE DESTINY
GUNDAM SEED ASTRAY
GUNDAM WING
GUNDAM WING: BATTLEFIELD OF PACIFISTS
GUNDAM WING: ENDLESS WALTZ
GUNDAM WING: THE LAST OUTPOST (G-UNIT)
GUYS' GUIDE TO GIRLS
HANDS OFF!
HAPPY MANIA
HARLEM BEAT
HONEY MUSTARD
I.N.V.U.
IMMORTAL RAIN
INITIAL D
INSTANT TEEN: JUST ADD NUTS
ISLAND
JING: KING OF BANDITS
JING: KING OF BANDITS - TWILIGHT TALES
JULINE
KARE KANO
KILL ME, KISS ME
KINDAICHI CASE FILES, THE
KING OF HELL
KODOCHA: SANA'S STAGE
LAMENT OF THE LAMB
LEGAL DRUG
LEGEND OF CHUN HYANG, THE
LES BIJOUX
LOVE HINA
LUPIN III
LUPIN III: WORLD'S MOST WANTED
MAGIC KNIGHT RAYEARTH I
MAGIC KNIGHT RAYEARTH II
MAHOROMATIC: AUTOMATIC MAIDEN
MAN OF MANY FACES
MARMALADE BOY
MARS
MARS: HORSE WITH NO NAME
MINK
MIRACLE GIRLS
MIYUKI-CHAN IN WONDERLAND
MODEL
MY LOVE
NECK AND NECK
ONE
ONE I LOVE, THE
PARADISE KISS
PARASYTE
PASSION FRUIT
PEACH GIRL
PEACH GIRL: CHANGE OF HEART
PET SHOP OF HORRORS

03.30.04T

ALSO AVAILABLE FROM  TOKYOPOP®

**For more
information visit
www.TOKYOPOP.com**

03.30.04T